The History of the University of Cambridge:
Texts and Studies

Volume 9

COMMEMORATION IN
MEDIEVAL CAMBRIDGE

The History of the University of Cambridge:
Texts and Studies

ISSN 0960-2887

Founding Editor
P. N. R. Zutshi
Former keeper of Manuscripts and University Archives
Cambridge University Library

COMMEMORATION IN MEDIEVAL CAMBRIDGE

EDITED BY

John S. Lee and Christian Steer

THE BOYDELL PRESS

CAMBRIDGE UNIVERSITY LIBRARY

First published 2018
The Boydell Press, Woodbridge
in association with
Cambridge University Library

ISBN 978 1 78327 334 8

The Boydell Press is an imprint of Boydell & Brewer Ltd
PO Box 9, Woodbridge, Suffolk IP12 3DF, UK
and of Boydell & Brewer Inc.
668 Mt Hope Avenue, Rochester, NY 14620, USA
website: www.boydellandbrewer.com

A catalogue record of this publication is available
from the British Library

The publisher has no responsibility for the continued existence
or accuracy of URLs for external or third-party internet websites
referred to in this book, and does not guarantee that any content
on such websites is, or will remain, accurate or appropriate

This publication is printed on acid-free paper

Printed and bound in Great Britain by TJ International Ltd, Padstow, Cornwall

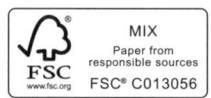

Contents

Illustrations

Map: Cambridge showing the parish churches, religious houses and colleges in the late Middle Ages. (Drawn for the editors by Sarah Wroot. Adapted from a map first published in *The Atlas of Historic Towns*, volume 2 © The Historic Towns Trust, 1975)

Black and white plates

The editors, contributors and publishers are grateful to all the institutions
and persons listed for permission to reproduce the materials in which they
hold copyright. Every effort has been made to trace the copyright holders;
apologies are offered for any omission, and the publishers will be pleased to
add any necessary acknowledgement in subsequent editions.

This publication has been made possible by grants received from the late Miss Isobel Thornley's Bequest to the University of London and the Francis Coales Charitable Foundation.

Acknowledgements

This collection of essays has grown out of a conference organised by the Monumental Brass Society and held at Trinity Hall, Cambridge, in April 2013. We are grateful to each of our contributors and to Rhun Emlyn, Rosemary Horrox, Robert Kinsey and Rebecca Oakes who, for different reasons, were unable to submit written versions of their lectures for this volume. We likewise extend our thanks to Claire Daunton who has brought her considerable depth of knowledge on the former masters of Trinity Hall together in her collaboration with Elizabeth New.

We also thank Martin Daunton, former Master of Trinity Hall, his wife Claire, and the college staff, and most especially Nicky Clarkson, for their hospitality and kindness during our stay. Paul Cockerham and Martin Stuchfield chaired sessions during the conference and, with Robert Kinsey, Nicholas Rogers, and the late Peter Heseltine, were our specialist guides during visits to King's, Queens', and Christ's chapels, and to the churches of Great St. Mary, St. Botolph, St. Bene't, St. Edward King and Martyr, and Little St. Mary. We likewise extend a grateful debt of gratitude to Caroline M. Barron, Jerome Bertram, Clive Burgess, and Anne F. Sutton for their support and specialist advice during the production of this volume; to Sarah Wroot for providing the map of medieval Cambridge; to Paul Everest, C.B. Newham, Maria Anna Rogers and Martin Stuchfield for their photographs; to Derrick Chivers and Janet Whitham for their rubbings; and to each of the institutions cited in the List of Illustrations for reproduction permissions. We likewise extend our thanks to Nick Bingham, Robert Kinsey and Caroline Palmer of Boydell & Brewer for their expert advice during the production of this volume, with a special mention in dispatches to Robert who generously produced the index.

John S. Lee
Christian Steer

Contributors

Sir John Baker QC, FBA, is Emeritus Downing Professor of the Laws of England, Cambridge, an Honorary Fellow of St. Catharine's College, Cambridge, and an Honorary Bencher of the Inner Temple and of Gray's Inn. He has written several books on English legal history.

Richard Barber has written widely on medieval literature and history including *The Holy Grail: The History of a Legend*, *Henry II* and the award-winning *The Knight and Chivalry*. His recent book *Edward III and the Triumph of England* was widely reviewed: the present paper arose out of research he has undertaken into the original knights of the Garter for that book. He founded Boydell & Brewer Ltd and subsequently directed it for forty years. He was awarded an honorary DPhil by the University of York in 2014.

Claire Gobbi Daunton has written on the patronage of late medieval stained glass and on parish patronage more broadly. She has recently explored the use of secular, ludic imagery in sacred spaces in the late medieval period in *Saints and Cults in Medieval England*, ed. Susan Powell (Donington, 2017).

Peter Murray Jones is Fellow Librarian at King's College, Cambridge. He contributed a chapter 'The College and the Chapel' to *King's College Chapel, 1515–2015: Art, Music and Religion in Cambridge*, edited by J. M. Massing and N. Zeeman (London, 2014).

John S. Lee is a Research Associate at the Centre for Medieval Studies at the University of York. His interests are in the economy and society of medieval England and local and regional history, particularly trade, markets, and urban communities. He has published *Cambridge and its Economic Region, 1450–1560* (Hatfield, 2005) and *The Medieval Clothier* (Woodbridge, 2018), together with articles in many academic journals, including *Urban History*, *Economic History Review*, and *The Local Historian*.

Elizabeth A. New is Senior Lecturer in medieval history at Aberystwyth University. She has published extensively on aspects of British medieval social, religious and cultural history, with particular interests in Christocentric devotion and in seals and sealing practices. She is Co-Investigator for the AHRC-funded Aberystwyth University/University of Lincoln 'Imprint: A Forensic and Historical Investigation of Fingerprints on Medieval Seals' project, and is a director of Sigillvm, the international association for the study of seals.

Susan (Sue) Powell is Emeritus Professor of Medieval Texts and Culture (University of Salford) and a Visiting Research Fellow at the Institute of English Studies, University of London, and the School of History, University of Leeds. She is an editor of manuscripts and early printed books, and her research focusses on religious and devotional texts and institutions. Her latest books are *Saints and Cults in Medieval England,* (Donington, 2017) and *The Birgittines of Syon Abbey: Preaching and Print* (Turnhout, 2017).

Michael Robson, a Fellow of St. Edmund's College, Cambridge, is the author of *Saint Francis: The Legend and the Life* (London, 1997), *The Franciscans in the Medieval Custody of York* (York, 1997), *The Franciscans in the Middle Ages* (Woodbridge, 2006) and *The Greyfriars of England (1224–1539), Collected Papers* (Padua, 2012). He edited *The Cambridge Companion to Francis of Assisi* (Cambridge, 2012) and *The English Province of the Franciscans (1224–c. 1350)* (Leiden, 2017) and he is the co-editor of three more volumes.

Nicholas Rogers is Archivist and Bye Fellow of Sidney Sussex College, Cambridge. He is a Vice-President of the Monumental Brass Society and a former Editor of its *Transactions.* He is also Honorary Curator of the Cambridge Antiquarian Society's collection of brass rubbings. He has written numerous articles on various aspects of late medieval art and culture.

Christian Steer is Honorary Visiting Fellow in the Department of History at the University of York. He has worked extensively on urban commemoration and has a particular interest in antiquarian and heraldic accounts of lost monuments. His most recent articles have discussed monuments of the dead in the Franciscan churches of Coventry and London, and patterns of commemoration in the city of London parishes of St. James Garlickhithe and St. Nicholas Shambles.

Abbreviations

AF	*Analecta Franciscana*
AFH	*Archivum Franciscanum Historicum*
BL	British Library, London
BRUC	A.B. Emden, *A Biographical Register of the University of Cambridge to 1500* (Cambridge, 1963)
BSFS	British Society of Franciscan Studies
CA	Cambridgeshire Archives, Cambridge Record Office
CCCA	Corpus Christi College Archives, Cambridge
CCR	*Calendar of Close Rolls*, HMSO, 46 vols. (London, 1892–1963)
CPR	*Calendar of Patent Rolls*, HMSO, 54 vols. (London, 1891–1916)
CUL	Cambridge University Library
Eccleston	A.G. Little, ed., *Fratris Thomae vulgo dicti de Eccleston Tractatus de adventu Fratrum Minorum in Angliam* (Manchester, 1951)
FS	*Franciscan Studies*, new series
KCA	King's College Archives
LMA	London Metropolitan Archives
LPL	Lambeth Palace Library
MBS	Monumental Brass Society
ODNB	*Oxford Dictionary of National Biography*, ed. H.C.G. Matthew and B. Harrison, 60 vols. (Oxford, 2004)
OED	*Oxford English Dictionary online*
RS	Rolls Series
SJCA	St. John's College Archives, Cambridge
SRS	Suffolk Records Society
THAR	Trinity Hall Archives, Cambridge
TMBS	*Transactions of the Monumental Brass Society*
TNA: PRO	The National Archives: Public Record Office
VCH	*The Victoria County History of the counties of England* (London, 1900–, in progress)

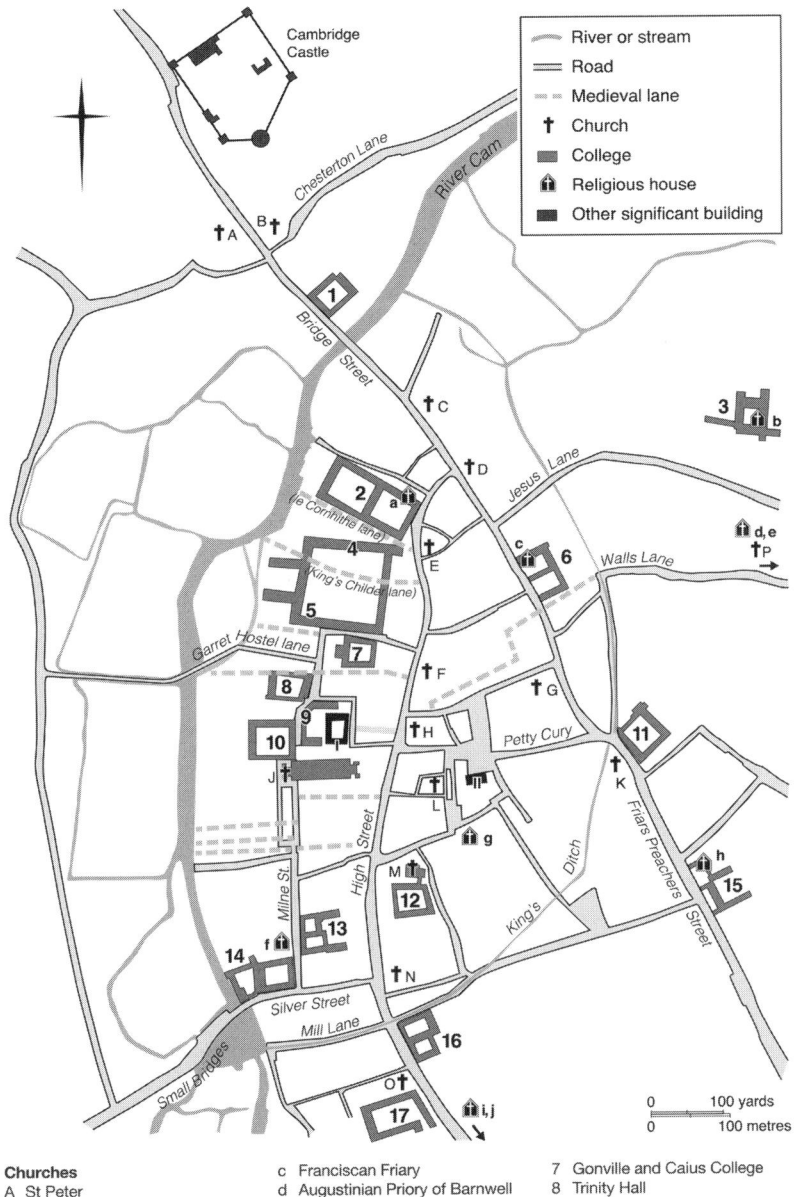

Legend

~~	River or stream
═══	Road
- - -	Medieval lane
†	Church
▨	College
⌂	Religious house
■	Other significant building

Cambridge Castle

Chesterton Lane

River Cam

Bridge Street

Jesus Lane

Walls Lane

(le Cornhithe lane)

King's Childer lane

Garret Hostel lane

Petty Cury

Friar's Preacher's Street

Ditch

King's

Milne St.

High Street

Silver Street

Mill Lane

Small Bridges

0   100 yards
0   100 metres

Cambridge showing the parish churches, religious houses and colleges
in the late Middle Ages.

Churches
A St Peter
B St Giles
C St Clement
D Holy Sepulchre
E All Saints in the Jewry
F St Michael
G Holy Trinity
H Great St Mary's
J St John Zachary
K St Andrew the Great
L St Edward King and Martyr
M St Bene't
N St Botolph
O Little St Mary's
P St Andrew the Less

Religious houses
a St John's Hospital
b Benedictine Nunnery of St
   Radegund

c Franciscan Friary
d Augustinian Priory of Barnwell
e St Mary Magdalene Leper
   Hospital, Stourbridge
f Carmelite Friary
g Augustinian Friary
h Dominican Friary
i Gilbertine Priory of St Edmund
j St Anthony and St Eligius
   Hospital

Colleges
1 Buckingham College, later
   Magdalene College
2 St John's College
3 Jesus College
4 King's Hall, later part of Trinity
   College
5 Michaelhouse, later part of Trinity
   College
6 Sidney Sussex College

7 Gonville and Caius College
8 Trinity Hall
9 King's College
10 University Hall, later Clare Hall
   (College)
11 Godshouse, later Christ's College
12 Corpus Christi College
13 St Catharine's College
14 Queens' College
15 Emmanuel College
16 Pembroke Hall (College)
17 Peterhouse

Other significant buildings
I   University Schools
II Guildhall

In Fellowship with the Dead

Christian Steer

How did the people of medieval Cambridge choose to be remembered after their deaths? They could opt for prayers, Masses and charitable acts, tomb monuments, liturgical furnishings and other gifts in the town's parish churches and religious houses, while the university and its colleges also provided intercessory services and resting places for the dead. The role of memory and commemoration in this English university town was explored in a weekend conference organised by the Monumental Brass Society at Trinity Hall, Cambridge, in April 2013. This collection of essays is based on several of those papers, examining the themes of 'Town and Gown', together with others, commissioned for this volume, which consider the celebration of the dead more broadly, the location (and loss) of tomb monuments, their purpose and iconography and the mnemonics used for 'pray and display'. The aim has been to explore what might have been distinctive about commemoration in medieval Cambridge and an important theme has emerged: the role of academic colleges, as part of the broader Church family and as commemorative institutions for founders and fellows. This dual role preserved the memory of the dead within the teaching of the living, although not all Cambridge men chose to be buried in their colleges. The example of Walter Crome, Cambridge fellow and London rector, ably demonstrates the multiplicity of commemoration as practised by college men in the later Middle Ages.

Walter Crome was fellow of Gonville Hall, Cambridge, and rector of St. Benet Sherehog in the city of London.[1] He drew up his will on 5 August 1452 and died in the summer of 1453.[2] Crome asked to be buried close to the tomb

---

[1] Gonville Hall was a Cambridge college first founded by Edmund Gonville, rector of Terrington St. Clement in Norfolk, in 1348, and re-founded in 1557 by John Caius as Gonville and Caius College.

[2] LMA, DL/C/B/004/MS09071/005, ff. 97–98v. On Crome see, for example, *BRUC*, p. 168; S. Lindenbaum, 'London After Arundel: Learned Rectors and the Strategies of Orthodox Reform', in *After Arundel: Religious Writing in Fifteenth-Century England*, ed. V. Gillespie and K. Ghosh (Turnout, 2011), pp. 187–208. C. Brooke, *A History of Gonville and Caius College* (2nd edition, Woodbridge, 1996), pp. 33–7; P.D. Clarke, ed., *The University and College Libraries of Cambridge*, Corpus of British Medieval Library Catalogues, 10 (London, 2002), pp. 254–9 and 683–4; J.C.T. Oates, *Cambridge University Library: A History* (Cambridge, 1985), pp. 25–9; M.R. James, *A Descriptive Catalogue of the*

of his predecessor Thomas Dale, who had died in 1442, in the chancel of their London parish church. He further directed that his grave was to be covered by a square memorial stone and engraved with an inscription recording his name and date of death. Neither Crome's nor Dale's tomb was recorded by the London antiquarian John Stow in the account of the church in his great *Survey of London*, first published in 1598.[3] These tombs, and many others from the church of St. Benet Sherehog, were probably destroyed during the iconoclasm of Edward VI's brief reign. But as well as his tomb monument, master Walter was likewise attentive to his funeral rites, requesting a set of seven-year anniversary services which were to mark not only his date of death but also his funeral service, with twelve chaplains in attendance at his burial, eight at his octave (that is the seventh day after his burial), and three at his respective anniversaries, which were to last for seven years. Crome further provided half the cost of a 'precious object' for the high altar, some 100s. (or £5), on condition that his parishioners matched the same sum. His vestment, made of Alexandrian cloth, he left to the church of St. Mary's, Hellesdon, Norfolk, whose parishioners were to pray for his parents and for all Christian souls.[4] Crome bequeathed two of his books to his eventual successor at St. Benet's but the bulk of his extensive library, some one hundred volumes, was divided between the common library of the University of Cambridge (ninety-three books) and Gonville Hall (seven). Several volumes had been provided during his lifetime with Crome's gift-inscription of 1444 written within.[5] It was not unknown for London rectors to own such extensive private libraries but the scale of Crome's collection from fifteenth-century London is unparalleled.[6] Other fellows gave just as generously to their newly built library at Gonville Hall (completed by 1441). For example, William Grene (d.1478), rector of St. Andrew Holborn, London, bequeathed a further twelve books to Gonville.[7] And like Crome a generation before, Grene chose burial in his London parish, siting his grave on the south side of the chancel.

Walter Crome and William Grene were fellows of Gonville Hall and remembered the college in their wills, yet they were buried in city of London churches. This is not surprising as it was the custom for London rectors to be buried within their parish church, usually close to the high altar in the chancel.[8] But what were the commemorative and burial strategies of

---

  Manuscripts in the Library of Gonville and Caius College, 2 vols. (Cambridge, 1907–08), i, pp. 118–22, 137–42, 385–6, 98–9 and ii, pp. 461–2.

[3] *A Survey of London by John Stow*, ed. C.L. Kingsford, 2 vols. (Oxford, 1908), i, pp. 260–1.

[4] Crome's *vestimentum de Borde Alisaunder*, bord Alexander, was a rich, striped silk originally from Alexandria and of some luxury.

[5] Oates, *Cambridge University Library*, pp. 26–9.

[6] R.A. Wood, 'The Ownership of Books amongst the London Rectors in the Late Fourteenth and Fifteenth Centuries', *Medieval Prosopography* 33 (2018), pp. 195–208; H. Kleineke, 'The Library of John Veysy (d.1492), Fellow of Lincoln College, Oxford, and Rector of St. James Garlickhithe, London', *The Library*, 17:4 (December 2016), pp. 399–423.

[7] LMA, DL/C/B/004/MS09071/006, f. 226–226v; *BRUC*, p. 270.

[8] An analysis of some 120 wills proved in the Archdeaconry and Commissary courts of London has revealed 85 percent of rectors requesting burial in the chancel. I am indebted to Dr. Robert A. Wood for this information.

Crome and Grene's contemporaries who had remained in Cambridge? Study of commemoration has revealed much about the strategies employed in preserving the memory of the dead.[9] This is seen not only in privately funded chantry and anniversary services but also, in the words of Caroline Barron, in the 'communal chantry', accessible through fraternity and guild membership.[10] The growing literature on the form, function and location of tomb monuments is impressive and adds another dimension to our understanding of late medieval commemorative practice. Such studies, by considering surviving and lost examples (through antiquarian and heraldic descriptions), have placed monuments to the dead in a broader – and far richer – commemorative context.[11] The parish, a natural anchorage for commemorative endeavour, has received particular attention.[12] It is notable that from about the late thirteenth century the introduction of chantries at the parochial level brought the celebration of the dead to the heart of parish life. Elsewhere, patterns of burial and commemoration in city cathedrals have revealed much about those interred within the body of the cathedral church, the side chapels and in the adjacent cemeteries, and the strategies they commissioned to aid their journey to Paradise.[13] We likewise learn of the importance of reserved zones for the exclusive use of, to borrow a phrase,

[9]   E.g. C. Steer, '"For quicke and deade memorie masses": Merchant Piety in Late Medieval London', in *Medieval Merchants and Money: Essays in Honour of James L. Bolton*, ed. M. Allen and M. Davies (London, 2016), pp. 71–89; C. Burgess, 'Chantries in the Parish, or "Through the Looking-glass"', in *The Medieval Chantry in England*, ed. J.M. Luxford and J. McNeill (Leeds, 2011), pp. 100–29; and *idem*, 'A Service for the Dead: The Form and Function of the Anniversary in Late Medieval Bristol', *Transactions of the Bristol and Gloucestershire Archaeological Society*, 105 (1987), pp. 183–211.

[10] E. Duffy, *The Stripping of the Altars: Traditional Religion in England 1400–1580* (London, 1992), pp. 141–54; G. Rosser, 'Communities of Parish and Guild in the Late Middle Ages', in *Parish, Church and People: Local Studies in lay religion 1350–1750*, ed. S. Wright (London, 1988), pp. 29–55; and C.M. Barron, 'The Parish Fraternities of Medieval London', in *The Church in Pre-Reformation Society: Essays in Honour of F.R.H. Du Boulay*, ed. C.M. Barron and C. Harper-Bill (Woodbridge, 1985), pp. 13–37, at p. 23.

[11] See especially the collection of essays in M. Penman, ed., *Monuments and Monumentality across Medieval and Early Modern Europe* (Donington, 2013) and C. M. Barron and C. Burgess, eds., *Memory and Commemoration in Medieval England* (Donington, 2010). N. Saul, *English Church Monuments in the Middle Ages: History and Representation* (Oxford, 2009) remains the standard work on tomb monuments of medieval England.

[12] E.g. J.S. Lee, '"'Tis the sheep have paid for all": Merchant Commemoration in Late Medieval Newark', *TMBS*, 19:4 (2017), pp. 301–27; N. Saul, *Lordship and Faith: The English Gentry and the Parish Church in the Middle Ages* (Oxford, 2017), pp. 161–83; N. Cartlidge, 'A Debate with Death: John Rudyng's Brass in St. Andrew's Church, Biggleswade', *TMBS*, 19:2 (2015), pp. 94–100; T.A. Heslop, 'The Alabaster Tomb at Ashwellthorpe, Norfolk: Its Workmanship, Cost and Location', in *Patrons and Professionals in the Middle Ages*, ed. P. Binski and E.A. New (Donington, 2012), pp. 333–46; C. Burgess, 'Obligations and Strategy: Managing Memory in the Late Medieval Parish', *TMBS*, 18:4 (2012), pp. 289–310; S. Badham and P. Cockerham, eds., *'The beste and fayrest of al Lincolnshire': The Church of St. Botolph, Boston, Lincolnshire, and its Medieval Monuments*, British Archaeological Reports, British Series 554 (Oxford, 2012).

[13] E.g. P. Cockerham, 'Bishops, Deans and Canons: Commemorative Contexts Across Two Centuries at Exeter Cathedral', *TMBS*, 19:4 (2017), pp. 277–300; C. Steer, 'The Canons of St. Paul's and their Brasses', *TMBS*, 19:3 (2016), pp. 213–34; and D. Lepine, '"A stone to be layed upon me": The Monumental Commemoration of the Late Medieval English Higher Clergy', in *Monuments and Monumentality*, ed. Penman, pp. 158–70.

the 'very special dead' and of the carefully planned management of grave space.[14] Abbeys, friaries and priories were also rich in the monuments of past founders, their families and descendants, friends, associates and retainers. Descriptions of tombs from these religious houses suggest they were mausolea of some magnificence with sumptuous monuments for donors lying alongside the brethren.[15] Moreover, such commissions were not confined to these great religious houses and it is noticeable how with their rise from the fourteenth century collegiate churches quickly came to house new sepulchres containing the bones of founders, their families and the chaplains who celebrated for them, many of whom enjoyed lavish tomb monuments.[16] In the late medieval period every ecclesiastical institution had a commemorative rationale at its core.

There remains, however, a lacuna in our appreciation of contemporary ecclesiastical institutions, namely the academic foundations at Cambridge and Oxford. These colleges represented a different type of Christian institution which, while collectively constituting a university, and evidently existing to satisfy a propaedeutic purpose, were also bound to provide commemorative services for their founders, fellows and benefactors. It is to be remembered that Cambridge existed as a university before the first college foundation of the late thirteenth century; it was not, in fact, until 1550 that the communities at Cambridge and Oxford converted into collegiate universities and by that time virtually every university student and teacher had become a member of a college.[17]

As Michael Robson points out in this volume, the colleges worked cheek by jowl with the teaching of the mendicant friars. The Franciscan *studium generale* in Cambridge was, for example, one of three schools established by the order within its English province and was held in high regard. All four orders of mendicants, like the colleges, offered commemoration and education and played a major role in establishing Cambridge as a university and especially in the study of theology. The monastic foundations at St. Edmund's Priory,

---

[14] Quote taken from P. Brown, *The Cult of the Saints: Its Rise and Function in Latin Christianity* (Chicago, 1981), pp. 69–85.

[15] E.g. C. Steer, 'Monuments of the Dead in Early Franciscan Churches *c.*1250–*c.*1350', in *The English Province of the Franciscans (1224–c.1350)*, ed. Michael J.P. Robson (Leiden, 2017), pp. 172–98; L. Slater, 'Defining Queenship at Greyfriars London, *c.*1300–58', *Gender and History*, 27 (2015), pp. 53–76; M. Carter, '"hys … days here liven was". The Monument of Abbot Robert Chamber at Holm Cultram (Cumbria)', *Church Monuments*, 27 (2012), pp. 38–52; and K. Stöber, *Late Medieval Monasteries and their Patrons: England and Wales, c.1300–1540* (Woodbridge, 2007), esp. chapter 3.

[16] E.g. D. Turner and N. Saul, 'The Lost Chantry College of Lingfield', *Surrey Archaeological Collections*, 98 (2014), pp. 153–74; C. Burgess, 'Fotheringhay Church: Conceiving a College and its Community', in *The Yorkist Age*, ed. H. Kleineke and C. Steer (Donington, 2013), pp. 347–66; N. Saul, 'Fotheringhay Church, Northamptonshire: Architecture and Fittings', in *The Yorkist Age*, ed. Kleineke and Steer, pp. 367–79; J.M. Luxford, 'The Collegiate Church as Mausoleum', in *The Late Medieval English College and its Context*, ed. C. Burgess and M. Heale (York, 2008), pp. 110–39; and N. Saul, *Death, Art, and Memory in Medieval England: The Cobham Family and their Monuments 1300–1500* (Oxford, 2001).

[17] C.N.L. Brooke, 'The Churches of Medieval Cambridge', in *History, Society and the Churches: Essays in Honour of Owen Chadwick*, ed. D. Beales and G. Best (Cambridge, 1985), pp. 49–76 at p. 61.

established by Gilbertine canons studying in Cambridge, and Buckingham College for Benedictine monks were likewise religious communities linked to the university. This dual role within college communities has been noted but not yet examined.[18] Studies of the academic colleges of the university have focused almost exclusively on their educational role, and up to this point their commemorative functions have generally been ignored. It is the purpose of this collection of essays to direct the spotlight on Cambridge and to consider the strategies of commemoration practised in the colleges in the centuries leading up to the Reformation. It cannot be the last word on the subject and it is hoped this innovative approach will open new avenues of research. This brief is ambitious, for surviving testamentary evidence is fragmentary at best and the material evidence of commemoration – brasses – has suffered centuries of neglect, damage and theft.[19] It should also be borne in mind, as noted by Nicholas Rogers in his chapter in this volume, that the academic population was a transient one.[20] Unless impeded by death, most fellows would move on to benefices elsewhere. Nevertheless, three important themes emerge from this study: place, benefaction and display; all played a part in the commemorative strategies adopted by their patrons and mirror the enterprises adopted by masters Walter Crome and William Grene. Colleges offered commemorative resources and, as in other institutions, those who sought to benefit could formulate strategies to suit their interests and circumstances, thereby expediting their salvation.

Many urban churches, on occasion, were often nothing more than building sites.[21] In Cambridge almost all parish churches were either rebuilt in whole or in part during the later Middle Ages. Construction work inevitably influenced the place of burial and the permanence of tomb commemoration: evidence from London suggests that many older incised slabs from the thirteenth century were used in the foundations of later church rebuilding work.[22] The college chapels in Cambridge were no different. Construction of the chapels at Pembroke and Gonville, for example, took a little under forty years to complete in the latter half of the fourteenth century. Building work on the

[18] E.g. Brooke, 'The Churches of Medieval Cambridge', p. 62; M. Campbell, 'Medieval Founders' Relics: Royal and Episcopal Patronage at Oxford and Cambridge Colleges', in *Heraldry, Pageantry and Social Display in Medieval England*, ed. M. Keen and P. Coss (Woodbridge, 2002), pp. 125–42 at pp. 127–30.

[19] The main series of Cambridge wills in the archdeaconry and consistory courts at Ely do not begin until the early sixteenth century and for the earlier period we are therefore reliant on surviving examples which were copied into the probate registers of the Prerogative Court of Canterbury. Similarly, the wills of university members proved in the Vice-Chancellor's court do not survive before the sixteenth century. On the brasses in Cambridge, W. Lack, H.M. Stuchfield and P. Whittemore, *The Monumental Brasses of Cambridgeshire* (London, 1995), pp. 20–83.

[20] N. Rogers, '"The Stones and all disrobed": Reasons for the Presence and Absence of Monumental Brasses in Cambridge' in this volume, pp. 152–64.

[21] A point most recently made in nearby Norwich: E. Rutledge, 'An Urban Environment: Norwich in the Fifteenth Century', in *The Fifteenth Century XII: Society in an Age of Plague*, ed. L. Clark and C. Rawcliffe (Woodbridge, 2013), pp. 79–99 at p. 91.

[22] E.g. J. Schofield, 'Excavations on the Site of St. Nicholas Shambles, Newgate Street, City of London, 1975–9', *Transactions of the London and Middlesex Archaeological Society*, 48 (1997), pp. 77–135 at pp. 101–3.

chapel at King's Hall, founded in 1317, did not start until about 1464 and was completed twenty-one years later. It was rebuilt during the sixteenth century. It is perhaps not surprising that at King's College, founded in 1441 – and with its foundation stone laid in 1446 – the imposing chapel endured a seventy-year construction programme, while glazing and furnishing went on into the 1540s.[23] And yet delayed building works, and the process of construction, were not the only influences on burials in medieval Cambridge: for example, Trinity Hall did not acquire the right to bury its dead until the mastership of Walter Hewke (1510–18) and for some colleges the right came even later. In the preceding centuries Hewke's predecessors, fellows, college servants and students had to be buried in the nearby parish churches of St. John Zachary and St. Edward's, or in one of the churches to which a college master or fellow was beneficed.[24] The men of Peterhouse were buried in the parish church of St. Mary the Less (or Little St. Mary's) where, for example, two memorial brasses survive for former masters.[25] Some colleges, such as Peterhouse and Corpus Christi, did not acquire chapels until after the Reformation. We do not have any surviving burial lists from the town's mendicant churches although we can derive some idea of the numbers buried in the Franciscan church.[26]

The memory of the dead was not exclusively managed through burial in a college chapel or in a related parish church. Colleges sometimes served as cenotaphs for their founders, who were in fact buried elsewhere but who nevertheless specified that their anniversary should be celebrated faithfully year after year. This could be extended to include their kin and other notable benefactors, as at King's where Peter Murray Jones here considers the exequies for the Lancastrian royal family celebrated alongside memorialisation for college fellows and patrons. Donors and friends were also remembered within the colleges, many of which maintained their own *liber benefactorum* for past patrons. The responsibility of the master to provide for his former college, and to serve as a 'role model' of benefaction, is demonstrated in the case studies here by Claire Gobbi Daunton and Elizabeth New. Masters not only provided for their colleges in different ways, but their acts of patronage also served as motivators for others desiring the benefits of college commemoration. They were remembered in special books of benefactors, resembling the bede rolls in parish churches, which recorded the names of special friends. These books of memory were not the only means by which donors could be remembered: more visible devices were also used, such as

---

[23] Brooke, 'The Churches of Medieval Cambridge', pp. 74–76; S. Bradley and N. Pevsner, *The Buildings of England: Cambridgeshire* (London, 2014), pp. 132–46.

[24] A point discussed elsewhere in this collection, see C. Gobbi Daunton and E.A. New, 'Patrons and Benefactors: The Masters of Trinity Hall in the Later Middle Ages', pp. 61–89.

[25] Their inscriptions are lost but these brasses are generally thought to commemorate John Holbrook (d.1436), Master of Peterhouse, Chancellor of the University and chaplain to Henry VI, and John Warkworth (d.1500) or Henry Hornby (d.1518), both of whom were masters of Peterhouse.

[26] M. Robson, 'The Commemoration of the Living and the Dead at the Friars Minor of Cambridge', in this volume, pp. 34–51.

the *tabula*, a (hanging?) board at King's. Evidence of such mnemonics has been found in churches in other towns and cities but the vulnerability of such boards, whether wooden, or on parchment within a wooden frame, has meant their almost complete loss.[27] What emerges from this study is the range of benefactions received by the Cambridge colleges, not only from their own men but also from the townsmen and their families, and those from further afield. In his discussion of the foundation of Corpus Christi College, Richard Barber has revealed an unlikely set of benefactors in the form of some of the wealthiest London merchants, such as Andrew Aubrey (d.1358). It would seem that these urban magnates had been encouraged to join the new Cambridge guild of Corpus Christi by John Tamworth, a successful forerunner of modern-day development directors. But prayers for donors were observed by the university and by all its colleges – for example at Peterhouse, where a weekly memorial mass was celebrated for the founder Hugh of Balsham, bishop of Ely (d.1286) and his eventual successor Simon Montacute (d.1345), along with Montacute's parents.[28]

The essays in this volume consider how founders, friends and benefactors of Cambridge colleges employed different forms of commemoration and remembrance, through chantries, anniversaries, prayers, *tabula* or books of benefactors. Absent from this discussion is the role played by tomb monuments placed over, or close to, the grave of the deceased. This is in part a consequence of a long foundation process, from Peterhouse in 1284 to the re-foundation of Buckingham College as Magdalene in 1542, and the prolonged building, and rebuilding, programmes of their chapels. As a result the college fellows not only worshipped in their local parish church but also chose, like Crome and Grene, to be buried and commemorated there. Urban churches were particularly vulnerable to loss, and a visit to, for example, St. Mary the Great reveals twenty-seven indents of lost brasses on the marbled floor: not one single medieval brass has survived.[29] Rogers has identified only forty-one surviving memorial brasses from medieval Cambridge and at least 152 lost ones. There were undoubtedly many more. Their loss, through building work, wear and tear, iconoclasm, neglect and theft, has swept away most of the material remains for town and gown buried in the town's churches.[30] The majority of their brasses are nothing more than shadows of their former selves.

---

[27] For such boards at King's College see P.M. Jones, 'Commemoration at a Royal College' in this volume, pp. 106–22. On the use of such *tabula* elsewhere, R. Marks, 'Picturing Word and Text in the Late Medieval Parish Church', in *Image, Text and Church, 1380–1600: Essays for Margaret Aston*, ed. L. Clark, M. Jurkowski and C. Richmond (Toronto, 2009), pp. 162–202; and V. Gillespie, 'Medieval Hypertext: Image and Text from York Minster', in *Of the Making of Books, Medieval Manuscripts, Their Scribes and Readers: Essays Presented to M.B. Parkes*, ed. P.R. Robinson and R. Zim (Aldershot 1997), pp. 206–29.

[28] See also Michaelhouse, Gonville Hall, St. Catharine's, Trinity Hall and King's College discussed further in J.S. Lee, 'Monuments and Memory: A University Town in Late Medieval England', pp. 10–33.

[29] Lack, Stuchfield and Whittemore, *Cambridgeshire*, pp. 64–8.

[30] Rogers, '"The Stones and all disrobed"'.

Those monuments which remain *in situ*, however, in the college chapels and parish churches of Cambridge, reveal how different masters and fellows chose to be displayed. Masters such as Walter Hewke went for a London-made product and one of some cost, his figure brass in the chapel of Trinity Hall measuring some 1356mm tall on a slab of 2710mm in height. We have no surviving information about how much was expended on the memorial, but it was probably in the region of about £10 plus carriage. Hewke entered Trinity Hall in 1490, was ordained sub-deacon in the same year and priest in 1491, and was admitted as doctor of canon law in 1495. He commissioned his brass during this lifetime and he chose to be commemorated as a priest wearing a cope with orphreys containing the twelve Apostles, fastened by a morse.[31] He was not dressed as a doctor of divinity. The type of dress displayed on brass memorials is a question which has received little scrutiny since Herbert Druitt's *Costume on Brasses* published over a century ago.[32] The remarks offered by Sir John Baker in this volume, in his comparison of scarlet robes, the formal dress of doctors of divinity and law, of judges and of serjeants at law, by drawing on surviving monumental brasses in Cambridge and beyond, address this neglect. The *capa clausa*, worn by doctors of divinity, is seen, for example, on the brasses for William Towne (d.1495) and John Argentein (d.1507), both fellows of King's College and the latter also its provost. The brass of Henry Hornby (d.1518) at the church of St. Mary the Less provides a fourth example of the *capa clausa*.[33] It is difficult to be certain in this case of the attribution to Hornby as this is one of several Cambridge brasses where the inscription plate has been removed from the slab and the identity lost. Hornby was one of Lady Margaret Beaufort's executors and served the King's Mother as dean of her chapel, secretary and then chancellor. He held a number of ecclesiastical appointments and was master of Peterhouse from 1501 to his death seventeen years later.[34] Other memorials for members of Lady Margaret's household were commissioned at her foundations of Christ's and at St. John's College. It is rare to have several extant examples for a particular aristocratic or royal household in such close proximity and the relationship between Lady Margaret, as founder, and the members of her circle is discussed further in Susan Powell's essay.

---

[31] Gobbi Daunton and New, 'Patrons and Benefactors'. Orphreys: a usually richly embroidered ornamental border, band or panel on a liturgical vestment. Morse: the clasp or fastening of a cope, frequently made of gold or silver, and set with precious stones (*OED*).

[32] H. Druitt, *Costume on Brasses* (2nd edition, London, 1970). A rare contribution to this discussion is K. Staniland, 'Civil Costume on Brasses', in *Monumental Brasses as Art and History*, ed. J. Bertram (Stroud, 1996), pp. 40–7. Cf. P.M. Walker, 'Fashioning Death: The Choice and Representation of Female Clothing on English Medieval Funeral Monuments 1250–1450' (Unpublished Ph.D., University of Manchester, 2013).

[33] On this identification, N. Rogers, 'Cambridgeshire Brasses', in *Cambridgeshire Churches*, ed. C. Hicks (Stamford, 1997), pp. 303–19 at p. 315. *Capa clausa*: literally 'a closed cope'. A cloak-like garment, closed up, with a single slit in the centre, and the distinctive dress of doctors of divinity. See below, J.H. Baker, 'A Comparison of Academical and Legal Costume on Memorial Brasses', pp. 90–105.

[34] *ODNB*.

Cambridge colleges, like other Church institutions, were supported by endowments provided by benefactors who, in return, were to be commemorated. They served as chantries for their founders and attracted later benefaction from within the college community and from further afield. Masters and fellows could choose one of a number of different means to secure their place in the collective memory of their college: Walter Crome, for example, could be buried under a tomb monument in a city of London church but remembered not only as a benefactor to the library of Gonville Hall but also as a major donor to the University Library. Colleges had a double focus, commemoration and education, and in their role as centres of learning they produced graduates able to work in the Church's ministry and advance the interests of the late medieval Church. Commemoration in a medieval Cambridge college, however, was about not only ensuring the memory of the dead, but also securing prayers for the deceased from those with whom he had studied and worked: it was a more stable and secure community than the parish.

CHAPTER 1

Monuments and Memory:
A University Town in Late Medieval England

John S. Lee

Commemoration can take the form of an action – a calling to remembrance, such as through prayer, or the form of an object – such as a memorial.[1] Many studies of late medieval commemoration have tended to examine the latter, exploring particular monuments in particular contexts, mostly in churches and cathedrals, as well as considering different workshops, styles and patrons. They have focused on the product of commemoration. Most have taken a traditional approach to this subject, simply discussing the tomb, or the window, or the chantry without reflecting on the overall message. There were, however, a myriad of different commemorative enterprises available. The role of the monument in the context of remembrance, the benefactor, charity and prayer is here explored within the university town of Cambridge. Studies of towns, such as Bristol, are well known and in recent years there has been a revived interest in urban commemoration which has 'opened up' ideas on the bigger picture and how intercessory prayer dovetailed with investment in church building, most particularly the monument, to achieve salvation.[2] New material on Boston, Coventry and York has revealed how urban elites and visitors sought appropriate commemorations for themselves and their families through a variety of differing and inter-connected strategies, while in London Christian Steer's study of St. James Garlickhithe has pieced together parts of the 'commemoration jigsaw' within this particular city parish, in which

---

[1] *OED*, 'commemoration'.
[2] We are indebted to the work of Clive Burgess. See for example his, '"For the Increase of Divine Service": Chantries in the Parish in Late Medieval Bristol', *Journal of Ecclesiastical History*, 36 (1985), pp. 46–65; 'Strategies for Eternity: Perpetual Chantry Foundation in Late Medieval Bristol', in *Religious Belief and Ecclesiastical Careers in Late Medieval England*, ed. C. Harper-Bill (Woodbridge, 1991), pp. 1–32; '"Longing to be prayed for": Death and Commemoration in an English Parish in the Later Middle Ages', in *The Place of the Dead: Death and Remembrance in Late Medieval and Early Modern Europe*, ed. B. Gordon and P. Marshall (Cambridge, 2000), pp. 44–65; and 'Obligations and Strategy: Managing Memory in the Late Medieval Parish', *TMBS*, 18:4 (2012), pp. 289–310.

different forms of commemoration served the interests of the living and the dead. Individual monuments, too, are now receiving fresh interpretations.[3]

In medieval Cambridge, the range of religious institutions to which benefactors could make gifts and entrust their commemoration expanded significantly. A burgess living in the town shortly after 1200 could choose to make a benefaction to one of sixteen parish churches, to either religious house (or both), or to one of the two hospitals. By 1300, Cambridge residents could also select one (or more) of the six houses of mendicant friars, or another religious house or hospital, as possible recipients.[4] By 1400, wealthy Cambridge citizens could also choose one of many guilds or several academic colleges to provide their intercessory services. Patterns of benefaction among medieval townspeople generally followed these trends, with new institutions commonly becoming the chief objects of attention.[5] The town was distinctive in having the presence of an academic community which grew in size and wealth during the later Middle Ages. The origins of the university are obscure, but they seem to have arisen following the migration of scholars during the temporary closure of Oxford University in 1209, after a dispute between the townspeople and university there. By 1225 these migrant students had achieved sufficient status to have their own chancellor in Cambridge, with powers delegated by the bishop of Ely, and in 1233 the *studium* or school for advanced study received papal recognition. The first college, Peterhouse, was founded in 1284 by Hugh of Balsham, bishop of

3   On Boston, S. Badham and P. Cockerham, eds., *'The beste and fayrest of al Lincolnshire': The Church of St. Botolph, Lincolnshire, and its Medieval Monuments*, British Archaeological Reports, British Series 554 (Oxford, 2012); on Coventry, C. Steer, 'Monuments of the Dead in Early Franciscan Houses, *c.*1250–*c.*1350', in *The English Province of the Franciscans (1224–c.1350)*, ed. M.J.P. Robson (Leiden, 2017), pp. 405–25 and P. Coss, *The Foundations of Gentry Life: The Multons of Frampton and their World 1270–1370* (Oxford, 2010), pp. 154–63; on York, C.M. Barnett, 'Commemoration in the Parish Church: Identity and Social Class in Late Medieval York', *Yorkshire Archaeological Journal*, 72 (2000), pp. 73–92; on London, C. Steer, '"For quicke and deade memorie masses": Merchant Piety in Late Medieval London', in *Medieval Merchants and Money: Essays in Honour of James L. Bolton*, ed. M. Allen and M. Davies (London, 2016), pp. 71–89 and his 'Burial and Commemoration in Medieval London, *c.* 1140–1540' (unpublished University of London Ph.D. thesis, 2013). New case studies include, for example, D. Lepine, '"Pause and pray with mournful heart": Late Medieval Clerical Monuments in Lincoln Cathedral', *TMBS*, 19:1 (2014), pp. 15–40; D. Harry, 'A Cadaver in Context: The Shroud Brass of John Brigge revisited', *TMBS*, 19:2 (2015), pp. 101–10; and J.S. Lee, '"'Tis the sheep have paid for all": Merchant Commemoration in Late Medieval Newark', *TMBS*, 19:4 (2017), pp. 301–27.
4   The religious houses were Barnwell Priory, a community of Augustinian canons, St. Radegund's Priory, a house of Benedictine nuns, and St. Edmund's Priory, a house of Gilbertine canons. The hospitals were those of St. John the Evangelist, and the leper hospitals of St. Mary Magdalene at Stourbridge and of St. Anthony and St. Eligius. The Franciscans (Grey Friars), Dominicans (Black Friars), Carmelites (White Friars), Augustinian (or Austin) Friars, the Friars of the Blessed Mary and the Friars of the Sack founded houses in Cambridge during the thirteenth century. See C.N.L. Brooke, 'The Churches of Medieval Cambridge', in *History, Society and the Churches: Essays in Honour of Owen Chadwick*, ed. D. Beales and G. Best (Cambridge, 1985), pp. 60–77.
5   R. Holt and G. Rosser, 'Introduction: The English Town in the Middle Ages', in *The Medieval Town: A Reader in English Urban History, 1200–1540*, ed. R. Holt and G. Rosser (London, 1990), pp. 1–18 at p. 13.

Ely. The second college, King's Hall, which became part of Trinity College in 1546, included the first collegiate provision for undergraduates, who otherwise usually resided in hostels. Seven further colleges followed during the fourteenth century.[6] Between the late fourteenth and early sixteenth centuries, the size of the university grew from between 400 and 700 to about 1,300 members, while the town's population declined, so that university members increased from being around one-sixth to one-third of the total population of Cambridge.[7] This rising proportion of university members led to the increasing dominance of the university within all aspects of town life. This included the built environment of the town, where the foundation of colleges from Queens' to St. John's during the fifteenth and early sixteenth centuries, together with the construction of university school buildings, created an academic quarter or campus to the west of the High Street. The impact of these religious and academic institutions remains an area ripe for further research. Although there are existing studies of the exercise of religious charity within Cambridge, concentrated on the hospital of St. John, a detailed study of the county's guilds and numerous histories of the colleges, many aspects of the pre-Reformation town and university of Cambridge remain surprisingly under-researched, despite scholarly interest over many years.[8] While there have been some studies of commemorative monuments in the university town of Oxford, its counterpart has received little attention.[9]

Exploring commemoration in medieval Cambridge requires a careful examination of the relationships that existed between town and gown. Most surveys of medieval and early modern Cambridge describe such relationships in terms of conflict. The title of Rowland Parker's book, *Town and Gown: The 700 Years' War in Cambridge*, captures this theme, but even the usually more measured tones of major reference works reflect this view. The *Victoria County History* claims that 'the story of the relations of town and gown was one of endemic border warfare, with recurrent crises'.[10] *Records of Early English Drama* suggests that 'Cambridge may serve as a perpetual challenge to the biblical

---

[6]   E. Leedham-Green, *A Concise History of the University of Cambridge* (Cambridge, 1996), pp. 2–4, 21–5.

[7]   J.S. Lee, *Cambridge and its Economic Region, 1450–1560* (Hatfield, 2005), pp. 28–9.

[8]   M. Rubin, *Charity and Community in Medieval Cambridge* (Cambridge, 1987); *Cartulary of the Hospital of St. John the Evangelist, Cambridge*, ed. M. Underwood (Cambridge Records Society, 2008); V. Bainbridge, *Gilds in the Medieval Countryside: Social and Religious Change in Cambridgeshire c.1350–1558* (Woodbridge, 1996). College histories include P. Lineham, ed., *St. John's College Cambridge: A History* (Woodbridge, 2011); D. Reynolds, ed., *Christ's: A Cambridge College Over Five Centuries* (London, 2005); J.M. Massing and N. Zeeman, eds., *King's College Chapel 1515–2015: Art, Music and Religion in Cambridge* (London, 2014).

[9]   A. Bott, *The Monuments in Merton College Chapel* (Oxford, 1964); J. Bertram, 'The Lost Brasses of Oxford, I: College Chapels', *TMBS*, 11:4 (1972), pp. 219–52; and J. Bertram, 'The Lost Brasses of Oxford, II: The Cathedral and City Churches', *TMBS*, 11:5 (1973), pp. 321–79.

[10]   R. Parker, *Town and Gown: The 700 Years' War in Cambridge* (Cambridge, 1983); 'The city of Cambridge: Town and gown', in *VCH: A History of the County of Cambridge and the Isle of Ely*, iii: *The City and University of Cambridge*, ed. J.P.C. Roach (London, 1959), p. 76.

maxim that a house divided cannot stand.'[11] Viewing the recurring complaints between the town and university authorities in isolation, such a perspective is not surprising. One could also note the violent clashes that occurred from time to time between townsmen and students, or the bitter disputes that arose between various mayors and vice-chancellors. This chapter, however, and the essays that follow take a different viewpoint and suggest that while occasional conflict did exist, co-operation between members of town and gown formed an important element of commemoration in medieval Cambridge, as well as in determining the development of the town more generally.[12] Cambridge society was made up of a complex web of interests and alliances, in which the town and gown were largely interdependent.[13] In short, co-operation was far more influential than conflict and underpinned several aspects of commemoration in this university town.

FORMS OF COMMEMORATION

The growing emphasis on the doctrine of Purgatory within the later medieval Church had a profound effect on the nature and scale of commemorative enterprises. Souls could be released from Purgatory through prayer, works of penance, alms-deeds and Masses, it was believed, as the image in a fifteenth-century Carthusian manuscript vividly depicts (Plate I). The wealthy arranged memorable funerals which included the *Placebo*, vespers for the dead recited on the night before the funeral, and the *Dirige* or dirge on the morrow, followed by the Requiem Mass and interment of the body. Knells would be rung, candles and torches burned, and members of the poor required to attend; they were attired in clothes provided from the deceased's estate and given doles of bread.[14] Hugh Chapman, for example, alderman and twice mayor of Cambridge, requested in his will of 1520 that ten priests, four clerks and four children in surplices sing *Dirige* and Mass at his burial, and 20*s.* worth of bread be given out in alms.[15]

Commemoration could include the re-enactment of particular aspects of these funeral rites. Many testators requested a monthly or yearly 'mind' (anniversary) during which the deceased would again be remembered with a Requiem Mass. Chapman required that the same number of priests, clerks and children who had attended his funeral attend his 'monthe day',

[11] A.H. Nelson, ed., *Records of Early English Drama: Cambridge*, 2 vols. (Toronto, 1989), p. 705.
[12] See also my account of the relationship between Trinity College, its predecessor colleges, and the town between the fourteenth and early eighteenth centuries: J.S. Lee, 'Trinity in the Town', in *A History of Trinity College, Cambridge*, ed. E. Leedham-Green and A. Green (forthcoming).
[13] A. Shepard, 'Litigation and Locality: the Cambridge University Courts, 1560–1640', *Urban History*, 31 (2004), pp. 5–28; A. Shepard, 'Contesting Communities? "Town" and "Gown" in Cambridge, c.1560–1640', in *Communities in Early Modern England: Networks, Place, Rhetoric*, ed. A. Shepard and P. Withington (Manchester, 2000), pp. 216–34.
[14] Burgess, 'Obligations and Strategy', pp. 296–7; E. Duffy, *The Stripping of the Altars: Traditional Religion in England 1400–1580* (2nd edition, London, 2005), pp. 354–76.
[15] CA, Archdeaconry of Ely, Will Register 1, f. 88. I am grateful to Honor Ridout for providing me with a transcript of this will.

when a bread dole would again be distributed.[16] Such ceremonies could include a solemn recreation of the funeral service: the parish hearse draped with a pall, torches or candles burned, bells rung, and the poor summoned to attend, as if the corpse were present once more. Some of these anniversaries or obits were endowed on a permanent basis, usually with income from land. Other obits were limited to a number of years and supported by monetary payments from heirs or executors. At least twenty obits were celebrated in Bassingbourn, a Cambridgeshire parish of about 500 souls, during the first forty years of the sixteenth century.[17] Maintaining these obits depended on the combined efforts of the clergy and leading parishioners.[18]

Testators could choose from a suite of remembrance aids, depending on their individual financial means. The cheapest service was the certen, where one's name was added to the prayers said during daily Mass, for an annual fee of around 4s. A trental (a series of thirty Requiem Masses) cost around 10s. Maintaining an altar light usually cost between 2s. and 4s. per annum.[19] The wealthy could afford to leave endowments to employ one or more priests to celebrate daily or weekly Masses for their souls, better known as chantries. Hugh Chapman, who was particularly conscientious when it came to his commemoration, required his executors to provide a priest to sing and pray for a year for his soul and the souls of his parents and relatives.[20] Creating a chantry was expensive as it required an appropriate endowment to provide annual income of around £6. Many chantries were thus of temporary duration, often no more than three years, but some were to be perpetual foundations, requiring an investment of at least £100 in order to support an annual income for a chantry priest.

The inclusion of the name of the deceased on a bede roll, or list of benefactors maintained by parish churches, guilds and colleges, ensured perpetual intercession and provided a vivid sense of continuity within these communities. Parishioners could have their names added by donating to the fabric or activities of the church, and churchwardens and priests were generally extremely conscientious in recording even modest benefactions.[21] The bede roll of St. Mary's guild in Cambridge, for example, included some 850 names followed by the *Kyrie* and collects. Following the Black Death of 1349 eighty-nine further names were added (Plate 1).[22] The hospital of St.

---

[16]   CA, Archdeaconry of Ely, Will Register 1, f. 88.
[17]   *The Churchwardens' Book of Bassingbourn, Cambridgeshire 1496–c.1540*, ed. D. Dymond, Cambridgeshire Records Society 17 (Cambridge, 2004), p. li.
[18]   Burgess, 'Obligations and Strategy', pp. 296–7; C. Burgess, 'A Service for the Dead: The Form and Function of the Anniversary in Late Medieval Bristol', *Transactions of the Bristol and Gloucestershire Archaeological Society*, 105 (1987), pp. 183–211.
[19]   K. Farnhill, *Guilds and the Parish Community in Late Medieval East Anglia, c.1470–1550* (York, 2001), pp. 73–4.
[20]   CA, Archdeaconry of Ely, Will Register 1, f. 88.
[21]   Duffy, *Stripping of the Altars*, pp. 153–4, 334–7.
[22]   O. Rackham, 'Why Corpus Christi?', in *Corpus within Living Memory: Life in a Cambridge College*, ed. M.E. Bury and E.J. Winter (London, 2003), pp. 9–17 at pp. 10–11; J. Hatcher, 'Commemoration of Benefactors Address, 4 December 2009: "For the Souls of the Departed in the Mortality and after the year of the Lord 1349 and after"', *The Letter* (Corpus Christi College, Cambridge), 89 (2010), pp. 14–23 at p. 19.

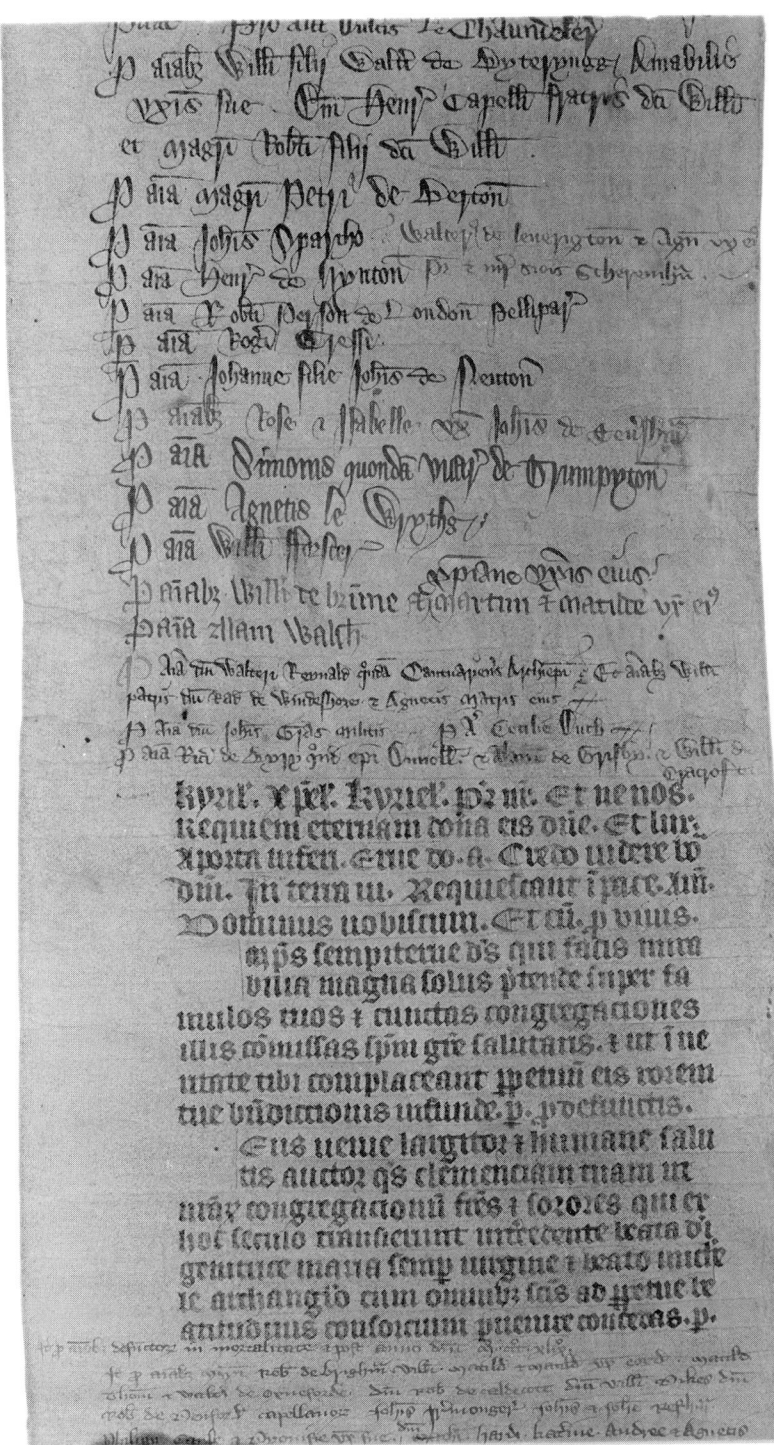

1: Corpus Christi College, Cambridge, bede roll of St. Mary's guild, Cambridge.

John possessed an account headed 'These are the names of the founders and other benefactors of this house for the souls of whom the Master and brethren have specially undertaken to pray.' The benefactors included Cambridge burgesses and three Cambridgeshire knights as well as Eustace, bishop of Ely, and Robert and Thomas Mortimer, who had created part of the hospital's original endowment.[23] At Peterhouse, as at other Cambridge colleges, the names of benefactors were entered onto a bede roll and recited at Mass several times a year. There was also an annual memorial service for benefactors and indulgences were granted to those who attended it.[24]

Commemoration was also practised through the commissioning of images and furnishings. Funerary images ranged from alabaster effigies on tomb chests commissioned by the wealthy, such as that of Hugh Ashton (d.1522) in St. John's College chapel, to slightly cheaper memorial brasses. These funerary images were generally located close to an altar which was often the designated site for intercessory Masses for the deceased and close to their grave. They may have operated as part of their subject's anniversary services and as a minimum they provided a focus for those attending the rites.[25] Ashton's tomb chest, for example, was made for his chantry chapel within the old chapel of the college, where his fellows and scholars were to say Mass for his soul and those of his patron Lady Margaret Beaufort, his parents and his benefactors.[26]

Monumental brasses for the dead survive in several Cambridge parish churches and college chapels. They were the products of an essentially urban industry, dominated by London workshops until the third quarter of the fifteenth century, when several regional centres of production emerged, including Norwich, Bury St. Edmunds and Cambridge.[27] The Cambridge-based workshop evidently produced its series of distinctive brasses between *c*.1506 and 1541, and examples of its products survive across the county. Urban examples survive in the town, such as the academic brasses of a doctor of divinity in Little St. Mary's church (*c*.1500); John Argentein (1507) and Robert Hacumblen (1528) in King's College chapel; former brasses now only surviving as indents in Great St. Mary's church (*c*.1525 and *c*.1530); priests in academical dress at Trinity Hall (*c*.1530), Christ's (*c*.1535) and Queens' (*c*.1535); and Nicholas Metcalfe's inscription (1537) in St. John's College.[28]

[23] Rubin, *Charity and Community*, p. 186.
[24] Rubin, *Charity and Community*, p. 278.
[25] Burgess, 'Obligations and Strategy', pp. 300–1.
[26] See below, Susan Powell, 'Cambridge Commemorations of Lady Margaret Beaufort's Household', in this volume pp. 123–51; C. Cross, 'Ashton, Hugh (d. 1522)', *ODNB*.
[27] S. Badham, 'Evidence for the Minor Funerary Monument Industry 1100–1500', in *Town and Country in the Middle Ages: Contrasts, Contacts and Interconnections, 1100–1500*, ed. K. Giles and C. Dyer, Society for Medieval Archaeology Monograph 22 (Leeds, 2005), pp. 169–72; M. Norris, *Monumental Brasses: The Memorials*, 2 vols. (London, 1977), i, pp. 177–95; N. Saul, *English Church Monuments in the Middle Ages: History and Representation* (Oxford, 2009), pp. 76–82.
[28] J.R. Greenwood, 'Haine's Cambridge School of Brasses', *TMBS*, 11:1 (1969), pp. 2–12; Norris, *Monumental Brasses*, i, pp. 186–8; W. Lack, H.M. Stuchfield and P. Whittemore, *The Monumental Brasses of Cambridgeshire* (London, 1995), pp. iii, 22, 25, 33–4, 36, 47–8,

The emergence of such regional workshops depended on local wealth (in the case of Cambridge generated by academic patrons), good river transport (provided by the navigable River Cam) and sufficient distance from London to ensure that carriage costs would be significantly cheaper. The identity of the craftsman or craftsmen who produced the brasses in Cambridge has not yet been determined, but the dates suggest that the work could have been carried out within the lifespan of a single master. Goldsmiths, coppersmiths, latteners, bellmakers and marblers were involved in producing brasses elsewhere, so the Cambridge workshop may not have specialised solely in monumental brasses.[29] A Suffolk workshop, possibly based in Bury St. Edmunds, may have supplied the brass of an unknown man in armour to Gonville Hall, now in the ante-chapel of Gonville and Caius College (*c.*1510).[30] Chirche's bell foundry in Bury, which supplied bells to St. John's Hospital, Great St. Mary's church and King's College, may also have produced brasses.[31] But even after the establishment of these regional centres of production, some patrons continued to order brasses from the London workshops, which probably supplied the brasses of Walter Hewke at Trinity Hall (engraved *c.*1510) and Thomas Fowler and his wife Edith at Christ's College (engraved *c.*1520).[32] This preference for London products is reflected in patterns of college consumption more generally, with many colleges, particularly the larger and wealthier institutions, looking to England's premier city to obtain top-of-the-range products, rather than sourcing within Cambridge or nearby provincial centres.[33]

Brasses were but one of several images which benefactors might choose for their commemoration. Glazing, rood screens and devotional images, wall paintings, internal and external carvings were likewise commissioned, and benefactors could use their initials, armorials, rebuses and other marks to identify their charitable contribution to the institution concerned in return for reciprocal prayer and commemoration.[34] The executors of Sir William Thorpe (d.1391), for example, completed the construction of the university's divinity school and paid for the glazing of the chapel above, where the souls of William and his wife Grace were commemorated alongside their family

---

59–60, 66, 68–71, 81–2; N. Rogers, 'Cambridgeshire Brasses', in *Cambridgeshire Churches,* ed. C. Hicks (Stamford, 1997), p. 315.

[29] Badham, 'Minor Funerary Monument Industry', p. 172; Norris, *Monumental Brasses,* i, p. 188. Lattener: a worker in or maker of latten, a mixed metal of yellow colour, either identical to, or closely resembling, brass (*OED*).

[30] The multi-media output of the Bury workshop is discussed by Nicholas Rogers, 'The Frenze Palimpsest', in *Tributes to Nigel Morgan – Contexts of Medieval Art: Images, Objects and Ideas,* ed. J.M. Luxford and M.A. Michael (Turnhout, 2010), pp. 223–40.

[31] Norris, *Monumental Brasses,* i, pp. 188–9; Lack, Stuchfield and Whittemore, *Cambridgeshire,* p. 28; Lee, *Cambridge and its Economic Region,* p. 193.

[32] Lack, Stuchfield and Whittemore, *Cambridgeshire,* pp. 81–2.

[33] Lee, *Cambridge and its Economic Region,* pp. 143–52; J.S. Lee, 'The Trade of Late Fifteenth-century Cambridge and its Region', in *The Fifteenth Century II: Revolution and Consumption in Late Medieval England,* ed. M.A. Hicks (Woodbridge, 2001), pp. 128–31.

[34] Burgess, 'Obligations and Strategy', pp. 303–4.

arms of Thorpe and Roos.[35] The rebus of Bishop John Alcock of Ely can still be found on the corbels in the hall and in the eastern windows of the library at Jesus College and is but one of many commemorative devices for the dead bishop, such as, for example, the chantry chapel where he is buried at Ely Cathedral.[36] Among the boldest of these commemorative images were those commissioned by the matriarch of the Tudor family. The lavishly carved coats of arms of Lady Margaret Beaufort (1443–1509), countess of Richmond and Derby and mother of Henry VII, still grace the gateways of her foundations of Christ's and St. John's. The plate that she bequeathed to both colleges was adorned with her heraldic badges. Elsewhere the lower walls of the ante-chapel in King's College acquired huge carvings of Henry VII's arms and badges, and the bosses in the fan vaulting also contain his Tudor rose and portcullis.[37]

Specific furnishings were given, often with a liturgical function, such as vestments, vessels, hangings and hearse cloths that would associate the donor with ceremonies observed within the church. Alderman Hugh Chapman asked for an altar frontal embroidered with flowers and three ash trees growing from three wells, a rebus commemorating John and Anne Asshewell (possibly his parents-in-law), whose souls Chapman's chantry priest was also to pray for.[38] From 1504, the University of Cambridge was required to celebrate an annual requiem service in Great St. Mary's church 'for the good and prosperous estate' of Henry VII. For this ceremony, a hearse was to be set in the middle of the church before the high crucifix and 'covered and appareled with the best and moost honorable stuffe to the said Universite belongyng for the same'. The hearse was symbolic, as both Henry and his wife, Elizabeth of York, were buried in Westminster Abbey. The hearse-cloth which was used for this purpose survives. It is decorated with a velvet cross on which the Tudor emblems of crowned roses and portcullises have been embroidered.[39] College and university libraries benefitted from bequests of manuscripts and printed books, as well as plate, money and property. Robert Hacumblen (1455/6–1528), master of King's College, asked to be buried near the chantry he had founded in the college chapel, and bequeathed to his college a brass lectern, which is still in the chapel, his 'chieff bookes', a

35   R. Kinsey, 'Each According to their Degree: The Lost Brasses of the Thorpes of North-amptonshire', *TMBS*, 18:4 (2012), pp. 311–33 at p. 331; R. Kinsey, 'The Location of Commemoration in Late Medieval England: The Case of the Thorpes of Northampton-shire', in *Memory and Commemoration in Medieval England*, ed. C.M. Barron and C. Burgess (Donington, 2010), pp. 40–57.

36   'The colleges and halls: Jesus', in *VCH: A History of the County of Cambridge and the Isle of Ely*, iii, p. 421.

37   R. Marks and P. Williamson, eds., *Gothic: Art for England 1400–1547* (London, 2003), pp. 160–1, 246–51.

38   CA, Archdeaconry of Ely, Will Register 1, f. 88.

39   This service was to take place on 11 February during the king's lifetime (when the requiem service was to be for his wife, Queen Elizabeth, who had died in 1503, and for his progenitors) and after his death, on the day of his burial: H. Tait, 'The Hearse-Cloth of Henry VII belonging to the University of Cambridge', *Journal of the Warburg and Courtauld Institutes*, 19 (1956), pp. 294–8. The item is in the Fitzwilliam Museum, Cambridge, object number AAL.3-2002.

paten 'with a schochyn of the 5 woundes' and £33 6s. 8d. for the celebration of Masses of the five wounds of Christ. His surviving memorial brass includes a shield with the five wounds and depicts him in doctor's robes holding a ribbon with an inscription which reads 'May your wounds, O Christ, be sweet medicine to me.'[40]

The later Middle Ages saw many bequests which were private acts of charity but also provided works of public utility. As well as the academic colleges, these included almshouses, hospitals, schools, bridges and roads, and water supplies.[41] In Cambridge townsmen and academics supported these works. Almshouses, for example, were founded by Thomas Jakenett, a burgess of Cambridge, and Agnes his wife in 1473, and also by Andrew Dokett, president of Queens', who specified in his 1485 will that his foundation was to be for three poor women who were to pray for his soul and those of the benefactors of his college.[42] Such bequests to support the poor were traditional acts of charity. The Cambridge scholar William Adam (d.1504), bachelor in civil law, left 40s. to build a house 'for loggyng and releyff (lodging and relief) of very pore people lyeing in the streetes of Cambrig that may not help them selff', but if the house was not constructed within eight years of his death then the bequest was to be spent on paving Jesus Lane.[43] Mercer John Herries of Cambridge (d.1418), mayor and MP for the town, left £100 to provide clothing and blankets for the poor, the blind and the deaf, as well as £10 to repair the 'vile road' from Cambridge to Barley and Barkway.[44] Thomas Pomell, another wealthy townsman, gave instructions to make a conduit in the market place but his executors refused to carry this out.[45] Testators making provision for such public works were undertaking good deeds as works of charity.[46]

INSTITUTIONS OF COMMEMORATION

The parish churches of Cambridge were places of commemoration for both townspeople and academics, reflecting the wider interaction between town and gown that took place in these buildings. Many of the clergy would have been university alumni, and the colleges acquired the right in several parishes to present the incumbent. Most importantly, many members of the university

---

[40] See below, Peter Murray Jones, 'Commemoration at a Royal College', pp. 106–22; N. Sandon, 'Hacomblen [Hacomplaynt], Robert (1455/6–1528)', *ODNB*; Lack, Stuchfield and Whittemore, *Cambridgeshire*, pp. 34, 36.

[41] J.S. Lee, 'Piped Water Supplies Managed by Civic Bodies in Medieval English Towns', *Urban History*, 41 (2014), pp. 369–93.

[42] 'The city of Cambridge: Almshouses', in *VCH: A History of the County of Cambridge and the Isle of Ely*, iii, pp. 146–7. M.G. Underwood, 'Dokett [Doket], Andrew (c.1410–1484)' *ODNB*.

[43] CUL, UA, Wills I, f. 11; *BRUC*, p. 3.

[44] R. Lovatt and M. Lovatt, 'The Religious Life of the Townsmen of Medieval Cambridge', in *Catholics in Cambridge*, ed. N. Rogers (Leominster, 2003), p. 18; E.M. Wade and L. S. Woodger, 'Herries, John (d.1418), of Cambridge', in *The History of Parliament: The House of Commons 1386–1421*, ed. J.S. Roskell, L. Clark and C. Rawcliffe (London, 1992), iii, pp. 356–7.

[45] TNA: PRO, C 1/299/52.

[46] Duffy, *Stripping of the Altars*, pp. 367–8.

would have worshipped alongside the townspeople not only as parishioners, but as members of colleges.

The colleges founded in the fourteenth century generally used neighbouring churches as places of worship, often adapting them to meet their particular liturgical needs. Hervey de Stanton (*c.*1260–1327), founder of Michaelhouse, completely rebuilt the adjacent parish church of St. Michael's after 1324. Like the abbey church of a monastery, St. Michael's gained an ante-chapel which served as a nave for parishioners, separated by a screen from the monastic chancel where members of the college prayed the canonical hours. The north choir aisle was used by Gonville Hall from its foundation in 1351 until its separate chapel was built in 1393. The church of St. Peter outside Trumpington Gate was similarly reconstructed to form the combined college chapel of Peterhouse and the parish church of St. Mary, to which it was rededicated in 1352. Thomas Cosyn, master of Corpus Christi College, built a south vestry and chapel linking St. Bene't's church with the college. The church of St. Edward King and Martyr acquired chapels for Trinity Hall and Clare between 1446 and 1466 to replace chapels lost when the church of St. John Zachary was demolished to create the new site for King's College.[47] Rebuilding of parish churches was another form of charity, benefaction and commemoration. It has been suggested that as many as two-thirds of all parish churches in England were substantially rebuilt or altered in the century and a half before the Reformation.[48] In Cambridge, such works were undertaken largely by the colleges as they adapted these buildings for their own requirements. Although these college-led schemes are among the best-documented examples of rebuilding in Cambridge parish churches, other works were funded by parishes or individuals. These included the south aisles of Holy Trinity church in Market Street. Many such additions to the church fabric served the liturgy of commemoration, including funeral chapels and chantry aisles, as well as towers to house the bells which summoned the faithful to Mass, funerals and anniversaries of the dead.[49] It has recently been argued that the remarkable series of rebuilding works in medieval Norwich during the fifteenth century inevitably led to a significant loss of earlier funerary monuments for the dead.[50] There can be little doubt that similar construction work in medieval Cambridge led to similar loss.

Although Cambridge colleges began to construct chapels within their own precincts in the later Middle Ages, this was a gradual process, and burials could only take place in college chapels which had been consecrated. Although King's Hall built and furnished an oratory between 1420 and 1424, a separate

---

[47] Brooke, 'The Churches of Medieval Cambridge'; A. Loewe, 'Michaelhouse: Hervey de Stanton's Cambridge Foundation', *Church History and Religious Culture*, 90 (2010), pp. 579–608 at p. 595.

[48] Duffy, *Stripping of the Altars*, p. 132.

[49] A.D. Brown, *Popular Piety in Late Medieval England: The Diocese of Salisbury 1250–1550* (Oxford, 1995), pp. 123–9.

[50] Christian Steer, 'Memory and Commemoration in Medieval Norwich', lecture presented at the 'Symbols in Life and Death' conference organised by the Monumental Brass Society, 18–20 September 2015, Norwich.

chapel was not started until 1464, and not consecrated until 1498–99,[51] hence the request of Richard Holme (d.1424), master of King's Hall, to be buried in the church of All Saints in Jewry. Although the church was demolished in 1864, an indent of a brass on the site is thought to be his lost memorial.[52] While Trinity Hall was granted permission for the building of a chapel in 1366, it was not consecrated until Walter Hewke's mastership (from 1510 until his death in 1518), over a century later. This enabled Hewke to be buried in the chapel where his fine, albeit restored, brass survives.[53] Elsewhere in Cambridge, Pembroke College was relatively unusual in obtaining permission to build a chapel as early as 1355. Some colleges did not acquire chapels until after the Reformation, such as Corpus Christi (1579) and Peterhouse (1628). But even after such rights had been secured, the early parish registers of Cambridge show that the colleges retained links with many churches, where fellows, scholars, servants and their families were baptised and buried.[54]

There are few Cambridge parish churches which contain any medieval brasses. Many have been lost.[55] The indent for the brass of Eudo de Helpringham (d.1329), a wealthy secular clerk who served as mayor and was also member of Parliament for Cambridge, is a rare fourteenth-century survival in St. Clement's church.[56] An indent on a Purbeck marble slab in the chapel of Jesus College is the only medieval monument from this particular college chapel to have survived and it contains a marginal inscription recording friar John de Pykenham, master of theology and 'prior of this place'. It is unclear where this slab was originally located.[57]

Only one of the sixteen parish churches of medieval Cambridge now contains any brasses for college fellows, the church of St. Mary the Less, known locally as Little St. Mary's, which also served as the college chapel for Peterhouse. A number of colleges' statutes specifically required burial of their fellows in their chapels and cloisters, although others did not secure the right of burial until after the Reformation. Much was destroyed on the orders of the Parliamentarian civil servant William Dowsing (d.1668).[58] It has also been argued that the sparsity of such brasses reflects the almost

---

[51] R. Willis and J.W. Clark, *The Architectural History of the University of Cambridge and of the Colleges of Cambridge and Eton*, 4 vols. (Cambridge, 1886, vols. 1–3 reprinted, 1988), iii, p. 512.

[52] See below, Nicholas Rogers, '"The Stones are all disrobed": Reasons for the Presence and Absence of Monumental Brasses in Cambridge', pp. 152–63. The indent was visible in 1970 but was gone by 1994: Lack, Stuchfield and Whittemore, *Cambridgeshire*, pp. 20–1.

[53] See below, Claire Gobbi Daunton and Elizabeth New, 'Patrons and Benefactors: The Masters of Trinity Hall in the Later Middle Ages', pp. 61–89.

[54] Lee, *Cambridge and its Economic Region*, pp. 69–71.

[55] Rogers, '"The Stones are all disrobed"'.

[56] Lack, Stuchfield and Whittemore, *Cambridgeshire*, p. 55.

[57] Rogers, 'Cambridgeshire Brasses', p. 317; Lack, Stuchfield and Whittemore, *Cambridgeshire*, p. 31, dates the stone to *c.*1300. No friar of this name is known, but there was a Friar John Pickering, D.D., Prior of the Dominicans in Cambridge, 1523–31: J.R. Moorman, *The Grey Friars in Cambridge, 1225–1538* (Cambridge, 1952), p. 202.

[58] Rogers, '"The Stones are all disrobed"'; T. Cooper, ed., *The Journal of William Dowsing: Iconoclasm in East Anglia During the English Civil War* (Woodbridge, 2001).

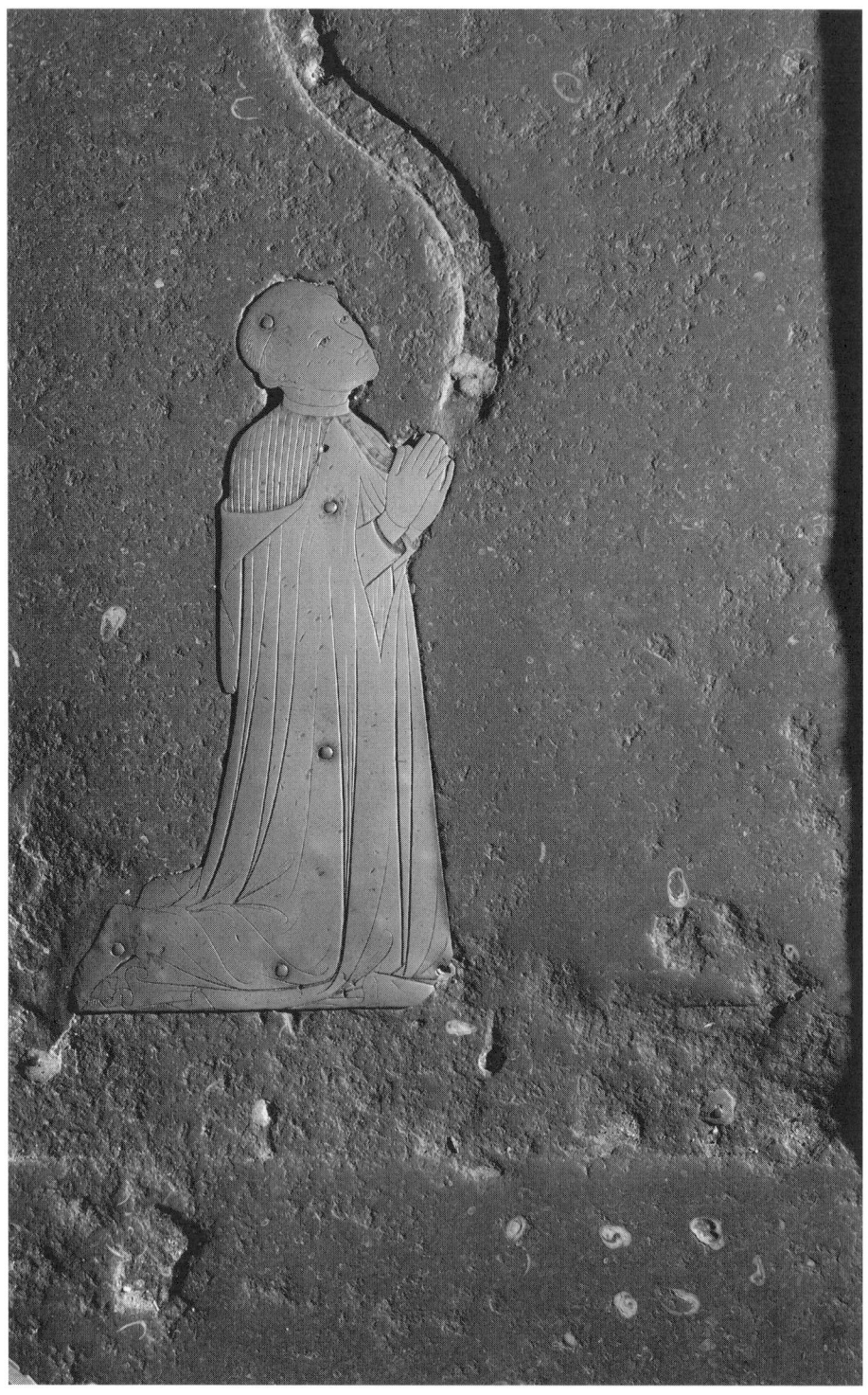

2: Brass of Richard Billingford (d.1432), St. Bene't's' church, Cambridge.

complete absence of an academic profession in the Middle Ages. Most fellows were anxious to obtain an ecclesiastical post outside the university as even a modest living offered better prospects than a meagre college fellowship: 'Only the unfortunate, or the exceptional, died in their colleges.'[59] Little St. Mary's contains the brass of John Holbroke (d.1436) and another brass of three-quarter-length format of a doctor of divinity which has lost its inscription but may commemorate either John Warkworth (*c.*1425–1500) or Henry Hornby (*c.*1457–1518), both masters of Peterhouse and both founders of chantries.[60] A brass commemorating Richard Billingford (d.1432) was stolen from the south aisle of St. Bene't's church in 2008 but has since been recovered (Plate 2). Holbroke and Billingford were college fellows who were doctors of theology and their brasses depict them wearing their academical dress. They also served as masters of their respective colleges, Peterhouse and Corpus Christi, as chancellors of the university and at the fringes of the royal court.[61]

Great St. Mary's formed the principal parish church for both the borough and university authorities by virtue of its location – 'equidistant from the Guildhall and the university's Schools ... shared and overlapping public space for each body'.[62] The university's official meetings, including disputations, generally took place there, as did annual ceremonies for the conferment of degrees until 1730 when the Senate House was constructed. A university chest was stored at the church in 1381 when it was looted during the Peasants' Revolt. At least eighteen men who were appointed mayor of Cambridge between 1450 and 1560 had connections with this church and eight of them had served as churchwardens or other officers for the parish.[63] Vice-chancellors, proctors and churchwardens organised fund-raising for the rebuilding of the church's nave around the 1490s. Dr. Thomas Barowe (d.1499), former fellow of King's Hall and lawyer and administrator to Richard III, gave £240 in 1495 to continue the rebuilding and pay for an obit in the church for the souls of the former king and his consort, parents and brothers.[64] Support for the rebuilding was also received from Henry VII and Lady Margaret Beaufort, as well as from ten bishops and thirty heads of religious houses.

'Canons and nuns who promised prayers in return for acres' was how Frederic Maitland described the religious houses of Cambridge, who received gifts of land from the townspeople, mostly 'in small parcels from small people'.

[59] R. Lovatt, 'Two Collegiate Loan Chests in Late Medieval Cambridge', in *Medieval Cambridge: Essays on the Pre-Reformation University*, ed. P. Zutshi (Woodbridge, 1993), pp. 129–65 at p. 129; Saul, *English Church Monuments*, pp. 201–3.

[60] Rogers, 'Cambridgeshire Brasses', p. 315; Lack, Stuchfield and Whittemore, *Cambridgeshire*, pp. 68–71; E.D. Kennedy, 'Warkworth, John (c.1425–1500)' and M.G. Underwood, 'Hornby [Horneby], Henry (c.1457–1518)', *ODNB*.

[61] See below, J.H. Baker, 'A Comparison of Academical and Legal Costume on Memorial Brasses', pp. 90–105; Lovatt, 'Two Collegiate Loan Chests', pp. 129–30; Lack, Stuchfield and Whittemore, *Cambridgeshire*, pp. 52–3, 68–9.

[62] Shepherd, 'Contesting Communities?', p. 223.

[63] Lee, *Cambridge and its Economic Region*, p. 71.

[64] A.F. Sutton and L. Visser-Fuchs, '"As dear to him as the Trojans were to Hector": Richard III and the University of Cambridge', in *Richard III and East Anglia: Magnates, Gilds and Learned Men*, ed. L. Visser-Fuchs (Richard III Society, 2010), pp. 130–42.

By the fourteenth century, the house of Augustinian canons at Barnwell Priory held around one-third of the total land in the town's East Fields; the other ecclesiastical and collegiate bodies held another third, leaving only a third to be held by townspeople.[65] The religious houses also received gifts from academics, such as Warkworth of Peterhouse, who made bequests to the monasteries of Ely, Crowland and Barnwell.[66] Barnwell Priory was to pay the annual stipends of two chaplains, students of theology in the University of Cambridge, who were to maintain a chantry founded by the executors of William of Kilkenny (d.1256), bishop of Ely. This is the earliest known chantry in Cambridge. The Cambridge alderman John Keynsham and Thomas King of Wisbech, two prominent merchants who established obits at the priory in 1502 and 1503–04 respectively, probably had personal connections with the prior of Barnwell, William Cambridge alias Rayson (d.1522), who was a member of an influential Cambridge family. Keynsham, who bequeathed his house in Bridge Street for the obit, appointed the mayor and borough officers as trustees and willed that a 'jonchett' be held immediately after the *Dirige*, when the mayor and other officers were to enjoy bread, cheese and ale and give alms to the poor. This supper long survived the dissolution of the priory, for in 1669 the mayor and aldermen still feasted on bacon and stewed prunes at this annual occasion.[67] Keynsham was one of several Cambridge burgesses who entrusted the borough government with arranging for exequies to be carried out and chose to fund them by bequeathing booths in Stourbridge Fair, a major annual trading event which brought merchants from many parts of England, including London and Coventry. By the turn of the sixteenth century, the borough treasurers were spending nearly £5 on these obits.[68]

The hospital of St. John was founded around 1200 by the burgesses of Cambridge, but quickly came under the patronage of the bishop of Ely. A community of scholars was established at the hospital in 1280 by Hugh Balsham, bishop of Ely (d.1286), but the two communities were unable to work together and the bishop removed the scholars in 1284 to form the college of Peterhouse.[69] The hospital, however, maintained contacts with both town and university through other means, including the provision of Mass for a town congregation and offering lodgings for a few members of the university.[70] Cambridge burgesses created two chantries at Holy Sepulchre

---

[65] F.W. Maitland, *Township and Borough* (Cambridge, 1898), pp. 59–63, 129–33, 161–3.

[66] Kennedy, 'Warkworth', *ODNB*.

[67] Rubin, *Charity and Community*, p. 191; 'Houses of Augustinian Canons: Priory of Barnwell', in *VCH: A History of the County of Cambridge and the Isle of Ely*, ed. L.F. Salzman (London, 1948), ii, pp. 234–49.

[68] CA, City/PB Box, X70/1–10, X71/1–10; Rubin, *Charity and Community*, p. 191. For Stourbridge Fair see Lee, *Cambridge and its Economic Region*, pp. 118–41 and J.S. Lee, 'The Role of Fairs in Late Medieval England' in *Town and Countryside in the Age of the Black Death: Essays in Honour of John Hatcher*, ed. S. Rigby and M. Bailey (Turnhout, 2012), pp. 407–37.

[69] R. Lovatt, 'Hugh of Balsham, bishop of Ely 1256/7–1286', in *Pragmatic Utopias: Ideals and Communities, 1200–1630*, ed. R. Horrox and S. Rees Jones (Cambridge, 2001), pp. 72–7.

[70] M. Underwood, 'The Impact of St. John's College as Landowner in the West Fields of Cambridge in the Early Sixteenth Century', in *Medieval Cambridge*, ed. Zutshi, pp. 169–71.

church as benefactors of St. John's Hospital during the thirteenth century, and another was created in St. Botolph's church in 1392. Other donors granted income just for the maintenance of a light in the hospital's chapel.[71] While there is little surviving evidence about poor or sick inmates at any period of the hospital's history, the institution's commemorative activities are better documented and even extended to paying 2*d*. for 'making a tombstone for a pauper' in 1485.[72]

There were also several monastic and mendicant foundations linked to the university which, unlike most of the secular colleges, surrendered their estates to the Crown during the Reformation. These included the house of Gilbertine canons of St. Edmund, Buckingham College for Benedictine monks and the Franciscan, Dominican, Carmelite and Austin convents in Cambridge. Their libraries were dispersed following their suppression and their history is piecemeal at best.[73] And yet the friars played a major role in academic study within the medieval university, particularly in theology, and remained popular with the laity. The Franciscans arrived in Cambridge during the 1220s and by 1230 they were in receipt of a mortuary roll from the Benedictine nunnery of Holy Cross and St. Mary and St. James at Castle Hedingham, Essex. Within twenty years the minister general admitted the order's friends and benefactors to the benefits of the friars' prayers, and a letter of fraternity followed as confidence in the friars' intercession grew.[74]

Dependent on charity, the friars were 'only as successful as the support and generosity of their benefactors in the town and elsewhere enabled them to be'.[75] The Cambridge friars were typical of their brethren elsewhere and received legacies from nobles and gentry, such as Dame Anne St. George de Foxton in 1523, from the local clergy, including Walter Smith, rector of St. Bene't's in 1488, and from the townspeople and scholars of Cambridge.[76] Henry Veysey, apothecary, left 10*s*. in 1503 to every order of friars in Cambridge to sing *Placebo* and *Dirige*, as well as 5 marks to the Blackfriars in the town to pray for him. William Adam, bachelor in law, gave 20*s*. in 1504 to each order of Cambridge friars 'commyng and helpyng me to the beriall of my body'.[77] The friars also attracted bequests from villages around Cambridge, stretching to Upwell twenty-nine miles to the north. Many were small gifts such as the single comb of barley left by John Sereman of Boxworth in 1521 to the orders

---

71 Rubin, *Charity and Community*, pp. 187–8, 192, n. 48.
72 M. Underwood, 'A Cruel Necessity? Christ's and St. John's, Two Cambridge Re-foundations', in *Pragmatic Utopias*, ed. Horrox and Rees Jones, pp. 84–96 at p. 89.
73 Zutshi, ed., *Medieval Cambridge*, p. 4; R.B. Dobson, 'The Monastic Orders in Late Medieval Cambridge', in *The Medieval Church: Universities, Heresy and the Religious Life*, ed. P. Biller and R.B. Dobson, Studies in Church History Subsidia 11 (Woodbridge, 1999), pp. 239–69; K.W. Humphries, ed., *The Friars' Libraries* (London, 1990), pp. 3–4 (Austin), p. 196 (Dominican) and p. 209 (Franciscan); Moorman, *Grey Friars*, pp. 127–42.
74 See below, Michael Robson, 'The Commemoration of the Living and the Dead at the Friars Minor of Cambridge', pp. 34–51, for details of the legacies given to the friars and their commemorative activities.
75 Lovatt, 'Religious Life', p. 12.
76 Moorman, *Grey Friars*, pp. 64–8, 246–59.
77 CUL, UA, Wills I, ff. 4v–6, 10–11v.

of friars in Cambridge who were to pray for his soul.[78] The Cambridge friars occasionally performed these services in village churches: in his will of 1519 John Cooke of Bottisham requested that a brother of the Friars Preachers of Cambridge sing a trental of Masses in the village church.[79] The privilege of burial in a friary church was much sought after and a number of Cambridge testators made provision for this. Some families had built relationships with particular orders over several generations: Hugh Rankyn requested in 1521 to be buried in Grey Friars church in Cambridge under the same stone as his father and grandfather.[80] We have no records of any memorial brasses from the Cambridge friaries, but we know that London's Black Friars was an extremely popular place of burial where there were over 100 recorded monuments in the friary church and probably many more.[81] The London Grey Friars was likewise a 'melting pot of the dead' with 682 monuments recorded in its burial register.[82]

Religious guilds or fraternities, devoted to a given saint or an aspect of the veneration of Christ, such as Corpus Christi, were popular in the second half of the fourteenth century and new guilds continued to be founded into the 1530s. One of their principal purposes was commemoration: they procured prayers and alms from their living members for the souls of their deceased members. Guilds also maintained lights in churches and promoted charitable and communal activities.[83] The Cambridge guilds were another type of institution with a commemorative purpose which engaged members from both town and gown. In the early sixteenth century, St. Katherine's guild at Holy Trinity church included a university bedell and doctor of law, the father of the president of Queens' College, and six men who had served as mayors of Cambridge.[84] The most striking instance of such town–gown co-operation was the foundation of Corpus Christi College, where as Damien Leader has noted 'the interests of town and university – a chantry for the citizens, and financial support for the scholars – produced a mutually agreeable solution'.[85] This was in the wake of the Black Death, which had arrived in Cambridge around Easter 1349, killing around half the population. In response to the plague came the foundations of Trinity Hall to provide canon and civil lawyers and Corpus Christi College to train priests and to provide prayers

---

[78] BL, Add. MS 5861, ff. 21–77v; CA, Archdeaconry of Ely, Will Register 1*, f. 44; J.S. Lee, 'Decline and Growth in the Late Medieval Fenland: The Examples of Outwell and Upwell', *Proceedings of the Cambridge Antiquarian Society*, 104 (2015), pp. 137–47 at p. 142.

[79] BL, Add. MS 5861, f. 67v.

[80] TNA:PRO, PROB 11/20, f. 135. Moorman, *Grey Friars*, p. 253.

[81] C. Steer, 'Royal and Noble Commemoration in the Mendicant Houses of London, *c.*1240–1540', in *Memory and Commemoration in Medieval England*, ed. C.M. Barron and C. Burgess (Donington, 2010), pp. 117–42 at p. 127.

[82] BL, Cotton MS Vitellius XII, ff. 274–316 printed in C.L. Kingsford, *The Grey Friars of London* (Aberdeen, 1915), pp. 70–144.

[83] Duffy, *Stripping of the Altars*, pp. 141–54.

[84] M. Siraut, 'Accounts of Saint Katherine's Guild at Holy Trinity Church, Cambridge: 1514–37', *Proceedings of the Cambridge Antiquarian Society*, 67 (1977), pp. 111–21 at pp. 114–17.

[85] D.R. Leader, *A History of the University of Cambridge*, i: *The University to 1546* (Cambridge, 1988), p. 86.

for the souls of departed guild members. Corpus was founded in 1352 by two town guilds which had amalgamated: the guild of the Blessed Virgin Mary and the guild of Corpus Christi. The first statutes of the college required the master, fellows and scholars, who were to be men of holy orders, to say Mass at St. Bene't's and St. Botolph's on feast days and to be present at the funerals of the brothers and sisters of the unified guild. The first members of the college were officers or chaplains within the guild.[86] The united guild is last recorded in the 1370s and the college inherited its property and plate, including a great horn and coconut cup, which are still in the college's possession.[87] In addition to its commemorative activities for townspeople and scholars, the college continued to lead the annual Corpus Christi day procession involving borough and university officials, which has been described as the 'most spectacular public event in the town's religious life during the late Middle Ages'.[88] While the links between town and gown in founding Corpus Christi College are well known, the involvement of wealthy and influential London merchants in establishing this commemorative institution is much more obscure. The notebook written by John Hardy *c*.1358 records donations and promises to the new guild of Corpus Christi by citizens of London. Previous historians, concerned with the local angle, have been puzzled by entries on a page headed 'Henry duke of Lancaster', listing a series of names which have been previously dismissed as probably a mixed bag of local men of modest standing. In fact, these names are those of some of the foremost citizens of London, including Andrew Aubrey, mayor of London, a merchant of fabulous wealth and political acumen.[89]

Corpus Christi College's other major patrons were Henry of Grosmont, first duke of Lancaster (*c*.1310–61), and his son-in-law John of Gaunt, duke of Lancaster (1340–99). It was Gaunt's support that provoked much of the hostility of the rebels towards the college in the Peasants' Revolt of 1381 and helps to explain why this institution, which was founded as 'a symbol of corporate unity and cooperation between town and gown',[90] became a target of attack. Grosmont had secured the royal licence for the new foundation and negotiated an exchange of sites for the new college, and Gaunt had successfully lobbied for the college to be granted permission to acquire additional lands and rents.[91] The rolls of Parliament, detailing the rising in Cambridge, refer to the college as 'the foundation of our most excellent lord of Lancaster'.[92]

---

[86] Hatcher, 'Commemoration of Benefactors Address'.

[87] Rackham, 'Why Corpus Christi?', pp. 10–12.

[88] M. Rubin, *Corpus Christi: The Eucharist in Late Medieval Culture* (Cambridge, 1991), p. 270.

[89] S. Thrupp, *The Merchant Class of Medieval London 1300–1500* (London, 1948), p. 322; See below, Richard Barber, 'The City of London and the Founding of the Guild of Corpus Christi', pp. 52–60.

[90] P.W. White, *Drama and Religion in English Provincial Society, 1485–1660* (Cambridge 2008), p. 106.

[91] TNA: PRO, C 143/367/3; C.P. Hall, 'The Gild of Corpus Christi and the Foundation of Corpus Christi College: An Investigation of the Documents', in *Medieval Cambridge*, ed. Zutshi, pp. 62–92 at pp. 80–4; Leader, *History of the University*, pp. 87–8.

[92] R.B. Dobson, ed., *The Peasants' Revolt of 1381*, 2nd edn. (London, 1983), pp. 240–1.

Gaunt was widely blamed by the rebels for the military failings and financial exactions of government, and many of his properties were targets during the revolt. In Cambridge, there were also riots by townspeople against the university, in which the university was forced to surrender its royal privileges and books and charters were ceremoniously burnt in the market place. This was not purely an attack against the university and colleges, though, as a number of prominent Cambridge men, such as John Blankpayn and Richard Maisterman, who had collected the poll tax, and Roger Harleston, member of Parliament, did not escape the rebels either.[93] There was a general wave of anti-clerical opposition, also expressed locally when rebels attacked Barnwell Priory. These attacks on the priory and Corpus Christi College, and the market-place riots against the university, were all protests against property and privilege.

The university and its colleges formed another major group of commemorative institutions in Cambridge. Historians have long debated whether the central purpose of the university colleges was as chantries or as educational institutions.[94] Contemporaries, though, are likely to have conceived their spiritual and academic aims as complementary. For example, the earliest known statutes of the university, dating to *c.*1250, make provision for observing the exequies of King Henry III and Hugh of Northwold, bishop of Ely, as well as for attendance at the funerals of deceased masters.[95] The master and fellows of Peterhouse were to attend weekly memorial Masses for the souls of the founder Hugh of Balsham, for Simon Montacute (1304?–45), the bishop of Ely, who had given statutes to the college, and for the souls of Montacute's parents and other benefactors.[96] The statutes of Michaelhouse required the fellows to pray for former kings and queens of England, personal benefactors of the founder Hervey de Stanton, and benefactors of the college and parish of St. Michael's.[97] At Gonville Hall, a detailed programme of worship was prescribed by William Bateman (*c.*1298–1355), bishop of Norwich, which required every fellow to hear or sing Mass daily, repeat the *Ave Maria* fifty times and pray for the college's benefactors.[98] And at nearby St. Catharine's, the founder Robert Wodelarke (*d.*1481?) detailed elaborate intercessory prayers within the college statutes that were to be offered for his soul and for those of his parents, for King Henry VI and for others.[99] Walter Hewke, master of Trinity Hall (d.1518), ordained that a priest-scholar

[93]   E.M. Wade, 'Cambridge Borough' and 'Blankpayn, John, of Cambridge', and 'Maisterman, Richard, of Cambridge and Duxford, Cambs.', in *The History of Parliament*, ed. Roskell, Clark and Rawcliffe, i, pp. 286–91; ii, pp. 249–50; iii, p. 670.

[94]   Brooke, 'The Churches of Medieval Cambridge', p. 62; A.B. Cobban, *The Medieval English Universities: Oxford and Cambridge to c.1500* (Aldershot, 1988), pp. 112–13; A. Cobban, *English University Life in the Middle Ages* (London, 1999), pp. 122–5.

[95]   M.B. Hackett, *The Original Statutes of Cambridge University: The Text and its History* (Cambridge, 1970), pp. 175–6, 216–17.

[96]   Cobban, *English University Life*, p. 122.

[97]   Loewe, 'Michaelhouse', p. 595.

[98]   M. Underwood, 'Religion and the University to 1535', in *Catholics in Cambridge*, ed. N. Rogers (Leominster, 2003), pp. 22–37 at p. 28.

[99]   Cobban, *English University Life*, p. 123.

was to pray for himself, his friends and for the souls of the founder William Bateman, Hewke's parents, Thomas Crane and for all Christian souls, and to celebrate the Mass of the Five Wounds of Jesus in the college chapel every Friday.[100]

Patronage frequently influenced the nature of benefactions and some colleges reflected the special devotions of their founders. King's College was founded in 1441 on a scale surpassing any other college in either Oxford or Cambridge: its members were expected to remember the king, his family and his royal ancestors in their liturgical practice. Henry VI, who was born on St. Nicholas' day, 6 December, initially dedicated King's as the royal college of St. Nicholas, later joining it with devotion to the Virgin.[101] The college's illuminated foundation charter depicts Henry VI kneeling in prayer, with members of the houses of Lords and Commons in the margin (Plate II). All are gazing towards the Virgin, encircled with angels, and St. Nicholas, interceding on their behalf.[102] King's was granted unique exemptions from university and ecclesiastical supervision or interference, including the establishment of its own probate jurisdiction. These records reveal late medieval practices commemorating donors to King's College, irrespective of whether they were royalty or commoners. Gifts and bequests included books, ecclesiastical vestments and jewellery. There were also memorial brasses and inscriptions in the chapel. Some forms of giving, like the endowment of chantries or annual sermons, were self-evidently commemorative; others might only be recorded in documents to be held in the treasury. These written records preserved at King's are as much commemorative as they are legal or administrative.[103]

College and university benefactors included royalty, nobility and gentry, senior churchmen, university personnel and townspeople.[104] It has been suggested that apart from Corpus Christi College, the colleges attracted little patronage from townsmen,[105] but this ignores the role of local men in the establishment of Queens' College. The efforts of Andrew Dokett (*c*.1410–84), rector of St. Botolph's, secured the patronage of Queen Margaret of Anjou and subsequently of Queen Elizabeth Woodville; he also made an endowment and bequests. Richard Andrew (or Spicer) was one of several parishioners of St. Botolph's who provided land for the initial site of the college. Andrew left property in return for an obit in St. Botolph's church with twenty-four priests present from the college fellowship. The college acquired its present site in 1447, largely from the gift of another burgess and parishioner, John Morris.[106]

[100] See below, Gobbi Daunton and New, 'Patrons and Benefactors', below.
[101] C.N.L. Brooke, 'The Dedications of Cambridge Colleges and their Chapels', in *Medieval Cambridge*, ed. Zutshi, pp. 7–20.
[102] Marks and Williamson, eds., *Gothic*, p. 162.
[103] Jones, 'Commemoration at a Royal College', below.
[104] A. Cobban, 'English University Benefactors in the Middle Ages', *History*, 86 (2001), pp. 288–312.
[105] Rubin, *Charity and Community*, p. 191.
[106] Underwood, 'Dokett', *ODNB*.

Yet a particular interest in academic benefaction, as a liturgical and mnemonic device for royal commemoration, endured into the early sixteenth century. The preoccupations of Lady Margaret Beaufort, the King's Mother, are well known. She was resident at Collyweston in Northamptonshire, so Cambridge was the closer of the two universities and easily accessible, not just from Collyweston but also from Hatfield, Croydon, London and Richmond, her other places of residence during those years. The connection had been fostered by John Fisher, first her confessor, then, as bishop of Rochester, her close confidant and advisor, and a man whose professional life had always been based in Cambridge: she met him first as senior proctor and before long he was advanced to life-chancellor of the university. The extent of Lady Margaret's association with Cambridge is mirrored through patterns of burial and commemoration expressed by her entourage and household, including brasses in Christ's to Edith Fowler and her husband Thomas, and to John Syclyng, the college's first master. Her funding of the Lady Margaret readership in divinity, for which the university covenanted to perform exequies, laid an enduring foundation for professorships and readerships even though the associated religious observances did not survive the Reformation. Lady Margaret's personal management of a second college was forestalled by her death in 1509, and it was Fisher, with the assistance of Henry Hornby and Hugh Ashton, the co-executors of her will, who effectively brought St. John's College to completion by 1511. Monuments for Hornby, her former chancellor, and Ashton, her receiver-general, were commissioned in Cambridge.[107]

While most academic benefactors in Cambridge were associated with institutions for higher education, some, including Lady Margaret, also made provision for teaching in grammar schools. In 1439, the London parish priest William Bingham (d.1451) had founded Godshouse to support the training of schoolmasters, and when the college was re-founded by Lady Margaret Beaufort in 1505 with additional endowments as Christ's College, six places were reserved for scholars to study grammar who were expected to teach in schools. Bishop Alcock's foundation of Jesus College in 1496 included an unspecified number of scholars to be educated in grammar. Although Alcock did not live to complete his plans, Lady Katherine Bray endowed the school in 1506 by securing the rectory of Great Shelford, five miles south of Cambridge, and its tithe income, enabling the school to provide free instruction.[108]

The university and colleges received donations in return for performing obits or memorial services in college chapels or churches in their patronage. Sir Robert Thorpe (d.1372) contributed towards the construction of the new divinity school at the university and after his death the project was continued by his nephew William Thorpe and his executors. In return, the university chancellor Eudo de la Zouche promised in 1398 to celebrate the obsequies of

[107] See below, Powell, 'Cambridge Commemorations'.
[108] N. Orme, 'The Medieval Schools of Cambridge, 1200–1550', *Proceedings of the Cambridge Antiquarian Society*, 104 (2015), pp. 125–36.

William and his wife annually in the new chapel above the school, and every graduate on his admission to the university was to say *De profundis* for the souls of William and his wife.[109] The university proctors were responsible for the due observance of these exequies and recorded them alongside those of other important benefactors in calendars in their books of statutes.[110] Richard Treton, executor to Sir Robert, and subsequently master of Corpus Christi College, left 100 marks to the college for the annual commemoration of Robert's soul, and 40 marks to each of the other seven colleges at Cambridge for annual prayers for the same purpose.[111] A century or so later in 1497, Edith Chamber of Cambridge left a messuage in St. Michael's Lane for the perpetual celebration of a daily Mass for her soul by a fellow of Michaelhouse who served as the parish chaplain and for yearly exequies with distributions to scholars and to the poor. The donation would default to the hospital of St. John if the original agreement could not be kept.[112] The colleges of Christ's and St. John's recognised the importance of sustaining the intercessory prayers of their predecessor institutions, and the fellows of these two colleges were required to pray specifically for the major benefactors of St. John's Hospital and Godshouse.[113] This dovetailed relationship between town and gown meant that college fellows would automatically have assumed the role of chantry priests.

The provision of loans at low interest, another form of charitable relief, also provided an opportunity for commemoration. Students in medieval universities sought credit with the expectation of obtaining more income after completing their studies, just as they do today. Nine university loan chests were founded in Cambridge in the fourteenth and fifteenth centuries. Loans were given against the security of an object which was marked and kept in the chest. Bishop William Bateman founded the Holy Trinity chest in 1354 with a capital of £100. Borrowers from the chest, deposited in the Carmelite friary, were to say the *Pater Noster* and the *Ave Maria* three times a day for the health of Bishop Bateman's soul – 'the charitable act of providing credit was expected to bear spiritual returns to the giver'. Founders were entered as benefactors of the university to be prayed for on their anniversaries and on the general benefactors' day.[114] There were also at least eleven college loan-chests of which nine were provided during the fifteenth century.[115] The Peterhouse chest was given by Thomas of Barnard Castle in 1420 and supplemented

---

[109] Kinsey, 'Location of Commemoration', pp. 46–7; H.P. Stokes, *The Chaplains and the Chapel of the University of Cambridge (1256–1568)*, Cambridge Antiquarian Society Publications, Octavo Series 41 (Cambridge, 1906), pp. 20–3. Stokes, and also Willis and Clark, *Architectural History*, pp. 10–11, confuse Sir Robert Thorpe with a contemporary of the same name who was master of Pembroke College.

[110] CUL, UA Collect. Admin. 3, pp. 11–16v.

[111] Kinsey, 'Location of Commemoration', p. 46.

[112] Rubin, *Charity and Community*, pp. 191, 280–1.

[113] Underwood, 'A Cruel Necessity?', pp. 84–96.

[114] Rubin, *Charity and Community*, pp. 284–6.

[115] G. Pollard, 'Medieval Loan Chests at Cambridge', *Bulletin of the Institute of Historical Research*, 17 (1939–40), pp. 113–29. On chests generally, see also E. Danbury, 'Security and Safeguard: Signs and Symbols on Boxes and Chests', in *Signs and Symbols*, ed. J. Cherry and A. Payne (Donington, 2009), pp. 29–41.

by John Holbroke in 1427, two successive masters of the college. In return, exequies and requiems were to be celebrated for Masters Thomas and Holbroke and two of their associates, William Noion and Thomas Pacchyng. From around 1500 the importance of these chests declined, with fewer loans and less orderly record-keeping. This seems to have reflected the growing standard of living of fellows, which made use of the loans less necessary, and the demise of the manuscript book, which had formed the principal form of pledge deposited in the chests. Registers of the loan chests of the colleges of Peterhouse and Corpus Christi survive, and Corpus Christi still possesses what is almost certainly Billingford's personal loan chest.[116] Richard Andrew established a similar chest for burgesses of Cambridge with a capital of 80 marks through his will made in 1459, from which they might borrow up to 26s. 8d. Each person receiving money was to say the psalm *De profundis* for the souls of Richard, his parents, wife and benefactors, and if the recipient was not literate then they were to say the Lord's Prayer, the angelic salutation and the Apostles' Creed.[117] Guilds also loaned money, usually exclusively to their members, and used the profits to fund their charitable activities. St. Katherine's guild was doing this in Cambridge in the early sixteenth century. Some guilds also hired out cattle or sheep.[118]

This essay has endeavoured to sketch out the varied aspects of commemoration in medieval Cambridge and the possibilities and challenges which were available in an urban setting. Commemoration took the form of both actions and objects: actions could include the provision of a monthly or yearly mind, a certen and a trental, maintaining a light, endowing a chantry priest or an obit. Objects included the commissioning of funerary images, such as tomb chests or memorial brasses, donating liturgical items, endowing a college or a loan chest, providing almshouses or other public works. Many acts of commemoration were recorded in bede rolls and records of benefactors, as well as through glazing, carving and other forms of decoration. And the act of commemoration could be displayed in a variety of institutions, including parish churches, religious houses, colleges and guilds. In Cambridge, the university provided additional opportunities for commemoration which were not generally available elsewhere. While many colleges were founded by royal and noble families and the senior clergy, Cambridge townspeople played a leading role in establishing two colleges, Corpus Christi and Queens'. The sacking of Corpus Christi College a generation later during the Peasants' Revolt reflected national grievances directed at John of Gaunt, the college's leading patron, rather than merely a local attack of a disgruntled townspeople against their academic neighbours barricaded behind stout gates. Indeed, an over-simplistic dichotomy of town and gown can mask a range of complex interrelations throughout society. These were two communities that lived side by side and the many forms of commemoration are testimony to this.

---

[116] Lovatt, 'Two Collegiate Loan Chests'.
[117] *Annals of Cambridge*, ed. C.H. Cooper, 5 vols. (Cambridge, 1842–1908), i, p. 210.
[118] Farnhill, *Guilds*, pp. 64–5, 67; Siraut, 'Accounts'.

The Reformation transformed many aspects of commemoration. The dissolution of the monasteries and chantries, and the suppression of the guilds, led to the loss or desecration of many funerary monuments, images and furnishings. One commemorative institution within Cambridge remained virtually untouched. The colleges escaped the threat of dissolution under the terms of the chantries acts of the 1540s through exerting pressure at the royal court and 'public recognition as deserving institutions which were entitled to special consideration'.[119] Commemoration within colleges survived, albeit in a modified form, and statutes of Elizabeth I required every college to assemble in its chapel after the end of each term and commemorate the founder and benefactors, followed by prayers preceded by the words, 'The memory of the righteous shall remain for evermore.'[120]

[119] T.A.R. Evans and R.J. Faith, 'College Estates and University Finances, 1350–1500', in *The History of the University of Oxford*, ii: *Late Medieval Oxford*, ed. J.I. Catto and R. Evans (Oxford, 1992), pp. 635–707 at pp. 701–2; V. Morgan and C. Brooke, *A History of the University of Cambridge*, ii: *1546–1750* (Cambridge, 2004), pp. 5–9.

[120] Morgan, *History*, p. 211.

CHAPTER 2

The Commemoration of the Living and the Dead at the Friars Minor of Cambridge

Michael Robson

In imitation of the apostolic community, the monastic world was centred on the celebration of the Divine Office and a life of self-abnegation within the cloister, where the individual lived, worked and prayed; one dimension of the monks' interaction with society was their intercession for founders, patrons and benefactors. By the later twelfth century a fresh understanding of the *vita apostolica* was gaining ground in western Europe, a concept that inspired St. Francis of Assisi to testify to the Gospel by engaging with society in a global cloister; his calling was to take Christian principles to the market place, the streets and the cross-roads. His followers divested themselves of their possessions and engaged in manual work in the towns and cities where they dwelt. This novel model of religious life was transplanted to England by nine penniless friars who landed in Kent during the late summer of 1224. Within a few years they were winning plaudits, initially for their testimony to the Gospel and then for their preaching, a ministry that became emblematic of their contribution to the local Church. Another conspicuous contribution lay in the realm of suffrages: a premium was placed on their intercession and members of the laity, the clergy and fellow religious eagerly sought their prayers. This study explores the order's establishment in Cambridge, the church of the Friars Minor in the town, the friars and intercession, the legion of testators and those interred in their church.

THE FRIARS' SETTLEMENT IN CAMBRIDGE

The Roman town of Cambridge had much to commend it to the friars through its ancient market close to the parish church of St. Mary, its network of a dozen or so parish churches in the thirteenth century,[1] the hospital of St. John the

---

[1] C.N.L. Brooke, 'The Churches of Medieval Cambridge', in *History, Society and the Churches: Essays in Honour of Owen Chadwick*, ed. D. Beales and G. Best (Cambridge, 1985), pp. 49–76 at pp. 50–1.

Evangelist[2] and the nunnery of St. Radegund. In addition, the growth of the schools of Cambridge into a university that offered a degree in theology[3] was a further attraction for the friars, who were already drawing students from Oxford University to their ranks. The friars were first welcomed to Cambridge by the burgesses about 1225 and they were initially accommodated on the site of the present Guildhall. Their first home was formerly occupied by Benjamin the Jew.[4] It was contiguous to a prison; the fact that the friary and the gaol shared a common entrance eventually became onerous to the friars. Henry III gave the friars 10 marks for the rent of the property which the burgesses purchased for the order's use.[5] Thomas of Spain, the first guardian of the community, was one of the cohort of continental friars who supplemented the work of the first group of friars in England.[6] The rapid growth of the order by the later 1230s and 1240s, however, made the friars' premises too cramped and by the middle of the century it was necessary to find another home in the town. As in other English towns, the friars relocated to a larger site.

The Cambridge friary was one of the largest in the English province; its stature and amenities may be gauged by the frequency with which it hosted the annual provincial chapters. It was a community with three focal points. First, it was like any other friary in East Anglia, ministering to the town and its environs, training recruits in the discipline of the religious life and supplying a theological education for those destined for the priesthood. The friars' municipal apostolate[7] was accompanied by the extra-mural activities of preaching tours throughout local towns and villages and the Fenland,[8] where they heard confessions inside their *limitatio*,[9] that is, the territory designated for their pastoral work. Secondly, the friary was the administrative head of the custody of Cambridge,[10] the geographical cluster of friaries under the direction of the *custos*,[11] that is, the senior friar who resided in the university

---

[2]   Cf. *The Cartulary of the Hospital of St. John the Evangelist, Cambridge*, ed. M. Underwood, Cambridgeshire Record Society, 18 (Cambridge, 2008).

[3]   D.R. Leader, *A History of the University of Cambridge*, i: *The University to 1546* (Cambridge, 1988) and A.B. Cobban, *The Medieval English Universities: Oxford and Cambridge to c.1500* (Aldershot, 1988).

[4]   J.R.H. Moorman, *The Grey Friars in Cambridge, 1225–1538* (Cambridge, 1952), p. 8, notes that, when the foundations of the Guildhall were being excavated in 1782, the remains of an old Jewish cemetery were unearthed with a tombstone bearing a Hebrew inscription.

[5]   *Eccleston*, p. 22. Cf. *Calendar of Fine Rolls of the Reign of Henry III Preserved in the National Archives*, II: *1224–1234*, ed. P. Dryburgh and B. Hartland (Woodbridge, 2008), no.194, p. 382. The mandate to the sheriff of Cambridge was dated 10 June 1231.

[6]   *Eccleston*, p. 10.

[7]   E.g., *Grace Book A: Containing the Proctors' Accounts and other Records of the University of Cambridge for the years 1454–1488*, ed. L.S. Mordaunt (Cambridge, 1897), p. 229.

[8]   R.L. Homan, 'Old and New Evidence of the Career of William Melton, O.F.M.', *FS*, 49 (1989), pp. 25–33.

[9]   CUL, EDR, G/1/1, Simon Montacute, f. 121. On 9 December 1342 John de Wetynge, a friar of Cambridge *et limitator insule Elien*, was appointed to hear the confessions of twelve people in the diocese.

[10] J. Röhrkasten, 'Friars and the Laity in the Franciscan Custody of Cambridge', in *The Friars in Medieval Britain*, ed. N. Rogers (Donington, 2010), pp. 107–24.

[11] P. Rutledge, 'The Will of Oliver Wyth, 1291', *A Miscellany*, Norfolk Record Society, 56 (Reading, 1991), no.152, pp. 9–30 at p. 23. The unnamed *custos* was a beneficiary of Wyth's will.

town and was supported by his vicar[12] and a team of counsellors and assistants. The custodial friaries were at Babwell, Colchester, Dunwich, Great Yarmouth, Ipswich, (King's) Lynn and Norwich. The friary at Walsingham was a later foundation by Elizabeth de Burgh.[13] Friars were members of a particular custody and moved from one house to another in that region, at the instigation of the custos. Thirdly, the *studium generale* attached to the friary was one of the three schools in the thirteenth century where a friar might enrol for the lectors' programme or proceed to the baccalaureate and doctorate in theology. The first of these trained friars to teach theology in the order's local schools and the second offered degrees in theology to those who would serve as regent masters in the university towns. The Cambridge school attracted masters and students from the friaries of East Anglia as well as neighbouring custodies in England and it drew friars from provinces overseas. On occasion friars taught theology elsewhere in the University.[14] By the early 1250s Adam Marsh, a friar at Oxford, recommended Cambridge as a suitable school of theology for friars from other provinces of the order.[15] The school's international status was echoed by the statutes of Benedict XII on 28 November 1336[16] and the general chapter of Assisi in 1354.[17] The friary interacted with the University of Cambridge whose constitutions ordained the occasions when special sermons were preached in the friars' church.[18]

THE FRIARS' CHURCH

Like their confrères in the other provinces of the order, the first friars in England frequented their parish churches. Initially the friars of Cambridge attended Mass and the Divine Office at one of the parish churches adjacent to the market square. Acting on Honorius III's decree of 3 December 1224, however, they erected a small and simple chapel where they prayed the Divine Office and celebrated Mass;[19] in each case, their communal devotions remembered the faithful departed. This chapel was subsequently adapted

---

[12] BL, Seals, xxxvi, 243, which has been assigned the date about 1244. It was discovered during the demolition of a wall in Cambridge about 1839–40.

[13] *Elizabeth de Burgh, Lady of Clare (1295–1360): Household and other Records*, ed. J. Ward, SRS, 57 (Woodbridge, 2014), pp. xxvii, 137–8. Cf. J. Lee-Warner, 'Petition of the Prior and Canons of Walsingham, Norfolk, to Elizabeth, Lady of Clare c.1345', *Archaeological Journal*, 26 (1869), pp. 166–73.

[14] KCA, Mundum Book, IX, ff. 38, 39, records payments to the master doctor of the Friars Minor for lectures delivered between 1499 and 1503. Leader, *History of the University*, i, p. 182.

[15] *The Letters of Adam Marsh*, ed. C.H. Lawrence, Oxford Medieval Texts (London, 2006–10), pp. 414–17.

[16] *Constitutiones Generales Ordinis Fratrum Minorum, II (Saeculum XIV/1)*, ed. C. Cenci and R.G. Mailleux, AF, 17, nova series, documenta et studia, 5 (Grottaferrata, Rome, 2010), IX, no. 3, p. 309.

[17] M. Bihl, 'Statuta generalia Ordinis edita in Capitulo generali an.1354 Assisii celebrato, communiter Farineriana appellata (Editio critica et analytica)', VI, no.17, in *AFH*, 35 (1942), pp. 35–112, 177–253, 111.

[18] *Documents relating to the University and Colleges of Cambridge*, 3 vols. (London, 1852), i, p. 400, n. 173.

[19] *Eccleston*, pp. 9, 22.

to the growing number of ordained friars from the later 1220s and the presence of the laity who began to hear Mass there. By the 1250s the friars had moved to a new site of six acres[20] on Bridge Street ('*in pontis vico*'),[21] in the parish of All Saints in the Jewry [22] where there was a lane of the Friars Minor ('*vicus fratrum minorum*').[23] The friars' church was mentioned when James, the excommunicated chaplain of Barnwell Priory, sought sanctuary there in 1267.[24] There was a further reference to it about twelve years later in the *Rotuli Hundredorum*.[25] Peter Salway suggests that the second church stood on the same land later occupied by the third almost 100 years later.[26]

This third church was not completed until the middle of the fourteenth century.[27] Edward I gave the friary 12*s*. 'for work' on 11 May 1304,[28] a term that might denote a donation to the new buildings that were being erected on the site of the present Sidney Sussex College. Almost half a century later, work on the friary and its range of domestic structures reached its completion, permitting the guardian to approach the diocese of Ely to have the new church and cloister blessed. In the absence of the bishop, William de Pecham, a vicar general, responded to the order's petition on 30 January 1349, licensing the dedication of the new church with the adjacent cemetery. The friars were given permission to engage any Catholic bishop for the ceremony and to have minor orders conferred on suitable candidates; they probably took the opportunity to arrange for the ceremonies to be conducted by one of their confrères who were serving as suffragan bishops in the various dioceses of England and Wales.[29] By the middle of the fourteenth century there were several friars in episcopal orders ministering in English dioceses. Thomas de Brakenberg, bishop of Leighlin, and Richard, archbishop of Nazareth, were active in the diocese of Ely in this period. The friars continued to acquire adjacent properties to enlarge their conventual complex. For example, Elizabeth de Burgh, Lady of Clare, left them £5 'for their works', denoting the church and additional projects on 25 September 1355.[30]

The friars' church, adorned with a belfry, was large enough for Parliament to be held there on 9 September 1388[31] and for the commencement

[20]   *Rotuli Hundredorum*, ed. W. Illingworth and J. Caley (London, 1812–18), 2 vols., ii, p. 360.
[21]   *The Works of John Caius, M.D. Second Founder of Gonville and Caius College and Master of the College 1559–1573*, ed. E.S. Roberts (Cambridge, 1912), p. 97.
[22]   CCCA, 01/G/1/17 (former reference: XXVII. 2).
[23]   CCCA, 01/G/1/11 (former reference: XXXI. 24) *in vico fratrum minorum in villa Cantebrig'*.
[24]   *Liber memorandorum Ecclesie de Bernewelle*, ed. J.W. Clark (Cambridge, 1907), pp. 125–6.
[25]   *Rotuli Hundredorum*, ii, p. 360: *ubi ecclesia eorum fundata est*.
[26]   P. Salway, 'Excavations on the Franciscan Site in Sidney, 1958', in *The Bull and the Porcupine* (1959), pp. 35–9, 36–7.
[27]   Cf. D. O'Sullivan, *In the Company of the Preachers: The Archaeology of Medieval Friaries in England and Wales*, Leicester Archaeology Monograph 23 (Leicester, 2013).
[28]   BL, MS Add. 8835, f. 5v. A similar term is understood as a royal donation for the building of the Black Friars in London. Cf. TNA: PRO, E403/59 and E403/72.
[29]   CUL, EDR, G/1/1, Thomas de Lisle, f. 17v.
[30]   *Elizabeth de Burgh*, pp. 141–9 at p. 145.
[31]   J.R. Harris, *The Origin of the Leicester Codex of the New Testament* (London, 1887), p. 29. *The Works of John Caius*, p. 82, reports that Parliament convened *in crastino nativitatis beatae Mariae virginis*.

ceremonies of Cambridge University in the early sixteenth century.[32] Dr. John Caius, the second founder of Gonville and Caius College, recalled in his *Historiae Cantebrigiensis Academiae ab urbe conditia* that the University functions held in Great St. Mary's had formerly taken place in the friars' church[33] and Dr. Thomas Fuller, D.D., described the church as 'the St. Mary's before St. Mary's'.[34] The University made an unsuccessful application to the crown to obtain the use of the friary and church in 1540.[35] Nonetheless, the conventual buildings and church had been demolished and their building materials were acquired by Trinity College within six years. Excavations at Sidney Sussex College in 1958 located part of the south aisle of the church, the nave (20 feet in width) and the north aisle (14 feet). A large quantity of stained glass from the late fourteenth century was recovered;[36] two fragments are displayed in the ante-chapel of Sidney Sussex College, thanks to the generosity of Professor Oliver Bulman, a fellow of the college (1945–74). A significant amount of later-fourteenth-century glass, but in a poorer state of preservation, was found during the 2014 excavation of the Master's Garden.

A distinctive feature of Franciscan architecture was the spacious nave to maximise room for those attending sermons.[37] The friars' churches of this period generally had several side altars or side chapels.[38] Contrasting his order's churches with the parish churches, William Woodford testified that the parish churches had two or three altars, while the friars' churches had ten or twelve.[39] Richard FitzRalph, archbishop of Armagh (1346–60), echoed the complaints of earlier reformers and critics when he protested that the friars built numerous sumptuous churches, cloisters, belfries, friaries and other fine edifices. His sermon at St. Paul's Cross, London, on 12 March 1357 alleges that the friars were not faithfully observing their Rule.[40] The ordained friars celebrated Masses each morning at these side altars. The

---

[32] *Grace Book B*, ed. M. Bateson, 2 vols., Cambridge Antiquarian Society, Luard Memorial Series, 2, 3 (Cambridge, 1903–05), i, p. 231; ii, pp. 69, 117, 118, 146, 231.

[33] *The Works of John Caius*, pp. 98–9.

[34] Thomas Fuller, *The History of the University of Cambridge from the Conquest to the year 1634*, ed. M. Prickett and T. Wright (London, 1840), no. 25, p. 66, and Thomas Fuller, *The History of the University of Cambridge, and of Waltham Abbey*, ed. J. Nichols (London, 1840), no. 25, p. 46.

[35] *Annals of Cambridge*, ed. C.H. Cooper, Cambridge Library Collection (Cambridge, 1852, 2009), i, p. 398.

[36] D.M. Wilson and J.G. Hurst, 'Medieval Britain in 1959', *Medieval Archaeology*, 4 (1960), p. 139.

[37] Cf. M.G. Underwood, 'The Impact of St. John's College as Landowner in the West Fields of Cambridge in the Sixteenth Century', in *Medieval Cambridge: Essays on the Pre-Reformation University*, The History of the University of Cambridge, Texts and Studies, 2, ed. P. Zutshi (Woodbridge, 1993), pp. 167–88 at p. 173. Master Eudo de la Zouche attended a sermon at the Franciscan church on Palm Sunday, 11 April 1378.

[38] *Acta Franciscana e tabulariis Bononiensibus deprompta*, ed. B. Giordani, I, AF, 9 (Florence, 1927), no. 113, pp. 39–40.

[39] E. Doyle, 'William Woodford, O.F.M.: His Life and Works together with a Study and Edition of his *Responsiones contra Wiclevum et Lollardos*', *FS*, 43 (1983), Q.61, pp. 17–187 at p. 179.

[40] Peterhouse Library, Cambridge, MS 223, ff. 35–43v at f. 40. In various places he appeals to the friars' Rule, adding that the *Regula Francisci precipit quod verba regule non glosentur*.

order's churches were resplendent with images of St. Francis and the order's saints, small shrines, statues of varying sizes, votive lights, flowers and sundry memorials to the faithful departed. Paintings,[41] stained-glass windows,[42] jewels, funeral monuments and the altars in the various chapels trumpeted the generosity of innumerable benefactors and reflected a concern to remember the faithful departed. Although there were several altars in the new church at Cambridge, only one is known by name, that dedicated to St. Barbara. There was at least one altar in the chancel. An ambiguous reference to burial 'before our lady' in the south aisle may denote a statue rather than an altar. Another testator requested burial in *'le cross alie, ante ymaginem Beate Marie'*.[43] The friars' church served the laity of the town and the University of Cambridge, providing Masses and confessions on a daily basis at particular hours.[44]

THE FRIARS AND INTERCESSORY PRAYER

Thomas of Eccleston (d.*c.*1258) delights in recounting the admirable example and sanctity of the first generation of friars and emphasises private devotions in their domestic oratories.[45] This fervour is exemplified by the three clerical friars of Cambridge who sang the Divine Office solemnly on the feast of St. Lawrence in their new chapel.[46] While St. Francis of Assisi was called to exercise an itinerant apostolate in Umbria, Tuscany, the Marches of Ancona and beyond those regions, he was continually attracted to the hermitages for prayer and contemplation. His fraternity was to be united in prayer and his Rule admonished friars to pray for the deceased.[47] When Elias of Cortona, minister general, announced the founder's death on the evening of 3 October 1226, he instructed friars to offer suffrages for his eternal repose.[48]

Suffrages were formalised at an early stage and the number of the deceased friars was read out at the general and provincial chapters. The friars' prayers were eagerly sought at an early stage and this is demonstrated by the suffrages that two ministers general, Haymo of Faversham (1240–44) and John of Parma (1247–57), granted to Romeo de Llivia, a Dominican of outstanding merit. Each priest in the order was required to celebrate a Mass in honour of the Holy Trinity for the pope and three Masses in honour

[41] *Eccleston*, p.38. C.L. Kingsford, *The Grey Friars of London: Their History with the Register of their Convent and an Appendix of Documents*, BSFS, 6 (Aberdeen, 1915), pp. 165–9. Thomas Wynchelsey, doctor of theology, commissioned paintings there in 1420.

[42] Kingsford, *The Grey Friars of London*, pp. 165–9 at p. 168, enumerates the donors of various windows, one of which was presented by the guardian, Henry de Sutton.

[43] TNA: PRO, PROB 11/11, ff. 67v–68.

[44] Cf. *Salimbene de Adam, Cronica a.1168–1287*, ed. G. Scalia, 2 vols., Corpus Christianorum Continuatio Mediaevalis, 125, 125a (Turnhout, 1998–99), pp. 634, 638.

[45] *Eccleston*, pp. 20, 25.

[46] *Eccleston*, pp. 9, 22.

[47] *Francesco d'Assisi Scritti*, ed. C. Paolazzi, Spicilegium Bonaventurianum, 36 (Grottaferrata, Rome, 2009), pp. 326–7.

[48] 'Heliae Cortonensis epistola encyclica de transitu Sancti Francisci', *Fontes Franciscani*, ed. E. Menestò, S. Brufani, G. Cremascoli, E. Paoli, L. Pellegrini and S. da Campagnola, Collana diretta da Enrico Menestò, Testi, 2 (Assisi, 1995), pp. 253–5.

of the Blessed Virgin Mary for the king of France and his family, for Guy Foulques, archbishop of Narbonne, and the Cistercians.[49] The earliest extant constitutions, promulgated by the general chapter of Narbonne in 1260, articulated the confrères' responsibility to pray for popes, monarchs and friars. Each priest was obliged to celebrate two Masses, one for the living and the other for the dead, for princes and prelates and all those recommended to the friars' intercession.[50] A local application of these general constitutions was the requirement that each friary should compile a *liber benefactorum* along with details of bequests. Donors' names were read out during the weekly chapters. The names of founders or co-founders[51] were recited annually.[52]

It is ironical that one of the earliest extant references to the friars' presence in Cambridge comes from the realm of suffrages. The friary received the mortuary roll of Lucy, foundress and first prioress of the Benedictine nunnery of Holy Cross and St. Mary and St. James at Castle Hedingham, Essex, by 1230.[53] Within seven years the friars elsewhere in the English province received alms of bread and ale and then 6*d.* for commemorating the anniversaries of an archdeacon and a canon of Chichester.[54] The friary at Cambridge was one of those communities that received the parchment roll soliciting prayers for the soul of Lucy de Vere, countess of Oxford, who had died on 3 February 1245.[55] The continuance of these practices is mirrored in the receipt of a mortuary roll from the prior and convent of Ely to request prayers for John Hotham, bishop of Ely, who died on 14 January 1337, '*titulus ecclesie fratrum minorum Cantebriggie*'.[56] The friars' network of domestic intercession is illustrated in Adam Marsh's letter to Robert de Thornham, *custos* of Cambridge, recommending John de Banbury, a deceased friar, to the prayers of the friars in East Anglia.[57]

Letters of fraternity, whose origins lay in the Carolingian period,[58] highlight another aspect of the friars' role as intercessors. John of Parma was the first minister general to grant the spiritual benefits of the order to members of

---

[49] F. Delorme, 'Diffinitiones Capituli Generalis O.F.M. Narbonensis (1260)', nn. 22–4, in *AFH*, 3 (1910), pp. 491–504 at p. 504.

[50] *Constitutiones Generales Ordinis Fratrum Minorum, I (Saeculum XIII)*, ed. C. Cenci and R.G. Mailleux, *AF*, 13, nova series, documenta et studia, 1 (Grottaferrata, Rome, 2007), no. 46, p. 26, XII, no. 1, p. 102.

[51] Fuller, *The History of the University of Cambridge from the Conquest to the year 1634*, no. 25, p. 66; Fuller, *The History of the University of Cambridge, and of Waltham Abbey*, no. 25, p. 46, attests that Edward I was the founder of the friary.

[52] *Constitutiones Generales Ordinis Fratrum Minorum, II (Saeculum XIV/1)*, XIII, nn. 1–3, p. 318.

[53] Cf. BL, MS Egerton 2849.

[54] Cf. *The Chartulary of the High Church of Chichester*, ed. W.D. Peckham, Sussex Record Society, 46 (Lewes, 1946), nn. 542, 548, pp. 140–1.

[55] *Fifth Report of the Royal Commission on Historical Manuscripts, Part 1: Report and Appendix* (London, 1876), pp. 321–2.

[56] A. Way, 'Mortuary Roll, sent forth by the Prior and Convent of Ely, on the death of John de Hothom, Bishop of Ely, deceased, January, A.D. 1336–7', *Cambridge Antiquarian Communications*, 1 (1851–59), pp. 125–39 at p. 139.

[57] *The Letters of Adam Marsh*, ed. Lawrence, ii, pp. 534–5.

[58] D.M. Knowles, *The Monastic Order in England: A History of its Development from the times of St. Dunstan to the Fourth Lateran Council, 940–1216* (Cambridge, 1963), pp. 475–9.

the laity, issuing letters under his own seal. Salimbene was careful to point out that this minister general merely responded to the petitions of the individuals concerned.[59] It is probable that one such petitioner and recipient was Martin of St. Cross, master of the hospital of Sherburn, Durham, and prebendary of Holme in the East Riding from 1256, who donated 100s. to the provincial chapter; specific mention was made of the charter of the minister provincial of the order. Eleven friaries, reflecting his geographical interests, benefited from his will, which was compiled between November 1259 and 9 August 1260.[60] Friars were, on occasion, granted letters of fraternity by both monastic and mendicant orders.[61] During the domestic chapter friars prayed for those whom they had admitted to a form of fraternity.[62] There are few surviving traces of such letters issued by the Cambridge Franciscans. Exceptions are the letters of fraternity granted to Andrew Dokett, president of Queens' College, in 1479[63] and to Thomas Semar of Walden in Essex, whose will was compiled on 20 May 1499.[64] The letter of fraternity granted to the master and fellows of Pembroke College, Cambridge, at an unspecified date in 1475 was issued by the minister provincial, William Goddard, STP, the elder.[65]

BENEFACTIONS AND PRAYERS

The thinly veiled economic dimension to the criticisms of the friars and their ministry was revealed in the complaint of the Augustinian canons of Barnwell, Cambridge, about 1250. The canons pointed out that the friars had quickly taken root in the town where their honeyed words ('*verbis mellitis*') had procured for themselves the burials, legacies and alms of rich citizens that had hitherto flowed to the monastery.[66] The potential source of alms was a weighty factor for the order in decisions about where to form a community[67] and in gauging the number of friars to be assigned there.[68] At an early stage the order was confronted by the economic reality of how to maintain a sizeable

---

[59] *Salimbene de Adam, Cronica a.1168–1287*, pp. 457–8.

[60] *English Episcopal Acta 29, Durham 1241–1283*, ed. P.M. Hoskin (Oxford, 2005), no. 111, pp. xxxvii–xxxviii, 97–101 at p. 97.

[61] Doyle, 'William Woodford', Q.23, p. 138, had letters of fraternity from the Augustinian canons and the Carthusians.

[62] Doyle, 'William Woodford', Q.57, p. 171.

[63] W.G. Searle, *The History of the Queens' College of St. Margaret and St. Bernard in the University of Cambridge 1446–1560*, Cambridge Antiquarian Society Publications, 9 (1867), pp. 54–5.

[64] G. Montagu Benton, 'Essex Wills at Canterbury', *Transactions of the Essex Archaeological Society*, new series, 21 (1933–7), pp. 234–69 at p. 254. He left 20s. to the friars to pray for his soul, describing himself as a brother of the order. Cf. *Wills of the Archdeaconry of Sudbury 1439–1474: Wills from the Register 'Baldwyne': Part II: 1461–1474*, ed. P. Northeast and H. Falvey, SRS, 53 (Woodbridge, 2010), no. 751, pp. 455–6.

[65] A.G. Little, *Franciscan Papers, Lists and Documents* (Manchester, 1943), p. 204. W.G. Clark-Maxwell, 'Some Letters of Fraternity', *Archaeologia*, 75 (1924–25), pp. 19–60, plate 6.

[66] *Liber memorandorum Ecclesie de Bernewelle*, p. 70.

[67] *Roberti Grosseteste episcopi quondam Lincolniensis Epistolae*, ed. H.R. Luard, RS, 25 (London, 1861), pp. 120–2.

[68] *Eccleston*, p. 36.

group of friars actively engaged in diverse forms of ministry in the diocese of Ely and the schools. The friary's international status as a *studium generale* merely increased the economic pressures.

Although the first friars received payment in kind, with the exception of money, by the middle of the thirteenth century, individuals or corporations paid cash for the friars' services; the stipend was assigned to the communal coffers. For instance, on 12 March 1352, Elizabeth de Burgh gave 15*s.* 4*d.* to a friar of Cambridge for illuminating one of her books.[69] Stipends were also disbursed to friars who preached before members of the nobility and the royal family. The unnamed guardian of Cambridge received 6*s.* 8*d.* on 4 March 1352 for preaching before Elizabeth de Burgh at Great Bardfield in Essex[70] and Robert de Denill, another friar from the town, delivered homilies before Queen Isabella at Hertford during the sacred *triduum* in 1358, earning 13*s.* 4*d.*[71] Three members of the friary appeared in a list of stipendiary chaplains in the deanery of Cambridge on 21 June 1406.[72] A regular source of income came from stole fees and this is mirrored in the payment made by Sir Peter de Ereswelle, the almoner of Elizabeth de Burgh, on 5 February 1352. He distributed £1 5*s.* to various religious houses of Cambridge to celebrate Masses for Sir Thomas de Cheddeworth.[73] Towards the end of the thirteenth century individual friars appeared in the probate registers;[74] alms were donated for a remembrance at the altar. For instance, on 3 December 1365 Gilbert Peckham, the fifty-eighth regent master in theology, received 40*s.* in the will of Thomas Ringstead, the Dominican bishop of Bangor, his former contemporary regent master at Cambridge.[75]

Italian sources yield much more information on contracts between benefactors and the friaries. Given the paucity of early-fourteenth-century wills, and the loss of the friars' registers and archives at the dissolution of the mendicant houses in 1538–39, such documents are scarce in England. Nonetheless, links between families and the order are borne out by the probate materials. Particular families arranged for Masses to be celebrated regularly, sometimes weekly or daily, for their deceased relatives. While the friars' new churches were under construction, funds were already arriving for family altars or chapels. Families enjoyed rights in relation to chapels[76] and they were expected to equip them with everything that pertained to the celebration of Masses on a frequent, if not daily, basis. In turn, such chapels

[69] TNA: PRO, E101/93/12, m.3.

[70] TNA: PRO, E101/93/12, m. 3.

[71] BL, MS Cotton Galba, E xiv, f. 34r.

[72] CUL, EDR, G/1/3, f. 161r.

[73] TNA: PRO, E101/93/12, m.3.

[74] Rutledge, 'The Will of Oliver Wyth, 1291', nn. 151–4, p. 23.

[75] P.N.R. Zutshi and R. Ombres, 'The Dominicans in Cambridge 1238–1538', *Archivum Fratrum Praedicatorum*, 60 (1990), pp. 313–73 at pp. 350–5; *Testamentary Records of the English and Welsh Episcopate, 1200–1413: Wills, Executors' Accounts and Inventories, and the Probate Process*, ed. C.M. Woolgar, Canterbury and York Society, 102 (Woodbridge, 2011), no. 31, pp. 179–82 at p. 180.

[76] L. Bourdua, 'Master Plans of Devotion or Daily Pragmatism? The Dedication and Use of Chapels and Conventual Spaces by the Friars and the Laity at the Santo 1263–1310', *Il Santo: Rivista Francescana di storia dottrina arte*, 51 (2011), pp. 491–510 at p. 498.

provided the burial place for their forebears. Some chapels were known by their family names rather the saints to whom they were dedicated.[77] The patrons of friaries displayed their coats of arms there.[78]

One of the ways in which the order's army of benefactors assisted the friars' ministry was by equipping them with the manuscripts to inform their studies and preaching. About 1295 Master John de Malebraunche, rector of Cherry Hinton and a fellow of Peterhouse, gave some quires of Thomas Aquinas's *Commentary on Aristotle's Ethics* texts to Walter de Bolevile, a Franciscan friar of Cambridge. Walter was at Oxford on 26 July 1300 when he was nominated for a licence to hear confessions in the archdeaconry of the university town.[79] Gifts of useful volumes were made on behalf of the souls of the deceased. The formula 'for the soul of N.' appears in several manuscripts from the fourteenth and fifteenth centuries. In return the friars made intercession for the named individual. For instance, Thomas, rector of Colveston, Norfolk, entrusted a heavily annotated Bible in verse to Thomas de Dudelington, a friar who flourished about 1328, for the soul of Sir William Rollesby. On the friar's death this book was to pass to the Cambridge Franciscans, where it was to remain in perpetuity.[80] A fourteenth-century hand commemorated those who had enabled Master Roger of Nottingham to obtain an astronomical text for the soul of Eve de Tattershall and for the souls of others whose alms had made it possible for him to procure this book.[81] Similarly, friars, especially those active in the schools, copied texts and volumes and enjoined successive readers to pray for them. One such was John de Holbech (Holbeche), probably at Cambridge in the late fourteenth and early fifteenth centuries, when he transcribed Nicholas of Lyra's *Postilla litteralis in uetus testamentum*. At the end of each book the colophon contains an injunction to pray for the scribe. The commentary on the book of Deuteronomy, for instance, concludes with this note, '... written by Friar John Holbeche of the order of Friars Minor. If anyone should use this book after his death, he should faithfully and devoutly say a *Pater Noster* and *Ave Maria* for his soul.'[82] Similarly, there is a comparable exhortation to recite the *Pater Noster* and *Ave Maria* for John's soul at the end of the second book of Maccabees.[83] John, probably a native of the southern part of the custody of York, was sent to Cambridge for higher studies and, while there, on 25 May 1411 he was licensed to hear confessions in the diocese of Ely.[84]

---

[77] Giogrio Vasari, *Le vite de' più eccellenti pittori, scultori e architettori nelle redazioni del 1550 e 1568*, ed. R. Bettarini *et al.*, 11 vols (Florence, 1966–87), ii, p. 98, mentions the Bardi, Peruzzi, Giugni and Tosinghi with the Spinelli chapels at Santa Croce in Florence.

[78] B. Jennings, *The Grey Friars of Richmond* (Richmond, 1958), p. 9.

[79] Peterhouse Library, MS 82, f. 133, the first leaf of a quire of twelve. I owe this reference to Professor Rodney M. Thomson; see his volume *A Descriptive Catalogue of the Medieval Manuscripts in the Library of Peterhouse, Cambridge* (Woodbridge, 2016), p. 44.

[80] BL, Sloane, MS 1726.

[81] CUL, MS Ii.III.3, f. 2v, *ex collacione fratris Rogeri de Notingham magistri*.

[82] Peterhouse Library, Cambridge, MS 85, f. 101vb.

[83] Peterhouse Library, Cambridge, MS 85, f. 235va.

[84] CUL, EDR, G/1/3, f. 260.

The friars were meticulous in their keeping of records concerning their houses and their obligations to individuals and the local community. Oblations for suffrages constituted a significant element in their domestic economy. The officials of the friary, perhaps the friar responsible for maintaining the *liber benefactorum*, received those who sought suffrages of various kinds. The weekly domestic chapter undoubtedly determined the scale of offerings for different forms of suffrages. Formal agreements or contracts concerning the number of prayers were made and deposited in the archives. Applications for particular types of Masses at specified altars by nominated friars and other forms of suffrages were initially approved by the community. The friars absent on preaching tours were fully aware of the customary offerings and communicated this information to those whom they encountered. For example, Masses and other forms of suffrages were stipulated by the will of Robert Arnolde of St. Neot's on 4 March 1504, in accordance with notes agreed with the community.[85] Similarly, Thomas Scotte of Great Shelford donated 10*s.* to the Friars Minor on 17 February 1521 and requested them to sing a trental of Masses for him two days after his death.[86] Some testators in the Cambridge area arranged for Masses to be celebrated in their parish churches by the visiting friars. On 25 April 1529 Edmund Boyer of Little Wilbraham, six miles east of Cambridge, made arrangements for a Franciscan to celebrate a trental of Masses for his soul in the church of St. John the Evangelist at Christmas, Easter and Whitsuntide.[87] The elaborate ritual surrounding terminal sickness, death and burial involved the friars, who were summoned to attend vigils and to participate in funeral processions and requiem Masses and burials. Requests for burial in the friars' cemetery or church were undoubtedly addressed to the guardian and a record was kept, particularly where testators wished to be commemorated by permanent memorials or to be interred in family vaults or next to parents and grandparents. The fragment of the account book for 1363–66 confirms the receipt of small amounts of money or payment in kind in return for the friars' prayers for the living and the dead, including deceased friars.[88]

PRAYERS FOR THE FAITHFUL DEPARTED: THE EVIDENCE FROM THE PROBATE REGISTERS

Probate registers from the diocese of Ely are impoverished compared with some English dioceses. Nonetheless, some wills remain in the episcopal registers and other local sources, as well as the probate materials from the adjacent diocese of London. Several inhabitants of Cambridge made bequests to the town's Friars Minor between the thirteenth and sixteenth centuries, including Alan de Welles, a burgher and parishioner of Great St. Mary's, on

[85] *Bedfordshire Wills proved in the Prerogative Court of Canterbury 1383–1548*, ed. M. McGregor, Bedfordshire Historical Record Society, 58 (Bedford, 1979), no. 46, pp. 60–1.
[86] BL, MS Add. 5861, f. 84v, formerly 164.
[87] BL, MS Add. 5861, f. 112r, formerly 219.
[88] Harris, *The Origin of the Leicester Codex of the New Testament*, pp. 23–7, Moorman, *Grey Friars*, pp. 242–5.

9 February 1316,[89] Thomas Lolleworth, a parishioner of St. Benet's, on 24 September 1383,[90] William Mast, a parishioner of All Saints, on 3 December 1432[91] and Peter Breynans, a stationer and binder of Cambridge, at an unknown date between 1502 and 1504.[92] The friars' presence at funeral ceremonies was requested by many testators. One such was Henry Veysey, apothecary, who asked them to attend his requiem Mass in Great St. Mary's, where he was to be interred in the south aisle. His will of 15 April 1503 left 10s. to each mendicant house in the town to sing a *Placebo* and *Dirige* for his soul and all Christian souls.[93] Robert Reson asked for burial in the parish of St Andrew on 27 April 1521, bequeathing 10s. to each friary for a trental of Masses.[94] While the vast majority of testators assigned alms to the friary, individuals were named as beneficiaries of wills. For example, on 21 September 1532, John Huyme asked for burial in the chapel of St. Saviour in the churchyard of the church of Sts. Peter and Paul on Castle Hill, donating 20d. to the unnamed Franciscan who was his confessor.[95] Members of the academic community were equally drawn to the Franciscans, among them Eudo Harleston, a parishioner of St. Clement, on 5 November 1403,[96] Master John Frisby (Frysby), cleric of King's Hall, on 26 August 1504[97] and Robert Morley, M.A., priest and fellow of Corpus Christi College and rector of St. Benet's parish, on 13 February 1518.[98]

Despite the intermittent bouts of tension between the friars and the secular clergy in the thirteenth and fourteenth centuries, many priests in Cambridgeshire valued the friars' prayers and remembered them in their wills. William de Outhorp, rector of Balsham, donated 40s. to the Friars Minor on 5 April 1346. Bequests were made to the other mendicant communities in the county town.[99] Robert de Muskham, rector of Over, left 40s. to each mendicant friary on 12 January 1386.[100] John de Sleaford, rector of Balsham, gave the friars 40s. on 8 September 1401.[101] John Fordham, bishop of Ely, was one of a cluster of prelates who gave alms to the friars. He assigned 66s. 8d. to each mendicant house of the town in his will of 3 October 1425[102] and

89 CCCA, CCCCo1/G/1/19 (former reference XXX1.28).
90 CCCA, CCCCo1/P/53 (former reference XXXI.92).
91 Jesus College Archives, Cambridge, Jesus/Nuns/Gray/144.
92 *Abstracts from the Wills and Testamentary Documents of Printers, Binders and Stationers of Cambridge from 1504 to 1699*, ed. G.J. Gray and W.M. Palmer (London, 1915), p. 1.
93 CUL, UA, Wills, I. 1501–1558, f. 4v.
94 CUL, UA, Wills, I. 1501–1558, f. 35v.
95 CUL, UA, Wills, I. 1501–1558, f. 54v.
96 TNA: PRO, PROB 11/2, f. 33v. He left 20s. to the friary.
97 CUL, UA, Wills, I. 1501–1558, f. 12v. He left 10s. to the Franciscans and 3s. 4d. to each of the other mendicant houses.
98 CUL, UA, Wills, I. 1501–1558, f. 32v. He left 6s. 8d. to each mendicant house in Cambridge.
99 Lincolnshire Archives, Lincoln, DIOC/REG/7, Episcopal Register 7, f. 214v.
100 LPL, Reg. Courtenay, Registers of Archbishop William Courtenay, I, f. 214v.
101 LPL, Reg. Arundel 1, Register of Archbishop Thomas Arundel, I, f. 187.
102 *The Register of Henry Chichele archbishop of Canterbury 1414–1443*, ed. E.F. Jacob and H.C. Johnson, Canterbury and York Society, 4 vols. (Oxford, 1937–57), ii, pp. 327–9.

John Hale, rector of Doddington, on 8 June 1458 bequeathed 10s. to the Franciscans for a trental of Masses.[103]

The legion of testators outside Cambridge testifies to the friars' itinerant ministry outside their town. William Swayn of Chesterton left 26s. 8d. to the four orders of friars on 4 May 1525.[104] John Grenelawe, a soldier of Hadenham, left each mendicant house in the town 10s. on 1 February 1431.[105] William Palgrave of Newmarket assigned 13s. 4d. to the friary in his will of 1 February 1452.[106] The sum of 2s. 6d. was given to each of the four houses of friars in Cambridge in the will of John Tebawde of Fordham on 2 July 1464.[107] Some wills shine a light on aspects of the friary's domestic life, such as indications of economic divisions within the community.[108] On 29 December 1409 Catharine de Burgh of Borough Green, Cambridgeshire, donated five quarters of wheat to each house of mendicant friars in the town. Five marks were provided for the Franciscans and 40s. were given to John Bradfeld, a member of that community. Six yards of russet were to be placed on her body for burial and afterwards given to a poor friar to pray for her soul.[109]

These Cambridgeshire legacies were accompanied by bequests from testators from adjacent counties: Huntingdonshire, Norfolk, Essex, Bedfordshire, Suffolk and Lincolnshire. One of the earliest wills in favour of the friary was compiled by William of Wendling, rector of Somersham, Huntingdonshire, between 1254 and 1259, making bequests to the friaries of Dunwich, (King's) Lynn, Norwich and Great Yarmouth. The Cambridge Franciscans were to receive 40s.[110] Oliver Wyth, a leading burgess of Great Yarmouth, Norfolk, was a wealthy testator and devotee of the spiritual sons of St. Francis. His will of 7 June 1291 commended his soul to the Blessed Virgin Mary, St. Nicholas and St. Francis, requested burial in his local friary and gave alms to the custodial friaries of Babwell, Cambridge, Colchester, Dunwich, Great Yarmouth, Ipswich, (King's) Lynn and Norwich. Several friars, some of them active at Cambridge in the last quarter of the thirteenth century, received sums of money, including Thomas de Brysingham, the thirteenth regent master in theology.[111] A similar predilection for the order was manifest in

---

[103] CUL, EDR, G/1/5, ff. 34v–35.

[104] BL, MS Add. 5861, f. 94, formerly 184.

[105] Jesus College Archives, Cambridge, Jesus/Nuns/Gray/360.

[106] *Wills of the Archdeaconry of Sudbury 1439–1474: Wills from the Register 'Baldwyne': Part I: 1439–1461*, ed. P. Northeast, SRS, 44 (Woodbridge, 2001), no. 499, p. 193.

[107] *Wills of the Archdeaconry of Sudbury 1439–1474: Part II*, no. 187, pp. 105–6.

[108] Rutledge, 'The Will of Oliver Wyth, 1291', no. 82, p. 20: *item eisdem fratribus xx.marc. solvendas pro necessitatibus eorundem et specialiter pro necessitatibus indumentis fratrum illius conventus qui tempore obitus mei magis indigebunt secundum disposicionem gardiani loci.* J. Röhrkasten, *The Mendicant Houses of Medieval London 1221–1539*, Vita Regularis, 21 (Münster, 2004), p. 152, cites evidence from 1390 when two testators mentioned the poorer members of the Friars Minor of London. John Scorfeyn mentioned *inter pauperimos fratres* and Matilda Cavendish ordained that her corpse be carried to the grave *per quatuor fratres minors qui sunt maxime egentes in domo eorum …*

[109] W.M. Palmer, *History of the Parish of Borough Green Cambridgeshire*, Cambridge Antiquarian Society, 54 (1939), pp. 87–9.

[110] N. Vincent, 'The Wonderful Will of William of Wendling (d.1270)', *Nottingham Medieval Studies*, 45 (2001), pp. 68–96 at pp. 89–93, argues that the will in its present form was never implemented.

[111] Rutledge, 'The Will of Oliver Wyth, 1291', no. 151, p. 23.

the legacy of Matilda de Vere, countess of Oxford, who left 10 marks to the friary in Cambridge in her will of 1366.[112] On 23 February 1378, Walter de Berney, a citizen of London, divided £10 equally between the Franciscans in Cambridge and Oxford[113] and on 23 March 1389 William de Wanton, a soldier, gave each of the four orders of friars in Cambridge 41*s.* 8*d.* to celebrate fifty Masses for his soul and those of all the faithful departed.[114] William Gunwardby, rector of the moiety of Houghton Conquest, bishop of Dunkeld and suffragan in the dioceses of Lincoln and Ely, compiled his will on 9 May 1457, when he made bequests to several religious houses and left two nobles to each friary at Cambridge.[115] John Barkere of Cowlinge, Suffolk, donated 10*s.* to his neighbouring friary of Babwell for a trental and the same amount to the Friars Minor of Cambridge in his will of 28 December 1470.[116] John Tynemouth was probably a former friar of Cambridge who subsequently joined the order of the Hospital of St. John. As the parish priest of Boston, Lincolnshire, and bishop of Argos, in his will of 1524 he bequeathed £5 to the Franciscans of Cambridge 'and they to pray for the soules that God wold have prayed for'.[117]

BURIALS AT THE FRIARS MINOR OF CAMBRIDGE

The link between burial and continuing intercession was of crucial importance to testators and led some of them to seek a final resting place among the friars. The interment of the laity in the friars' churches was one of the grounds of the protracted dispute between the mendicant orders and the secular clergy from the middle of the thirteenth century.[118] By that stage the Dominicans and Franciscans stood accused of burying the people of Cambridge, to the financial detriment of local parishes and religious houses. Beyond that date the Franciscans started to enlarge their convents with churches and adjacent cemeteries. Benefactors, members of the Third Order and others attracted by the mendicant revolution in spirituality started to request burial in their cloisters. Information regarding burials at Cambridge is culled from archaeological evidence, indulgences summarised in the episcopal registers, the probate registers, assorted wills and chronicles. These diffuse sources offer some information on the laity who were laid to rest in the friars' church and cemetery. A more realistic picture is supplied by the incomplete list of 765 burials in the Friars Minor of London.[119]

Franciscans were buried in either the order's churches or cemeteries. The names of deceased friars of Cambridge were relayed to the annual provincial

[112] Montagu Benton, 'Essex Wills at Canterbury', pp. 263–4.
[113] LPL, Reg. Sudbury, Register of Archbishop Simon Sudbury, f. 101r.
[114] London Metropolitan Archives, DL/A/A/004/MS09531/004 (former reference Guildhall Library MS 9531/4), f. 433v. His will was proved on 31 August 1389.
[115] *Bedfordshire Wills*, no. 13, pp. 17–18.
[116] *Wills of the Archdeaconry of Sudbury 1439–1474: Part II*, no. 490, pp. 290–2.
[117] TNA: PRO, PROB 10/3 and 11/21, ff. 211v–212.
[118] *Salimbene de Adam, Cronica a.1168–1287*, pp. 613, 637–8, 640–1.
[119] Kingsford, *Grey Friars*, pp. 7, 40, 75, 134. CUL, EDR, G/1/2, f. 56v. Master Edward Burnell, rector of Cottenham, on 30 March 1386 requested burial at the Friars Minor of London, bequeathing £40 to the city friary.

chapters, where special prayers were recited '*pro fratribus defunctis*'. Two such lists are extant and name John Berme, Stephen Cayl, Andrew de Ballynges and Stephen de Stouemerchet whose passing was communicated in 1304 and 1327.[120] Geoffrey de Massingham, Roger de Alby and Roger de Baldiswell were probably friars of Cambridge at the time of death and they featured in the domestic necrology or martyrology. Although the friary's necrology is no longer extant, additional sources confirm that Dr. Richard Conington, a former regent master at Oxford and then Cambridge before becoming minister provincial, was buried at the latter friary *c.*1331.[121] Information from other friaries indicates that the friars were interred under inscribed gravestones of varying sizes and decorations.[122] Deceased friars, too, benefited from the prayers of their neighbours. Robert de Staunton may have been resident at the local friary when he was sent to the Roman Curia to procure the business of Pembroke College; he died at the papal court on 5 May, probably in 1357, and thereby earned himself a place in the necrology of the countess of Pembroke's new foundation.[123]

The cemetery and the cloister at Cambridge were mentioned by the vicar general on 30 January 1349 in the permission for the dedication of the new church. Reflecting on the archaeological evidence of the neighbouring friary of Walsingham, Professor Salway interprets the evidence of the 1958 excavation of Cloister Court at Sidney Sussex College as an indication of a lay cemetery. Four burials were located, including the skeleton of a child aged seven or eight. Dr. Fuller, whose connections with Sidney Sussex College began in 1629, testified that the site of the friars' church was still visible, adding 'I have oft found dead men's bones thereabouts.'[124] Later in that century more skeletons were found during the construction of Cloister Court.[125]

The small extant group of references to burials in the Cambridge identifies some wider patterns. For instance, information regarding the burial of Sir Richard of Freyle, knight, in the friars' church survives only in the form of an indulgence of 20 days granted by John Dalderby, bishop of Lincoln, on 19 March 1302 to those who prayed for the deceased knight.[126] The brief will

[120] A.G. Little, 'Records of the Franciscan Province of England (Cotton Charter, XXX, 40)', in *Collectanea Franciscana*, I, ed. A.G. Little, M.R. James, H.M. Bannister, BSFS, 5 (Aberdeen, 1914), pp. 141–53 at pp. 151–2.

[121] *Eccleston*, p.54.

[122] Kingsford, *Grey Friars*, p.72. Discussed in C. Steer, 'The Franciscans and their Graves in Medieval London', in *The Franciscan Order in the Medieval English Province and Beyond*, ed. M. Robson and P. Zutshi (Amsterdam, 2018), pp. 115–38.

[123] J. Ringrose, 'The Medieval Statutes of Pembroke College', in *Medieval Cambridge*, ed. Zutshi, pp. 93–127 at p. 118.

[124] Fuller, *The History of the University of Cambridge from the Conquest to the year 1634*, no. 25, pp. 65–6, and Fuller, *The History of the University of Cambridge, and of Waltham Abbey*, no. 25, p. 46.

[125] P. Salway, 'Sidney before the College', in *Sidney Sussex College, Cambridge: Historical Essays in Commemoration of the Quatercentenary*, ed. D.E.D. Beales and H.B. Nisbet (Woodbridge, 1996), pp. 3–34, 9, 23. Cf. K.R. Dark, 'Archaeological Survey at Sidney Sussex College Cambridge 1984', *Proceedings of the Cambridge Antiquarian Society*, 74 (1985), pp. 81–4; Wilson and Hurst, 'Medieval Britain in 1959', p. 139.

[126] Lincolnshire Archives, Lincoln, DIOC/REG/3, Episcopal Register 3, f. 43v.

of Roger Mason, a parishioner of the adjacent parish of St. Radegund, on 5 July 1392 requested burial '*inter fratres minores Cantebr*'. A bequest of 10*s.* was paid to the friars and 5*s.* to the high altar of his parish church for wax to burn before the body of Christ. The testator's cottage in Nunn's Lane was to be sold to discharge his debt. His executor was his wife, Felice, who was instructed to dispose of the proceeds '*pro anima mea prout ei melius videbitur expediri*'.[127] The will of Master John Roucliff (Rondyff), rector of St. Mary the Virgin at Great Shelford, on 1 July 1492 illustrates the strong family bonds with the Friars Minor. His relatives in Yorkshire forged strong connections with the order and several of them were interred in the Franciscan church of York. In turn, this rector requested burial in the friars' church at Cambridge '*in le cross alie, ante ymaginem Beate Marie, si illuc bene portari poterit*'. The sum of £3 was left to the friary for burial and £1 was bequeathed to each of the other three mendicant orders in the town. Several religious houses in East Anglia benefited from the will, as did different parish churches in the environs of Cambridge.[128]

A cluster of burials reflects patterns to be found elsewhere in the English province. The will of John Hermer (Henner), a mason and probably a parishioner of All Saints, on 6 February 1508 requested burial among the 'grey freeres before our lady in the south aisle'. It is unclear whether he asked for burial in front of a statue or an altar. The sum of 13*s.* 4*d.* was left to the friars, perhaps to meet the burial expenses; the same amount was given to each of the other mendicant houses in the town. Bequests were also made to the Benedictine monasteries of Bury St. Edmunds and Westminster Abbey.[129] The will of Thomas Fyneham on 13 January 1518 is rich in information regarding the friary and some of its members. The testator asked for burial in the chancel, making an offering of 40*s.* to the friary for the costs of his funeral; the same sum was left to the four orders of friars for suffrages. In addition, the substantial sum of £20 was bequeathed to Robert White, a member of the community, to defray the costs of his exhibition at Oxford or Cambridge in return for offering Masses for him for the space of four years. In addition, the guardian and his vicar and four friars were each to receive 4*d.* for accompanying his body to burial. Another friar was to be designated to celebrate a daily Mass at the altar where the testator was interred between the rather late hours of 10am and 11am for the space of a year in return for a daily stipend of four pence. The sum of 10*s.* was assigned to Robert White for his religious habit. Master William Barle, a clerk, was instructed to celebrate Masses for the testator for a period of three years in the parish of All Saints and chapel of King's Hall and sometimes at the Friars Minor. The testator's cousin John Fyneham of Wells was responsible for providing the friars with three sets of vestments and other ornaments for the service of God. Robert White, described as a clerk, was given one of the testator's featherbeds and

---

[127] Jesus College Archives, Cambridge, Jesus/Nuns/Gray/29.
[128] TNA: PRO, PROB 11/11, ff. 67v–68. *Testamenta Eboracensia: or Wills registered at York*, ed. J. Raine and J.W. Clay, Surtees Society, 6 vols. (London, 1836–1902), iv, pp. 102–7, at p. 107, n.
[129] TNA: PRO, PROB 11/16, f. 108v.

a bolster and blue cover for the bed and was a witness to the codicil of the will on 22 January.[130] The practice of members of a family seeking burial in a particular chapel or before an altar is exemplified in the will of Hugh Rankyn, alderman of Cambridge and probably a parishioner of Holy Sepulchre or St. Clement, on 22 September 1521, stating that he wished to be buried under the same stone as his father and grandfather. Hugh Rankyn set aside 40s. for the repair of the friars' church. The guardian was to receive 8d. and each member of the community was given 4d. to accompany his body to the grave.[131] The will of another municipal official, Nicholas Simond (Symond), a goldsmith and burgess in St. Benet's parish, Cambridge, reflected the friars' outreach and many of the late medieval conventions regarding burial. His will of 14 July 1533 made the following provision:

> I Nicholas Simond otherwise called Goldsmythe of the Towne of Cambridge goldsmythe and Burges … First I bequeathe my soule to allmightye God to our blessed ladye St Marye and to all the holye company in heaven and my bodye to be buryed in the churche of the Fryers maiors other wise called the graye fryers in Cambridge before the alter of St. Barber in the same churche. Itm I bequeathe for my buriall there for breaking of the church 10s. Itm I give and bequeathe to the warden and covent of the same grey [fryers] to fetche my bodye to the sayd grave to burye me other 10s. … Itm I will have iiij Fryers of every order one to beare my bodye from St. Bennets churche after my suffrags sayd to the gray Fryers. To every of the same fryers 12d. …[132]

Injunctions to commemorate the faithful departed, especially deceased friars, founders and benefactors, were central to the life of the friary and its daily *horarium*. Suffrages for the dead were offered in the refectory and the reading of the convent necrology at the community's weekly chapter and each evening after dinner. The earliest extant constitutions of the order enacted that each priest should celebrate a requiem Mass annually; the other friars were bound to recite psalms or the *Pater Noster*. There were also specific instructions about the solemn celebration of the office for deceased friars and benefactors thrice annually.[133] The constitutions of Narbonne in 1260 reaffirmed this statute, that is, that this office should be solemnly celebrated the day before the feasts of St. Mary Magdalene (21 July) and St. Michael the Archangel (28 September) and on the Monday after Septuagesima Sunday. Clerics should celebrate Mass, Vespers and the vigil with nine lessons. The other members of the community were required to pray the *Pater Noster* one hundred times.

---

[130] TNA: PRO, PROB 11/19, ff. 38–40.

[131] TNA: PRO, PROB 11/20, ff. 135–135v.

[132] W.D. Sweeting, 'Cambridge Friars in 1533', *Fenland Notes and Queries: A Quarterly Antiquarian Journal for the Fenland, in the Counties of Huntingdon, Cambridge, Lincoln, Northampton, Norfolk, and Suffolk*, 5 vols. (Peterborough, 1891–1909), iv, no. 712, pp. 71–2.

[133] *Constitutiones Generales Ordinis Fratrum Minorum, I (Saeculum XIII)*, nn. 48, 46, 23, pp. 11, 26, 46.

Similarly, office should be celebrated for friars' parents on the last day before Advent.[134]

The friars' churches contained the graves of several friars, their benefactors and those who turned to them for spiritual direction and support. Numerous funeral slabs, monuments and gravestones marked the final resting place of both benefactors and friars as well as the graves of their confrères who had shouldered positions of responsibility in the fraternity. The graves of the men and women of Cambridge provided the friars with a constant reminder of the generations of their community's benefactors for whom Masses were offered and prayers recited at their place of burial in the church or cemetery on a weekly basis. Prayers were similarly offered for them in the friary's weekly chapter. The priests of the community, in addition, celebrated Masses at side altars where people were buried in order to commend the deceased to their Creator.

The craftsmen, farmers, merchants, nobles, prelates, priests, scholars, soldiers and tradesmen of medieval Cambridge and its surrounding towns and villages valued the friars' intercession. While generations of men and women attended the church of the Friars Minor to hear the celebrated preachers, others went there to pray for the living and to participate in the elaborate ceremonial surrounding death and burial, the month's mind and anniversaries. Each day the priests of the community prayed for the living and the faithful departed *ad altare* in a church teeming with monuments to earlier generations. The incomplete diocesan and probate registers of the diocese of Ely illustrate the vast amount of detail on the legacies given to the friars and supply information about the rhythm of the friary's life along with the pastoral activities of its members. Above all, they are a testament to the friars' role in the commemoration of the people of Cambridge and their deceased relations, friends, colleagues and neighbours.

[134] *Constitutiones Generales Ordinis Fratrum Minorum, I (Saeculum XII)*, nn. 1, 6, 7, p. 102.

CHAPTER 3

The City of London and the Founding of the Guild of Corpus Christi

Richard Barber

The notebook written by John Hardy in about 1358 is the most valuable evidence for the background to the foundation of Corpus Christi College, and has long been known to historians of the university of Cambridge.[1] It is in effect an informal set of accounts, recording donations and promises to the new Guild of Corpus Christi, and the expenses incurred, most of which concern local citizens. Previous historians, focussing on the local angle, have been puzzled by entries on a page headed 'Henry duke of Lancaster', which contains names of one or two men associated with him, and then a series of other names which were dismissed by the first editor as probably of men of modest standing, of whom there was no other record. In fact, these names are those of some of the foremost citizens of London, including Andrew Aubrey, mayor of London and not only a wealthy man but an important political figure of his generation. This chapter reviews what we know about this group of Londoners, and tentatively suggests possible reasons for their involvement with the college's foundation, highlighting John of Tamworth, the head of the king's chancery, and his role in the process, which Hardy acknowledged by calling him the chief promoter of the college's cause.

Hardy's notebook is a paper booklet of thirty-six pages, written over a period of almost a decade. This is the source of most of our detailed knowledge about the Guild of Corpus Christi from 1350 to 1358, the period when the idea of founding a new college was conceived and put into effect. It was printed very accurately in 1903 by Mary Bateson, though the order of pages was incorrect when she worked on it. It has been cleaned and restored in recent years, and the leaves have now been correctly reordered.[2] John Hardy, as a stationer, was a professional scribe, and his work is reasonably systematic, particularly as the entries are more in the nature of memoranda than of an organised account of the transactions that took place. Catherine

---

[1] CCCA, Minutes of the Gild of Corpus Christi, CCCCo1/G/2/1.
[2] *Cambridge Gild Records*, ed. M. Bateson, Cambridge Antiquarian Society, Octavo Series, 39 (Cambridge, 1903).

Hall, the college's archivist for many years, has skilfully analysed the contents of the manuscript and the way in which they are organised, beginning with the minutes of the meeting in January 1350 at which two treasurers were elected, and a number of people, either individuals or families, were admitted to the guild.[3] At this point, the guild had evidently been in existence for at least a year, as payments for the procession and festivities on the previous Corpus Christi day are recorded.[4] In the course of the following pages, three figures come to the fore as the men who are planning the guild's future; in addition to John Hardy himself, they were William Horwode, mayor of Cambridge, and Henry de Tangmere, the town receiver. By March 1352, they had negotiated a merger with the Guild of St Mary, which had existed since the thirteenth century; evidence of this is the appointment of John Hardy as proctor for the two guilds, to act for them jointly, on 26 March of that year.[5]

Up to this point, the guilds are purely Cambridge institutions, with a local membership. But in November 1352, when the formal royal licence for the union of the guilds is issued, the alderman of the new united organisation is named as Henry, duke of Lancaster. The duke has no other known connection with Cambridge, and this move has always been puzzling.[6] At this point in the notebook, his name appears on a new right-hand page, headed simply 'London'. Below it is the name of Henry Walton, his treasurer from 1348–53, a trusted servant who later acted as his lieutenant of the county palatine of Lancaster when the duke was abroad,[7] and then a sequence of other names, all evidently written at the same time. However, it is the names which come after this that reveal a fascinating aspect of the college's history which has hitherto been ignored. The list reads as follows:

> John Clement of Tamworth and Alice his wife, Henry and Matilda parents of the said John, entered the fraternity. He was and is the best counsellor and helper in all the business pertaining to the gild or college in London; and the said John gave the college a chalice and a vestment with all that belonged to it.
> Simon Franceis citizen of London and Matilda his wife entered the fraternity.
> Andrew Aubri citizen of London entered the fraternity and gave etc.
> Henry de Lacy serving the said Andrew entered the fraternity and gave half a mark
> Walter Neel and Alice and Katerina wives of the said Walter and of John Doxenford entered the fraternity and gave the procurator 20s and promised alms of £40 to the said gild.

3   C. Hall, 'The Gild of Corpus Christi and the Foundation of Corpus Christi College: An Investigation of the Documents', in *Medieval Cambridge: Essays on the Pre-Reformation University*, ed. P. Zutshi (Woodbridge, 1993), pp. 71–2.
4   Corpus Christi day was on 18 June in 1348. It was a moveable feast, celebrated on the Thursday after Trinity Sunday.
5   *Cambridge Gild Records*, ed. Bateson, p. 139.
6   K. Fowler, *The King's Lieutenant: Henry of Grosmont, First Duke of Lancaster 1310–1361* (London, 1969), p. 27.
7   Fowler, *The King's Lieutenant*, p. 177.

Alice de Boseham of London entered the fraternity and gave alms of 20s 6d for wax. 6d was paid to the treasurer and 20s to Hardy.

John de Trumpiton of London and Alice his wife entered the fraternity and gave as alms a piece of silver with which to make two ewers for holy water for the college and 20s in silver and wax. The wax was paid to the treasurer and they are to pay the money after the feast of the exaltation of the Holy Cross; he gave the piece of silver to J. Hardy.

Robert de Linham of London entered the fraternity and gave 20s in alms and is to pay the money after the feast of Corpus Christi. The wax was paid to the treasurer.[8]

In a different hand with larger script, possibly that of John Hardy on a separate occasion, further names have been added at the bottom of the page:

Simkin Simeon squire of the duke of Lancaster entered the fraternity.

Sir Thomas Haselarton, knight, and lady Alice his wife entered the fraternity.

Sir John Rotseie of Harlton, knight, and lady Cecilia his wife entered the fraternity.

Reginald de Wygenhale and Agnes his wife entered the fraternity and gave 30s in alms and wax. The wax was paid to Hardy and they were given until the feast of Corpus Christi to pay the 30s. The whole sum was paid to John of Teversham, chaplain, by the hand of John Hardy in the presence of the master and Sir Thomas Caumpes.

These records also reveal details of the network of Duke Henry and Sir Walter Mauny (whose name appears later in the notebook) as founder members of the Order of the Garter. One might expect to find a link with John Clement of Tamworth, the name that came after that of Henry Walton, Lancaster's treasurer, particularly as Tamworth is not far from Leicester, the centre of Henry of Lancaster's estates and his chief castle. The duke was on good terms with the townsmen of Leicester, who sent him wine when he hunted nearby and rewarded the messengers whom he sent to them with news of his exploits overseas: on his return from Aquitaine in 1347, they gave a dinner in his honour.[9] But John Clement of Tamworth is not in the surviving Lancaster records, though there is a Sir Nicholas de Tamworth who served with the duke in 1359–60 on the Reims campaign, and he could be from the same family.[10]

John Hardy makes it clear that John Clement of Tamworth had been one of the key figures in the establishment of the guild and college. This is the only entry where Hardy allows himself a comment, rather than simply noting the fact of entry into the guild, the amount paid on entry, and any future gifts promised. John Clement was in fact in a position to be of considerable

[8] *Cambridge Gilds*, ed. Bateson, pp. 49–50; my translation.
[9] Fowler, *The King's Lieutenant*, p. 194.
[10] K. Fowler, 'Henry of Grosmont, first duke of Lancaster, 1310–61' (unpublished Ph.D. thesis, University of Leeds, 1961), appendix, p. 260; he was contracted in 1355, but did not serve.

assistance to the fledgling guild. He appears as John of Tamworth in T.F. Tout's monumental work on the administration of the medieval kings of England.[11] Tout describes him as 'the first clerk of the Crown of whom we have full knowledge',[12] a man occupying a key legal position within chancery, with responsibility for drafting the legal documents required by the king and his ministers. In 1344, he was already an experienced clerk of long standing, and in 1350 he is singled out for a special reward as clerk of the chancery, because of the 'great expenses which he incurred in the sustenance of the clerks in the aforesaid office since the cessation of the last deadly pestilence',[13] costs incurred in 'serving us and our people'.[14] It seems that he was running a small training school for chancery clerks, whom he maintained until they were ready to start work in the chancery office. By 1368, he was married, an unusual but by no means unknown state, particularly for clerks whose main work was in the public service.[15] He was a man of property, and the first purchases date from shortly after the royal grant of 1350: he acquired houses in Chancery Lane, London, including the New Inn, which was later to become one of the inns of court.[16] On his death in 1375, his will names three children, and also implies that he dealt in timber, as he left a 'shout', or barge, and all his timber to his son William. He was evidently a man at home in the worlds of both the royal administration and the merchants and property owners of the city.

The entries which follow come from the highest levels of exactly that group, the wealthiest citizens of London. This list, which in the past was characterised as 'people doubtless worthy but entirely undistinguished' with a 'yawning gap between their social standing and that of the Duke',[17] contains nothing less than two mayors of the city of London, one of them the richest man in fourteenth-century England, the widow of another mayor and two sheriffs of the city. The guild which founded Corpus Christi College was intimately linked through these members with the city of London.

The first name is that of Simon Fraunceys.[18] He is noted as entering the guild with his wife Matilda, but no note of his offering is recorded; however, the same applies to Henry of Lancaster, and it may be that they were offered membership simply because of their influence. Simon Fraunceys first appears in the records as the most important of seven cloth merchants who supplied materials for Edward's coronation in 1327.[19] We next hear of him as a member of a diplomatic mission sent to Flanders in 1335 with the task of settling longstanding trade

---

[11]   He can be identified as John Clement of Tamworth since his wife Alice is named in both the records of the guild and in his will (*Calendar of Wills Proved and Enrolled in the Court of Husting, London A.D. 1258–A.D. 1688*, ed. R.R. Sharpe 2 vols. (London, 1890), ii, p. 167).

[12]   T.F. Tout, 'The Household of the Chancery and its Disintegration', in *Essays in History presented to Reginald Lane Poole*, ed. H.W.C. Davis (Oxford, 1927), p. 72.

[13]   *CCR, 1349–1354*, p. 173.

[14]   Related grant on patent rolls: *CPR, 1348–1350*, p. 470.

[15]   In 1388, an ordinance against married chancery clerks excepted Tamworth's successors and their subordinates. Tout, 'The Household of the Chancery', p. 82.

[16]   There is no continuous history of its use as a lawyers' inn: it reappears as an inn considerably later, in the early sixteenth century.

[17]   Hall, 'The Gild of Corpus Christi', p. 81.

[18]   S. O'Connor, 'Fraunceys, Simon (d.1358), *ODNB*.

[19]   Lisa Monnas, 'Textiles for the Coronation of Edward III', *Textile History* 32, 2001, 2–35.

disputes there. A detailed record of the mission's negotiations survives in the National Archives and shows that the count of Flanders was highly reluctant to come to terms; in the end, the envoys had to return with very little to show for their efforts. The appointment shows that Fraunceys was highly regarded by the government.[20] He was mayor in 1342–43 and again in 1355–56, and was one of the London representatives on the king's council and in parliament in the 1340s. He was a member of the Mercers' Company, a merchant, financier and landowner and may have been related to another mayor of London, Adam Fraunceys, though there is no definite proof of this. Simon died in 1358 and was buried in the priory of Holy Trinity Aldgate where his tomb was recorded by the herald Thomas Benolt in *c.*1505.[21]

Simon Fraunceys became mayor for the first time on the death in office of John de Oxenford in 1342, and another entry concerns Walter Neel, who was an executor of Oxenford's will. In 1353, Neel left an annuity of £5 for a chaplain to celebrate a daily Mass at St. James Garlickhithe in the city of London 'for my soul and the souls of Katherine my late wife, Alice my wife,[22] my father, my mother, John de Oxenford and all my other benefactors'.[23] This same group reappears in the Corpus Christi fraternity, where Walter gives 20*s.* and promises the very substantial sum of £40. Walter Neel was sheriff of London in 1338, and was a member of the cornmongers' company.[24] John de Oxenford had been sheriff in 1323–24, and was a vintner. It looks as if these men were part of a network within the city; Neel and Oxenford were both aldermen for Castle Baynard ward. Neel seems to have had connections with Hamo Hethe, bishop of Rochester; he is recorded in connection with the business of the diocese in 1320 and 1330.[25] He died in 1361 and was buried near de Oxenford's tombstone in St. James Garlickhithe.[26] But he undoubtedly appeared in the records of the Corpus Christi guild because of his status in London.

The name below that of Simon Fraunceys is of the most important figure in the city in the 1340s. Andrew Aubrey (d.1358) was mayor in 1339–41, at a critical moment in London's history.[27] He was probably born around 1300, and was factor to Thomas Enfield, a wealthy trader in pepper. When Enfield died in 1328, Aubrey married his widow, the classic move on the ladder to fortune; his tax bill in 1332 was one of the highest in London. He was

[20] H.S. Lucas, 'Diplomatic Relations between England and Flanders from 1329 to 1336', *Speculum*, 11 (1936), pp. 59–87, pp. 65 ff.

[21] College of Arms, London, MS CGY 647, f. 20v.

[22] He had married Alice clandestinely in 1330 at Islingham. *Registrum Hamonis Hethe, Diocesis Roffensis, A.D. 1319–52*, ed. C. Johnson, Canterbury and York Society, XLVIII, 2 vols. (Oxford, 1948), i, p. 252. He was at Islingham on 13 September (*Registrum Hamonis*, i, p. 438).

[23] *Registrum Hamonis*, i, p. 485.

[24] He is described as 'bladarius', which means cornmonger: John Stow, *A Survey of London*, ed. C.L. Kingsford, 2 vols. (Oxford, 1908), ii, p. 325.

[25] *Registrum Hamonis*, i, pp. 84, 438.

[26] Stow, *Survey*, i, p. 245. On John de Oxenford and Walter Neel see C. Steer, '"For quicke and deade memorie masses": Merchant Piety in Late Medieval London', in *Medieval Merchants and Money: Essays in Honour of James L. Bolton*, ed. M. Allen and M. Davies (London, 2016), pp. 71–89.

[27] P. Nightingale, 'Aubrey, Andrew (d. 1356)', *ODNB*.

evidently a shrewd and efficient businessman, as he was named auditor of the city's accounts in 1337. At the same time, he became one of the London members of parliament, and engaged in the highly lucrative but politically vulnerable wool trade with Flanders. One of the means by which Edward III financed his wars in France was by seizing wool for resale at a profit, and Aubrey suffered from this in 1338 when £156 worth of his wool was taken by the king at Antwerp. The king's actions and the costs of the war led to a crisis in which Aubrey played a pivotal role. Edward returned unexpectedly from Flanders in the autumn of 1340, determined to dismiss the administration in England because they had failed to provide him with the money to pursue his campaign. He arrived at midnight at the water gate of the Tower of London, and found the constable of the Tower absent. According to the *French Chronicle of London*, the king sent at once for Aubrey to speak with him; the mayor fell to his knees as soon as he entered the king's room, but the king told him to get up and to arrest eight members of the royal council responsible for the crisis, which he did.[28]

The failure of the king's finances also led to severe strains within the city, and Aubrey was mayor when these difficulties degenerated into open riots. He was attacked personally in 1340 during street fighting between two of the companies, and although his assailant was a member of a prominent city family, Aubrey petitioned the king for a sentence of execution, arguing that this was needed to ensure the mayor's future safety and authority. In the absence of a response, because the king was at war in Flanders, he summoned a large assembly of citizens, who condemned him to death, and on this authority his attacker was immediately executed, without the king's warrant. The king later ratified Aubrey's action, and Aubrey went on to develop a considerable commercial empire with his family, and to found what became the Grocer's Company. At the height of his prosperity in 1348, a single cargo owned by him was valued at £2,000. In 1349, he and his son John went on pilgrimage to Rome to mark their survival of the plague, and Aubrey was mayor once again in 1351, at the time when the entry in the Corpus guild records was probably made. Aubrey's name is followed by that of his 'servant' Henry de Lacy. The Latin word is *serviens*, which could mean either apprentice or steward. Given Aubrey's status in the City, he is less likely to have had apprentices than a steward. Furthermore, when Lacy witnessed Aubrey's will in 1349 he was recorded as a 'grosser' or wholesaler, which implies he was already of some standing.[29] He subsequently appears in a grant by Aubrey's son in 1364 as a pepperer, like his master.[30] He is evidently a lesser figure than the great man who had employed him, but nonetheless an influential citizen.

We have already discussed Walter Neel, and after him three other Londoners are named: Alice de Boseham of London, John of Trumpiton of London and his wife Alice, who gave silver plate to the college, and Robert de

---

[28] *Chroniques de London*, ed. G.J. Aungier, Camden Society Old Series, 28 (London, 1844), p. 84.

[29] *Calendar of Wills Proved and Enrolled in the Court of Husting, London*, ii, pp. 1–6.

[30] *CCR, 1364–1369*, pp. 92–3. He also witnessed a transaction by the younger Aubrey in 1356: *CCR, 1354–1360*, p. 321. He was dead by 1376: *CCR, 1374–1377*, p. 351.

Linham of London. For these, we have little information. John de Boseham was sheriff of London in 1378–79, and Alice may have been related to him. William de Trumpiton, whose will was enrolled in 1350, had a brother named John.[31] And for Robert de Linham we have nothing. With these names, the 'London entry' ends.

The duke of Lancaster's squire, Simeon Simkin, and two other knights are then recorded, in a larger and coarser hand, which is probably a later addition, by either John Hardy or someone else. 'Simeon Simkin' conceals a much more important figure than a mere squire. Simon Simeon was Lancaster's chamberlain, and 'most trusted confidant',[32] who had been in his father's service since at least 1329. We first meet him in the duchy records hunting with Henry, then aged twenty, in the autumn of 1330. He was in Henry's retinue in Scotland as an esquire in 1336, and thereafter served him in both peace and war until the duke's death: he was an experienced soldier who had fought in Flanders and had been captured there, and he went on crusade to Prussia with the duke in 1352. He was a valued administrator and became the duke's chamberlain in 1354. His name may have been added in that year, when he returned from a pilgrimage to Jerusalem. In 1356, the duke joined a fraternity at Newstead in Oxfordshire, and asked that Simeon should also be admitted.[33] Later he was one of the duke's executors at his death in 1361, and went on to serve John of Gaunt.[34] The other men named with Simon Simeon are almost unknown: we can only guess that Sir Thomas Haselarton is evidently related to Walter Haselarton, who served with Henry, duke of Lancaster, in 1354–55 in Brittany, and again on the Reims campaign in 1359–60, and to Sir Simon Haselarton who also served the duke on the Reims expedition.[35]

Sir Walter Mauny's name appears as a rough note some pages later; there is merely a list of the names of his family, divided into *vivi* and *mortui*; it is the relations of his wife, Margaret of Brotherton, heir to the earldom of Norfolk, who are the *mortui* whose names are to be included in the guild's prayers. Mauny is generally known for his swashbuckling appearances in the pages of Froissart; but there is also a very different side to him. He was a wealthy man, even as a young knight, and was able to lend Edward III £4,000 in 1340. By 1352 he had also inherited the family estates in Flanders, and in 1354 he made a splendid marriage to Margaret of Brotherton, daughter and co-heir of the earl of Norfolk and a granddaughter of Edward I. Mauny himself was well acquainted with London and its merchants, both because he had mercantile interests in Flanders, where his family estates were, and because of his friendship with Michael Northburgh, bishop of London, which had led him to create a large cemetery for plague victims just outside the city walls in Smithfield.[36] This major benefaction later became the church of the London

[31] *Calendar of Wills Proved and Enrolled in the Court of Husting, London*, ii, pp. 308–9.
[32] Fowler, *The King's Lieutenant*, p. 27.
[33] R. Somerville, *History of the Duchy of Lancaster*, i: *1265–1603* (London, 1953), p. 358.
[34] Fowler, *The King's Lieutenant*, pp. 27, 176, 179, 217.
[35] Fowler, 'Henry of Grosmont', appendix, p. 252.
[36] *Calendar of Wills proved and enrolled in the court of Husting, London*, ii, pp. 61–2.

Charterhouse. It was here in 1372 where Mauny was later buried and where he was commemorated by his funerary monument – probably sculptured effigies – for himself and his wife Margaret. It may be that he too was part of this group of prominent citizens.

The presence of this group of London founders in the Cambridge guild raises all sorts of questions as to their motives for being involved in the creation of the college. This chapter concludes by reflecting on some of these queries in order to identify future strands of research that will be needed before the make-up of this group of founders can be fully assessed. There is a good reason for John of Tamworth: just as William Bateman founded Trinity Hall specifically as an institution to educate canon lawyers, Tamworth may have been anxious to find a source of new recruits to the royal service.[37] As to the others, they may well have been recruited by Tamworth, in view of Hardy's praise for his efforts on the guild and college's behalf. There is also the possibility that there were business links of some kind with men such as Henry of Tangmere; in this case the analogy would be with the grandiose church of Salle in Norfolk, built in a remote rural site with the support of the Coventry guilds who bought the local wool.[38] It may simply have been that the membership of a Corpus Christi guild was a sought-after privilege: 'famous fraternities like Corpus Christi of York attracted members from all over England, and some merchant fraternities offered membership and the related benefits to substantial merchants from other towns'.[39]

The next question is why this London connection does not appear to have had any real impact on the college. There are no sums of money promised against the names of the two mayors, though Aubrey's entry ends 'and he owes etc.', as if there had been an offer, but the writer did not think it would come to fruition. Again, we can only speculate. Perhaps these names were there simply to add lustre to the list of founders; the lesser personalities all have specific amounts against their names. Perhaps also the problems which London merchants faced because of royal policy in the early 1350s, when they lost many privileges, made them less interested. Furthermore, there were very large numbers of new foundations during this period, which all competed for attention. Aubrey had founded a chantry in London in 1348, building a chapel next to the church of St. Antonin, home of the fraternity of pepperers which he had joined the previous year. Lancaster and Mauny were both involved with the religious fraternity of St. George's Windsor, the Order

---

[37] Most Cambridge colleges concentrated on theology; Trinity Hall was unique in having a stated purpose as 'a perpetual college of scholars of civil and canon law'. Corpus would thus parallel Trinity Hall in being intended to supply recruits to serve in the royal administration. See *Documents relating to the University and Colleges of Cambridge*, 3 vols. (London 1852), ii, p. 415. On the foundation of Trinity Hall, see Claire Gobbi Daunton and Elizabeth New, 'Patrons and Benefactors: The Masters of Trinity Hall in the Later Middle Ages' in this volume, pp. 61–90.

[38] E. Duffy, 'Salle Church and the Reformation', in his *Saints, Sacrilege and Sedition: Religion and Conflict in the Tudor Reformation* (London, 2012), pp. 83–108 at p. 86.

[39] M. Rubin, 'Religious Culture in Town and Country: Reflections on a Great Divide', in *Church and City 1000–1500: Essays in Honour of Christopher Brooke*, ed. D. Abulafia, M. Franklin and M. Rubin (Cambridge, 1992), pp. 3–22 at p. 6.

of the Garter and its college, and had their own projects. Lancaster founded a large college at Leicester beginning in 1353, and all these had to be endowed. Henry gave the manor of Barton and the advowson of Grantchester to Corpus, and the advowson of Uttoxeter to St. George's. The college at Leicester had vast endowments by comparison: five manors and five advowsons. Two of the advowsons were later exchanged for more modest Welsh churches, but 1,000 marks of annual rent were added at this point.[40]

There is a further possibility, which is that the 'London connection' was largely the work of John of Tamworth, and that it was less an exercise in recruitment than in fundraising. Caroline Barron has suggested that in the wake of the Black Death a large number of wills failed because the heirs named in them had died, and the estates were therefore in the gift of the executors – if indeed they themselves had survived – for charitable purposes.[41] A foundation such as Corpus Christi College with its guild association was ideal as a means of ensuring that prayers were said for the soul of the testator, particularly as the testators could be enrolled *post mortem* as members of the guild. John of Tamworth would have been very well placed to suggest the college as a worthy recipient of their largesse, and John Hardy's acknowledgement of him as the college's 'best helper and counsellor' in all business in London seems to confirm this idea.

The identification of this hitherto anonymous group of founders, and the realisation of their importance, begs as many questions as it solves. One important point to emerge in this study is the extent to which medieval benefactors employed different commemorative strategies – and not confined to a funerary monument near their grave – to benefit their soul in the afterlife. The use of chantries and obits elsewhere is well known but this essay has revealed the way in which a number of prominent Londoners, and those who may have died intestate, chose to be patrons of a Cambridge guild and be beneficiaries of another part of a rich spiritual armoury. It is particularly striking how an executor such as Walter Neel 'signed up' not only himself and his wives Alice and Katherine, but also his fellow London parishioner John de Oxenford who had died many years before, and for whom he served as executor. If I may risk a speculation, it seems possible that John of Tamworth's 'sales pitch' may have centred on the idea that they were patronising not only a guild, but a college which would train the clerks sorely needed to ensure that the chantry services could be maintained. This would have had enormous resonance given the high mortality of clergy in the Black Death. But now that the presence of these Londoners has been revealed, we can at least begin to discuss such possibilities, and shed more light on the origins of Corpus Christi College.

[40] Fowler, *The King's Lieutenant*, p. 189.
[41] *Pers. comm.*, January 2013. I am most grateful to Professor Barron not only for this suggestion, but also for notes of relevant documents. I would also like to record the debt I owe to the late Professor Christopher Brooke, who encouraged me to work on a general history of Corpus, which, alas, did not come to fruition, but from which this article arose. He was kind enough to comment in detail on an earlier draft, intended originally for the College *Letter*.

CHAPTER 4

Patrons and Benefactors: The Masters of Trinity Hall in the Later Middle Ages*

Claire Gobbi Daunton and Elizabeth A. New

The foundation by William Bateman (*c.*1298–1355) of the college of the Most Holy Trinity in Cambridge, to be known as Trinity Hall (Plate 3), raises important questions.[1] This was undoubtedly an act of both patronage and benefaction; borne out of short-term necessity, it went on to have long-term consequences. But the college's longevity is a triumphant memorial not only to its founder: the institution and its buildings are testimony to the work and memory of Bateman and of his many successors. This essay considers three particular Masters whose careers provide an opportunity to interrogate the complementary concepts of patronage and benefation.

Bishop Bateman was an active and effective clerical administrator working on an international stage as a papal diplomat; but he was also a Norfolk man and his principal post for a significant part of his career was that of bishop of Norwich.[2] His family background (he was the son of a citizen of Norwich who had built up the family's wealth and local influence) and his network of connections rooted him firmly in his own locality, whilst the connections established there helped him to make his mark within a much broader setting.[3] Nothing, however, could have prepared him for the onslaught of the Black Death across East Anglia.[4] Bateman's return to England from the papal

---

* The authors wish to thank Ann Rycraft, Ginny Swepson and also Dominique Ruhlmann, Librarian, and Alex Browne, Archivist, at Trinity Hall, Cambridge, for their help in the preparation of this article.

1 Trinity Hall was established by Bateman in 1350 as 'The College of Scholars of the Holy Trinity of Norwich' specifically to serve his own diocese. The link with the diocese was silently omitted in 1559 when the college was granted a new charter by Elizabeth I. The college has remained on the site acquired by Bateman in the centre of Cambridge.

2 R.M. Haines, 'Bateman, William (*c.*1298–1355)', *ODNB.*

3 C. Crawley, *Trinity Hall: The History of a Cambridge College, 1350–1975* (Cambridge, 1976), pp. 4–5.

4 For evidence of the plague's effect in the region see J. Aberth, 'The Black Death in the Diocese of Ely: The Evidence of the Bishop's Register', *Journal of Medieval History*, 21 (1995), pp. 275–87.

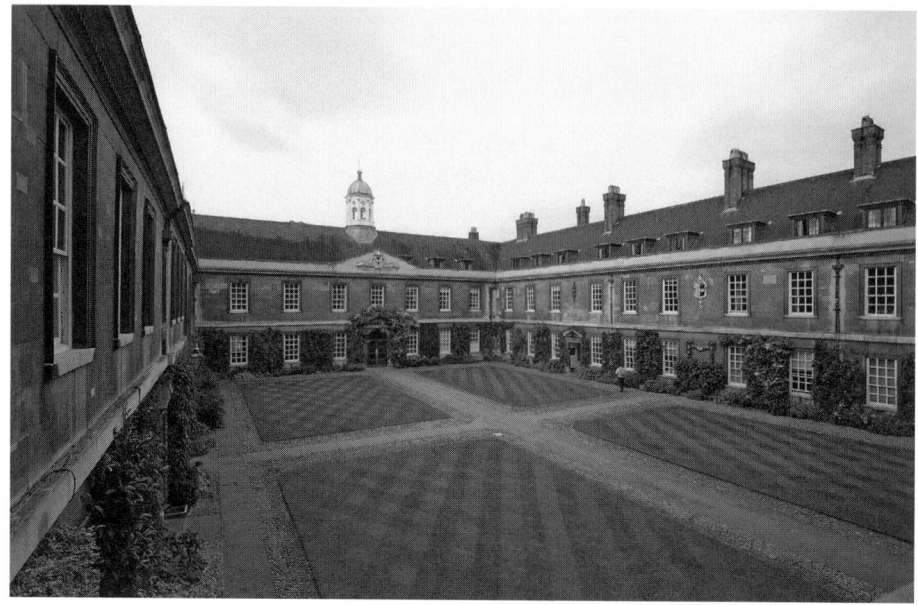

3: Trinity Hall, Cambridge.

court at Avignon and his response to death amongst the clergy were acts of decision and strategy, as well as of necessity.[5]

The bishop's foundation of Trinity Hall in 1350 was rooted in his knowledge of his diocese and its needs at a time of great challenge. At this moment he was able to appreciate with acuity the importance of maintaining and increasing a priesthood whose well-trained members could follow in his own footsteps.[6] It is, of course, possible that Bateman had already planned to establish an institution for training clergy in higher level administration before his hand was forced by the onset of pandemic. One might then consider his foundation of the college as an act of strategic patronage. It was one with far-reaching consequences well beyond what he could have imagined; and consideration of the general concept of patronage will bring into sharper focus these longer-term consequences.

PATRONS AND BENEFACTORS IN THE MIDDLE AGES

The most basic meaning of the term 'patronage', as the act of a father, takes us immediately into the religious sphere. Spiritual fatherhood is embedded in the Judaeo-Christian tradition: the Jewish God as protector of his people, chastising but forgiving;[7] and God as Father, one element of the Triune God of Christianity, the Father all-powerful but also part of an intimate redemptive

5   *The Register of William Bateman, Bishop of Norwich, 1344–1355*, ed. P.E. Pobst (Woodbridge, 1996), pp. xxxi–xxxii.
6   L.E. Boyle, 'Aspects of Clerical Education in Fourteenth-century England', in *The Fourteenth Century*, ed. P. E. Szamarch and B.E. Levy (New York, 1977), pp. 19–32.
7   Zechariah 2: 8–10.

process.[8] The medieval Church was influenced also by the Greco-Romano notion of patronage absorbed in the early days of Christianity. Here fatherly protection, or personal patronage towards dependants, and more general patronage towards the wider public were made evident. Personal and public patronage, civic euergetism, were put on display in order to cement a system in which the figures dispensing the patronage were in charge; and the system depended on all players taking on their allotted roles. The giving of support or gifts was intended to foster or maintain dependence.[9] In the Christian Church these two strands came together and were cemented within the hierarchy of the Church and in its reach to the wider community of believers.[10]

A distinction can, however, be made between acts of patronage and those of beneficence, between the role of the patron and that of the benefactor. Within an overarching system of patronage, heavenly and earthly, the medieval Church survived on acts of beneficence and kindness. Donations by generous benefactors, whose wealth and influence in life and in death founded monasteries and built churches, hospitals and almshouses, were made of out of love of God and neighbour, but also from a desire to be remembered, to be well thought of, or to maintain status, and as an act of charity.[11] They created a benefit for the individual; generosity and a concern for spiritual welfare in life and beyond death went hand in hand.

Further care needs to be taken when considering appointments to benefices in the late medieval period. Here the meanings of concepts such as 'patronage' and 'beneficence' come sharply into focus. An appointment to a benefice, a living, a parish, a livelihood, was not an act of beneficence on the part of a bishop or other senior figure; it was an act of patronage: the bishop wanted men he could trust, with whom he could work and over whom he would be able to exercise control. The effective functioning of the medieval Church relied on this control and it was within this context that William Bateman operated. There was a professionalised system of giving and receiving favours, of dependence and obligation, and this could be compared with the celestial system of dependence and obligation that was at the heart of the Christian religion.[12] If the pope was at the apex of dependency in the earthly church, the Trinity was his celestial counterpart: the granting of prayerful wishes, the relief from suffering after death, the protection of family, and the spiritual nourishment of the sacraments and pious devotions all led, eventually, back

[8]   Mark 1: 10–11.
[9]   K. Lomas and T. Cornell, eds., *Bread and Circuses: Euergetism and Municipal Patronage in Italy* (London, 2003). See particularly the essay by John Patterson, 'The Emperor and the Cities of Italy', pp. 89–103.
[10]   In his recent book, *The Ransom of the Soul* (Cambridge, MA, 2015), Peter Brown considers the importance of euergetism in the classical period and its adoption into Christian thought and practice, especially pp. 85–8.
[11]   For example, the essays by Michael Robson, 'The Commemoration of the Living and the Dead at the Friars Minor of Cambridge', pp. 34–51, and Richard Barber, 'The City of London and the Founding of the Guild of Corpus Christi', pp. 52–60 in this volume.
[12]   A local example of how this system of patronage operated is described in R.M. Haines, 'Associates and *Familia* of William Gray and his Use of Patronage whilst Bishop of Ely, 1458–1474', *Journal of Ecclesiastical History*, 25 (1974), pp. 225–48.

to the Trinity, just as all ecclesiastical dependency led, eventually, back to Rome.

The personnel of the late medieval Church were the agents integrating the institution within its society. The clergy were responsible for overseeing attempts to maintain the Christian view of society, and as agents of the institution had the duty to protect its property and rights. They could engage in a variety of specialised careers – such as lawyers and administrators – alongside their cure of souls and the spiritual welfare of their parishioners.[13]

THE FOUNDATION OF TRINITY HALL

Within this system it was no more than Bishop Bateman's professional duty to find a way to replenish his diocese after the Black Death with priests who were capable of administering within it. One might suggest that Bateman was fortunate in his timing: the impact of the plague was such that he had the opportunity to take an entirely new approach to the professionalisation of clergy; and he seized this opportunity eagerly. The institution he founded was to be dedicated to scholarship, to learning, and particularly to the development of academic expertise in the law, ecclesiastical and civil. Further, it was to be a community that offered the discipline and mutual support of scholarly pursuits to those who were members. Bateman's foundation was to provide administrators; not all those who were to be scholars were to become priests. The bishop would certainly have wanted to ensure that the diocese of Norwich was able to withstand any future problems. It was a departure from the foundation of colleges formed earlier in the fourteenth century – colleges of priests – whose main aim was to pray for souls and to have a pastoral outreach within an overall parochial framework.

The innovative nature of Bateman's foundation was also somewhat different from other Cambridge foundations of that period. The statutes of Clare College, founded by Elizabeth de Burgh, countess of Ulster and Lady of Clare, more than a decade before, were promulgated in 1359 and set out the purpose of her foundation:

> Our purpose is that through their study and teaching at the university they should discover and acquire the precious pearl of learning, so that it does not stay hidden under a bushel but is displayed abroad to enlighten those who walk in the dark paths of ignorance.[14]

Corpus Christi College, founded in 1352 in the years immediately following the outbreak of plague, was the product of an agreement between two town guilds, the guilds of Corpus Christi and the Blessed Virgin Mary.[15] These guildsmen and women wanted their institution to train priests. Since so many members of the clergy had died in the plague there was a serious shortage of

[13] R.N. Swanson, *Church and Society in Late Medieval England* (Oxford, 1989), p. 27.
[14] Clare College Cambridge Archives, CCGB/1/1/5.
[15] CCCA, CCCCo1/GF/1. On the foundation of the college see Barber, 'The City of London and the Founding of the Guild of Corpus Christi', above.

priests to perform the sacraments and to ensure that the ecclesiastical life of the town continued.

As a response to the consequences of the plague, the foundational aims of Trinity Hall were perhaps more specifically professional than those of Clare or Corpus Christi College. The aim was to train canon and civil lawyers, initially to be at the service of the diocese of Norwich, to administer the diocese and to ensure that their fellow priests carried out their spiritual and secular duties in conformity with the law. Bateman wanted a diocese well run, according to the law. He went about achieving this aim in a professional manner. And crucial to survival was funding. Once again Bateman was focussed and thorough. He had control of the income of several benefices in Norfolk and he committed this income to the setting up of his college: funding from his own purse and from his family was, no doubt, added to the mix. Here, one might add that the Greco-Roman concept of patronage was to the fore: funding within one's personal control was being used to further one's own goals which were clearly intended to serve the wider public good and ensure that one's name and reputation, and those of one's family, were held in high regard. In short this was an act of patronage, charity and personal commemoration, established on a lavish scale and far grander than commemoration expressed through any funerary monument. The wider public good in this case, however, could primarily be defined as the wider good of the Church – and the donor (Bateman) – and an act of patronage always in the service of the ultimate patron, God.

On the question of funding Bateman paid particular attention to the matter of an adequate endowment. At the moment when Trinity Hall was being established, Gonville Hall in Cambridge, founded by his associate and fellow-priest Edmund Gonville, was in severe financial difficulties. Bateman stepped in, as patron and protector, to put Gonville Hall on a firmer financial footing and to ensure its survival.[16] Bateman's patronage of these two institutions – Trinity Hall and Gonville Hall – established them as places of professional training and learning. This he considered one of the principal expressions of his role as bishop. To appreciate the significance of this interpretation, it is helpful to consider Bateman's contemporary and fellow member of the English episcopate, John Trillek (1308–60), bishop of Hereford from 1344 until his death sixteen years later.

Trillek was of a similar age and background to Bateman and his episcopate also spanned the plague years.[17] But Trillek, by contrast, had immediate access to ecclesiastical patronage from the time of his birth. His uncle Adam Orleton was bishop of Hereford in the formative days of Trillek's career, and both the pastoral and academic aspects of Trillek's development as a cleric were undertaken under the watchful eye of Orleton. Just as Bateman came to notice as a papal administrator and diplomat, so Trillek came to be

---

[16] C.N.L. Brooke, *A History of Gonville and Caius College, Cambridge* (Woodbridge, 1985), pp. 10–14.

[17] D.N. Lepine, 'Trillek, John (c.1308–1360)', *ODNB*. W. Dohar, *The Black Death and Pastoral Leadership: The Diocese of Hereford in the Fourteenth Century* (Philadelphia, 1995), pp. 55–78.

distinguished for his work within the diocese of Hereford as a good pastor, someone who worked hard to ensure effective training of the clergy and attention to the daily operation of parishes. Having himself experienced a university education in Oxford and Paris, Trillek, like Bateman, supported priests of his diocese during their time of study in Oxford.[18] Nor was Trillek without links to the papal curia. One might be tempted to judge Trillek the more effective bishop and senior cleric, since his obvious devotion to diocesan pastoral affairs is clear. This is perhaps to take too narrow a view of the higher clergy of this period: managing the internal affairs of a diocese in various ways and representing a diocese in a broader context were essential parts of the role of bishop. Trillek and Bateman played to their own personal strengths: and both were clearly effective patrons within their dioceses.

Whatever their difference of approach to carrying out their respective roles, patronage of higher education was important: Trillek encouraged his priests in their studies; Bateman gave his attention to Trinity Hall and Gonville Hall. Both understood the value of their patronage: the sustenance of their dioceses and the maintenance of their own good name before their priests and people and before God. For neither is there an extant will so it is not possible to know how closely their own personal bequests reflected their professional and spiritual lives, but this comparison gives some context to Bateman's work.[19]

THE MASTERS OF TRINITY HALL AND THEIR COMMEMORATIONS

Bishop Bateman's foundation was fortunate in the century that followed. Successive Masters built up the endowment of the college through direct benefaction or through their persuasive friendships and connections with others. It became the norm that Masters should bequeath money and property to the college to ensure it survived and flourished, and successive wills bear that out. The most notable of these was Simon Dalling.

Simon Dalling

Dalling was already a fellow, and trained in civil and canon law, when he was appointed Master in 1443, a post he appears to have held for ten years since his successor, Simon Thornham, was appointed in 1453.[20] Simon Dalling's understanding of the role followed closely that of the founder. Bateman's challenge was to provide priests trained in the law for his diocese: Dalling's challenge was to sustain Bateman's institution when Henry VI came buying land for the building of his college adjacent to Trinity Hall and could not be refused. In 1445 Dalling was able to exchange what was then low-lying

---

[18]   Dohar, *The Black Death*, pp. 124–6.
[19]   Trillek is commemorated by a fine monumental brass in Hereford Cathedral (1360), see E.A. New, 'The Brass and Seal of John Trillek (d. 1360), Bishop of Hereford: Comparative Thoughts', *TMBS*, 19:1 (2014), pp. 2–14.
[20]   *BRUC*, p. 175.

land close to the River Cam and the church of St. John Zachary for land and adjoining property, including the church of St. Edward King and Martyr, close to the market place, and its living. The church was used by both Trinity Hall and Clare College, each college having its own chapel within the church, but it was in the gift of Trinity Hall. The consequent income from this and from land purchases was sufficient to sustain the endowment and increase the number of fellows and scholars.[21] This expansion enabled the college to take a significant step forward from Bateman's original foundation.

Willian Dalling and Simon Thornham

In the succeeding decades this pattern continued with Masters Simon Thornham (d.1472) and William Dalling (d.1501, nephew of Simon). Both were Norfolk men of similar backgrounds with benefices in Norfolk and Cambridgeshire, whose tenures as Master covered the period 1453 to 1501. Thornham was well connected in the diocese of Norwich, serving in Norwich itself first as Master of the Hospital of St. Mary Magdalen and then as dean and canon of the College of St. Mary in the Fields. He held these posts as well as many rural livings.[22] William Dalling, in particular, was a significant benefactor to Trinity Hall, bequeathing to the college items of silver and furniture in his room, as well as land in Cambridgeshire. The former were to be sold to fund a set of black Mass vestments and a cope for use at the funerals of benefactors; and the proceeds of the sale of land he owned were to be used by the college to commemorate him on the feast of St. William (8 June).[23] It is worth noting that William Dalling requested burial at the church at Over, Cambridgeshire, a living he appears to have held at least since 1490. At this time burial in the college chapel was not possible since it was not yet consecrated.[24] The fact that Masters or Fellows might be buried where they held livings was not necessarily to the detriment of the college; rather it was one of the ways in which the college, the city of Cambridge and surrounding areas maintained contact with each other: the reach of colleges and university was wide.

An investment in the future of the college was also an investment in the memory of the Master and these men were rich enough to have goods and property for the college to realise. By the early sixteenth century the role of the Master, as both patron and benefactor, was well established. That a Master should seek out opportunities for raising income, and increase the profile of the college, together with providing funds out of his own pocket, is evident from the careers of these three fifteenth-century Masters. But it was some time before the college was to have another sponsor of this ilk in the person of Walter Hewke, Master from 1510 to his death (probably in 1518). It will become clear from the discussion of Hewke's role as Master (considered below) that one can read the provisions of his long and remarkable will as

---

[21]   Crawley, *Trinity Hall*, pp. 20–3.

[22]   *BRUC*, p. 585.

[23]   *BRUC*, p. 175.

[24]   See below, note 60, for comment on the burial of Walter Hewke, first Master to be interred in the college chapel.

expressions of patronage and benefaction, which dovetail with Bateman's original long-term intentions for his college.

Edward Shuldham

The importance of Walter Hewke as college benefactor and friend is brought into sharp focus by comparison with his two immediate predecessors, Edward Shuldham (d.1503)[25] and John Wright (d.1518) who had trained as lawyers at Trinity Hall.[26] These men were markedly different from other Masters for their rectorships were outside Cambridgeshire and Norfolk:[27] Shuldham died in office, in 1503, after only one year as Master; and Wright, who succeeded him after a short interregnum, resigned seven years later in 1512 and died in 1518. They left wills and the two documents bear comparison. Shuldham's will of 1499 (Appendix 1) gives detailed instructions concerning liturgical arrangements for his burial and for keeping the anniversary of his death[28] Wright's document of 1518 (Appendix 2) has no such preoccupations concerning the ceremonies surrounding burial or memorial.[29] The two documents are also distinct from each other: one is written in Latin and in a careful copyist's hand typical of the late fifteenth century and the other is in English and written in free-flowing secretary hand of the second decade of the sixteenth century.

Although only twenty years separate these two documents, even their physical appearance gives a strong indication of the similarities and differences between the two men. Shuldham and Wright asked to be buried in parish churches in Hertfordshire (Therfield and Clothall respectively), to which they left money and vestments, with legacies to friends and family. It is striking that although they were university men, trained as lawyers, books do not figure largely in either will and are certainly not significant items of bequest. Shuldham's will, made before he became Master of Trinity Hall in 1502, does not appear to have been altered before his death in 1503; and this short tenure of office suggests an unexpected death.[30] The will makes no specific mention of Trinity Hall, the only direct link being through John Wright, an executor, described as rector of Clothall in Hertfordshire. But Shuldham left money for institutions in Cambridge and the rich detail of his will reveals something of the character chosen to be Master of Bateman's foundation at the beginning of the sixteenth century; it deserves close

---

[25] The spelling 'Shouldham' is used for the Norfolk village of that name; the family name is rendered 'Shuldham', as used in Edward Shuldham's will and that of other members of that family in the late medieval period.

[26] *BRUC*, pp. 526–7 and 603.

[27] The list of livings held by Shuldham in particular is extensive and includes Southoe and Buckworth in Huntingdonshire, Cranfield in Bedfordshire and Therfield in Hertfordshire, in addition to his canonry at Newarke College and prebendary at Lincoln Cathedral. Wright was clearly very attached to his living at Clothall, Hertfordshire, and had strong links with the town of Baldock, as will be shown below.

[28] TNA: PRO, PROB 11/13 ff. 201v–202.

[29] Huntingdonshire Archives, Huntingdon, AH15/1/2, Archdeaconry Wills, vol. 2, p. 183.

[30] The will is dated 28 November 1499 and was proved on 21 August 1503.

scrutiny. Shuldham was clearly wealthy, well connected and pious, and his network of connections was extensive. It is most likely that he was part of the extended eponymous family of gentry landowners of north-west Norfolk, with manors in Shouldham, Marham and Narborough. Remaining sources provide somewhat contradictory evidence concerning his possible relationship to the various branches of the Shuldham family, particularly to Thomas Shuldham of Narborough (d.1472) and Thomas Shuldham of Marham (d.1514), both members of the local gentry.[31] It is, however, likely that family connections would have assisted him in his profession and provided him with some of the income to which his testamentary bequests bear witness. And it is significant that he made a bequest of 40s. for the purchase of a cope for the church of All Saints, Shouldham. Membership of a prosperous gentry family would also explain why he was not beneficed before he went up to Cambridge. His several ecclesiastical livings would also have brought him a significant income.

Master Shuldham evidently had particular attachments to, and affection for, his parish of Therfield in Hertfordshire and religious houses nearby.[32] His wish to have anniversary Masses said in the University of Cambridge and the fact that he wanted a Cambridge-trained scholar to be hired as chantry priest at Therfield suggest that he also maintained links with his place of training, though these links do not feature prominently in his last testament. And he had interests elsewhere too. The first bequest in Shuldham's will is to Lincoln Cathedral. He was briefly canon there, and it was a poor prebend, but both he and Wright were careful to mention their diocesan mother church in their wills. In his study of English secular cathedrals in the late Middle Ages, David Lepine notes that canon and civil law were amongst the most popular subjects studied by canons.[33] In addition to the appointment to the cathedral chapter, Shuldham was the bishop of Lincoln's commissary in the archdeaconry of Huntingdon in 1492 and a commissary of Bishop Smith of Lincoln in 1498.[34] Shuldham was also a canon of Newarke College in Leicester, a prestigious religious institution founded in 1330 by Henry, earl of Lancaster, kinsman of Edward III, well known for his personal piety.[35]

---

[31] F. Blomefield, 'Clackclose Hundred and Half: Shouldham', in *An Essay towards a Topographical History of the County of Norfolk: Vol. 7* (London, 1807), pp. 414–27; http://www.british-history.ac.uk/topographical-hist-norfolk/vol7/pp414-427 [accessed 20 August 2015]. The wills of relevant members of the Shouldham family are at Norfolk Record Office, Norwich Consistory Court will registers 10, 11, 25: Betyns 137 (1468); Jekkys 268 (1472); Popy 523 (1504). Other documentation for the Shouldhams can be found in the Hare Collection in the Norfolk Record Office, HARE 2817, 199X5, HARE 2818, 199X5. We are most grateful to Christine M. Hood of Norwich for her help with genealogical enquiries and related material.

[32] His will includes specific mentions of the Augustinian priory in the Hertfordshire town of Royston and the Grey Friars in Bedford and Cambridge.

[33] D. Lepine, *A Brotherhood of Canons Serving God: English Secular Cathedrals in the Late Middle Ages* (Woodbridge, 1995), p. 58.

[34] Private communication from David Lepine, to whom we are grateful.

[35] 'College of the Annunciation of St. Mary in the Newarke, Leicester', in *VCH: A History of the County of Leicestershire*, ed. W.G. Hoskins and R.A. McKinley (London, 1954), ii, pp. 48–51l; http://www.british-history.ac.uk/vch/leics/vol2/pp48-51 [accessed 23 August 2015].

Shuldham's rectories, which were rich, would have provided some element of knowledge and experience at parish level, as well as increasing his income substantially; and his Cambridge fellowship ensured that he maintained his university links. In terms of appointments and ecclesiastical connections, Shuldham was building up a 'career portfolio' which no doubt influenced his appointment as Master of Trinity Hall.

Edward Shuldham was named as executor and beneficiary in the will of William Bathcombe (d.1487), doctor of canon law in the University of Cambridge and vicar of the church of Holy Trinity, Cambridge.[36] It is notable that Bathcombe made a bequest to the poor of Marham, where the Shuldhams held a manor, perhaps suggesting that his friendship with Edward Shuldham extended beyond their university acquaintance.[37] Shuldham's own testamentary expressions of personal piety were made in a number of specific forms. Bequests of vestments, or whatever was necessary, were made for two well-known local Marian shrines, one at White Hill, near the south Cambridgeshire village of Haslingfield, and another at the Augustinian priory of Barnwell on the outskirts of the town. The first, in a prominent position within the surrounding countryside, must have served as a local landmark as well as a place of pilgrimage. Little is known of its origins or operation, but it was, perhaps, also a staging post for pilgrims on the way to Walsingham.[38] The chapel at Barnwell was much better known. At times it served as lodgings for royalty and other significant pilgrims or visitors, as well as a popular burial place for the wealthy of the area.[39]

The Shuldham family retained strong connections with a number of religious foundations. Several kinswomen, including Anne, Katharine and Barbara – each a member of a different female religious order – received a bequest of 10*s.* each, and separate bequests were also made to their religious houses.[40] In addition, religious houses in different parts of Bedfordshire and Huntingdonshire with which Shuldham had been associated received generous donations. For example, funds were bequeathed for an image of St. Peter in Chains at the church in Cranfield, Bedfordshire, and an image of St. Leonard in the church of Southoe, Huntingdonshire, dedicated to that saint. Shuldham seems to have had a particular devotion to St. Leonard, evident in donations to the saint's image in the college in Leicester as well as in Southoe.[41] One unusual bequest was that to the convent at Barking, where

---

[36] *BRUC*, p. 44.

[37] TNA: PRO, PROB 11/8 ff. 79v–80v.

[38] J. Spain, *The Pilgrimage to Our Lady of White Hill: Antiquaries, Local Historians and the Formation of an Historical Tradition* (Cambridge, 2013).

[39] 'Houses of Augustinian Canons: Priory of Barnwell', in *VCH: A History of the County of Cambridge and the Isle of Ely*, ed. L.F Salzman (London, 1948), ii, pp. 234–49; http://www.british-history.ac.uk/vch/cambs/vol2/pp234-249 [accessed 7 February 2016].

[40] The communities concerned were the Augustinian priory at Campsey Ashe in Suffolk, the convent of Poor Clares at Denny near Cambridge and the Benedictine houses at Elstowe in Bedfordshire and Barking in Essex.

[41] In 1485 the college was granted the Hospital of St. Leonard at Leicester by Lord Hastings, in return for an annuity of £20. This might account for Shuldham's mention of an image of St. Leonard in the college. See note 35.

his sister Elizabeth was abbess.[42] The Benedictine abbey of Barking was a royal foundation and one of the richer houses of the country, but Shuldham's bequest indicates a certain austerity.[43] He left money for the annual payment of coal for the fires in their dormitory, specifically stating that the bequest was to ensure that the nuns would be warm in winter after they had said the early morning office of Matins. This mixture of human concern for the comforts of daily life with attention to spiritual needs, of formality with informality, and of concern for family and the wider community adds to the picture of Shuldham as a deeply spiritual person. A further indication of his spirituality and pastoral concern is his desire to be buried not in the place of importance in the chancel, as was often the case with rectors of his stature, but rather in the nave, close to the font, at the rear of the church.

Shuldham was clearly much influenced in his early years by his contact with the community of Ramsey Abbey. Of all the individuals mentioned in Shuldham's will, one merits particular attention: John Wardeboys, abbot of Ramsey from 1473 until his death in 1489, who was an Oxford-trained theologian. Shuldham requested that his executors pay for a priest to say Masses for his soul in the University of Cambridge, and that he should also remember the souls of his parents and his 'most special lord', John Wardeboys. Master Shuldham followed this with a number of bequests to the abbey of Ramsey and to the individual monks there. Ramsey Abbey was a significant landholder in north-west Norfolk, and there may well have been a family connection with it, as there clearly was with Barking.[44] It is possible that Shuldham attended the abbey school and was perhaps taught by John Wardeboys. Further, the wealthy livings Shuldham held at Therfield in Hertfordshire and Cranfield, Bedfordshire, were in the gift of Ramsey Abbey.[45] The little we know of Abbot Wardeboys comes from his own expression of piety inscribed in a copy of Higden's *Polychronicon* (in translation):

> Halt your step, fix your eyes upon our tomb,
> You who go there, remember John Wardeboys.
> Pour out your prayers for me, if you be moved to piety.
> The earth grasps my body, my mind takes its rest

---

[42] Elizabeth Shuldham was abbess from 1479 until her death earlier in 1499. Members of the community there were each left 20*d.*, in addition to the benefaction of £13 6*s.* 8*d.* for the purchase of coal.

[43] 'Houses of Benedictine Nuns: Abbey of Barking', in *VCH: A History of the County of Essex*, ed. W. Page and J. Horace Round (London, 1907), ii, pp. 115–22; http://www.british-history.ac.uk/vch/essex/vol2/pp115-122 [accessed 24 August 2015].

[44] 'Houses of Benedictine Monks: The Abbey of Ramsey', in *VCH: A History of the County of Huntingdon*, ed. W. Page, G. Proby and H.E. Norris (London, 1926), i, pp. 377–85; http://www.british-history.ac.uk/vch/hunts/vol1/pp377-385 [accessed 24 August 2015].

[45] 'Parishes: Therfield', in *VCH: A History of the County of Hertford*, ed. W. Page (London, 1912), iii, pp. 276–84; http://www.british-history.ac.uk/vch/herts/vol3/pp276-284 [accessed 26 August 2015]. 'Parishes: Cranfield', in *VCH: A History of the County of Bedford*, ed. W. Page (London, 1912), iii, pp. 275–9; http://www.british-history.ac.uk/vch/beds/vol3/pp275-279 [accessed 12 February 2016].

If you look, behold! the Rector and Abbot of the present monastery lies
dead:
Nature commands, thus life requires.
The image following shows the year and day when the holy Father scatters
the weak from the earth.
In the arms above: ravens feeding on the sun, the motto Wisdom.
At the mouth: O Christ, have pity upon your deserving John Wardeboys.
At the feet: You who passes through here, remember John Wardeboys.[46]

This inscription appears to replicate that on Wardeboys tomb. It suggests that
the dead abbot was commemorated by an effigy of himself alongside a
personal epitaph – distinct from formulaic 'hic iacet' texts – with his armorials
displayed above, a scroll from his mouth and a request for prayers from future
visitors to his monument.

Abbot Wardeboys' evident Christocentric piety and his injunction to
viewers of his tomb that they should invoke the name of Christ in remembrance
of him are replicated by Shuldham's own piety. He is unusually prescriptive
about the different elements of the liturgical commemorations he is
supporting. He is not only ensuring that prayers will be said for his soul at
different times and in different places (Cambridge, Royston, Therfield), but
he is also linking these very specifically to the liturgical seasons (Christmas,
Easter, Pentecost) as a reminder to the faithful of particular feasts, such as, for
example, the Assumption, and particular devotional practices. This detailed
attention to very specific commemorative devotional practices is somewhat
unusual and is perhaps the mark of a man, trained as a lawyer, who gave
attention to detail.

There is also an acknowledgement of popular, vernacular piety in
Shuldham's choice of words to be used at his anniversary, which was to be
held at his tomb. His grave, before the font in the nave of Therfield church,
was where his chantry priest – who was to be dressed in his alb – was to
celebrate Shuldham's obit by saying 'of your charite praye for the soule of
Edward Shuldham and all christen soules' followed by the *De Profundis*. The
Master also left a bequest for a sermon to be preached, presumably also in
the vernacular, to the people after one of the anniversary Masses held in the
priory of Royston. There was money for images of the dedicatees of churches
for which he held rectorships, which would have added to the beauty and
devotional ambience of those buildings, as well as serving as prompts to
prayer. These were acts of both patronage and benefaction by a Master of
Trinity Hall.

---

[46] BL Royal MS 14 CIX f. 8v. The volume is inscribed 'Liber Iohannis Wardeboys Bachilaurei
theologie et abbatis' (f. 1r). The inscription clearly notes that Wardeboys was abbot at
the time of his death, thus indicating that the volume in question belonged to him and
not, as sometimes stated, to John Laurence of Wardeboys who was abbot at the dissolution, but who at the time of his death (1541) was living out his post-abbatial retirement
in Burwell in Cambridgeshire where he was buried and commemorated with a figure
brass.

There is little in Shuldham's will to suggest sustained academic pursuits. One of the first requests in his will was for a Mass to be celebrated in the 'University of Cambridge' for himself, John Wardeboys and his parents. Edward Shuldham did not make specific mention of the college in his will; and his books were recorded alongside his general household goods and similar possessions. Unlike previous Masters, Shuldham did not bequeath any land or property to the college and yet he was a wealthy man. His largesse was directed to the places he knew best and to those associated with them; and for the most part these were not in Cambridge. Two clerics were amongst his beneficiaries, William Wellys and John Partrych/Partryk, but there is little evidence to identify anything concerning their careers.[47]

John Wright

It is tempting to make much of the contrast in style and detail between the will of Edward Shuldham and that of his successor John Wright – a simpler, less formal statement. But this would overlook a number of similarities between the two documents. Both men acknowledged an allegiance to the diocese of Lincoln with bequests to the cathedral and both are clearly attached to their Hertfordshire parishes. They are concerned for relatives and friends as well as for those who had served them. The spiritual attraction of Christocentric devotion appears to have been important, and was physically expressed in Wright's fine monumental brass (Plate 4). Wright, for example, bequeathed 20*s.* to the Brotherhood of Baldock, or the Guild of the Holy Name of Jesus, a much patronised and wealthy body in the town, in close proximity to his parish of Clothall.[48] This suggests he was involved with activities of the guild; and the supervisor of his will, Master Richard Druell (or Drewell), who held the manor of Clothall, was a guild member.[49] Indications of Edward Shuldham's personal devotion can be seen by his own request for the Mass of the Five Wounds of Christ to be celebrated, expressive of devotion to the suffering humanity of Christ and particularly apposite for a priest whose principal duty lay in the re-enactment of Christ's death in the saying of the Mass.[50]

[47] *BRUC*, p. 627, records a William Wellys for whom a grace was granted to study law and the arts in 1501. Of John Partrych, who is described in Shuldham's will as rector of Datchworth in Hertfordshire, little is known. There is a brief entry in *BRUC*, p. 443, for a cleric of this name, indicating 'inception' in Cambridge in 1459.

[48] The Brotherhood of the Holy Name of Jesus, as the guild was known, was founded in 1459. It was popular with the leading laity and clergy of the town, who supported it with lifetime gifts and testamentary bequests, until its eventual demise in 1550. See 'Parishes: Baldock', in *VCH: A History of the County of Hertford*, ed. W. Page (London, 1912), iii, pp. 65–73; http://www.british-history.ac.uk/vch/herts/vol3/pp65-73 [accessed 24 August 2015].

[49] We are grateful to Brendan King of the Baldock Local History Society for access to his work on the Jesus Guild and on the history of Baldock more generally. Elements of this work are accessible in *The Baldock Mail*, issues 189 and 190 (April and June, 2009).

[50] For the introduction of the feast of the Holy Name and accompanying liturgical celebration, see R. Pfaff, *New Liturgical Feasts in Later Medieval England* (Oxford, 1970), pp. 85–90.

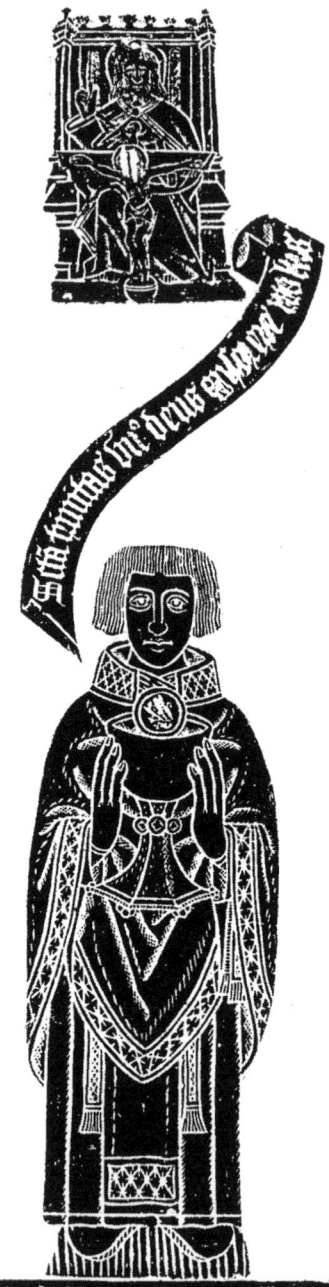

4: Brass of John Wright (d.1519), St. Mary the Virgin, Clothall, Hertfordshire.

The will of Master Wright displays nothing of the personal piety and attention to liturgical convention that are so apparent in Shuldham's extensive instructions. The institutions with which he was associated received a token benefaction, but much of his will is taken up with legacies to family and to his servants. Neither the monetary bequests nor the gifts in kind are of any great value (they range from 20*d.* to 13*s.* 4*d.* alongside gifts of brass pots and other household goods) but they betray a similar level of intimacy when compared to Shuldham's instructions. But one particular bequest stands out for its high value: 'Item to the Trinite halle in Cambrige x *l.*'. This is the largest bequest given by Wright but the purpose of this £10 is vague and there are no instructions concerning the use of this legacy. What is striking is that Wright had resigned the post of Master in 1512, some seven years before he drew up his will. We do not know why Wright resigned, but his generous bequest in 1519 suggests a continuing association with, or obligation to, the college, with little personal involvement. Wright did what was expected of him as a former Master and remembered his college: but he did not ask for special remembrance and nor did he ask that his gift be publicly recognised. The bequest of £10 can be seen as a genuine act of benefaction, the doing of a good deed as death approached.

Wright makes no mention of any other engagement with scholarly activities or with the University of Cambridge, and his executors and the supervisor of his will do not appear to have had any close connections with Cambridge: rather they were local Hertfordshire men. Richard Druell, noted above, was appointed supervisor of Wright's will: he was a member of the local gentry. Other executors and witnesses – Richard Parker, John Bamford, John Cok – are cited in Baldock's churchwardens' accounts and were evidently local men of some standing.[51] John Smyth, described as 'bayly of Baldock', is cited in charters as a 'chandler' and 'yeoman'.[52] Wright was buried in the chancel of the church of St. Mary the Virgin in Clothall where he is commemorated by a figure brass. His memorial – a product of a London workshop – contains a Latin inscription describing Wright as a priest, a graduate and a one-time Master of Trinity Hall. The text concludes with request for divine intercession:

Hic iacet Joh[ann]es Wright c[ler]icus in decretis bacallarius collegio sive aule sancta trinitatis Cantebr[igia]' quond[am] mag[ist]ri sive custos aceciam hui[us] eccl[es]ie de Clothall quondam rectoris qui obyt xii die maii A[nn]o d[omi] ni mil[les]imo quingentesimo xix cuius a[n]i[m]e p[ro]picietur deus. amen.[53]

(Here lies John Wright, clerk, with the degree of bachelor, one-time master or guardian of the college or hall of the Holy Trinity, Cambridge and rector of this church of Clothall who died on the twelfth day of May in the year of Our Lord 1519, on whose soul may God have mercy.)

---

51 We are grateful to Brendan King of the Baldock Museum and Local History Society for these details.
52 BL, Add. Ch. 35381–35402.
53 Wright died on the same day he drew up his will, 12 May 1519.

Over the head of the figure of Master Wright is a prayer scroll which is placed beneath a striking 'seat of mercy' image of the Trinity, *S[an]cta Trinitas un[um] deus miserere nobis* (Holy Trinity, one God, have mercy on us).[54] The most striking aspect of this funerary monument is the figure of Wright: he is dressed in Mass vestments and holds up a rather exaggeratedly large chalice and host. Whilst the inscription marks out his academic status, the image illustrates very clearly his Eucharistic piety and his vocation.[55] He was above all else a priest, a servant of his Lord, God.

In the early part of the sixteenth century the benefactions of Edward Shuldham and John Wright reveal the relationship between scholars and clergy. Their wills, though only snapshots and formulaic, indicate that both Wright and Shuldham were men of their time and their profession. The exercise of patronage and benefaction was important to both, but with different emphases, and, as suggested above, with different outcomes for Trinity Hall from the bequests of either their immediate predecessors or successors. The connections between the two men are evident in their wills: Wright is named by Shuldham as an executor; and they appear to have had a servant in common in the person of Thomas Parish (otherwise Praise) to whom both left legacies. Clearly, they also had their college affiliation and legal training in common, as well as their training as priests in the diocese of Lincoln and their neighbouring Hertfordshire parishes of Clothall and Therfield, both close to the town of Baldock. Their bequests to the institutions with which they were associated were a matter of conscience and of practical consideration. Their membership of their parishes, colleges and other religious communities was a constant reminder to them of their position in the body of the Communion of Saints: supporting others so that they supported you with their prayers in life and death was part of everyday life in the late medieval period. But unlike other members of the clerical establishment, former Masters of a Cambridge college would become part of the memory and commemorative custom of their institution and receive the prayers of generations of scholars to follow. This enabled such men to spread their commemorative net much wider and seek the prayers of friends and kinsfolk across a much larger area.

THE MEMORIAL BRASS OF MASTER WALTER HEWKE (D. 1518)

Of Walter Hewke, the twelfth Master of Trinity Hall, we know considerably more than of his two immediate predecessors. He made sure this would be the case through his acts of charity, and his recording of them, not least in

---

[54] The image of the Trinity shows God the Father seated on a throne of mercy with the Holy Spirit in the form of a dove above the throne, hence the description given to this type of image of the Trinity. See D. Marmion and G.E. Thiessen, *Trinity and Salvation: Theological, Spiritual, and Aesthetic Perspectives* (Bern, 2009), p. 130. Most were destroyed at the time of the Reformation since reformers believed it was idolatrous to depict the Trinity in this manner.

[55] W. Lack, H.M. Stuchfield and P. Whittemore, *The Monumental Brasses of Hertfordshire* (Stratford St. Mary, 2009), pp. 164–7 (illustrated p. 167).

his long and detailed will. The fact that the college later had to go to some lengths to prove entitlement to his bequest has added to the documentation on Hewke. He neatly combines the themes of patronage and benefaction, and of lifetime support and long-term commemoration. Furthermore, his story – and his memorial – shed interesting light on individual donors and communal memory.

Walter Hewke, like Bateman two centuries before, was from the diocese of Norwich, and while it is tempting to speculate that Walter was a member of the Hewke family of Booton, a small village north-west of Norwich where a John Hewke was commemorated by a now lost memorial in 1471, this remains uncertain.[56] Young Walter emerged into the historical record when he entered Trinity Hall to study canon law in July 1490; he was ordained sub-deacon in the same year and priest in 1491.[57] Hewke was admitted to the fellowship of Trinity Hall in the same year and to the degree of doctor of canon law in 1495, suggesting that he was an exceptionally gifted scholar. In 1501 he was also appointed rector of the college living of Holywell in Huntingdonshire, a benefice he held until his death.[58] Hewke was elected Master in 1512, following the resignation of John Wright, and died in office in early 1518.[59] Of his time as Master we have little record, although one of his first acts was to oversee a renovation of the college chapel and have the building consecrated.[60] Trinity Hall's chapel was licensed in 1352, but although papal dispensation to celebrate Mass and Divine Service there was granted in 1366, the building itself remained unconsecrated and dependent on the church of St. John Zachary, and members of college were often buried in that church or in St. Edward's (of which Trinity Hall held the advowson).[61] The concern for practical and liturgical matters and the identity of the college is in keeping

[56] J. Venn, *Alumni Cantabrigienses: A Biographical List of All Known Students, Graduates and Holders of Office at the University of Cambridge, from the Earliest Times to 1900*, Part 1: *To 1751*, 4 vols. (1922–27), ii, p. 363. An original copy of Hewke's will survives as Trinity Hall Archives (hereafter THAR), THAR/6/1/2/3, and as a registered copy, TNA: PRO, PROB 11/19 ff. 69–69v. The will is transcribed in full (although with a few minor errors) in *Warren's Book*, ed. A.W.W. Dale (Cambridge, 1911), pp. 237–43. Richard Hewke was named as one of the parties in the transfer of land and property next to the Dolphin Inn to Walter Hewke in 1516, THAR/8/2/2/16/1. None of the late fifteenth- or early sixteenth-century individuals named Hewke whose wills survive in the Norwich Consistory Court records can securely be associated with Master Walter. We are grateful to Christine M. Hood for this information. Blomefield, 'Hundred of South Erpingham: Boton', *An Essay towards a Topographical History of the County of Norfolk*, vol. 6 (1807), pp. 352–9; http://www.british-history.ac.uk [accessed 10 April 2013]. Blomefield names the wife of John Hewke (or Newke) as Margaret, daughter of Richard Springwell.

[57] Venn, *To 1751*, ii, p. 363; *BRUC*, p. 303. It is possible that Hewke was younger than twenty-four, the canonical age for ordination, at this point since scholars were sometimes ordained under age; see Lepine, *A Brotherhood of Canons*, p. 66.

[58] Venn, *To 1751*, ii, p. 363; *BRUC*, p. 303.

[59] Venn, *To 1751*, ii, p. 363; *BRUC*, p. 303; *Warren's Book*, p. 237.

[60] THHR/2/4/1/4; Crawley, *Trinity Hall*. p. 32; 'The Colleges and Halls: Trinity Hall', *VCH: A History of the County of Cambridge and the Isle of Ely*, iii: *The City and University of Cambridge* (1959), pp. 362–71; http://www.british-history.ac.uk/vch/cambs/vol3/pp362-371#h3-0005 [accessed 10 April 2013].

[61] Crawley, *Trinity Hall*, p. 32; *Warren's Book*, pp. 59–60; 'The Colleges and Halls: Trinity Hall'.

with what else we know about Master Walter, and the consecration of the chapel enabled burial within the college for the first time.

Hewke made his will and testament on 1 May 1517 'in good and hole memorie and good health of body'.[62] The pious preamble is conventional, with Walter's soul commended to God, the Blessed Virgin and the whole company of heaven, but the rest of the document is far from standard. First, there is the stipulation that his body is to be buried 'where it shall please God I may assign it', followed by his instruction that 'my gravestone that is redy bought and paide for to be laide over my body shortely after my descease with the Image and other Scriptures made therefore'. With this, we can be quite certain that the original plate for Hewke's extant memorial brass was of his own choosing, carefully acquired by, as well as made for, the man it commemorates (Plate 5).[63]

Master Walter's memorial is a large and impressive example of an early sixteenth-century monumental brass.[64] The figure is wearing a cope with orphreys depicting the twelve Apostles, fastened by a morse (or clasp) engraved with Christ blessing, and has a low academic cap on his head. There are two scrolls with inscriptions above the figure and a four-line foot inscription which reads:

> *Gloria, fama scolis, laus, artes, cetera mu[n]di*
> *vana nimis, valea[n]t – spes michi sola Jhesus*
> *Suscipe Walteru[m] bone Jhesu in fine dier[um]*
> *Qui obyt Anno D[omi)ni Mil[les]imo quingentesi[m]o x …*

('If there be any fame in the schools, praise of arts or other exceeding vain things of the world, let them fare well. My only hope is Jesus. Lift up Walter, good Jesus, at the end of days. Who died A.D. 151-')

The first part of the inscription is the same as that on the brass of William Towne, Doctor of Theology (d.1496), in King's College chapel.[65] Hewke would have had ample opportunity to see this memorial, and take note of the inscription's suitability for the theologically discerning academic. The date

---

[62] THAR/6/1/2/3. Hewke wrote his own will. The copy now in Trinity Hall could be the original but is more likely to be a probate copy since it does not appear to have been sealed and has the grant of probate attached.

[63] The head was lost by 1729 and the current plate is a late nineteenth-century restoration modelled on the *c.*1510 London-made brass commemorating John Gygur, warden of Merton College, Oxford (d.1504), at the Collegiate Church of the Holy Trinity, Tattershall, Lincolnshire, C.G.R. Birch, 'Note on the Brass of Dr. Walter Hewke, Trinity Hall, Cambridge', *TMBS*, 2:6 (1895), 223–4. On the Tattershall brass see M. Norris, *Monumental Brasses: The Memorials*, 2 vols. (London, 1977), i, pp. 167–8 and H.J. Clayton, *The Ornaments of the Ministers as Shown on English Monumental Brasses*, Alucin Club Collections 22 (London, 1919), pp. 126–7, fig. 56.

[64] W. Lack, H.M. Stuchfield and P. Whittemore, *The Monumental Brasses of Cambridgeshire* (London, 1994), p. 81.

[65] J. Mason Nealno, ed., *Illustrations of Monumental Brasses*, 5, Cambridge Camden Society (Cambridge, 1842), p. 8; Lack, Stuchfield and Whittemore, *Cambridgeshire*, pp. 31–2, 36; the brass is here identified as 'early Suffolk (?)' style.

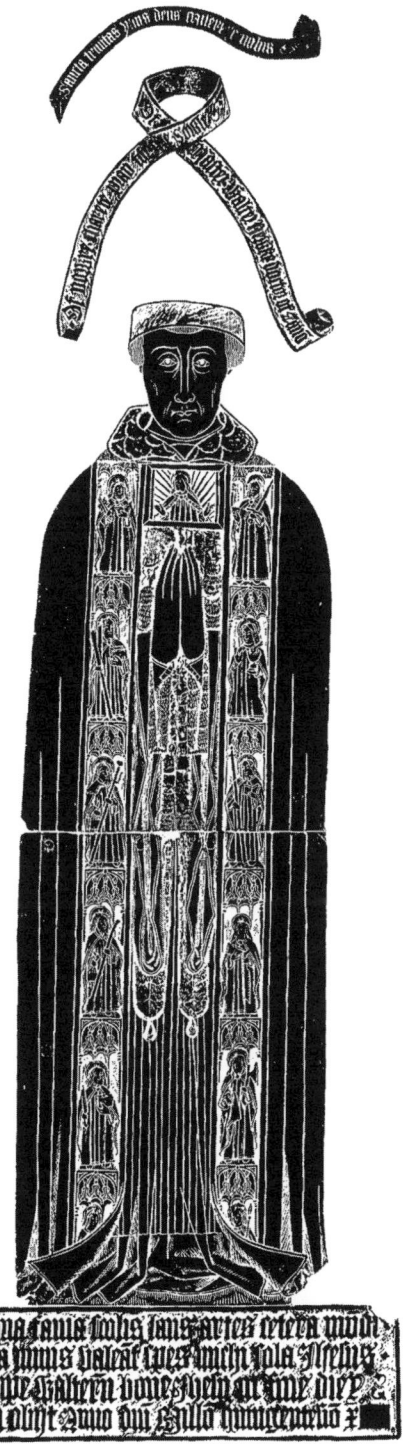

5: Brass of Walter Hewke (d.1518), Trinity Hall chapel.

of death on Hewke's brass has been left unfinished, and the fact that it was not filled in after his death may suggest a dispute between the college and Hewke's executor (his kinsman Richard Hewke), who was responsible for this important matter.

The lower of the two scroll inscriptions is of a piece with the text-block at the foot but is in English: 'Of yowr Charete pray for ye sowle of Master Walter Hewke Doctor of Cano[n Law]'. The use of the vernacular is slightly puzzling, since the principal audience would have been highly educated and Latinate, but Hewke may have wanted to ensure that his petition reached non-academic visitors, college servants or the youngest scholars just starting their studies. His grave would evidently not have a restricted audience. The final inscription on Hewke's memorial differs from the others in several ways and is evidently a later addition. The scroll is narrower and the wording smaller, with the letters punched intaglio, black against the metal, and the inscription fairly generic, if appropriate for the college: '*Sancta Trinitas unus Deus miserere nobis*' (Holy Trinity, one God, have mercy on us). It was probably added to the slab during its later history.[66]

The brass is without question the high-quality product of a London workshop,[67] and this metropolitan provenance is unsurprising. Hewke was Master of the lawyers' college at Cambridge, with an important alumni network and with contacts based in London. We have no record of Hewke being in London but it is quite likely that he visited in person when commissioning his monument, or at the very least sent a trusted representative to negotiate on his behalf. Others have shown that the patrons of brasses and other funerary monuments took a lively interest in what was in fashion and where the best could be bought.[68]

Hewke requested that his memorial brass be laid without delay following his burial. The circumstances of his death, and whether he had time to confirm the preferred location of his grave, are unknown, but he was buried directly in front of the high altar.[69] This was entirely appropriate, for not only was he Master and, as shall be seen, a significant benefactor, but he had ensured that from thenceforth members of Trinity Hall could be buried within their own college.

In his will, Hewke dealt quickly and efficiently with what was to happen to his body after death, but no details were provided concerning his funeral rites.[70] Instead, the majority of the main will, along with a Latin codicil, is occupied with details of a major bequest to the college, establishing a chantry-cum-fellowship. Hewke stipulated that a 'prest seculer' (ruling out a monk or friar) was to pray for himself and his friends, and for the souls

---

[66] We are grateful to Jerome Bertram for his comments on this brass.
[67] Almost certainly London Workshop F, possibly very early London Workshop G: Norris, *Memorials*, i, p. 167; Lack, Stuchfield and Whittemore, *Cambridgeshire*, p. 81.
[68] For example, N. Saul, 'Patronage and Design in the Construction of English Medieval Tomb Monuments', in *Patrons and Professionals in the Middle Ages*, ed. P. Binski and E.A. New (Donington, 2012), pp. 316–32.
[69] *Warren's Book*, p. 71.
[70] THAR/6/1/2/3.

of the founder William Bateman, Hewke's parents, Thomas Crane (as yet unidentified) and all Christian souls, and to celebrate the Mass of the Five Wounds of Jesus in the college chapel each Friday. An annual commemoration was to be held on his anniversary (changed to the first Monday in May in the codicil).[71] 'Doctor Hewks prest' had special responsibilities but was not, despite initial appearances, a standard chantry priest. Instead, the man chosen for this position was to be 'vertiouse good and abyll in wyt and manners' and prepared to study canon or civil law, and, moreover, he was to be expected to be admitted as doctor of one or both laws within ten years of his election to the fellowship. That Hewke was as concerned for the academic opportunities of his priest as for the commemoration of his own soul is clear from detailed instructions about the duties and conduct of the fellow. When selecting a candidate, preference was to be given to a scholar of Trinity Hall who was already a priest and a Cambridge graduate, presumably to encourage the successful completion of a higher degree. Furthermore, once elected, Hewke's fellow was not to serve as curate of St. Edward's, nor as steward of the college, specifically to ensure that he was not distracted from his studies. There was also a proviso that if a Rogation Day coincided with the commemoration of Hewke's anniversary (as might happen if Easter fell early), the latter was to be postponed until the Tuesday so as not to clash with the universal observance. This reflects not only a scrupulous priest and canon lawyer, but also a man with deep Christocentric devotion, since Hewke requested the celebration of the Mass of the Five Wounds each Friday, while the inscriptions on his memorial specifically invoke Jesus. The cult of the Holy Name and Christocentric devotion more generally were fashionable among educated clerics at the time, as seen with the humanist John Colet, among others.

While Hewke's fellowship and perpetual commemoration were based upon faith, they were supported by very real assets. In order to provide for 'Hewk's prest', Master Walter bequeathed to his college the Griffin Inn and two neighbouring tenements with gardens in Bridge Street, along with two tenements with gardens and yards next to the Dolphin Inn 'at the corner' by Grey Friars.[72] This was (and is) prime real-estate in the heart of the town and demonstrates that Hewke engaged with the urban community beyond the confines of his academic stronghold, albeit for the long-term benefit of gown rather than town. Hewke seems to have acquired the Griffin in about 1512, perhaps after his election as Master, purchasing it for £100 sterling.[73] At about the same time Hewke acquired four other properties for a total of £57, presumably the tenements abutting the Griffin, and in 1516 he acquired property and land in Jesus Lane.[74]

---

71 *Warren's Book*, p. 238; THAR, MS 20, The Master's Statute Book, unfoliated leaves, five from end.
72 THAR/6/1/2/3; *Warren's Book*, p. 238; Crawley, *Trinity Hall*, p. 24 n. 2.
73 THAR/8/2/2/12/2/2. The long paper roll is stitched Chancery fashion, but the membranes are at present unnumbered.
74 THAR/8/2/2/12/2/2. According to the testimony of a Thomas Hobbys of Eaton, aged about twenty-five at the time of the deposition, he had been present when Hewke had

In his will, Hewke was quite clear about the bequest of these properties to Trinity Hall, but the college had serious concerns about the Griffin and its appurtenances following their benefactor's death. The only document relating to the Griffin prior to Hewke's death now preserved among the college archives is a 1507 bargain and sale, suggesting that a deed or deeds had been mislaid (a particular embarrassment for the lawyers' college). Within months of Hewke's death, the college therefore went to a great deal of trouble to compile an extensive record of sworn depositions confirming the late Master's rights to the properties and his intention to leave them to the college. The effort put into collecting the depositions clearly had the desired effect, and probate was granted by the Prerogative Court of Canterbury on 11 August 1518, enabling the college to take possession of Hewke's properties. In this context, the placing of Hewke's monument in the centre of the chapel makes particular sense, with the college wishing to remember him, and to show others how their benefactors were honoured.

Within twenty years of Hewke's burial and the appointment of his first priest-scholar, however, the fellowship and monument faced danger as a result of the upheavals of the Reformation, although both survived more-or-less intact. The liturgical commemoration and prayers ceased, but the fellowship presumably survived because it was for civil as well as canon law. Perhaps because Hewke's fellow was no longer required to undertake clerical duties and could therefore be supported with fewer funds, Trinity Hall sold the Griffin Inn to the town authorities in 1560/61, a somewhat ironic decision considering the trouble they had gone to in order to secure it only forty years previously.[75]

That Hewke's memorial brass also survived the events of the mid-sixteenth and mid-seventeenth centuries is surprising, since the image includes depictions of the Apostles and the inscription explicitly seeks prayers for the deceased. It is probable that during the reign of Edward VI, the memorial was protected by the conservative Stephen Gardiner (Master 1531–51), who had studied at Trinity Hall while Hewke was Master.[76] In the 1640s the memorial faced its greatest threat in the form of a visitation by the Puritan William Dowsing, although he is said to have found little 'Popery' at Trinity Hall.[77] This would imply that Dowsing missed the inscription on Hewke's memorial, and it is possible that this was somehow covered during the iconoclast's visitation. What makes the survival of the Catholic inscription more puzzling, however, is that Hewke's memorial was in fact attacked, with the figure quite literally defaced.[78] This is exactly the same treatment meted out to images

---

acquired the Griffin and the 'howses' 'vj or vij yeres past'. Two houses were purchased from Hugh Rankyn for £30 and two from Robert Smyth clerk, deputy of John Smyth clerk, for £27 'or therabowt'. The purchase of the land in Jesus Lane is detailed in THAR/8/2/2/16/1.

[75] Crawley, *Trinity Hall*, p. 24 n. 2.

[76] 'The Colleges and Halls: Trinity Hall'.

[77] *Warren's Book*, p. 81.

[78] Warren noted that the 'head of the ye Drs Figure is now off', wryly commenting that this was done in the time of Cromwell's 'Rebellion' by 'people of those times in abhorrence, as they pretended, of Superstition': *Warren's Book*, p. 78.

of saints, and it is tempting to speculate whether Dowsing mistook the richly vested suppliant figure for such a representation.[79] Master Walter's role as benefactor to the college probably also helped prevent more extensive damage. Thomas Eden (Master 1625–45) was a Parliamentarian,[80] making Trinity Hall less suspect than some Cambridge colleges, and one can imagine Dowsing being allowed to erase the face of the 'saint' while discreetly not saying anything about the Catholic inscriptions, perhaps emphasising that the memorial commemorated a benefactor and should be preserved with limited damage.

Hewke's monument remained reasonably intact and in its original position until 1729 when, as part of the refurbishment of the chapel, the memorial was moved into the ante-chapel. William Warren took this opportunity to investigate the grave in the hope of finding something to confirm the exact date of Hewke's death, which is missing from the inscription on the brass.[81] Instead he found that only bones remained, the size of which led Warren to conclude that Hewke was 'a Tall man', before he had the remains reburied in situ with 'all decency & tender regard to ye memory of our Benefactor'.[82] Hewke's endowment continued to support a fellow until the early twentieth century, with the last named incumbent elected in 1904.[83] In 1915, as a result of several fellowships being vacant (presumably because of the Great War) and scholarships under-resourced, the Governing Body decided to transfer funds from those fellowships to support students, and thus, after 400 years, Hewke's direct benefaction of a named individual ceased.

CONCLUSION

The story of Walter Hewke provides a number of important insights into patronage, benefaction, and commemoration in Cambridge on the eve of the Reformation. He was responsible for the consecration of the chapel, while his brass is a remarkable testament to the memorialisation of benefactors in the most literal sense, especially since it was saved from damage or destruction on at least two occasions. Meanwhile, the financial provision made by Hewke, and safeguarded by the college through the remarkable depositions list, reveals the hard-headed pragmatism necessary for long-term benefaction. The Reformation set in train a process which would not only sweep away many of the beliefs of the medieval Church, but which also redefined, over the longer

---

[79] Such rapid collective amnesia regarding Catholic iconography is evidenced elsewhere. The 1608 seal matrix of the city of Durham shows a heart-shaped object with flames at the top affixed to the chest of a bishop, presumably because the craftsman did not recognise that the image on the medieval seal he was copying was St. Cuthbert holding St. Oswald's head: E. New, 'Seals and Status in Medieval English Towns: A Case-study of London, Newcastle and Durham', in *Good Impressions: Image and Authority in Medieval Seals*, ed. N. Adams, J. Cherry and J. Robinson (London, 2008), pp. 35–41 at p. 35, fig. 1.

[80] 'The Colleges and Halls: Trinity Hall'.

[81] *Warren's Book*, pp. 74–5.

[82] *Warren's Book*, p. 75.

[83] *Warren's Book*, p. 170.

term, the primary purpose of colleges. But beyond the differences of creed, all colleges realised the fundamental importance of patronage and benefaction for their survival as places of learning and teaching. In the case of Trinity Hall the move away from training canon and civil lawyers to concentration on the latter was achieved easily, and its change from clerical to secular Masters was similarly smooth.

Benefactions such as that of Hewke for a scholar priest, aimed at providing for his soul's progress to heaven, could be turned to secular use without difficulty. Masters were expected to provide for the future by building up the 'fabric' of the college whilst in office, and to leave it more financially secure for generations to come when their term came to an end, either through death or resignation. What William Bateman's vision achieved within the first two centuries after the foundation of his college was to embed in the community a belief in and loyalty to its original intention: the training of scholar lawyers in the college, long into the future. Given the institutional changes and challenges it has faced, Bateman's decision to place his college under the patronage of the Holy Trinity has clearly proved to be the most efficacious benefaction of all.

TRANSLATION OF THE WILL OF EDWARD SHULDHAM
DATED 28 NOVEMBER 1499

1. In the name of God, Amen. On the 28 day of the month of November in the year of Our Lord 1499, I Edward Shuldham, clerk in holy orders, of sound mind and good memory, make my will in this manner.

2. First, I commend my soul to Almighty God, to the Blessed Virgin Mary and to all the saints and body to be buried in the centre of the nave of the church of Therfield before the font.

3. Item I leave to the repair of the mother church of Lincoln 6s. 8d.

4. Item I leave to the chapel of St. Mary of Whitehill a vestment or something needed for that chapel, to the value of 13s. 4d.

5. Item I leave to the chapel of St.Mary of Barnwell an altar cloth or something needed for that chapel, to the value of 6s. 8d.

6. Item I leave to dames Katherine Shuldham of Campsey, Barbara Shuldham of Elstowe and Anne Shuldham of Denney, nuns, 20s. to be divided equally between them.

7. Item I leave to the convent nuns of Sion [Abbey], 13s 4d.

8. Item I leave to the brothers of that place [Syon Abbey], 10s.

9. Item I wish that an honest priest, a master graduate of arts or a scholar in sacred theology should celebrate Mass for three whole years following my death, in the University of Cambridge, for my soul, for remembrance of the soul of my most especial lord in grace, master John Wardeboys, formerly abbot of Ramsey, [for the souls] of my mother and father, and of all my benefactors and of those to whom I am in any way indebted or have obligations or amendments to make, whether living or dead.

10. And that the first five Masses in whatever year of the said term of years should celebrate the five wounds of Christ, the Holy Spirit and the Assumption of the glorious Virgin Mary, and after celebrating I wish that he should approach the town of Therfield on the vigil of the birth of Our Lord or before if he pleases and staying there, that he should celebrate divine service in the said church as he is wishes, daily up to the day after the Epiphany of Our Lord. And in the same way that he should go to that town on the vigil of Palm Sunday and should remain there until the day after Low Sunday, and similarly on the vigil of Pentecost up to the day after Trinity Sunday and on the vigil of the Assumption of St. Mary the Virgin until the day after that feast, in the same manner on the said particular feasts for the said three years.

11. And I wish that on whatever day this priest has celebrated Mass for my soul in the church of Therfield aforesaid that after the Mass, in his alb, he should go to the head of my tomb and say in the common language

'Of your charity, pray for the soul of Edward Shuldham and all Christian souls' and that he should say the 'De Profundis'. And on Rogation Monday, in each of the three years while [this] is proceeding, the priest should preach or cause to be preached a sermon to people gathered in the conventual church at Royston if this is acceptable to the Lord Prior that it should be done there, or in another place.

12. And I leave to the same priest celebrating for his stipend in whatever year, £6.

13. Item I leave to the Friars Minor of Bedford so that they celebrate a trental for my soul and the souls of those mentioned above, 10s.

14. Item I leave to the Friars Minor of Cambridge, in the same manner, 10s.

15. Item I leave £3 6s. 8d. for the purchase of coal for burning in the dormitory of the monastery in Barking in wintertime after matins and at other times so that the devoted nuns there might warm themselves, and not otherwise nor in any other way elsewhere is it to be spent, in each year 3s. for a term of twenty-two years.

16. Item I leave to each nun in the monastery of Barking, 20d.

17. Item I leave to Dame Margaret Shuldham my sister, £3 6s. 8d.

18. Item I leave to the religious house of Ramsey in gratitude for their benevolence to me most generously given that moved by charity they pray for my soul, namely £3 6s. 8d. to the lord abbot; 6s. 8d. to the lord prior, and the remainder of a sum of £3 6s. 8d. to be divided amongst each and every monk of that monastery.

19. Item I wish that a new tabernacle be made for the image of St. Peter in the chancel of the church at Cranfield at a cost of 10s.

20. Item I wish that a new tabernacle be made for St. Leonard at Southoe at a cost of 26s. 8d.

21. Item I wish that an image of St Leonard in a certain tabernacle be situated in whatever churches of the mother church of Lincoln, and in the college of new work in Leicester and in the chapel of the hospital at Ilford, the price of whatever image with the tabernacle 6s. 8d.

22. Item I leave to Henry Shuldham, son of Edward Shuldham my nephew, £10 that he might become a student and I wish that the said sum of money should remain in the hands of my executor or executors and I ask them that the said money be placed for his benefit.

23. Item I leave to the church of All Saints of Shuldham a cope, price 40s.

24. Item I leave to the fabric of the church of Southoe 40s.

25. Item I remit to Thomas Paryse £8 13s. 4d. owed to me by him.

26. Item I leave to John Benet £8.

27. Item to Thomas Beynton £3 6s. 8d.

28. Item I leave to John Fichwyn 40s.

29. Item I leave to John Osborne 26s.

30. Item I leave to Hugh Pygot 40s.

31. Item I wish my books and all my utensils and household goods noted down in my inventories, other than those I have detailed in my inventories to be delivered to those to whom I have left them just as I have detailed

their names in my aforesaid inventories, so that if anything from these goods should be lost or should not come into the hands of my executors the said executors are not forced to pay back the price of the value of that which is lost.

32. The residue to be sold by my executors to pay for my burial and tomb and other expenses incurred and should go to recompense my executors whose names are given below.

33. I give and bequeath to my executors named below [the request] that they buy, from that residue, a set of vestments of velvet, that is to say, for the celebrant priest, for the deacon and the subdeacon, and a cope for divine service in the church of Therfield aforesaid in future, at a price of £20, if the said residue is sufficient for this, otherwise at a lower price according to how it seems to my executors.

34. And if the residue of my said goods amounts to a sum greater than £20 needed to buy the aforesaid set, then I wish that such residue remaining be spent by my executors on two vestments to be bought and given to the churches of Cranfield and Boxworth of white colour, each at a price of at least 40s. and these things done. The residue, if there be, should be spent towards the building of a certain church house or roads in the parish of Therfield aforesaid in accordance with the wish of my executors whom I ordain and constitute, master John Wright, Bachelor of Arts, rector of Clothall, Sir John Partrych, rector of Dachewell and Thomas Paryse, my servant. And I leave to Master John and Sir John Partrych for their labours, each of the said, 40s. and to the said Thomas Paryse for his work £3 6s. 8d.

35. With faith in the foregoing and trust in my aforesaid witnesses, I have signed the order and constitution and the following [things] with my own hand on the aforesaid day and year, with these witnesses William Wellys, Robert Smyth, John Benet and Thomas Beynton.

This will was enrolled in the register of the Prerogative Court of Canterbury (TNA: PRO, PROB 11/13 ff. 201v–202). Probate was granted on 31 August 1503.[1] A copy of Shuldham's will may be found in Canterbury Cathedral Archives, CCA-DCc/Register/F, ff. 189–190.

---

[1]   In the transcription above, paragraph numbers have been inserted for ease of reference.

TRANSCRIPTION OF THE WILL OF MASTER JOHN WRIGHT DATED 12 MAY 1519

The will is headed 'Testamentum Dr Johannis Wright   Dxxxiiii'
There is a marginal note 'Sir Johannis Wright'.

1. In the name of God Amen, the xiith day of the moneth of May the yere of our lord god mccccccxix, I John Wright, clerk, p[ar]son of the parissh church of Clothall w[ith]in the dioc[ese] of Lincoln of hole mynd and memory beyng, make this my testament and last will in man[er] and forme folowyng,

2. ffirst I beque[a]th my sowle to almyghty god, to o[ur] lady saint mary and to all the sayntes, my bodie to be buryyd in the chauncell of Clothall and

3. I beque[a]th to the sayd church my chales, my masse booke, my vestyment, ii alter clothes staynyd and xxs.

4. Item to the church of Lincoln xiid.

5. Item I bequeth to ev[er]y sonne and daughter of my susters Isabell and Margaret except M[aste]r Simon ev[er]yone vis viiid.

6. Item to the reparation of the church of Ufford, xxs.

7. Item to Thomas Parissh my serva[u]nt ii kine, x q[uart]ers of malt, x shepe, and xxs of money, a brasse pot and a payre of shetes.

8. Item to Agnes Johnson my serva[u]nt ii kine, x q[uart]ers of malt, a brasse pot, a payre of shetes, and x ewes and xxs of money.

9. Item I will that ev[er]y prest beyng present at my buryng have xxd.

10. Item I beque[a]th to Thomas Hoga[n] my serva[u]nt a ewe iiis iiiid in money and all my clothe that came from the fuller and aray hym w[it]h all.

11. Item to ev[er]y godson and goddaughter I have a ewe, iiis iiiid.

12. Item to Elizabeth Baron my goddaughter xxd.

13. Item to the Trinite halle in Cambrige xli.

14. Item I beque[a]th to M[aste]r Richard Baron my gret federbed.

15. Item to Edward Baron a doct[o]r that wrigth uppon the decretallis called abbot.

16. Item to John Baron my c[o]urse of Civill.

17. Item I bequeth to the brotherhed of Baldock xxs in money.

18. The residew of my goodes not beque[a]thed I committ holely to the disposicion of myn execut[or]s whom I make Sir Harry Haw, p[ar]son of Astwick, Richard Baron, gentilma[n] and Richard Parker that they dispose for the we[a]lth of my sowle as it shall beste beseme unto them and as they will awnswer before God and I beque[a]th to eche of them for theyre labo[u]rs v m[ar]kes.

19. Also I will that M[aste]r Richard Druell esquyer be sup[er]visor of this my testament and he to have for his labo[ur]s v m[ar]kes so that he be good helpyng and kynd to myn executors about thexecucion of this my testament.

20. Thes being witnes Ser Roger Hatfeld, vicar of Russhden, John Sumt[e]r, bayly of Baldock, John Bamford, John Cok and Thomas Parissh prayed to bere witness and severally desired.

This will was enrolled in the Archdeaconry Court of Huntingdon (Huntingdonshire Record Office, Archdeaconry Wills, vol. 2, f. 183). Probate was granted on 20 June 1519.[1]

---

[1]   In the transcription above, paragraph numbers have been inserted for ease of reference. Contractions are expanded and indicated by square brackets.

CHAPTER 5

A Comparison of Academical and Legal
Costume on Memorial Brasses

J.H. Baker

The history of English legal costume is now reasonably clear,[1] and it might be supposed that the history of academical dress would be even clearer, but in fact that is far from being the case. There has been a great deal of confused antiquarianism, and the only book on the subject – by an author who also managed to confuse the history of legal dress almost beyond recovery – made things worse rather than better.[2]

Written sources are not as helpful as might be supposed. The few medieval regulations which survive from Oxford and Cambridge used words well understood at the time but not defined or explained with helpful diagrams. The same is true of secondary sources such as wills and inventories. But the proposition to be made in this essay is that more can be learned from lateral investigations, by comparing brasses with paintings, monuments and written sources, by considering what happened to the various forms of dress as they evolved in later periods, and by drawing parallels with legal dress. Brasses are a plentiful source of illustration, but many academical figures are anonymous and therefore of limited use as evidence for the dress appropriate to particular degrees; allowance must also be made for a measure of artistic licence or ignorance which prevents us from relying on brasses in the same way that we might rely on photographs or paintings from the life. For the present exploratory purpose, the concentration will be on scarlet robes – the

---

[1] For judges see J. Baker, 'English Judges' Robes 1350–2008', in *Collected Papers on English Legal History*, ed. J.H. Baker (Cambridge, 2013), ii, pp. 812–31. For barristers see 'The Mystery of the Bar Gown', *ibid.*, pp. 857–67. For serjeants at law see J.H. Baker, *The Order of Serjeants at Law*, Selden Society Supplementary Series, 5 (1984), pp. 67–83. See also J.H. Baker, 'An Outline History of the Legal Robes now Worn in England and Wales', in *Court Dress: A Consultation Paper issued on Behalf of the Lord Chancellor and the Lord Chief Justice* (1992), appendix 1, [19–30] (unnumbered pages); T. Woodcock, *Legal Habits: A Brief Sartorial History of Wig, Robe and Gown* (London, 2003).
[2] W.N. Hargreaves-Mawdsley, *A History of Academical Dress in Europe until the end of the Eighteenth Century* (Oxford, 1963). The companion volume on legal dress was published at the same time.

formal full dress of doctors of divinity and law, of judges of the benches,[3] and of serjeants at law. There are examples of the later black undress gowns on brasses, but the black doctoral gown is not in obvious ways different from that worn by laymen in the Tudor period.

Doctors at Cambridge and Oxford now have two principal orders of dress, the festal gown of scarlet cloth faced with silk[4] and the undress black gown. The scarlet hood is worn with either gown, on occasions when hoods are worn. Until the nineteenth century there was a third form of dress known at Cambridge as the congregation habit. This still survives at Oxford as the convocation habit, and a vestige lives on at Cambridge for a different purpose, which will be noticed later. This habit is the principal form of academical dress seen on brasses. There is no connection with the present festal gown, the origins of which are less clear.[5] The term 'habit', still used at Oxford for the full dress, was also used for the judges' formal full dress in the fifteenth and sixteenth centuries.[6]

By the mid-thirteenth century all universities enjoined the wearing of the 'scholastic habit'. This was not a matter of dressing up on special occasions, but a matter of good order and communal discipline, like a monastic habit or a military uniform. The black gown continued to perform that function at Cambridge until the 1960s, when it could be seen in the streets and in the University Library as well as in lectures and supervisions, but over the last fifty years it has gradually been abandoned for everyday purposes. In the Middle Ages academical dress seems to have been universal throughout Western Europe, and of a broadly standard character, subject to variations attributable to local robemakers. The earliest Cambridge statutes (*c.*1240–50), which derive from those of Paris (1215), required regent doctors and masters to wear either the *capa clausa* or the *pallium* at lectures, disputations, inceptions and funerals.[7] Those are still occasions on which academical dress

3 I.e. the courts of King's Bench and Common Pleas. The third court of common law in Westminster Hall was the Exchequer. The barons of the Exchequer wore similar robes but without facings. A painting of the Court of Chancery *c.*1460 (Plate IV) (Inner Temple MS. Add. 188) shows that in that court the lord chancellor and master of the rolls wore academical dress.

4 An exception is the festal gown of the Cambridge doctor of philosophy, which is of black stuff or silk faced with scarlet cloth. The reason for the distinction is that, since arts and philosophy are in academical parlance synonymous, the Ph.D. is really an examined M.A. This reasoning did not prevail at Oxford, where the D.Phil. gown is scarlet.

5 See J.H. Baker, 'Doctors wear Scarlet: The Festal Gowns of the University of Cambridge', *Costume*, 20 (1986), pp. 33–43.

6 J. Baker, *The Men of Court: A Prosopography of the Inns of Court and Chancery and Courts of Law*, Selden Society Supplementary Series, 18 (2012), i, p. 677; ii, pp. 1022, 1085, 1296, 1553 (*habitus* in Latin).

7 M.B. Hackett, *The Original Statutes of Cambridge University: The Text and its History* (Cambridge, 1970), p. 203: '*In theologia decretis et artibus regentes capis clausis uel palliis in leccionibus et disputacionibus ordinariis utantur. in eodem habitu ad incepciones et exequias decenter incedentes.*' The corresponding Oxford statute shows that the underlying purpose was to ban the use of sleeved copes: ibid., p. 79 ('*nullus regens in artibus, uel decretis, uel theologia, in capa manicata lectiones legat ordinarias, et in pallio uel capa clausa*').

is worn – when giving lectures,[8] and when attending Tripos examinations, graduations and memorial services, though these are all now usually black-gown occasions. The earliest medieval regulations do not mention colour, but other evidence shows that these garments were already in the thirteenth century black for masters and scarlet for doctors.[9] The scarlet garments were lined or faced with miniver – that is, the fur of ermine without the tails – which was also used by judges (and peers[10]) on their scarlet robes.

The word *pallium* is confusing because it also denotes the archbishop's Y-shaped pall, and the word *capa* (or cope) likewise has a distinct ecclesiastical meaning, well illustrated in that sense on brasses. But there is nothing especially ecclesiastical about the academical cope and *pallium*. Both were cloak-like garments, resembling the scarlet mantle of peers and judges, which was called *chlamis* in Latin,[11] or 'cloak' in the English of fifteenth- and sixteenth-century testators.[12] The judge's cloak, however, was open down to the ground at the right-hand side, and was worn over the cowl part of the hood (Plate 6),[13] whereas the academical copes were closed up, apart from slits for the arms, and were worn under the hood.

The *capa clausa* had a single slit in the centre and was the distinctive dress of doctors of divinity, perhaps because it was a form of dress prescribed for the clergy on formal occasions by provincial constitutions of 1222.[14] The hood as worn with this cope by doctors of divinity was folded outwards so that the miniver lining was fully displayed falling over the shoulders; indeed, over time, the miniver would take over completely. There are four illustrations of this dress on Cambridge brasses. The earliest is taken from a brass (Plate 2 in

[8]   When the writer began teaching at Cambridge it was *de rigueur*, at any rate in the Law Faculty, to wear a gown when lecturing. The writer continued to do so until his retirement, but he is informed that only one colleague now observes this immemorial custom.

[9]   As to black see Hackett, *Cambridge Statutes*, p. 80, n. 2 (citing a Parisian statute of 1215); *Statuta Antiqua Universitatis Oxoniensis*, ed. S. Gibson (Oxford, 1931), pp. 39, 292 (*capa nigra* to be worn by regent masters). The black *capa clausa nigra* of a master of arts is shown as the dress of the proctors in the Cambridge University charter of 1292. Red for doctors of law is mentioned in an early-fourteenth-century Cambridge statute: *Statuta Academiae Cantabrigiensis* (Cambridge, 1785), p. 70, no. 147.

[10] I.e. for their parliamentary robes, which probably date from the fourteenth or fifteenth century. Bishops' parliamentary robes are also of scarlet, with a miniver cape or hood similar to the *capa clausa* of medieval doctors of divinity.

[11] J. Fortescue, *De Laudibus Legum Anglie*, ed. S.B. Chrimes (Cambridge, 1942), p. 128 ('*iusticiarius factus, loco collobii clamide induetur, firmata super humerum eius dexterum*'); Baker, *The Men of Court*, ii, p. 1553 ('clamis' in a judge's will of 1508).

[12] Baker, *The Men of Court*, i, p. 677 (will of Anthony Fitzherbert, whose brass is at Norbury, Derbyshire, 1538); ii, p. 1022 (will of Thomas Littleton, whose brass was formerly in Worcester cathedral, 1481), p. 1455 (will of Humphrey Starkey, whose brass was formerly in St. Leonard's, Shoreditch, 1486), and pp. 1583–4 (the will of Thomas Urswyk, whose brass is at Dagenham, Essex, 1479); Baker, 'English Judges' Robes' (above, n. 1), pp. 818, 819. In the Judges' Rules of 1635 they are called mantles: *ibid.*, p. 820.

[13] This is shown on many brasses, the earliest being that of John Cassy (d.1400), chief baron of the Exchequer, at Deerhurst, Gloucestershire. The brasses are consistent in this regard, though there are a few representations of the hood worn over the mantle, e.g. the figure of William Howard (d.1308) in a fifteenth-century window at Long Melford, Suffolk; it is possible that these were errors.

[14] Hackett, *Cambridge Statutes*, pp. 80, 81 n. 2. It was also, in its black form, the dress of regents in arts and survives as the Cambridge proctorial 'ruff'.

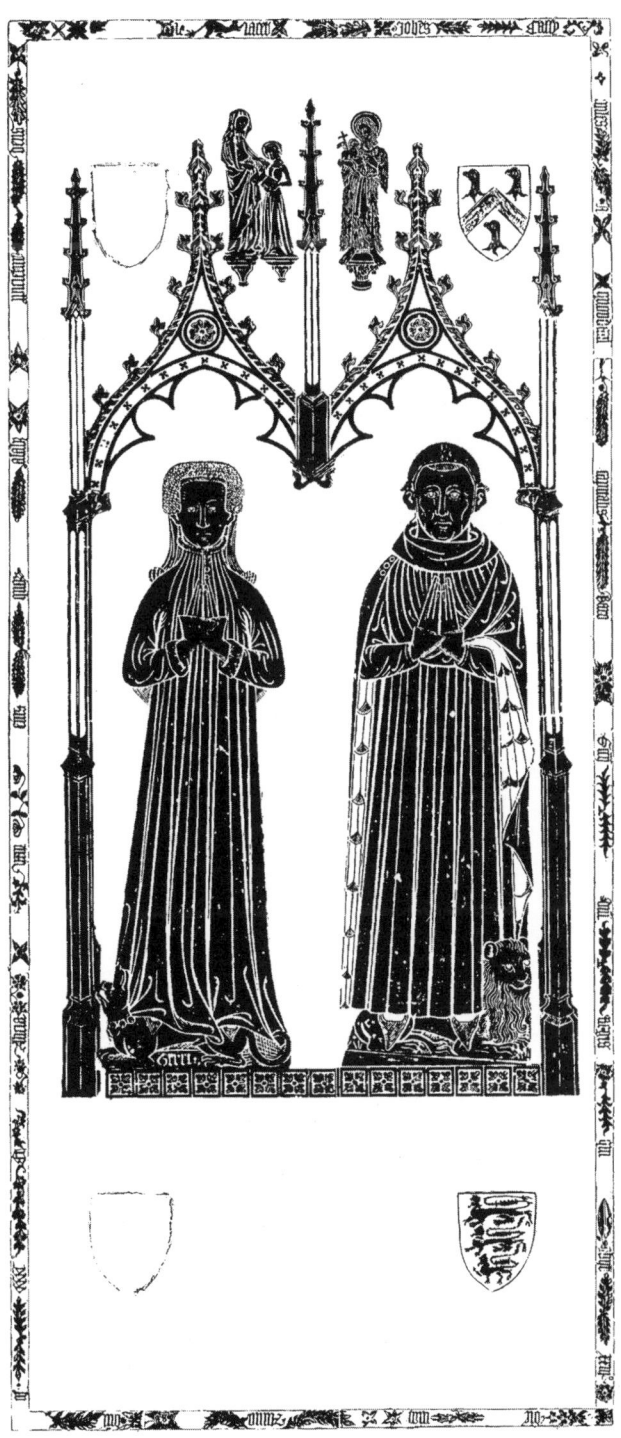

6: Brass of John Cassy, chief baron of the Exchequer (d.1400),
the Priory Church of St. Mary, Deerhurst, Gloucestershire.

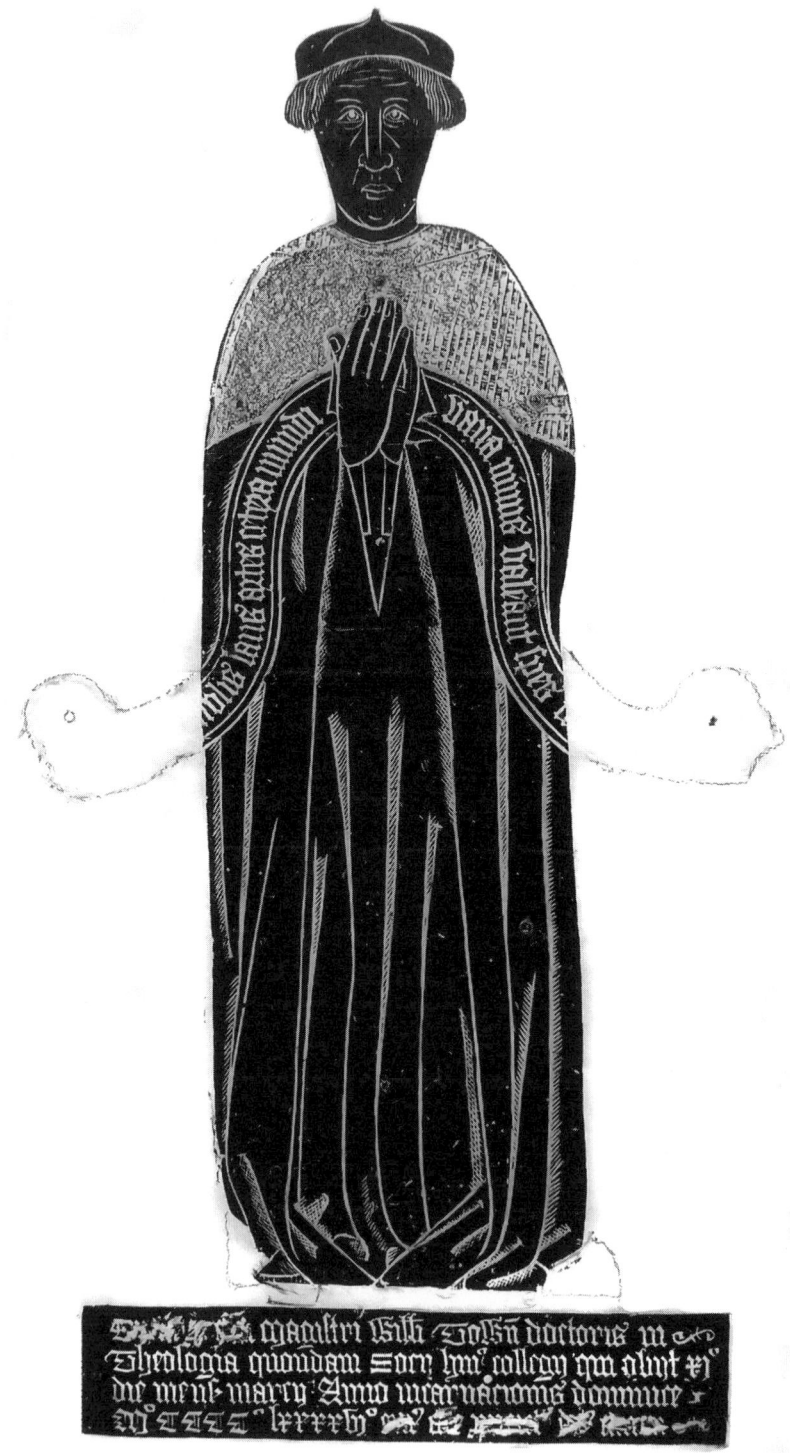

7: Brass of William Towne (d. 1496), King's College chapel, Cambridge.

chapter 1) in St. Benet's church (Richard Billingford, 1432) and there are two later examples (Plates 7 and 8a&b) in King's College chapel (William Towne, 1496, and John Argentein, 1507); there is also an anonymous one in Little St. Mary's.[15] The same dress was worn by divines at Oxford, where an example is to be found in the chapel of New College (Thomas Hylle, 1468). It seems also to have been kept up in France, as may be seen from the portrait of Cardinal Jean Rolin (*c*.1480) in the Musée Rolin at Autun. Rolin seems to have been a doctor of law, which is not helpful for the present analysis, though he may have worn the cope as a doctor of decretals. An English doctors of decretals is seen in the same dress on a brass at New College (William Hautryve, 1441, Plate 9), though this has a hood of the same type as that of a doctor of law.

This dress continued in use as the most formal habit for a doctor of divinity at Cambridge until the nineteenth century and is shown in a number of paintings in college collections. Over the course of time it came to be completely open in front, but fastened at the top with hooks and eyes, and the miniver hood was turned into a sort of cape attached to it. By the end of the nineteenth century it was worn at congregations of the Regent House only by the vice-chancellor or his deputy, and by regius professors and their deputies when presenting candidates for higher degrees. This practice continues; but the habit is no longer the dress of a particular degree, since it is used whether or not the wearer is a doctor of divinity. It is understood that the Oxford habit was deprived of its miniver facings centuries ago.

The doctor of civil law had a distinctively different costume, namely the garment known as the *capa manicata furrata* (furred sleeved cope).[16] Possibly it was related to the *pallium*, though the nature of that garment is obscure and the early Cambridge statute referring to the *capa clausa* and *pallium* omits to mention regents in civil law.[17] The civil lawyers' cope had two slits for the arms, so that it was a *pallium* (as Dr. Michael Hackett defined it), but with false sleeves hanging to the ground, which made it *manicata*. The hood was worn with the scarlet cowl over the shoulders and most of the miniver falling behind from a v-shape at the neck, like a judge's hood. There is a good illustration of this dress on a brass at New College, Oxford (John Lowthe, who died in 1427, Plate 10).[18] There is a less clear Cambridge example on the Lyndwode brass (1419) at Linwood (Lincolnshire), one of the figures in the group of sons being the great canonist William Lyndwode of Gonville Hall;[19] perhaps the reason why he does not wear the *capa clausa* (like Hautryve) is that he was a doctor of both laws. Three Cambridge brasses showing the same dress – at Christ's College, Queens' College and Trinity Hall – are all anonymous, and so it cannot be proved that they are all doctors of law, but

[15] Possibly John Warkworth (d.1500) or Henry Hornby (d.1518), both of whom were masters of Peterhouse College.

[16] It is so described in a fourteenth-century Cambridge statute: *Statuta Academiae Cantabrigiensis* (1785), p. 70, no. 147 (to be worn by jurists and regents in medicine when lecturing or performing magistral acts).

[17] Hackett, *Cambridge Statutes*, p. 147.

[18] The name has sometimes been misread as Sowthe.

[19] It is now very worn. There is a drawing of it in J.H. Baker, *Monuments of Endlesse Labours: English Canonists and their Work 1399–1900* (London, 1998), p. 45.

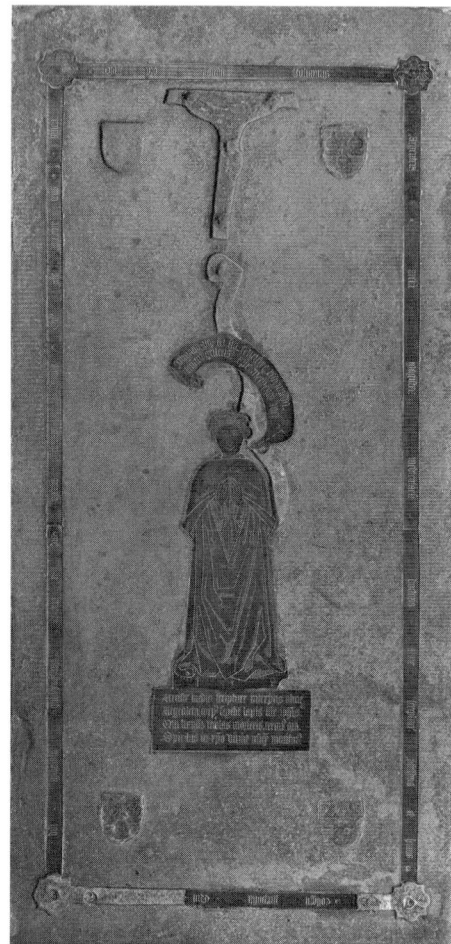

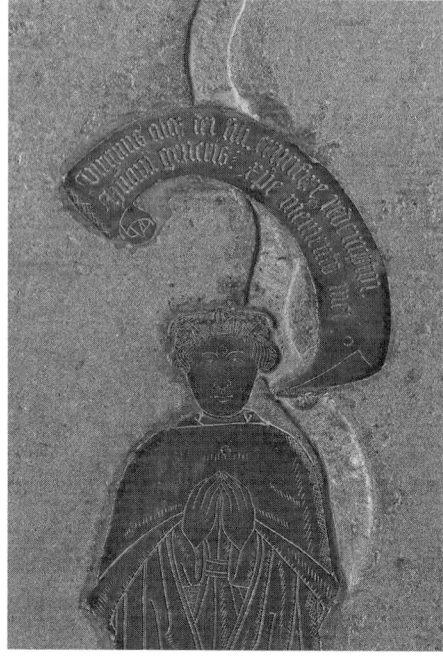

8b: Brass of John Argentein (close up).

8a: Brass of John Argentein (d.1507),
King's College chapel, Cambridge.

Trinity Hall was a college for lawyers and in any case the contrast with the brasses of known doctors of divinity at Cambridge is telling. The Trinity Hall example shows clearly the hanging sleeves, though the other two do not, because they were not very visible from the front. The habit is more clearly represented, in three dimensions, on the wall-monuments of Dr. Thomas Legge (1607) and Dr. Stephen Perse (1615) in the chapel of Gonville and Caius College. David Loggan's engraving of academical dress at the end of the seventeenth century, from his *Cantabrigia Illustrata*, shows the two distinct divinity and law habits very clearly.[20] Later illustrations may be seen in college

[20] The cope of the doctor of divinity is still not wholly open at the front. By this time, of course, there were no degrees in canon law and therefore only one kind of doctor of law. The Cambridge doctorate in law is abbreviated as LL.D., but in the Latin of the Senate House it is *doctor in iure*, in the singular.

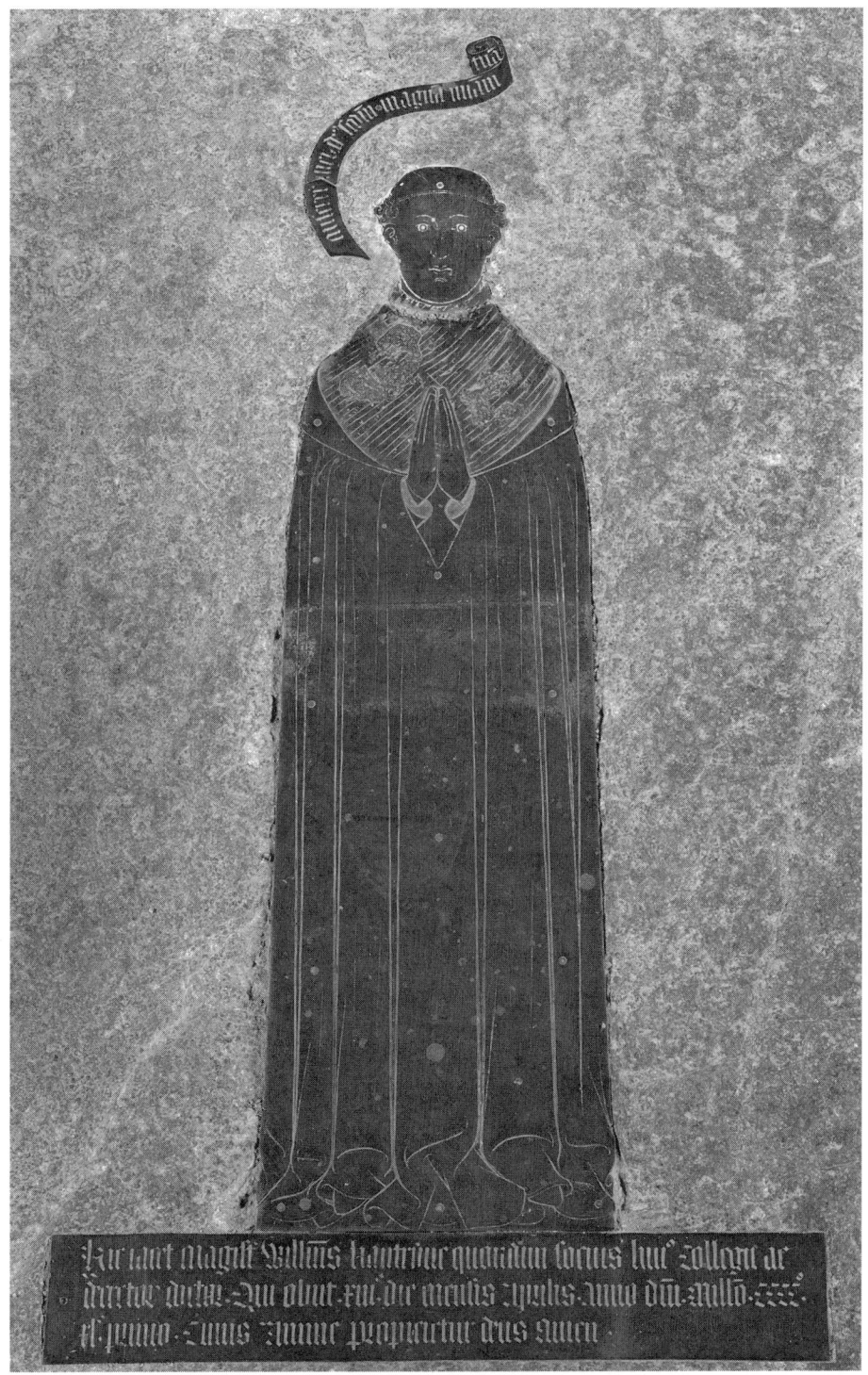

9: Brass of William Hautryve (d.1441), New College chapel, Oxford.

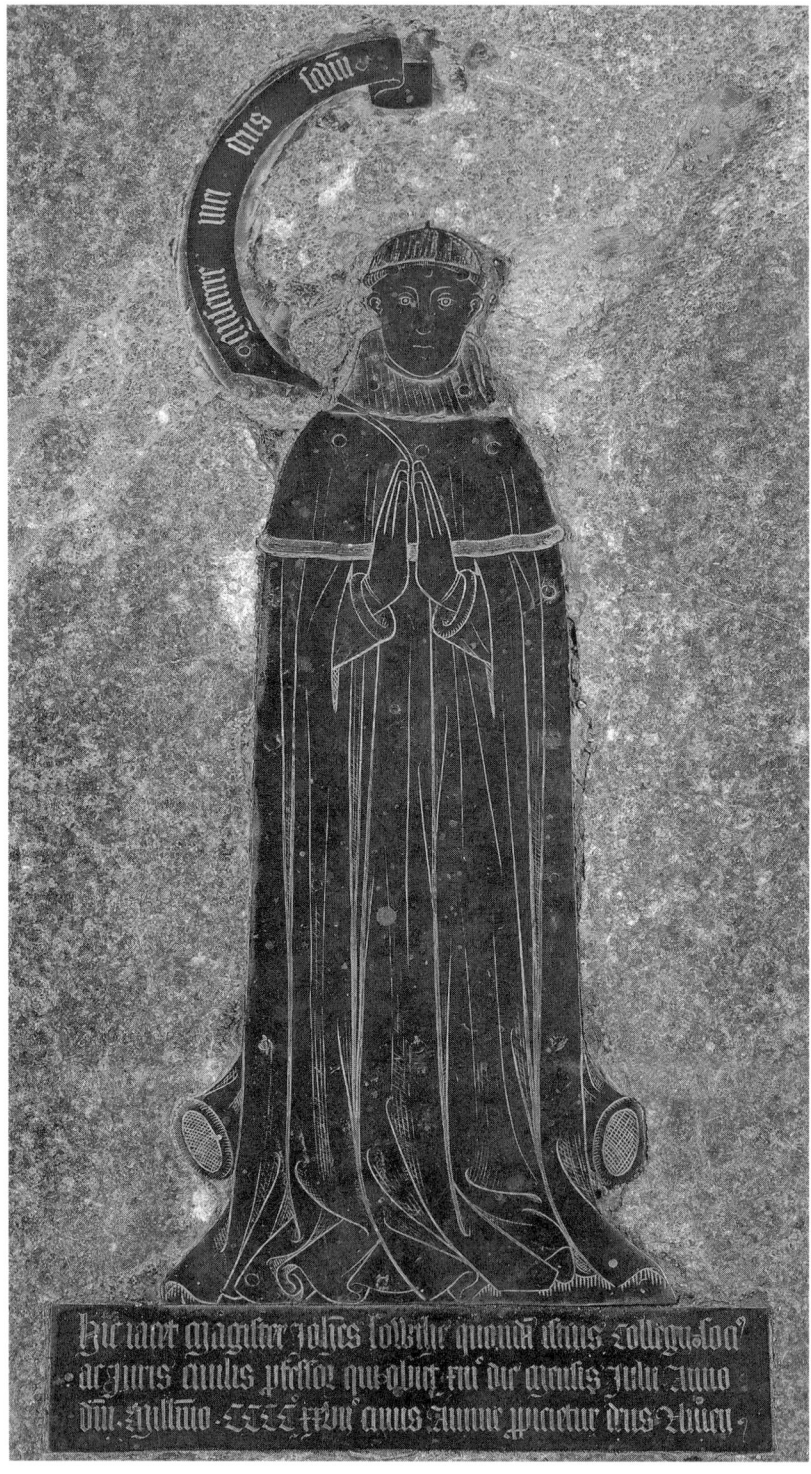

10: Brass of John Lowthe (d.1427), New College chapel, Oxford.

portraits. This dress also continued in use until the nineteenth century, but it then disappeared completely. The latest illustration known to the writer is an engraving of Dr. John Lee (d.1866), though he was probably wearing it as an advocate of Doctors' Commons. For some arcane reason, or perhaps for no reason other than ancient usage, the later practice of the Court of Arches – where scarlet was required for advocates as well as judges – was that Cambridge doctors wore the congregation habit furred with miniver, whereas their Oxford counterparts wore festal gowns faced with silk.[21]

It may be no coincidence that most of the surviving brasses showing the habit are from churches and chapels in Cambridge and Oxford. Doubtless it was a form of dress not much worn outside the university (and the Court of Arches). Country parsons were more likely to wear a less formal garment, either a coloured tabard or a white surplice, with the hood. The full dress of both the doctor of divinity and the doctor of law is now, at both universities, the scarlet festal gown, which is open in front and has silk facings instead of miniver. The origin of this is probably the *collobium* or tabard, which is seen on the brass of Eudo de la Zouche (d.1414), doctor of laws and chancellor of the University, in St. John's College chapel, Cambridge (Plate 11). It corresponds with the tabard worn by serjeants at law – seen on the brass of Thomas Rolf (d.1440) at Gosfield, Essex (Plate III) – which Sir John Fortescue writing in the 1460s described as a *collobium*.[22] The serjeants' tabard had distinctive *labellae* or lapels in front, but these were usually covered by the hood; it is difficult to understand the Gosfield brass, which shows the lapels lying in front of the hood, except on the supposition that the engraver must have made a mistake. The *collobium* was not peculiar to doctors and lawyers – it is also seen on the brasses of masters and bachelors, sometimes with furred sleeves.

An alternative possibility is that the festal gown was simply a long robe with the sleeves elongated and turned back to show the lining. The judges' and serjeants' robes evolved in that way. The brass of John Broke (d.1522) in St. Mary Redcliffe, Bristol, shows a robe with wide sleeves over a longer robe or cassock, and so it might represent a development of the *collobium*. On the other hand, judges' robes were of the same pattern and are not shown with an under-robe. The portrait of Serjeant Bendlowes (d.1564) in St. John's College, Cambridge, provides an obvious parallel with academical festal dress, the main difference being that serjeants had given up using any lining whereas doctors used a cerise-coloured silk. Two brasses of doctors of law from around 1530 appear to represent the festal gown with wide sleeves. Dr. William Taylard (Offord Darcy, Huntingdonshire), who took his doctorate in law from Cambridge in 1502, seems to have a hood with a silk lining, whereas

<hr/>

[21] Baker, *Monuments of Endlesse Labours*, pp. 90, 114.
[22] Fortescue, *De Laudibus*, quoted in n. 10, above. For the equivalence of tabard and *collobium* in academical parlance see A.B. Cobban, *The King's Hall* (Cambridge, 1969), p. 197. Bishop Bateman's statutes for Trinity Hall and Gonville Hall required the master and fellows of each to wear long tabards or ankle-length gowns: *Documents relating to the University and Colleges of Cambridge* (Cambridge, 1852), pp. 129, 419 ('*cum longis tabardis seu epitogiis talaribus*').

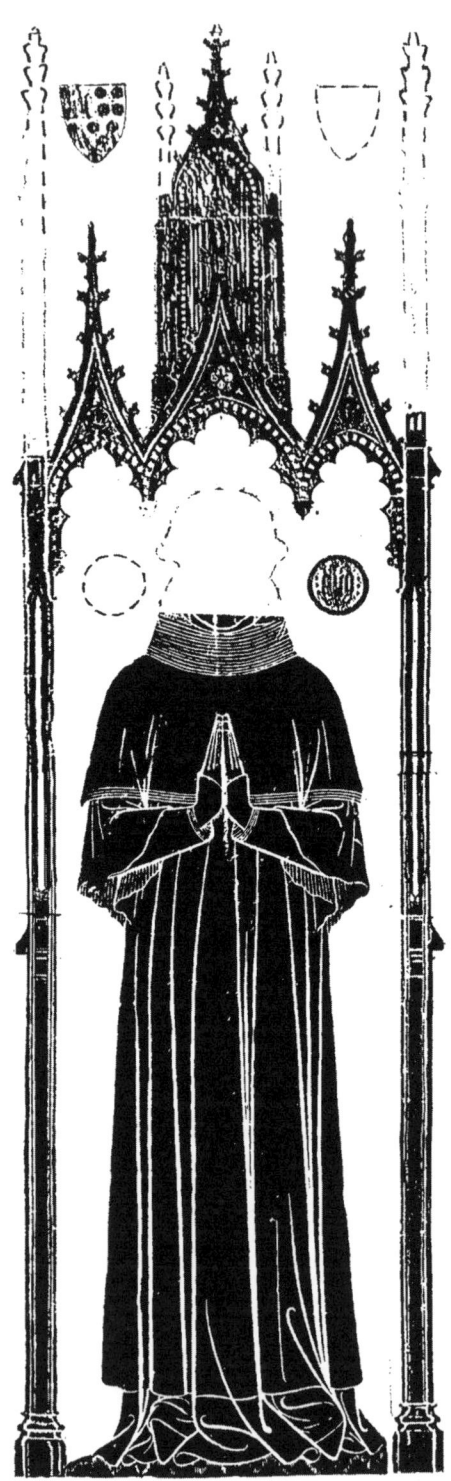

11: Brass of Eudo de la Zouche (d.1414), St. John's College chapel, Cambridge.

Dr. Brian Roos (Childrey, Berkshire), a doctor in decrees from Valence (in Dauphiné), incorporated at Oxford, has his hood lined with fur, although no fur is shown on the sleeves. Perhaps at first there were winter and summer orders of dress, as with judges, who until 2008 wore miniver facings only in winter.

In a Cambridge regulation of 1577 it was stated to be the old custom for doctors to wear *togae murice tinctae* (scarlet gowns) in public on red-letter days, and a year later it was ordered that none but doctors should wear their hoods lined with silk, 'as doctors usually do'.[23] This shows that the festal gown had by then become the norm for red-letter days, and indeed the list of scarlet days in 1577 is almost the same as today's – until very recently Cambridge dons wore scarlet when lecturing on All Saints' Day or when examining on Ascension Day. In Tudor wills and inventories, the scarlet gown, usually faced with silk, is distinguished from the 'habit' faced with miniver.[24]

There is one further aspect of academic and legal dress which deserves mention and that is the squared hood. It occurs on at least ten brasses around 1480–1530 and has caused much puzzlement; some have wrongly called it a scarf, and some have even thought it an item of ecclesiastical dress. Examples are the figure of William Warham on his father's brass (1487) at Church Oakley, Hampshire; George Rede (Annunciation plate dated 1492) at Fovant, Wiltshire; an anonymous figure at North Creake, Norfolk (*c.*1500), where the cowl and tail are fastened with a button; the second son of Robert Baynard (1501) at Lacock, Wiltshire; the second son of Sir Thomas Barnardiston (1503) at Great Cotes, Lincolnshire; William Smyght (1510) at Ashby St. Ledgers, Northamptonshire, in whose case it seems to be worn over a scarf; Robert Godfrey (1518), Bachelor of Laws, at East Rainham, Norfolk; Richard Bethell (1519) at Shorwell, Isle of Wight, where the tail only is pinned; and a doctoral instance, similarly pinned, in the figure of John Yslyngton S.T.P. (*c.*1520) at Cley, Norfolk. A late occurrence, on the brass of William Lawnde (*c.*1530) at Northleach, Gloucestershire, seems to show it with a surplice (Plate 12).

---

[23] *Statuta Academiae Cantabrigiensis* (1785), p. 353. The regulation was still in force when the statutes were printed in 1877.

[24] E.g. the following from Cambridge: *Testamenta Eboracensia; or Wills registered at York*, ed. J. Raine and J.W. Clay, vol. iv (Surtees Society, 53; Durham, 1869), p. 285 (Martin Colyns D.Cn.L., 1509: '*j toga scarleta cum caputio duplicata cum viridi sarsenet ... j toga scarleta duplicata cum waterd damask ... j toga scarleta cum caputio penulata cum menyver ... j scola habita cum capucio penulata cum menyver*'); vol. v (Surtees Society, 79), p. 253 (William Melton D.D., 1528: 'a gowne of rede scarlet furred with menyvere and a hoode ... a scole abite furred with menyvere'); TNA:PRO, PROB 11/30 f. 277 (Edward Wygan D.D., 1545: 'a skarlett gowne facyd with black say ... a doctors habytt ...'); CUL, UA, Vice-Chancellor's Court, inv. 1541/2 (Geoffrey Blyth D.C.L., 1542: 'a skarlett gowne with an hoode lyned with changeable sarsenet ... a skarlett cope with an hood furred with mynyver ...'); *ibid.*, inv. 1567 (Robert Beaumont D.D., 1567: 'a skarlet gowne and hoodde lyned with tawney sylke ... a doctors cope of bristol redd ...'); *ibid.*, inv. 2/77, f. 2 (Thomas Ithell LL.D., 1579: 'a scarlet gown and a hoodde ... his doctors coope and hoodde of bristol redd ...'); *ibid.*, inv. 1587 (John Hatcher M.D., 1587: 'a scarlet gowne faced with red damaske ... an habite and hood of skarlet ...'); *ibid.*, inv. 23 June 1598 (Thomas Preston LL.D., 1598: 'a scarlett gowne and a whood ... a hood and habbitt of scarlett faced with miniver ...'); *ibid.*, inv. 1635/6 (John Smithson LL.D., 1635: 'one scarlett gowne, 1 habitt, 1 coape and one hoode all of scarlett').

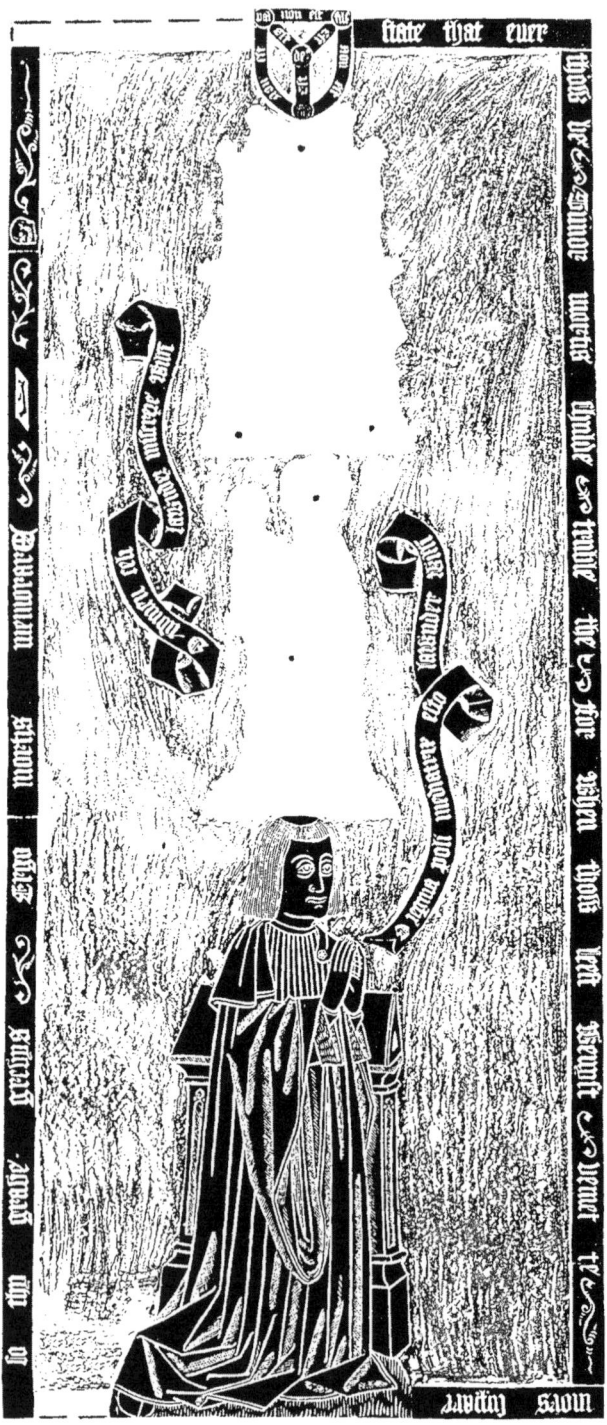

12: Brass of William Lawnde (c.1530), St. Peter and St. Paul, Northleach, Gloucestershire.

These may be compared with painted illustrations of the same fashion. The earliest is a miniature of the Court of Chancery, dating from *c.*1460, in which the tonsured masters in ordinary are shown in undyed robes, with hoods around the shoulders, while the chancellor wears the scarlet *pallium* and hood of a doctor of laws (Plate IV).[25] Another is the figure of John Schorn, a clergyman celebrated for tricking the devil into a boot, on the rood screen at Gateley, Norfolk (Plate V). These may all have been clerics, but there is nothing technical or ecclesiastical about the garment.[26] It is simply a hood worn scarfwise round the neck rather than over the head, perhaps sometimes (in the case of clergy) a miniaturised version of the hood adapted for the purpose, and sometimes secured with a brooch. The regulations for King Henry VII's court provided that on formal occasions the king should wear a furred hood pulled ('sliven') over his head, and rolled at the neck, but that at evensong and meals he would take off his mantle and wear the hood laid about his shoulders, the cowl and tail fastened together with a brooch on the breast, 'in doctors wise'.[27]

The same fashion was adopted by judges and serjeants at the same period, and they called it a 'casting hood'.[28] It was a less formal order of dress, and therefore not often shown on early portraits. Indeed, there are no legal examples on brasses. The legal casting hood came to be suspended from the right shoulder by the tail, or liripipe, with the bulk of the hood (full-sized) hanging limp down the back rather than lying on the left shoulder. It is still worn by judges, with the tail passing over the black scarf and tucked into the black cincture. Here we see a direct parallel with the 1510 brass for William Smyght (Plate 13), at Ashby St. Legers; and the two orders of dress are exactly paralleled in academical and royal dress. Full dress required a hood over the shoulders (as it still does for judges), replaced in everyday dress by a black scarf and a hood worn with the tail over one shoulder. The parallel with clerical dress was noted as late as 1635 in the Judges' Rules for dress made in that year, which observed in passing that the judges of the previous generation considered it a lay usage to wear the tail on the right shoulder (as judges still do), whereas priests wore it on the left.[29]

---

[25] Inner Temple MS. Misc. 188. No hanging sleeves are visible.

[26] In the Rolin painting mentioned above, Jesus Christ's father Joseph (a carpenter) is wearing a hood in the same way.

[27] *Collection of Ordinances and Regulations for the Government of the King's Household*, ed. J. Nichols (1790), pp. 119–121 ('... [on Twelfth Night] the Kinge must change his mantle when hee goeth to meate, and take of[f] his hood and lay it about his necke and claspe it before with a riche owche'); *Joannis Lelandi Antiquarii de Rebus Britannicis Collectis*, ed. T. Hearne, iv (1770), p. 235 ('[at evensong the king wore] the Hode aboute his Showlders, in Doctors wise').

[28] Baker, *Serjeants at Law* (above, n. 1), pp. 79–80.

[29] W. Dugdale, *Origines Juridiciales* (3rd edn., London, 1680), pp. 101–2: 'The Scarlet Casting-Hood is to be put above the Tippet [scarf], on the right side; for Justice Walmesley [d.1612] and Justice Warburton [d.1621], and all the Judges before, did wear them in that manner; and did declare, that by wearing the Hood on the right side, and above the Tippet, was signified more temporal dignity; and by the Tippet [*sic*] on the left side only, the Judges did resemble Priests.' The last word 'Tippet' must be a slip for the casting hood. The word continues to cause confusion.

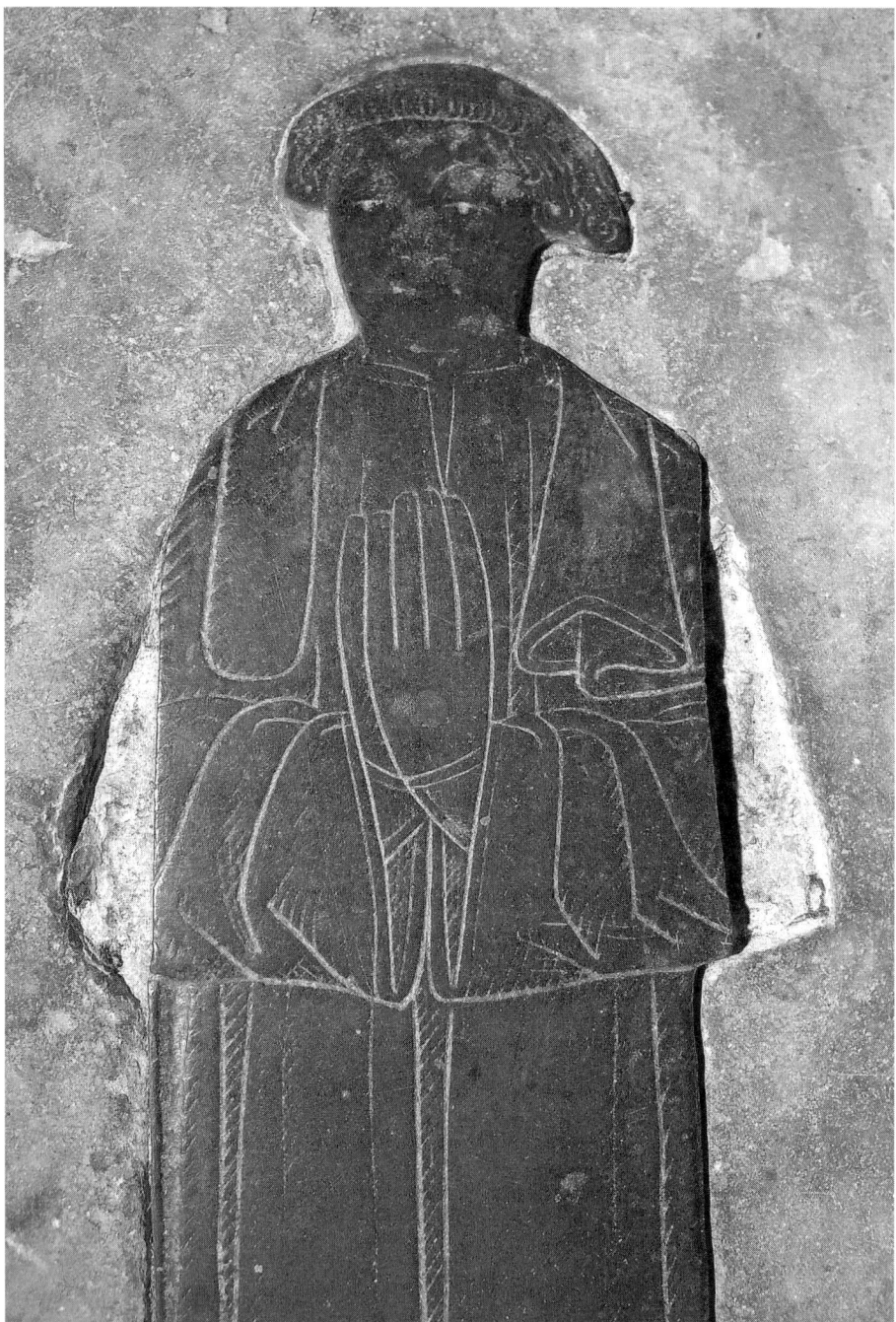

13: Brass of William Smyght (d.1510), the church of the Blessed Virgin Mary and St. Leodegarius, Ashby St. Ledgers, Northamptonshire.

The casting hood went out of use for academical purposes, probably because it was replaced by the fashion of wearing the hood hanging down the back – turning the front of the cowl into a mere neckband. But it survives in the dress of the proctors at Cambridge, who have two unique forms of full dress:[30] the congregation habit, with the hood flourished and worn over a remnant of the *capa nigra* of the master of arts; and the *ad clerum* habit, worn for University sermons and a few other occasions, with the hood 'squared' and worn wrapped over both shoulders. The squared hoods in use when the writer served as a proctor (in 1980) were of some age; they were made without the neckband in front, and if put on over the head still had a distinct cowl like a medieval hood.

This contribution may not have made things much clearer, but the story would become even more complex if it took in the brasses of masters and bachelors. The main point is that there was more consistency in the various forms of academical dress seen on brasses than some writers have allowed, and that we might move closer to understand them if more use were made of parallel forms of evidence.

[30]   See J.H. Baker, 'The Dress of the Cambridge Proctors', *Costume*, 18 (1984), pp. 86–97.

CHAPTER 6

Commemoration at a Royal College

Peter Murray Jones

The commemorative practices of a college founded by Henry VI, crowned king of England in 1429 and king of France in 1431, were inevitably different to those of any other Cambridge college. They reflected the personal and express wishes of the royal founder in respect of his family and himself, and they also reflected the scale and diversity of the endowments he and his successors made to his college. The commemorative practices of other donors who wished to be associated with the royal college, and of individual members of the foundation, were in turn influenced by those of the founder. But at the same time the way in which Henry VI framed his foundation, and the statutes he gave to the college, were modelled on the practices of his own father Henry V and those of William Wykeham, the founder of Winchester College and New College, Oxford. This applied as much to commemoration as to other features of the new foundation.[1]

FOUNDATIONS

The College of the Blessed Virgin Mary and St. Nicholas was the first college at Oxford or Cambridge set up by a reigning monarch. Its foundation, with that of its sister Eton College, may have been the first independent initiative by the young Henry VI. Remarkably, he decided to lay the foundation stone of his new college at Cambridge with his own hands, and the ceremony took place just ten weeks after the acquisition of the site, on Easter Sunday, 2 April 1441. The inspiration for this novel act of commemoration may have been his father Henry V's laying of the foundation stone of the Bridgettine abbey of Syon in 1415. Henry VI repeated the act of laying the foundation stone for his other college of Eton on 11 June 1441, two months later. The ceremony attending these royal foundations probably followed the liturgy laid down in pontificals like that of William Durandus written in the late thirteenth century. There would have been a blessing of the stone, with the king taking the role

---

[1] I should like to acknowledge the invaluable help of the archivist of King's College, Patricia McGuire, in the writing of this chapter. Elisabeth Leedham-Green provided a prompt and helpful reply to my enquiry about Henry Veysey.

normally assumed by the bishop, on the analogy of a baptismal rite. The stone would then have been lowered into the foundation trench. The unique survival of the two painted foundation stones found at the base of the London Guildhall's new civic chapel – from 1441–42, naming two benefactors – gives an idea of what form the King's and Eton stones may have taken. Indeed, it is possible that the mayor and aldermen of London were emulating the king when they held their blessing ceremony and laid their foundation stones shortly afterwards. In terms of commemoration, as Nick Holder says, 'The foundation stone thus becomes a physical, almost contractual, symbol of the benefactor's generosity.'[2]

There is in fact a contemporary, or near-contemporary, account of the foundation ceremony of the original college building (now known as Old Court, lying to the north of the present King's College chapel) in 1441. It is recorded in Latin and English verses written at the end of a fifteenth-century King's College register.[3] The Middle English translation of the Latin verse runs:

> Seint Nicholas is whos day was born henry the sext our sovereign lord the kyng
> After that his excellence at Eton had leyd the anoynted stone
> Here stablisshed this werke hys clergy tenderly remembryng
> The yere of oure lorde a thousand foure hundred fourty and one
> The secunde day of Aprill that tyme Sunday in the passion
> The xix yere of reigne here kneling on his knee
> To the honour of seint Nicholas first founded this edification
> With whom in heven to be laureat graunt might the holy trinitee

The writer of these verses clearly supposed that the young king had laid the foundation stone of Eton before that of Cambridge, but the precise order of events is not entirely certain. However, things are a lot clearer as to the placing of the foundation stone. Opposite the poem is a note in Latin which reads in translation: 'This stone was placed in the right or southern tower of the gate opposite Clare hall.' The exact siting of the stone is here carefully recorded for posterity. If there is ever an archaeological dig under the gate to the Old Court of King's, which still stands opposite Clare, now forming the entrance to the Old Schools, the main university offices, there must be a very good chance of finding this foundation stone.

Three years after the laying of the college foundation stone, Henry VI wrote to Abbot William Curteys of Bury St. Edmunds inviting him to preside at the laying of the first stone of the first college chapel, to be held on 29

---

[2]   This paragraph is based on Nick Holder, 'Medieval Foundation Stones and Foundation Ceremonies', in *Memory and Commemoration in Medieval England*, ed. C.M. Barron and C. Burgess (Donington, 2010), pp. 6–23.

[3]   KCA, KC/56, f. 16. See R. Willis and J.W. Clark, *The Architectural History of the University of Cambridge, and of the Colleges of Cambridge and Eton*, 4 vols. (Cambridge, 1886), i, pp. 321–2; H.M. Colvin, *The History of the King's Works*, 6 vols. and map vol. (London, 1963–82), i, p. 269.

September 1444, as the king was unable to attend. This second foundation stone was presumably laid under the high altar of the chapel, sited to the north of the present chapel, at the climax of a similar ceremony to that held in 1441 for the college foundation. But the king was already developing a much more ambitious scheme for both college and chapel. As a result, a much larger chapel was planned as part of a great court to the south of Old Court, and this time the king was able to attend the laying of its foundation stone in person. The ceremony took place on 25 July 1446, St. James's day, and Henry laid the first stone on the site of the future high altar. Once again the act of laying the stone is commemorated in Latin verses written in the same King's College register. The second set of verses refers to the anointed foundation stone as laid by the king's sacred hand. Precise directions are again given as to its placing: '*Ex orientali medio si bis septem peditimtim/ Mensurare velis inuenies lapidem*' ('Fourteen paces from the eastern end in the middle/ you shall measure to find the stone'). It was thus buried fourteen paces from the east end in the middle of the chapel.[4] This register is bound in soft vellum with thirteenth-century flyleaves. The poems recording the laying of stones by Henry VI in 1441 and 1446 are situated on a parchment leaf between copies of the papal bulls establishing the college's freedom from other ecclesiastical jurisdictions and the composition between the college and the university. They are clearly not afterthoughts in this register book; they were deliberately placed and elegantly written in the fifteenth century to stand between documents that established King's College's unique jurisdictional status in Cambridge.[5]

In founding his colleges at Eton and Cambridge, Henry VI and his advisors had followed the model of the foundation of New College, Oxford (1379) and Winchester College (1382) by William of Wykeham, bishop of Winchester. But whereas William of Wykeham had set himself against commissioning lavishly illuminated charters for his new foundations, the king was not so minded. The charter upon Act of Parliament, dated 16 March 1446, confirmed the founder's earlier gifts to King's and conferred many additional privileges upon the college (Plate II). Both this charter and the similar one for Eton (dated 5 March 1446) were illuminated that same year by the London artist William Abell.[6] The script of the body of the charter was written by the chancery scribe John Broke, with the exception of its calligraphic penwork heading, with interlaced letter forms and elaborate cadels, which is by an unknown scribe. The elaborate iconographic programme of the illumination at the head of the charter commemorates the act of foundation itself. The king, wearing a closed crown and an ermine-lined mantle, is depicted within

---

4   William Cole records a failed attempt to find the stone c.1770, possibly because they were searching in the wrong 'bay' of the chapel. See Willis and Clark, *Architectural History*, i, p. 465.

5   KCA, KC/56, f. 16. See Holder, 'Medieval Foundation Stones', p. 22; Colvin, *History of the King's Works*, i, p. 271.

6   For his biography see H. Combes, 'William Abell: Parishioner, Churchwarden, Limnour, Stationer in the Parish of St. Nicholas Shambles in the City of London', *The Ricardian*, 12 (2000), pp. 120–32.

the calligraphic letter H of 'Henricus', kneeling at a prie-dieu, holding the charter and gesturing to a scroll inscribed *'Fiat ad laudem gloriam et cultum tuum'* ('Be it done to thy praise, glory and worship'). Behind him are the Lords Spiritual and Temporal, headed by the lord chancellor, Archbishop Stafford, and Cardinals Beaufort and Kemp. Below, heading a group of sixteen members of Parliament, is the speaker of the House of Commons, holding a scroll inscribed in Law French *'Prient lez comunes'* ('The Commons request'). This is echoed by the Lords: *'Et nous le prioins auxi'* ('And we also request it').

Henry's prayer is directed to the patrons of the college, shown above him in heaven. St. Nicholas intercedes with the Blessed Virgin, who is shown being borne up by angels to be crowned by the Trinity. She appears as a Madonna of Mercy mediating the grace of the Trinity to the assembled Parliament and the king below. Above the figure of the king, angels are shown bearing a giant crown over the royal arms and a scroll reading *'Henricus sextus rex et fundator huius regalis collegii'* ('Henry VI King and Founder of this royal college'). Other half-angels to each side hold the arms of St. Edward the Confessor and St. Edmund, patrons of the Lancastrian dynasty.[7] The image as a whole links earth to heaven and the king to his royal forebears, to the dedicatees of the chapel, St. Nicholas and the Virgin, and finally to the Trinity. The act of foundation is interpreted as a dynamic moment of prayer and intercession, and it is this moment that is commemorated by the illuminated charter.

PRAYERS, MASSES, ANNIVERSARIES

In 1443 Henry VI took over the task of issuing statutes to his new college from the commissioners he had first appointed for the task in 1441. A new commission arrived in Cambridge in 1447 with statutes that reflected the now expanded vision of the college. The first provost, William Millington, refused to swear obedience to them, and was deprived of office. These statutes no longer survive, so it is not certain what the stumbling block was for Millington. New statutes were brought to the college in 1453, and it is these statutes (with small alterations in 1459) which are known as the founder's statutes and were in force until 1861. The founder's statutes were modelled on William of Wykeham's statutes for New College, Oxford. Those statutes made provision for the commemoration of William of Wykeham and his family, the royal family, the benefactors of the college and the souls of the faithful departed, as well as laying down the rules that were to govern the foundation. Similarly, the founder's statutes for King's stipulate that every morning and evening the members of the college must say prayers for the souls of the king, for those of its benefactors and for the faithful departed. The next statute specifies the seven masses that are to be said daily in chapel in perpetuity. The second

---

7   This description follows N. Rogers, 'Charter upon Act of Parliament for the Foundation of King's College, Cambridge', in *The Cambridge Illuminations: Ten Centuries of Book Production in the Medieval West*, ed. P. Binski and S. Panayotova (London, 2005), pp. 379–81. See also J. Saltmarsh, 'The Muniments of King's College', *Proceedings of the Cambridge Antiquarian Society*, 33 (1933), pp. 83–97.

of these is a requiem for the soul of the founder, those of his parents and all benefactors. The names of these benefactors are to be written down on a *tabula* (board). The anniversary of the founder's death is to be celebrated each year and allowances are made to the members of the college, according to their status, and including the choir and bellringers, for their participation in these celebrations. The obits of Henry V, of Catherine his queen and of Queen Margaret, Henry VI's wife, are also to be commemorated. During the Christmas season exequies are to be held for all benefactors. Four times a year, apart from these anniversaries, exequies are also to be held for the souls of the king, his parents and all benefactors.[8]

The college's Mundum Books (the primary financial record at King's) show that these instructions were complied with, at least so far as the anniversary exequies were concerned. From 1456–57 there are annual entries for Queen Catherine (4 January), Henry V (31 August) and for benefactors of the college (20 December). From 1466 Cardinal Henry Beaufort was added (though he had died in 1447, and had not featured by name in the statutes), and from 1472–73 Henry VI himself, somewhat more than a year after his death in the Tower of London on 21 May 1471. The fact that the prime mover in his death, Edward IV, was back on the throne does not seem to have inhibited this commemoration of Edward's rival. While the college had lost many of its estates in the 1460s after Edward seized the throne, he had made no attempt to interfere with the founder's statutes, which made provision for Henry's commemoration after his death. As well as the primary commemoration on 21 May there were exequies performed for the founder on four other occasions in the year (on or near 14 December, 10 April, 22 June and 27 September) as well as an additional celebration in the public schools, paid for by King's College. The obit of Queen Margaret, Henry's wife, was celebrated on 3 August annually from 1483, the year after her death. Thomas Rotherham, archbishop of York and a former vice-provost of King's, died on 29 May 1500 and exequies for him were held at King's in 1501 (although thereafter the records indicate only the ringing of a bell at most). This was in accord with the undertaking the college made in May 1475 to provide prayers and suffrages in honour of its benefactor, and then obsequies upon his death.[9]

For all of these exequies there are records of those who celebrated them, with payments appropriate to their rank. These payments varied according to the occasion, with the primary exequy for the founder being the most expensive. Typically, on that occasion the provost was paid 20*d.*, the vice-

---

8   J. Saltmarsh, 'The Founder's Statutes of King's College, Cambridge', in *Studies presented to Sir Hilary Jenkinson*, ed. J. Conway Davies (London, 1957), pp. 337–60; *idem*, 'The Colleges and Halls: King's', in *VCH: A History of the County of Cambridge and the Isle of Ely, iii: The City and University of Cambridge*, ed. J.P.C. Roach (London, 1959), pp. 376–408; http://www.british-history.ac.uk/vch/cambs/vol3/pp376-408 [accessed 15 March 2016]. Statute 41 deals with prayers for the royal family, benefactors and the faithful departed.

9   The Mundum Books are in KCA, KCAR/4/A/3. I have examined the sequence from the beginning in 1448 to 1554. The 'Anniversarium' of Archbishop Rotherham is documented in KCA, Ledger Book I (KCAR/3/3/1/1/1), f. 86.

provost 12*d.*, fellows in orders 10*d.*, those not in orders 6*d.*, conducts (chaplains) 8*d.*, scholars and clerks 6*d.*, and the sacrist 3*s.* 4*d.* for ringing the bell. Later, choristers were added to the bill. Of course it cannot be known for certain that all those itemised were always present at the masses celebrated, but the fact that the financial record varies from service to service in terms of the number of celebrants rewarded suggests that it was more than just a record of a regular (but unearned) stipend.[10]

There is remarkable consistency in these records from the reign of Edward IV to that of Queen Mary. It would appear that religious changes in the state or the financial difficulties of the college made little or no difference. Each term was marked by observance of the obits of those specified by the founder or added after his death. From 1504 onwards the Mundum Books also record payments for the 'Memoriale' of Henry Veysey, who is listed among the exequies for the grand figures of the college, but who seems to have been only a Cambridge apothecary. However, he must have been a very rich apothecary, for he gave the college £40. In return the college accepted him amongst its benefactors and guaranteed a requiem mass and collects, to be celebrated in perpetuity.[11] His 'Memoriale' was celebrated four times a year in King's from 1503/04 onwards to judge from the Mundum Books.

In the cases of other individuals to whom an anniversary was allowed at King's, as recorded in Ledger Book 1, there is no equivalent financial record to show that the anniversaries were in fact celebrated in the college. Nevertheless, we know that such commitments were made for Henry VII by Provost John Doget and the fellows of the college in 1499–1500; prayers and suffrages were to be said during his lifetime, and then others for his soul after his death, together with the appropriate exequies and requiem masses in perpetuity. More detailed arrangements were specified for memorialising the king under the seal of the next provost, John Argentein, in November 1503. An anniversary had been allowed for his mother Lady Margaret, countess of Richmond, in 1498. A number of other prominent benefactors were commemorated, the first of whom was William Waynflete, bishop of Winchester (August 1459). Others included Richard Foxe, bishop of Durham and later of Winchester; and Sir Reynold Bray, the chancellor of the duchy of Lancaster, who had been brought up in the service of Lady Margaret; and Sir Robert Brudenell, chief justice; and Sir William Gascoigne, treasurer in the household of Cardinal Wolsey (both these last names were directed to be entered in the college's table of benefactors). Some less obviously powerful individuals were added to the list of benefactors for whom prayers, suffrages, exequies and masses were to be celebrated. Dr. Roger Marchall was remembered in this way because of the books he had given to the College Library (1475). The anniversary allowed to the judge Sir Robert Rede in 1490 included provision for his name to be 'written in the tables of our benefactors'. Not all those commemorated were benefactors from outside.

[10]   KCA, KCAR/4/A/3/1/1/6, Mundum Book 1469–74, f. 107 (20 December 1473).
[11]   KCA, Ledger Book 1, f. 189v, dated 23 January 1502/03.

The obits of provosts John Chedworth, Walter Field and John Doget were also to be regularly celebrated according to the earliest college Ledger Book.[12]

TESTAMENTS AND BENEFACTIONS

Ledger Book 1 is the primary legal register of the college, begun in 1451, and it contains copies of deeds of all kinds relating to college property, presentation to college livings, admissions of provosts and letters to the king and others. Between 1449 and 1794, King's was permitted to exercise probate jurisdiction within the precincts of the college. The wills of members of the college, servants, tradesmen and tenants were proved in its court, which also granted, where appropriate, letters of administration. Ledger Book 1 thus also includes copies of the wills of many individuals, some of which made provision for the commemoration of obits within the college chapel. An early example is the will of William Warmystre or Warminster, a fellow of King's, dated 13 October 1457. He directed that his body should be buried in the college cemetery, with his body lying so that the head was to the east side of the cross in the middle. He left books to the college library and to another fellow, Edmund Arnold, and 3s. 4d. for a silver spoon with his name engraved on it to the college, as well as 20s. There were 10s. for oblations to the high altar of the chapel and 6s. 8d. for oblations elsewhere. As regards his exequies, he left 6d. to the priest who sang his requiem mass, 4d. for masters, 3d. for bachelors, and for ungraduated fellows, 2d. for scholars, and 1d. for each chorister who participated.[13] Later wills of fellows take a similar form, except that the burial is directed to take place in the 'new Chapel' rather than the cemetery.[14] The will of John Welschott, fellow, is dated 9 June 1525. He first provided 6s. 8d. for a light before the image of the Blessed Virgin Mary standing in the body of the chapel. Then he gave the college £13 6s. 8d. to pay for a fellow priest to say an annual mass for his soul, for that of his father and for those of his good friends. Another £6 13s. 4d. was to pay for a *Dirige* to be sung, one at his burial, one at his month's mind and the third at his twelve month's mind. In addition,

---

[12] Ledger Book 1, ff. 168v, 188 (Henry VII), 161v (Lady Margaret), 27 (Waynflete), 172 (Foxe, Bray), 256 (Brudenell), 268v (Gascoigne), 86 (Marchall), 142 (Rede). The background to the grant for Henry VII is explained in M. Condon, 'God Save the King! Piety, Propaganda and the Perpetual Memorial', in *Westminster Abbey: The Lady Chapel of Henry VII*, ed. T. Tatton-Brown and R. Mortimer (Woodbridge, 2003), pp. 59–97 at p. 81.

[13] Ledger Book 1, f. 17v. See A.N.L. Munby, 'Notes on King's College Library in the Fifteenth Century', *Transactions of the Cambridge Bibliographical Society*, 1 (1951), pp. 280–6 for Warmystre's book donations.

[14] See similar covenants for John Hogekyns (1480; printed at length), John Plente (1483), William Towne (1499) and William Scales (1508), in *Documents relating to the Additional Endowments and Trust Funds of King's College, Cambridge* (Cambridge, 1875), pp. 5–8. All of these were still in effect in 1578/79, according to the College Mundum Books (I owe this observation to Dr. Patricia McGuire, archivist, King's College, Cambridge).

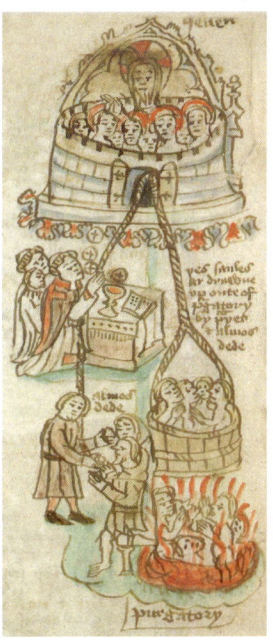

I: Souls being drawn out of Purgatory through prayer, alms and masses. Carthusian manuscript, possibly from Mount Grace Priory, Yorkshire, c.1460.

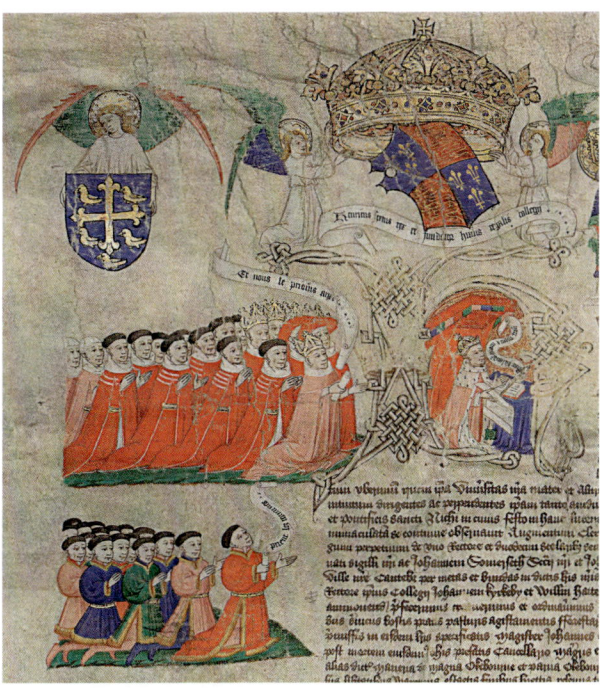

II: Foundation grant by Henry VI of lands and privileges to benefit his King's College of St. Nicholas and Our Lady at Cambridge, 1446. Illuminated by William Abell.

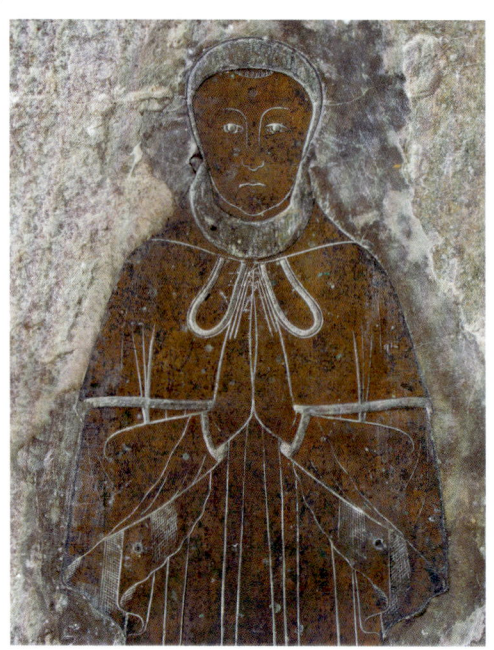

III: Brass of Thomas Rolf (d.1440), St. Catherine's church, Gosfield, Essex.

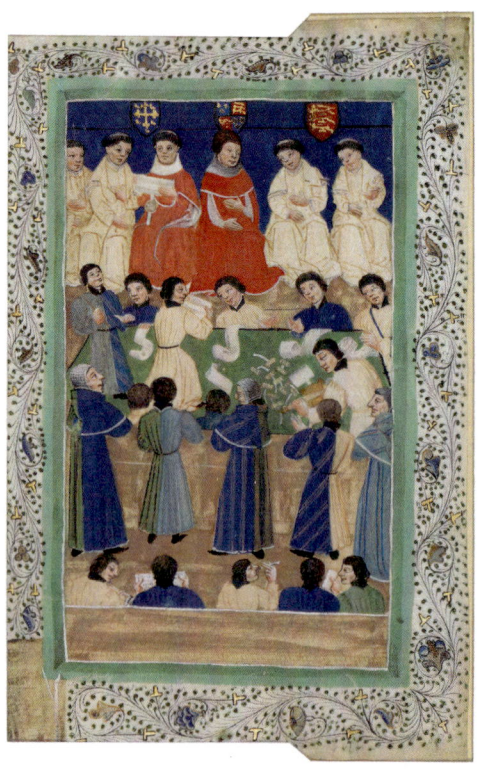

IV: Court of Chancery at Westminster Hall, *c.*1460.

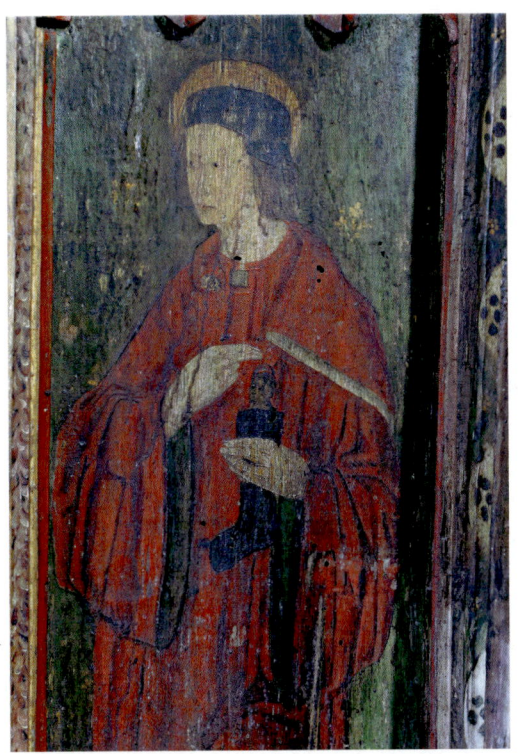

V: John Schorn shown on the rood screen at St. Helen, Gateley, Norfolk.

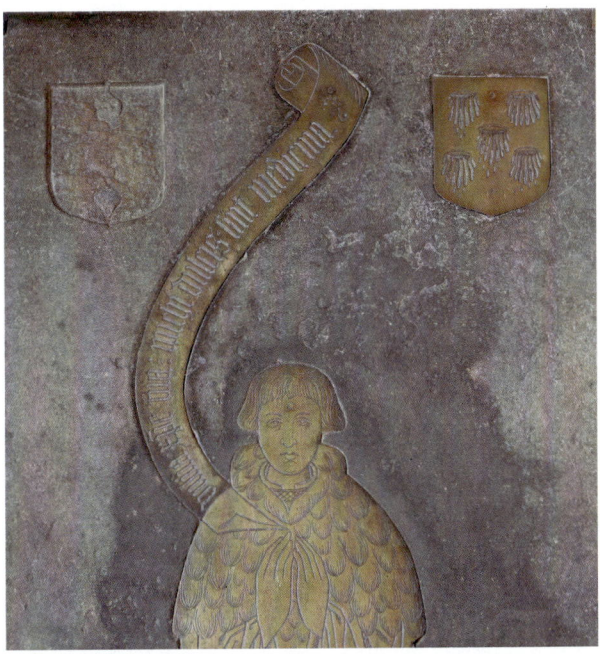

VI: Brass of Robert Hacumblen (d.1528), King's College chapel, Cambridge.

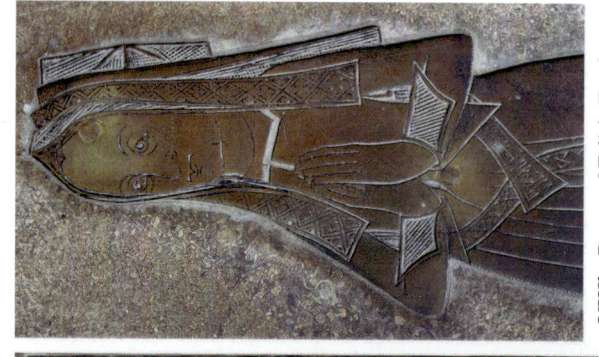

VIIIb: Brass of Edith Fowler (close up).

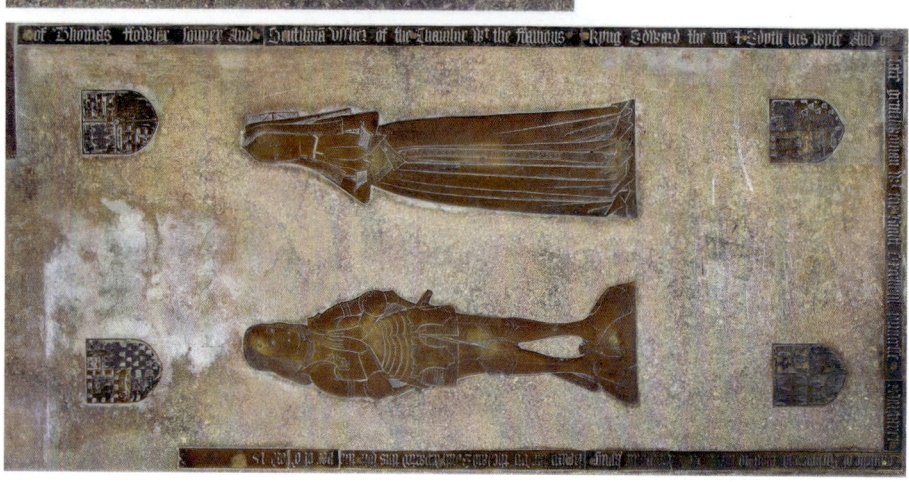

VIIIa: Brass of Edith Fowler (d. before 1514), gentlewoman, and her husband Thomas (d.1506), Christ's College chapel, Cambridge.

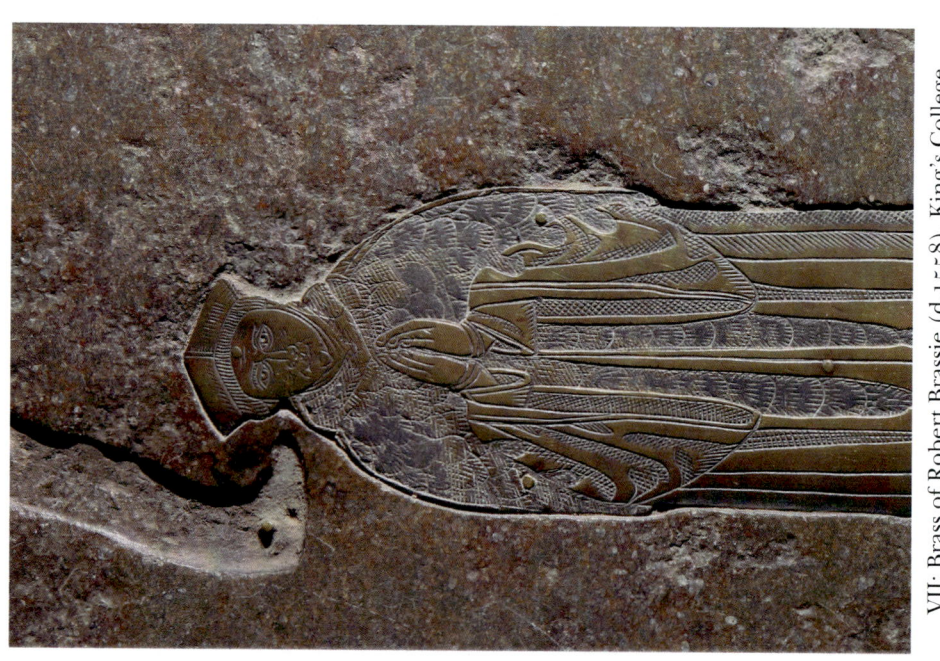

VII: Brass of Robert Brassie (d.1558), King's College chapel, Cambridge.

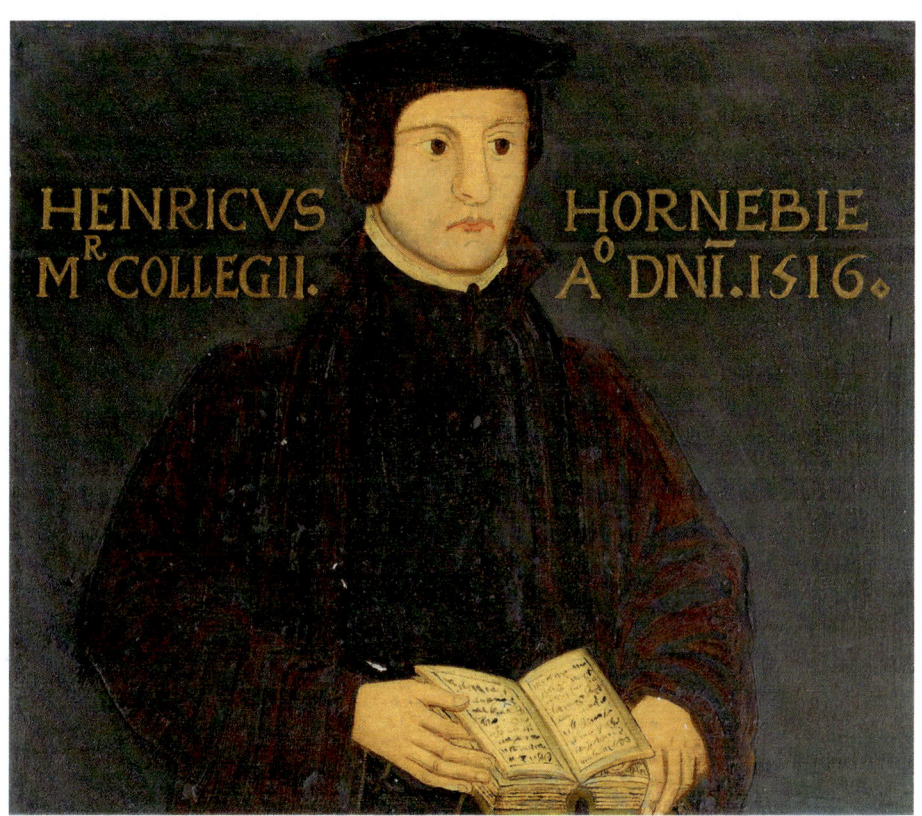

IX: Portrait of Henry Hornby, dated 1516.

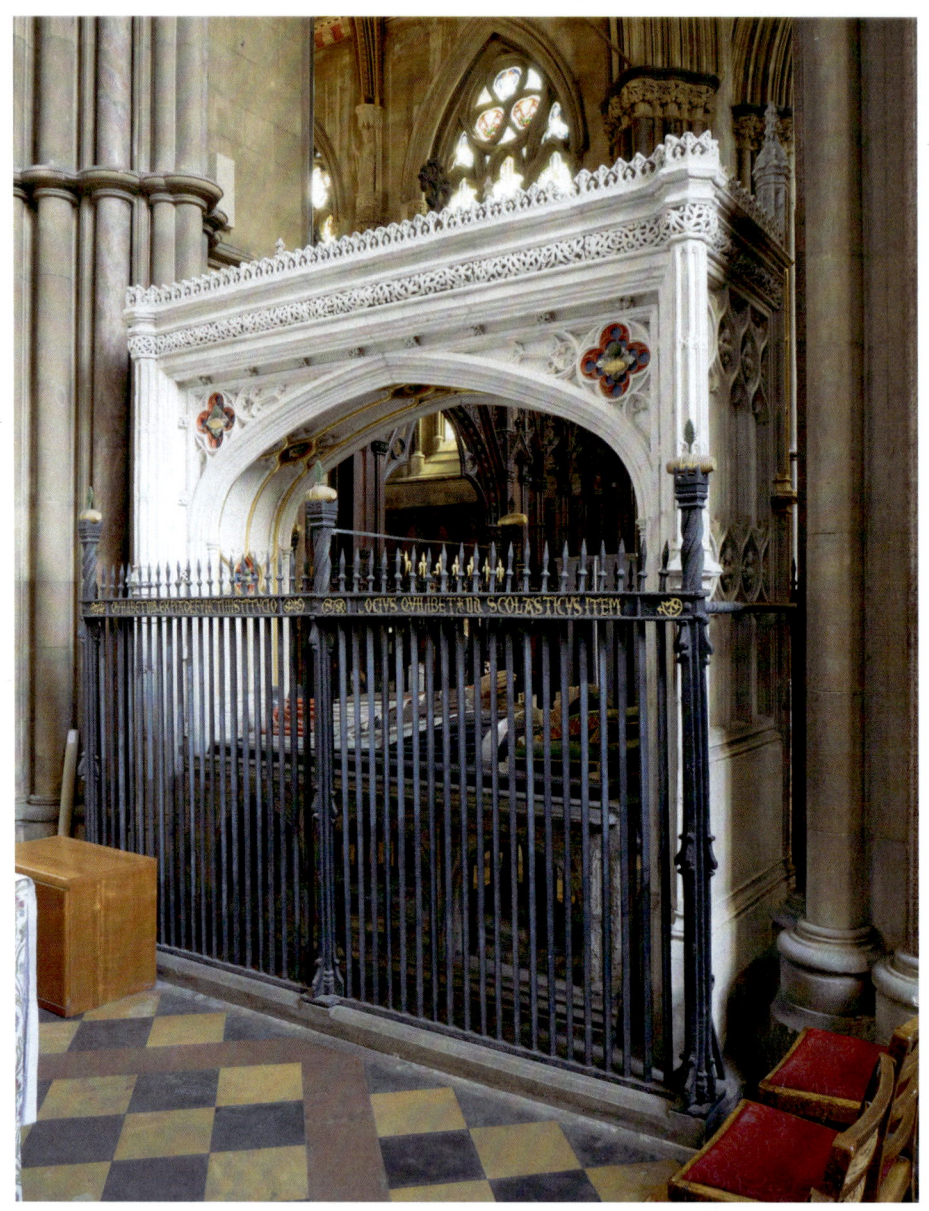

Xa: Tomb monument for Hugh Ashton (d.1522), archdeacon of York, receiver-general and controller of the household of Lady Margaret Beaufort, St. John's College chapel, Cambridge.

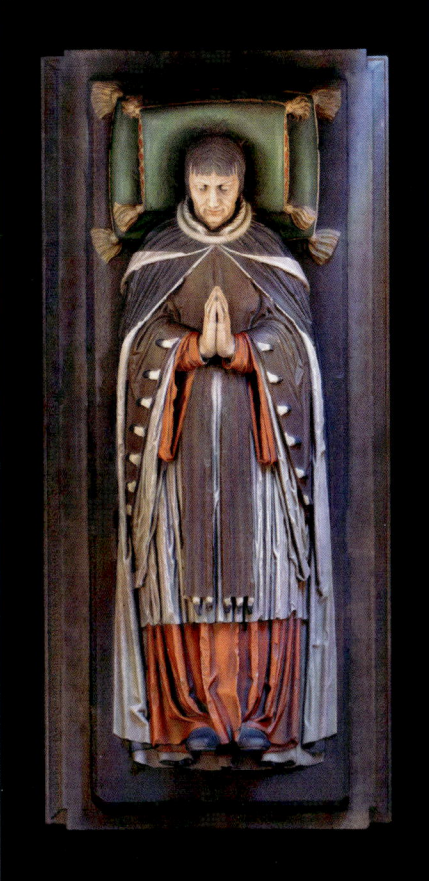

Xb: Sculptured effigy of Hugh Ashton placed above the cadaver, St. John's College chapel.

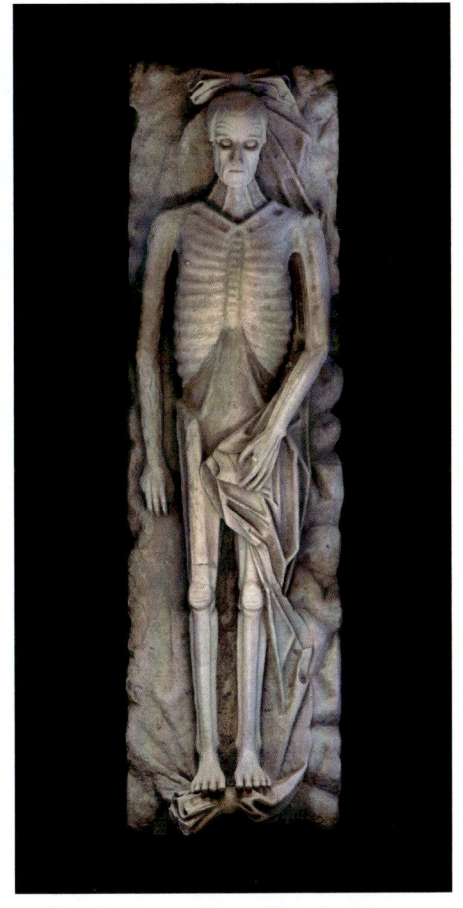

Xc: Cadaver effigy of Hugh Ashton (d.1522), St. John's College chapel.

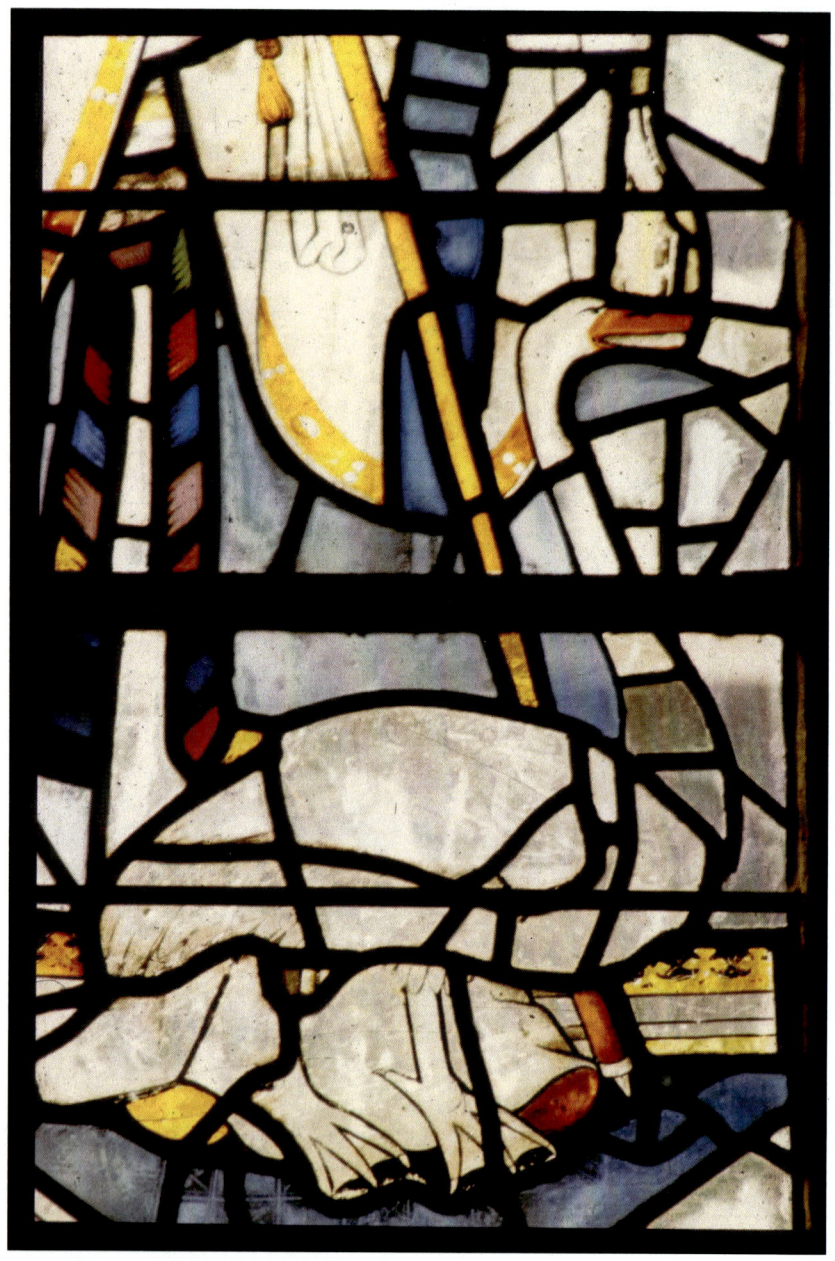

XI: Figure of St. Hugh, with a swan at his feet, St. Michael-le-Belfry, York, in light a of window sIV (third from the east in the south wall).

the four orders of friars in Cambridge were to receive 40s. to sing four trentals for him, and £4 was to be distributed to the poor.[15]

A number of references have been made already to the practice of recording the names of benefactors in 'tables' to commemorate their generosity. The earliest surviving list of benefactors to King's is to be found in a book bound in fifteenth-century oak boards, which may indeed represent the 'tables' mentioned. The list of benefactors is impressively written in a contemporary book hand. A later, but probably also fifteenth-century, hand has provided marginal annotations to the names of the benefactors. The list begins in Latin with the founder, who 'erected, made and founded' the college, and endowed it in perpetuity with spiritual and temporal possessions, out of his 'most gracious munificence'. The remainder of the list comprises benefactors of the college. It begins with the first provost, William Millington, who enhanced the college with his righteous way of life and sound doctrine, but, as the entry has it, 'he left' – in fact he was deprived of office in 1447. Cambridge University's chancellor John Langton is second; he procured the foundation of the college within the university and laboured to endow the chapel with books, chapel plate, vestments and precious objects.[16] Nicholas Close, one of the six original fellows nominated by the founder in 1441, comes next; he was the official master of works at the college in 1446 and a royal chaplain, later to become bishop of Coventry and Lichfield. But in the table of benefactors he is commemorated for the provision of books for study in the library, which only came to the college after his death (intestate) in 1452. John Chedworth, the second provost, later bishop of Lincoln, is remembered for his services to the governance of the college and for forgiving 100 marks which the college owed him. Henry, Cardinal Beaufort, and bishop of Winchester, gave £100 to the college 'in memoriam', and as we saw above, he was indeed commemorated with an obit from 1466 if not before. Ralph Holland, alderman of London, also gave £100; no explicit reason is given for his beneficence, but he did receive two tenements in Watling Street from the Crown, so this may explain his generosity to the royal college. The last on the list is Henry Somer, chancellor of the Exchequer, and knight of the shire for Cambridgeshire, whose executors Henry Langley and John Dunham forgave the debt of 100 marks owed by the college to Somer, who died in 1450. The latest death recorded in this one leaf of the list was in 1452.[17]

[15]   Ledger Book 1, f. 268v. A list of individual wills proved at King's College is described at http://www.kings.cam.ac.uk/sites/default/files/archives/probate-records-index.pdf [accessed 13 April 2016]. The pattern of observances is similar to that described for Bristol churches in C. Burgess, 'A Service for the Dead: The Form and Function of the Anniversary in Late Medieval Bristol', *Transactions of the Bristol and Gloucestershire Archaeological Society*, 105 (1987), pp. 183–211.

[16]   KCA, KCA/344, Purveyance by Langton of Chapel books, 1443; KCA/345 vestments, c.1445.

[17]   KCA, KCE/716; a transcription by John Saltmarsh is to be found in KCHR/3/12. For the individuals named, see *ODNB*.

INVENTORIES AND DONATIONS

The earliest surviving inventory of college possessions, *c.*1453–57, records the chapel plate, service books and the numerous vestments and other ornaments used in the chapel (this was of course the 'old' chapel, not the present building). Many of the items listed correspond to the purveyances of John Langton and constitute the original fittings acquired by the college through the royal prerogative. The manuscript containing the inventory also contains a transcript of Henry VI's original charter to King's and letters patent granting the college lands and reversions (ff. 13–26), an inventory of books under the heading '*Libraria*'[18], a list of provosts and scholars of King's from the foundation down to *c.*1522 and a badly damaged inventory including pledges in college chests. There are many blank leaves in the manuscript and it seems to have been kept unbound but sewn into gatherings. It was designed to be kept up to date, with entries to be added to the initial drafts made in one elegant display hand of the mid-1450s. The format is of large leaves of parchment with wide margins, 450 × 300mm, and a ruled written area of 297 × 175mm. The 'book' as a whole suggests an attempt to impress the viewer as much as to record information.[19]

From a commemorative point of view it is the additions made to the inventory of chapel gear that are most remarkable.[20] Whereas the original entries do not refer to donors, the added entries are often records of donation. The name most frequently mentioned is that of John Doget, provost of King's 1499–1501. He gifted:

> Two gilded images, one representing the Church and the other the Synagogue
> A little cross of silver-gilt with a stone in the foot
> A gilded and enamelled pyx
> Two large gilded candelabra
> A gilded holy water bucket and sprinkler
> A table (hanging image) with relics
> A large gilded monstrance with stones in the foot and a cross on top
> A vestment of white damask with books and chalices and orphreys of purple sarsenet

---

[18]   See P.D. Clarke, ed., *The University and College Libraries of Cambridge*, Corpus of British Medieval Library Catalogues, 10 (London, 2002), pp. 282–304; M.R. James, *A Descriptive Catalogue of the Manuscripts other than Oriental in the Library of King's College, Cambridge* (Cambridge, 1895), pp. 69–83.

[19]   KCA, KCA/684, ff. 3–12 (inventory), 13–26 (Henry VI's charter), 58–65v (books), 70–77 (list of members of the foundation), 81 (pledges). The 1453–57 inventory was published by G. Williams in 'Ecclesiastical Vestments, Books, and Furniture, in the Collegiate Church of King's College, Cambridge, in the Fifteenth Century', *The Ecclesiologist*, 20 (1859), pp. 304–15; 21 (1860), pp. 1–7; 24 (1863), pp. 99–102. Williams left out additions to the inventory subsequent to the original scribe's activity. These additions were transcribed by M.R. James and W. St. John Hope in a copy of Williams's article: KCA, Coll 2/23.

[20]   KCA, KCA/684, ff. 3–12, *passim*.

Other donations of metalwork are recorded from John Day (admitted 1453), Provost John Argentein, John Benett (adm. 1457), Robert Hacumblen (later provost), John Cokke (probably Coker, adm. 1455), John Barbour (not identified) and William Bowes (adm. 1479; this name corrected from Doget), and of vestments from Master Ashwell (not identified), Richard Young (Yonge, adm. *c.*1482), John Argentein, John Rokelyff (Rowclyff, of King's Hall), John Benett (see above) and John Regnold (Reynold, adm. 1457). Amongst the donors of chapel books were Argentein again, John Boston (adm. 1447, two books), Thomas Bower (adm. 1446), Grove (not identified) and John Welles (Wellys, adm. 1457). Exceptionally one breviary is recorded as '*donatum per Johannem Fray*' (possibly John Freys of St. Edmund's Priory, Cambridge) in the original listing rather than as an addition. Apart from the last, the donors, where identified, seem to have been members of the college or connected institutions like King's Hall.

It is no surprise that provosts John Doget, John Argentein and Robert Hacumblen loom so large amongst the recorded donors. Their incomes were of a different order of magnitude to those of other members of the college; they lived in the Provost's Lodge in aristocratic style. The same pattern of recording donations occurs in subsequent inventories of chapel goods. Some items listed in the earlier inventory are no longer present in the next inventory of 1506, probably as a result of the college's comparative impoverishment in Edward IV's reign from 1465/66 onwards. But those items donated by the individuals named in the earlier inventory are not included among those pledged or lost by 1506. And there are new donations by 1506 from members of the college, including provosts Doget and Argentein again and other officers: William Clerke, identified as receiver of the college (from 1469, d.1505/06), Robert Smith, sub-bursar, and James Denton (adm. 1486, bursar 1498–1500, later King's chaplain). Geoffrey Blythe (adm. *c.*1479, bishop of Coventry and Lichfield from 1503) gave a mitre with twenty finials or crockets, for the use of the boy-bishop celebrated on St. Nicholas's day in accordance with the college statutes.[21] The most striking donation, however, was that of a pax, listed as a *textus* of the Gospels with the Angelic salutation to Mary on the cover, given as a memorial (*pro memoria*) of William Stertour (adm. 1468, bursar 1488–89) and Lady Margaret Rede (wife of Sir Robert). The entry records that it cost £20, towards which Lady Rede gave £4 and Master Sterter £10. This memorial is otherwise unrecorded by the college, and it indicates the use of the inventory books to record gifts that were no doubt intended by their donors to memorialise themselves.[22]

---

[21] KCA/22, f. 23.

[22] KCA/22, f. 10. Originally the scribe wrote Anna Re-, which was subsequently crossed out and replaced by Margarete Rede. If Lady Rede was in fact Anne Rede, this might be the wife of Sir William Rede of Boarstall; her maiden name was Donne, and she was portrayed as a child by Hans Memling in the Donne Triptych (National Gallery). See 'Parishes: Boarstall', in *VCH: A History of the County of Buckingham*, ed. William Page (London, 1927), iv, pp. 9–14.

Subsequent inventories were made in 1529 and 1535.[23] The most sumptuous new donations in the 1529 inventory were made by Provost Hacumblen. He gave one chalice inscribed with '*Orate pro anima Roberti Hacumblen*' ('Pray for the soul of Robert Hacumblen') on the bottom and in the paten an inscription '*Benedicamus patrem*' ('Let us bless our Father'). A second gifted chalice has a design of the five wounds of the Passion in the paten and the sacred name on the foot.[24] The five wounds motif on the second chalice is repeated on Hacumblen's memorial brass (Plate VI) in the side-chapel given his name in the new chapel that he had done so much to bring to completion. He also gave two new copes embroidered with roses. The vestments section of the inventory concludes with a 'Memorandum that such ornaments as belong to the Hacomblen chapell be not expressed in this bok ... Here nor yet the ii gret brasse deskes with ii standers of brasse.' One of these brazen desks is the lectern that now stands in the chapel choir, engraved with the name of Robert Hacumblen.[25] The 1536 inventory has detailed descriptions of two statuettes of the Virgin, given by Provost Doget but not recorded before, and another of Henry VI inscribed on the back with the name of James Denton (the royal chaplain). A statue of St. Nicholas is inscribed on the base with 'Hacomblen' and the prayer '*beate Nicholae te colentem protege*' ('Blessed Nicholas protect you as you worship'). Another of the Virgin with a wide crown on her head, a sceptre in her right hand and her Son on her left has the word 'Hacumbleyn' on the back of the foot, and around it '*Intercede pro nobis Virgo Maria*' ('Intercede for us Virgin Mary').[26] Hacumblen clearly designed that his gifts should associate his own name with the intercessions of the college's patron saints, for his own soul and for those who contemplated and prayed before the images. But while his memorial brass and the glass in the windows of the side-chapel remain nearly intact, these statues have since disappeared.

MEMBERS OF THE FOUNDATION

The earliest of the two volumes discussed above contains a list of the provosts and scholars of King's from the foundation down to 1524.[27] As a form of record of the statutory membership of the college, this list, in order of admission, may be distinguished from the administrative records that mention those drawing stipends or present at meals (the Mundum and Commons Books) and the

---

[23] These are inserted within the same paper book, bound in soft vellum, as the 1506 inventory (KCA/22). Although not as elegantly presented as the first college inventory (KCA/684), this is still a spaciously designed book with a variety of flourished capitals and a use of display scripts. The inventories from 1506 onwards were transcribed by M.R. James and W. St. John Hope, and are now to be found in Coll 2/23 and KCA/687.

[24] One chalice is also described in his will in Ledger Book 1, f. 278v, as transcribed in N. Pickering, 'Provost Robert Hacumblen and his Chantry Chapel', in *King's College Chapel 1515–2015: Art, Music and Religion in Cambridge*, ed. J.M. Massing and N. Zeeman (London, 2014), pp. 96–113.

[25] KCA/22, f. 45. The lectern is pictured in Pickering, 'Provost Robert Hacumblen', Ill. 64 (at p. 96).

[26] KCA/22, ff. 70–70v.

[27] KCA/684, ff. 70–77.

notarised records of admission ceremonies, which survive in the Protocollum Books from 1500 onwards. For each entry the county of origin of the individual is given where known, and the town is often added. But this information is supplemented, usually by a later hand, with further detail relating to an individual's subsequent career. Thus the entry for John Freeman, of Beverley in Yorkshire, who was admitted scholar in 1445, tells us that he became a clerk of the Privy Council, and was married.[28] The list seems to function as a memorial of members of the college kept up by fellows with knowledge of the subsequent careers of their predecessors admitted earlier (much as the King's College published Register of Admissions functions today). The original entries were written by several hands of different generations before tailing off in 1524.

Although abandoned at this point, the list was not forgotten. It became the foundation of the work begun by Thomas Hatcher (d.1583), who had been elected from Eton College and admitted at King's in 1555. He was a fellow of the college from 1558 to 1566. At some time before 1562 he began his '*Catalogus praepositorum, sociorum, et scholarium Collegii Regalis Cantabrigiae, a tempore fundationis ad annum 1572*' ('Catalogue of the Provosts, Fellows and Scholars of King's College Cambridge from the date of the foundation to the year 1572').[29] He made use of donor information in the inventories and King's library books, as well as inscriptions in stone and glass, to supplement the information he gained from the list and the Protocollum Books from 1500. He recorded college traditions and gossip about individuals as well as their appointments and writings; thus the college records were only the scaffolding for the expanded catalogue. The first 869 entries up to 1562 were written by Thomas Hatcher himself, though later additions were made to these entries, and continuations of the work were added by John Scott, Edward Hinde and George Goad.[30] Hatcher's work was the subject of a '*Distichon Apostrophicon*' by Ralph Winterton, of King's College, physician and author (1601–36): '*Defuncti vivunt, redeunt et Tempora Prisca/ O Hatchere tuo munere, Scotte tuo*' ('The dead live, they return with former times/ O Hatcher, O Scott, through your gift)'. Ultimately the catalogue fell into the hands of the King's antiquary William Cole, and he made it the basis of his 'Historiette or Account of the Provost, Fellows, and Scholars of King's College in my 13, 14, 15, 16 vols. of my collections for the County of Cambridge'.[31] A contemporary of Cole's, Anthony Allen, separately made use of Hatcher's catalogue to construct his

---

[28]   KCA/684, f. 70. John Freeman's entry in *BRUC*, cites this inventory volume as its source for his career after Cambridge.

[29]   Copies are to be found in Cambridge, Gonville and Caius College MS 173/94; BL, Harley MS 6114, Harley MS 6865, Add. MS 5954, and Add. MS 5955. For Hatcher, see *ODNB*.

[30]   John Scott, notary public and 'coroner of King's College' according to William Cole, fl.1617–21; Edward Hynde, adm. 1595, Fellow 1597–1622; George Goad, adm. 1620, Fellow 1623–47, see *ODNB*.

[31]   BL, Add. MS 5814, f. 3v (c. 1748). Cole's considerable collections for the history of King's College and the county of Cambridgeshire found their way to the British Museum (afterwards BL). He recorded Winterton's distich after the title of Hatcher's catalogue, which Cole continued up to 1746, on f. 6.

own '*Skeleton Collegii Regalis Cantab[rigiae]*: Or a Catalogue of all the Provosts, Fellows and Scholars, of the King's College of the blessed Virgin Mary and St. Nicholas in the University of Cambridge; since the Foundation thereof Anno 1441 *usque ad extremam. Anno 1750*'.[32]

CHANTRIES AND BURIALS

The new chapel, whose foundation stone was laid by Henry VI in 1446, was not completed structurally until 1515. The glass was installed in stages between 1515 and 1547 (except the Last Judgement in the west window, which was not installed until 1879). The original plan for the new chapel had included six side-chapels between the buttresses of the ante-chapel, three on the north and three on the south. In the founder's will of 1448 they are called 'closets', which meant especially a place of private devotion. The king must have envisaged private chantries for the singing of masses for other individuals taking place alongside the use of the chapel choir (where there were three altars) as a great chantry for the royal family. Before 1461 the design of the building was changed to allow for the creation of a total of eighteen side-chapels. Eight of the new side-chapels were designed for ceremonial use and probably contained altars of their own. We know of four side-chapels which were definitely used as burial sites and chantries for one fellow and three provosts of King's College. In the cases of William Towne, a fellow of the original foundation, who died on 11 March 1495, and Provost John Argentein, who died on 2 February 1509, we have surviving memorial brasses in their side-chapels (Plates 7 and 8a&b in chapter 5). These men died and were commemorated before the completion of the new chapel building. Accordingly, we do not have evidence of a design for furnishing a complete side-chapel as a memorial chapel. But in the cases of Provost Robert Hacumblen, who died on 8 September 1528, and Provost Robert Brassie, who died on 10 November 1558, we know that their wills made explicit provision for side-chapels devoted to their memory.[33]

In the case of William Towne, we do not have a will so cannot be sure of his express intention in regard to his memorial brass. But we do have a deed establishing his '*Anniversarium*', dated 10 May 1499, that is, more than four years after his death. In it, his executors gave 160 marks to establish an annual commemoration of his death. There is no mention of the memorial brass or of a specific location for the commemoration. The extant brass is dated 1496, so in Towne's case was probably executed and installed before the anniversary obit was established. It is located in the second side-chapel from the east on the northern side of the chapel. The stone slab is now broken. The obit was nevertheless most likely to have been celebrated in the side-chapel containing his brass. The brass shows him as a doctor of divinity, with a cap and a fur-lined tippet over his shoulders. There is a scroll held between his

---

[32] A manuscript now in the Library of King's College (no pressmark).
[33] P.M. Jones, 'The College and the Chapel', in *King's College Chapel 1515–2015*, ed. Massing and Zeeman, pp. 161–79 at pp. 162–3.

breast and praying hands, with the following distich: '*Gloria fama scolis laus artes cetera mundi/ vana nimis valeant spes [mea sola deus]*' ('Glory, fame in the schools, praise, the other arts of the word are vain things valued too high. My hope is in God alone'). The last three words are missing, but not defaced. This inscription is also found on the brass of Dr. Walter Hewke, *c.*1510, of Trinity Hall, Cambridge. The first and last parts of the obituary inscription below the figure have been roughly crossed out in an effort, presumably, to remove offensive text during the Commonwealth.[34] The words crossed out are '*Orate pro anima*' ('Pray for the soul') and '*cuius anime propitietur deus*' ('may God have mercy on his soul'), which would have been unacceptable to strict Protestants. The remaining words below the image describe Towne as a fellow and doctor of divinity, and give his date of death.[35]

For Provost John Argentein, we have a will dated 27 January 1507. He wished to be buried where his executors pleased, but '*coram imagine aliqua Jesu Christi crucifixi saluatoris nostri*' ('beside a picture of our saviour Jesus Christ on the cross'). This image of the Crucifixion is now missing from the brass, but clearly occupied a space above the image of Argentein and connected with the scroll from his mouth. He then gives precise instructions for a stone '*non egregius aut sumptuosus*' ('not splendid or sumptuous') with his image, hands folded in prayer to the crucifix. He specifies the verses proceeding from his mouth, '*Virginis atque dei fili crucifixi* [on the brass, '*crucifixe*'] *redemptor/ humani generis christe memento mei*' (Christ crucified son of God and of the Virgin, redeemer of human kind, remember me)'. Below the image these verses were to be cut: '*Artiste medici scripture interpretis alme Argentein corpus sepelit lapis iste Johannis/ Qui transis recolas moneris termini ora/ Spiritus in christo viuat nunquam moritur*' ('The body beneath this stone is that of John Argentein, Master of Arts, physician, and preacher of the word/ Whosoever passes, remember, be reminded of your end, pray. The spirit lives in Christ and never dies'). These instructions were followed in full. The image shows Argentein wearing a doctor of divinity's hat. Three shields surviving (of four), not specified in the will, display the arms of Argentein: *Gules, three covered cups argent*. There is a marginal inscription fillet with Evangelists' symbols at the corners retaining traces of red enamel (those for Matthew and Mark are missing). As in the case of Towne, the brass is located in a side-chapel at the east end, in Argentein's case the first on the south of the chapel.[36]

---

[34] T. Cooper, ed., *The Journal of William Dowsing: Iconoclasm in East Anglia during the English Civil War* (Woodbridge, 2001), p. 186.

[35] KCA, Ledger Book 1, ff. 167v–168. J. Wilson, *Memorabilia Cantabrigiae: or, An account of the different colleges in Cambridge: biographical sketches of the founders and eminent men, with many original anecdotes, views of the colleges, and portraits of the founders* (London, 1803), pp. 85–6; P.J. Heseltine, *The Figure Brasses of Cambridgeshire* (St. Neots, 1981), no. 12 (ill.), p. 21; W. Lack, H.M. Stuchfield and P. Whittemore, *The Monumental Brasses of Cambridgeshire* (London, 1995), pp. 31, 32 (ill.), 36.

[36] John Argentein, *ODNB*. KCA, Ledger Book 1, f. 212. Heseltine, *Figure Brasses*, no. 13 (ill.), p. 21; Lack, Stuchfield and Whittemore, *Cambridgeshire*, pp. 33 (ill.), 36; Royal Commission on Historical Monuments, *An Inventory of the Historical Monuments in the City of Cambridge*, 2 vols. (London, 1959), p. 116 and Plate 5. This is now the All Souls Memorial Chapel.

Robert Hacumblen's side-chapel, the second from the west on the south side of the chapel, was already furnished and in use by the time he made his will in 1528. He describes it as the 'midyll Chapel on S. side which I have honored att myn owne proper coste and charge'. The walls may have been fully panelled because in 1742 William Cole described them as 'wainscoted'. A wooden stall with desk and some wooden panelling survive in Hacumblen's chantry. No trace of the altar on the east wall survives, but Cole noted 'Holes in the East Wall' which he considered evidence of its placing. The vault features a large central Tudor rose with a poppy head, gilded in gold against a blue background. Traces remain in the stonework of red and blue paint, and Cole described the roof as 'elegantly gilt with gold and painted red and blew with stars on it'. The stained-glass windows of the chantry were finished in the 1520s, and most of the surviving glass is original. The inside windows are devoted to the Virgin Mary, with the upper lancets filled with saints and other images connected to the Virgin. These saints are mentioned as intercessors for Hacumblen in his will. There are many quarries with the letters 'R H' for Hacumblen. His brass memorial has the inscription '*Vulnera Christe tua michi dulcis sint medicina*' ('O Christ, may your wounds be sweet medicine to me') on a scroll rising from his praying hands, and a marginal inscription-fillet like that of Argentein's. The chantry is dedicated to the cult of the wounds of Christ, and the surviving shield on his brass images the five wounds. Hacumblen's will requests that Masses of the Five Wounds be said for him.[37]

The chantry chapel of Provost Robert Brassie is also mentioned in his will. In the original document, dated 27 July 1558, Brassie required: 'And yf it shall please god that I deceasse in Cambridge then I wyll my bodye to be buryed in the myddes of the south chappell next beneythe the Roodeloft in the kynges Colledge Churche …'. He also gave the college 40 marks and the tenancies and leases he held of a Mr. Lodge and John Martyn, conditional on his not having during his lifetime spent the equivalent on the ornament of the chapel. In the rider to his will of 7 November 1558, he changes the sum of 40 marks to £30:

> Which I wyll to be bestowed upon Candellstyckes with Inscription of my name in the bygger sort of letters. I wyll that the forseyde Chappell be anownred [adorned] to the doble sum before mencyonyd yf yt wyll not other wyse be brought to the example of hacumblen's chappell. And in the border of the doore to be kervyd '*Orate pro anima Roberti brassye quondam prepositi huius collegii* [Pray for the soul of Robert Brassye, former Provost of this College]'. And to have a stone of blue marble whyth an image of brasse in hit about the breadth of a foote in the habit of the provost in the quere with inscription in the mouthe '*deus propitius esto mihi peccatori*' ['God have mercy on me, a sinner'] with other thynges as

---

[37] This paragraph is based on Pickering, 'Provost Robert Hacumblen'; his brass is ill. p. 75. See also Heseltine, *Figure Brasses*, no. 14 (ill.), p. 21; Lack, Stuchfield and Whittemore, *Cambridgeshire*, pp. 34 (ill.), 36; Royal Commission on Historical Monuments, *City of Cambridge*, p. 116 and Plate 5.

is semelye with letters R B dyspersyd in the waulys of the chappell as is convenient in the payntynge …

His preferred plan was thus to imitate the furnishings and adornment in Hacumblen's chantry next to his. But he then made provision for a scheme of burial in the middle of the chapel if there was not enough money to fit out the side-chapel in the manner described.[38] Brassie died seven days before Queen Mary, and thus his chantry chapel was the last to be endowed in this fashion. The chapel was instituted as he had intended next to the rood loft (or screen), and in the eighteenth century William Cole recorded that the '*Orate pro anima* …' inscription specified by Brassie was still on the outside of the door to this side-chapel, written in Gothic characters on parchment and covered with horn. The stone slab, with his memorial brass inset (Plate VII), remains today, showing Brassie in cap, surplice, almuce and stole. The scroll next to his mouth would presumably have read '*Deus propitius esto mihi*', but is now missing. Underneath the image is '*Hic iacet Robertus Brassie sacrae theologiae professor quondam prepositus huius collegii qui ab hac vita decessit decimo die Novembris Anno Domini 1558*' [in Roman numerals] ('Here lies Robert Brassie D.D., former provost of this college, who died on 10 November 1558').[39]

The surviving evidence of King's College memorials in the form of tomb slabs, glass, brass monuments and schemes of decoration is confined now to the great chapel (and the buried foundation stones). Much of this evidence is now covered up, or difficult to view, unlike the post-medieval memorials in the chapel which are much easier to see for the visitor.[40] The pre-Reformation liturgies which would have made up the daily and festal practices of commemoration in King's College have disappeared altogether, leaving behind only written and illuminated evidence in the form of foundation documents, statutes, wills, registers and inventories. Many of these documents, however, are not just historical records of commemoration practices once held in the chapel and the college but were intended to be commemorative in themselves. The best written and decorated examples were made for display purposes and to provide a permanent and visible memorial to the piety of donors from Henry VI onwards, to record and to aid intercession for the souls of those commemorated, and to commemorate the lives and deeds of members of the foundation.

A remarkable feature of the commemorative practices of King's College in the first century and more of its existence is that despite violent changes of political regime, reformations and restorations of liturgy and religion, there seems to have been surprising consistency and reluctance to

---

[38] Will of Robert Brassie: KCA, Ledger Book 1, ff. 414–15.
[39] KCA, Ledger Book I, ff. 414–15v. Jones, 'The College and the Chapel', p. 163; Lack, Stuchfield and Whittemore, *Cambridgeshire*, p. 36, ill. 35; Royal Commission on Historical Monuments, *City of Cambridge*, p. 116, Plate 5.
[40] For example, the great wooden screen between choir and ante-chapel, built in 1533–36 in the form of a triumphal arch, commemorates the marriage of King Henry VIII and his Queen Anne Boleyn, with intricate carvings of their intertwined initials and family badges.

abandon established anniversaries. Necessarily the abolition of Purgatory and of intercession meant a break with the elaborate liturgical practices (both communal and private) of seeking salvation characteristic of the pre-Reformation Church. But the evidence of the college's records strongly suggests that commemoration of the founder and his family, of important donors from the foundation onwards, and the recording of the lives of members of the foundation were not interrupted as might have been expected.

CHAPTER 7

Cambridge Commemorations of
Lady Margaret Beaufort's Household

Susan Powell

Lady Margaret Beaufort (1443–1509) is familiar to both scholars and the general public as the grand matriarch who engineered the marriage of her son, Henry VII, to Elizabeth of York, and in doing so united the warring Houses of Lancaster and York. Her household papers at St. John's College, Cambridge, date from 1498,[1] when, at the age of fifty-five, Lady Margaret separated from her husband, Thomas Stanley, first earl of Derby, and ran her own household as *femme sole*.[2] Stanley was her third husband. Her first husband, Edmund Tudor, had died before their son, the future Henry VII, was born and after only six months of marriage. Her second (almost immediate) marriage, to Henry Stafford, son of Humphrey, first duke of Buckingham, was longer lasting but produced no offspring. Her third marriage covered her years of maturity, from 1472, when she was approaching thirty, to 1504, when Stanley died. He had been steward to the household of Edward IV when she married him, and after Bosworth he became constable of England and high steward of the duchy of Lancaster, but his lands and principal estates were all in the north-west.[3] Lady Margaret herself owned land and property over a

[1] I am engaged in editing these documents for the British Academy, in their Records of Social and Economic History series. I wish to express my gratitude to the Master and Fellows of St. John's College, Cambridge, for their hospitality and generosity during the period I have been working on this project, and for permission to publish details of the accounts. Personal, as well as professional, thanks go to the former archivist, Malcolm Underwood, for answering many of my questions and sharing with me his unrivalled knowledge of the St. John's College archives. To his book, co-authored with Michael K. Jones, I am much indebted: M.K. Jones and M. Underwood, *The King's Mother: Lady Margaret Beaufort, Countess of Richmond and Derby* (Cambridge, 1992).
[2] The separation was probably planned soon after the execution for treason of Stanley's brother William in 1495, which was followed by a visit of the king to his mother and stepfather at Lathom and Knowsley.
[3] His principal residences in the north were at Lathom (three miles north-east of Ormskirk) and Knowsley (seven miles from Liverpool). For the burial of his first wife and other members of his family at St. James Garlickhithe, near his London residence, see C. Steer, 'The Plantagenet in the Parish: The Burial of Richard III's Daughter in Medieval London', *The Ricardian*, 24 (2014), pp. 63–73 at pp. 64–7. Although Stanley and Lady Margaret were frequently at court, the northern affiliations of her household are important (see below and S. Powell, 'Lady Margaret Beaufort as Patron of Scholars

123

wide area of the Midlands and even in the south-west,[4] but in 1498 she took a vow of chastity (confirmed at Stanley's death) and established a household at Collyweston in Northamptonshire, four miles south-west of Stamford.[5] As far as is known, she never returned to the north-west of England, although Stanley had his own rooms at Collyweston and visited occasionally until his death in 1504.[6]

It is with her separate establishment that Lady Margaret comes into her own, for us at least, because it is from then that we have most evidence of her daily life:[7] most of her household accounts (1498–1509); the accounts of James Morice, her clerk of works; numerous individual documents; and inventories of her chapel and household goods, as well as her executors' accounts. The household accounts are those of her secretary and dean of chapel, later chancellor, Henry Hornby (1499–1509); her respective cofferers, James Clarell (1498–99), Miles Worsley (1502–09), and Robert Fremingham (1509);[8] the treasurer of her household, William Bedell (1506–07); and her chamberlain, Roger Ormeston (1501–02).[9]

During these last ten years of her life Lady Margaret became closely involved with Cambridge. Cambridge was the closer of the two universities to her Midlands estates and easily reachable, not just from Collyweston but also from Hatfield, Croydon, and London, her other places of residence during these years.[10] Several members of her household had Cambridge associations or acquired them through her service.[11] Henry Hornby had graduated B.A., M.A., and D.D. at Cambridge between 1479 and 1495/96 and was master of Peterhouse from 1501 until his death in 1518. It is likely that Lady Margaret knew him from an early date – the George Hornby who was her keeper of horses in 1483 may have been his father.[12] If so, he was born close to her manor at Maxey Castle, perhaps in East Deeping or Baston, to whose churches he

and Scholarship', in *Patrons and Professionals in the Middle Ages*, ed. P. Binski and E.A. New (Donington, 2012), pp. 100–21).

4   For a list of Lady Margaret's vast estates (augmented in her son's Great Grant after Bosworth), see Jones and Underwood, *The King's Mother*, Appendix 2, pp. 262–7.

5   She already owned the manor there, as well as land and property in the area, principally Maxey Castle (Lincs.), which she had inherited from her father by right of his mother Margaret Holland.

6   He himself was buried at the Austin canons house at Burscough in Lancashire, with his two wives either side of him, although they themselves were buried elsewhere (for Eleanor Neville see note 3 above, and for Margaret Beaufort see further below). Despite attempts by Stanley's great-grandson Edward Stanley, third earl of Derby, to save the priory at the dissolution, it was suppressed and the family tombs removed to the parish church at Ormskirk.

7   Some evidence of Lady Margaret's earlier life is preserved in the Stafford accounts at Westminster Abbey (see Jones and Underwood, *The King's Mother*, *passim*).

8   From 1506 called treasurer of the chamber.

9   The dates are those of the extant accounts. For these men, see Jones and Underwood, *The King's Mother*, *passim*; Powell, 'Lady Margaret Beaufort as Patron', *passim*.

10   Hatfield was the palace of her stepson, James Stanley, bishop of Ely; Croydon was the palace of William Warham, archbishop of Canterbury; her London residence was Coldharbour.

11   M.G. Underwood, 'The Lady Margaret and her Cambridge Connections', *Sixteenth Century Journal*, 13 (1982), pp. 67–82.

12   Jones and Underwood, *The King's Mother*, p. 276; *ODNB*.

left bequests in his will.[13] When Lady Margaret set up house at Collyweston in 1498, Hornby was her secretary and dean of chapel.[14] Late in 1504 he became chancellor of her household after the elevation to the see of Exeter of her previous chancellor, Hugh Oldham.

Oldham was a Lancashire man and had probably started service as a cleric in the household of another Lancashire man, Laurence Booth, bishop of Durham. He appears to have spent time at Oxford in the 1480s, since he claimed eight years' study at Oxford in order to incept as a bachelor of civil (and perhaps canon) law at Cambridge in 1493.[15] By 1488 he was rector of Lanivet in Cornwall and secretary to the keeper of the royal hanaper, William Smith, who had risen through the patronage of the king and his mother and who became bishop of Lincoln in late 1495. This is probably the route by which Oldham became receiver of Lady Margaret's west-country estates by 1492 and her chancellor by 1502,[16] but he may have been known to her during her years with Stanley in the north of England and he is venerated in Manchester as the founder of Manchester Grammar School.[17] In the south he was a principal benefactor of the Oxford college of Corpus Christi, founded by Richard Foxe, bishop of Winchester, a colleague of Oldham.

Until his elevation to Exeter, Oldham had handled the receipts of Lady Margaret's estates with another member of her household, Hugh Ashton; thereafter Ashton became sole receiver-general and was controller of the household by 1508. He is regularly recorded in her Collyweston accounts,[18] but it seems likely that he was personally known to her in her Stanley years, since he had been employed by the Manchester collegiate church as early as 1464.[19] A Lancashire man like Oldham, he was not, it seems, trained at either university but was (again like Oldham) a very capable administrator.[20] His

---

[13] See further below.

[14] In the earliest accounts (James Clarell, 24 June 1498–12 January 1499) he is called 'master secretorye' until 22 December when he becomes 'master deane' (SJCA, D91.17, p. 61). (In quoting from the accounts, u/v and i/j are normalised, expansions are italicised, and capitalisation is minimal but modern.)

[15] *ODNB*.

[16] This had taken place 'by 1503', *ODNB*, but he is called chancellor in SJCA, D91.20, p. 5 ('Item receyved the xxvii day of M*arche* [1502] by a byll of allowanc*e* of m*aister* chauncellers m*aister* Hughe Oldoms').

[17] See L. Wooding, 'Manchester College from Foundation to Reformation', in *The History of Manchester Collegiate Church and Cathedral*, ed. J. Gregory (Manchester, forthcoming).

[18] The earliest reference in the SJCA accounts is the entry for 14 November 1498: 'Wedynsdaye. Item payde to sir Hew Assheton for the kepynge of a yonge woman that wul be a nonne … xix s. vi d.' (D91.17, p. 56). The earliest reference to his duties as receiver appears to be 19 November 1500: 'Item receyved the xix day of the said moneth of sir Hugh Ashton of the landes of Frongnalles in Kent' (SJCA, D102.10, p. 23).

[19] Jones and Underwood, *The King's Mother*, pp. 106, 151 and *sub* Ashton, p. 268. The source is F.R. Raines, *The Fellows of the Collegiate Church of Manchester*, ed. F. Renaud (Manchester, 1891), pp. 21–6 at p. 22. He was the son of Sir William Ashton of Croston in Lancashire and was still connected with the Manchester college in 1492. His *ODNB* biographer, Professor Claire Cross, does not mention Manchester but does see his rise to prominence as the result of a probable encounter with Lady Margaret in Lancashire, *ODNB*.

[20] Perhaps on the strength of this, he was incorporated M.A. of Oxford on 13 October 1507 (Raines, *The Fellows of the Collegiate Church of Manchester*, p. 23 ('Oct. 23th'

Cambridge degree of bachelor of canon law was awarded him in 1508 with a dispensation from study, presumably through Lady Margaret.

Of the others of her household mentioned above, Oldham's cousin Roger Ormeston had also been known to Lady Margaret as early as 1492 and was her chamberlain from at least 1501 until his death in 1504, when her kinsman Sir John St. John II of Bletsoe (d.1525) took over. Ormeston's early life is unknown, but he had been in Lady Margaret's service for some time, having been constable of her Corfe Castle estate in 1492–93; in 1504 he became steward of the University of Cambridge (undoubtedly through his connection to Lady Margaret) but died the same year.[21] Likewise, William Bedell had been her receiver in the 1480s and 1490s before becoming permanent treasurer by 1498.[22] Nothing is known of either Bedell or the cofferers, Clarell, Worsley, and Fremingham, in relation to Cambridge, but others of her household had Cambridge connections. John Fothede, her controller 1504–06, was master of Michaelhouse as early as 1498, took his doctorate in 1508, and was University preacher in 1509–10,[23] and Robert Bekinsall, her almoner by 1508, had been a fellow of Michaelhouse and junior proctor of the University. Lady Margaret supported his studies for the degree of bachelor of divinity in 1502,[24] he was appointed president of Queens' College in 1508, and in 1509, after her death, he became almoner to Queen Katherine.[25]

However, the man closest to Lady Margaret after her son (and in some ways before him) was none of these. He was John Fisher, a graduate of Michaelhouse himself and president of Queens' College before Bekinsall.[26] Lady Margaret had met Fisher in 1494/95 when he was senior proctor.[27] They soon developed a personal and working relationship, a partnership in which they worked together to use her money for the education and improvement of poor scholars, particularly of the north of England. (Fisher came from Beverley in Yorkshire and Lady Margaret, as we have seen, was familiar with the north of England and valued northerners as her senior household servants.) Fisher took his doctorate in theology in 1501 and became vice-chancellor of the University; in 1502 he was the first Lady Margaret reader in divinity at Cambridge; in 1504 he became bishop of Rochester and chancellor of the University, an office he then held for life.

erroneously for 'Oct. 13th'), citing Anthony à Wood, *Fasti Oxonienses, or Annals of the University of Oxford by Anthony à Wood* (London, 1815–20), p. 645). Compare Hooker's comment on Oldham as 'a man having more zeal than knowledge' (cited *ODNB* by Nicholas Orme) with Claire Cross's *ODNB* description of Ashton's expertise in administration and estate management despite no formal university education. Practical men were what Lady Margaret sought as her servants.

[21]   Jones and Underwood, *The King's Mother*, p. 280.

[22]   Jones and Underwood, *The King's Mother*, pp. 105, 109, 269. See also the *ODNB* entry by Laura Wood (forthcoming).

[23]   Jones and Underwood, *The King's Mother*, p. 274.

[24]   SJCA, D91.20, p. 24. For her regular support of scholars at both universities, and even in Paris and Orléans, see Powell, 'Lady Margaret Beaufort as Patron', pp. 104–6.

[25]   Underwood, 'The Lady Margaret and her Cambridge Connections', p. 74.

[26]   Jones and Underwood, *The King's Mother*, pp. 273–4; *ODNB*. See too R. Rex, *The Theology of John Fisher* (Cambridge, 1991).

[27]   Underwood, 'The Lady Margaret and her Cambridge Connections', p. 68.

During these years Lady Margaret was closely involved with Cambridge. By 1498 she was funding out of her own income the Lady Margaret readerships in divinity at both Oxford and Cambridge. By 1503 these were formally established, Fisher being her first Cambridge reader and Dr. John Roper at Oxford.[28] In the same year she was associated with the king and queen in the foundation of Jesus College, Cambridge,[29] and she secured lands from her ward, Edward Stafford, third duke of Buckingham, for Queens' College, Cambridge,[30] where, as we have seen, her own men, Fisher and then Bekinsall, held the post of president from 1505. In 1504 she endowed University preacherships only at Cambridge; in the same year a licence was granted for the foundation of her own college, Christ's College, created out of the existing God's House, which had been founded in 1439 to train grammar school masters. For this purpose money was diverted from Westminster, to the chagrin of the abbey. Christ's was founded (or re-founded) in 1505, but work was still underway at her death on 29 June 1509.[31] At that time her second Cambridge foundation was still in the early stages and is only mentioned as a codicil to her will.[32] The foundation of St. John's out of the twelfth-century Hospital of St. John the Evangelist took much longer to achieve than had Christ's – its foundation charter was signed in 1509 but it was not until 1516 that the college held its opening ceremony. Its existence was in the end secured almost entirely through the efforts of Fisher, with Hornby also involved. However, it was Fisher who was by far the most active of her eight executors in securing the future of her second foundation.[33]

CAMBRIDGE COMMEMORATIONS

Of those of Lady Margaret's immediate circle who were associated with Cambridge, the most intact extant memorial in Cambridge is to Hugh Ashton at St. John's College. A brass at Little St. Mary's may be that of Henry Hornby.

[28]   R. Rex, 'Lady Margaret and her Professorship 1502–1559', in *Lady Margaret Beaufort and her Professors of Divinity at Cambridge 1502 to 1649*, ed. P. Collinson, R. Rex and G. Stanton (Cambridge, 2003), pp. 19–56 (at pp. 19–27 for Fisher's role).
[29]   Underwood, 'The Lady Margaret and her Cambridge Connections', p. 69.
[30]   Jones and Underwood, *The King's Mother*, p. 214.
[31]   For the most concise description of Lady Margaret's founding of Christ's, see Jones and Underwood, *The King's Mother*, pp. 215–22. For full details see A.H. Lloyd, *The Early History of Christ's College, Cambridge: derived from contemporary documents* (Cambridge, 1934). Of interest is D. Starkey, 'A Royal Saint at Work: Henry VI, Henry VII and the Tudor Transformation of Cambridge', in *Saints and Cults in Medieval England*, ed. S. Powell (Donington, 2017), pp. 80–100.
[32]   For the will, dated 6 June 1508 and transcribed from the Grant of Probate, see St. John's College [T.G. Bonney], *Collegium Divi Johannis Evangelistae 1511–1911* (Cambridge, 1911), Appendix, 'The Will of the Foundress', pp. 101–26 (124/145–125/148 for the added details of St. John's).
[33]   Her executors were Richard Fox (bishop of Winchester), Charles Somerset, Lord Herbert (chamberlain to Henry VII), Sir Thomas Lovell (his treasurer), Sir Henry Marney (chancellor of the duchy of Lancaster), and Sir John St. John II (her own chamberlain), as well as Fisher, Hornby, and Ashton. For Fisher's pre-eminent role in the foundation of St. John's, see R. Rex, 'The Sixteenth Century', in *St. John's College Cambridge: A History*, ed. P. Linehan (Woodbridge, 2011), pp. 5–92, *passim*.

There is little physical evidence of Fisher's chantry, since he was executed as a traitor in 1535.[34] However, there is ample textual evidence, and Fisher's memorial will be discussed below, as well as the commemorative brasses to two masters of Lady Margaret's foundations: John Syclyng, master of God's House and first master of Christ's, and Nicholas Metcalfe, master of St. John's 1518–37. As already noted, Hugh Oldham left her service in 1504 to become bishop of Exeter. This is where he died in 1519 and where he is commemorated, in an elaborate chantry chapel at the south end of the retrochoir.[35] It has a contemporary wooden door and a reredos flanking the Mass of St. Gregory with the Annunciation and the Nativity, the tomb itself amply adorned with shields bearing his arms.[36] However, this account will begin with another member of Lady Margaret's household, not one of her officers, but someone frequently mentioned in her accounts. This person is commemorated with a floor brass at Christ's College, Cambridge, and, most unusually for such a commemoration, is a woman.[37]

Edith Fowler

Edith Fowler was one of Lady Margaret's gentlewomen and was responsible for her daily needs.[38] She appears first in Miles Worsley's accounts for 1502–05, and in all the accounts thereafter,[39] much more frequently than any other of Lady Margaret's women and usually in relation to repayments for sums paid out on Lady Margaret's behalf to a variety of different people in different circumstances. For example:

> Item delyvered to maistres Foler for a reward yeven unto a servand of my lady Wauce the xxiiii day of February ... xx d. [24 February 1502]
> Item delyvered the xvii[th] day of January unto maistres Fowler for a reward yeven unto maister Morgance doughtur at hir maryage ... x s. [17 January 1503]

34   He was tricked into denying the Act of Supremacy, or saying as much, and convicted of high treason. Richard Rex, *Henry VIII and the English Reformation*, 2nd edn. (Basingstoke, 2006), pp. 14–15 provides a concise and lucid explanation.
35   B. Cherry and N. Pevsner, *The Buildings of England: Devon* (New Haven and London, 2nd edn., 1989; repr. with corrections 1991), p. 380.
36   'Sable, a chevron or between three owls argent.' This is still, with the arms of the Exeter see, the coat of arms of Manchester Grammar School.
37   The brass is shared with her husband, who was not a member of Lady Margaret's household. 'The remarkable feature of the brass ... lies in its being the only example known of a monumental brass to a married couple in any college of Cambridge or of Oxford' (A.H. Lloyd, 'Two Monumental Brasses in the Chapel of Christ's College', *Proceedings of the Cambridge Antiquarian Society*, 33 (1933), pp. 61–82, at p. 63).
38   Lady Margaret Beaufort's ladies were Lady Jane and Lady Willoughby; her gentlewomen were mistresses Clifford, Parker, Fowler, Stanhope, Jane, and Radcliff; her chamberers were Perott Doren and Jane Walter (Lloyd, 'Two Monumental Brasses', p. 66 and note 3; Records of Lord Chamberlain's Department, Henry VII (TNA: PRO, LC 2/1, f. 96)).
39   Note that there are no extant cofferer's/treasurer's accounts between 12 January 1499 (the end of SJCA, D91.17) and 2 February 1502 (the start of SJCA, D91.20).

Item paid unto maistres Foler for a reward yeven unto maistres Parkers <nurse *canc.*> nurse ... xx d. [around 23 March 1504]

Item the <v *canc.*> xxviii day of January delyvered unto maistres Foler for a reward yeven unto Marmyon at his goyng to the courte ... xx s. [28 January 1505]

Item the xvii[th] day of January delyvered unto maistres Foler for a reward yeven to my lady Maneres at hir beyng with my ladys grace at Croydon ... xl s. [17 January 1506]

Item the xi[th] day of Aprell delyvered to maistres Foller for a reward yeven unto Cony my lord of Derbies servand for the bryngyng worde of the delyverance of my lady Derby ... vi s. viii d. [11 April 1507]

Item delyvered unto maistres Foller for a reward yeven unto the prior of the charterhowse in Coventre ... vi s. viii d. [around 29 January 1508]

Item to maistresse Fowler for money by hir paied to the wief of Roger Notte of Hatfeld for expense of <Roger *canc.*> Reignald my ladies ydiot the first night of his commyng ... vi d. [around 10 April 1509][40]

Mistress Fowler appears to have had special responsibility for Lady Margaret's own chamber, where items such as spices would have been kept, as in the entry in the one extant Latin roll, the accounts of William Bedell for 1506–07:

In croco. Nichil hic – tamen memorandum pro croco remanente in custodia magistre Fouler

(Saffron. Nothing here – however, remember the saffron remaining in the custody of mistress Fowler).[41]

After Lady Margaret's death she was held responsible by the executors for money and items in her mistress's bedchamber and private rooms, as in the heading to a list of precious objects in the 'Book of the Revestrie': 'Certayn juelles founde in Mastres Fowlar kepyng'.[42]

The brass is in the south-eastern corner of the ante-chapel but was probably moved there in the eighteenth century from a chapel on the north side (with so little care that it faces west, not east (Plates VIIIa&b)).[43] The marginal inscription, which is in English, is damaged and lost completely at the top,

[40] SJCA, D91.20, pp. 13, 63, 150; D91.21, pp. 9, 92; D91.19, pp. 16, 70; D102.1, f. 9v.

[41] SJCA, D91.16, sheet 25.

[42] SJCA, D91.15, f. 55v. This is a book kept in the vestry at Collyweston, the fair copy and final version of an inventory of chapel stuff and other household plate and service books annotated by Fisher, of which the draft is D102.13.

[43] For a detailed discussion of the brass and the Fowlers (as of the Syclyng brass to be discussed later), see Lloyd, 'Two Monumental Brasses', on which the discussion of the Christ's College brasses depends. Lloyd (p. 61, note 1) refers to an earlier brief mention of the brass in the *TMBS*, 2:7 (1896), p. 264. For a modern description of the chapel, see Royal Commission on Historical Monuments, *An Inventory of the Historical Monuments in the City of Cambridge*, 2 parts (London, 1959), i, pp. 28–32 (brass p. 29), and for a modern description of the brass, see W. Lack, H.M. Stuchfield, and P. Whittemore, *The Monumental Brasses of Cambridgeshire* (London, 1995), p. 22 (p. 23 for a drawing of the brass).

probably due to the depredations of William Dowsing on his visit of 2 January 1644.[44] Starting from the top right and running down the right side, what is left reads:

> of Thomas ffowler squyer and Gentilma*n* Vssher of the Chambir w*ith* the ffamous kyng Edward the iiii[th] & Edyth his wyfe And of late gentilwoman w*ith* the Right Excellent princesse Countesse of Richmound mod*er* to the most victoryouse kyng henry the vii[th] the seid Edith departed this lyff the yer of o*ur* lord 15...

There is no date of death for either Thomas or Edith, and the unfinished date for the latter led A.H. Lloyd, who investigated the brass thoroughly, to suggest that the tomb is a cenotaph (as is that of Hugh Ashton to be discussed later). He also discussed at length the four shields on the tomb (actually two shields duplicated) and the genealogy of Thomas Fowler and his third wife, Edith, née Dynham, which the shields commemorate.

Thomas's elder brother, Sir Richard Fowler (d.1477), was chancellor of the Duchy of Lancaster under Edward IV.[45] As the brass states, Thomas himself was a squire of the body and gentleman usher of the chamber to the same king, and, as Lloyd notes, he performed the same duties for Richard III.[46] Lloyd argues that it was not therefore Edith's husband who found favour with Lady Margaret (quite the reverse) but Edith's own family, and he speculates that the connection might have been through Edith's uncles, one of whom was a trustee of the marriage settlement between Lady Margaret and Stanley and another of whom she presented to the rectory of Amersham, Buckinghamshire.[47] It was Edith who served in Lady Margaret's household, although her husband was certainly well known to both Lady Margaret and Stanley from the court of Edward IV, where Stanley had been steward. Edith alone was a legatee of Lady Margaret's will, Thomas being already dead, and she was left £10 per annum from Lady Margaret's lands at Maxey.[48] In

---

[44] 'We pulled down divers pictures, and angels, and the steps ... Orat. pro anima on the brasen eagle' (T. Cooper, ed., *The Journal of William Dowsing: Iconoclasm in East Anglia during the English Civil War*, (Woodbridge, 2001), p. 188). For the circumstances of Dowsing's destruction, see P. Lindley, *Tomb Destruction and Scholarship: Medieval Monuments in Early Modern England* (Donington, 2007), pp. 114–26.

[45] Lloyd, 'Two Monumental Brasses', p. 64.

[46] Lloyd, 'Two Monumental Brasses', p. 67.

[47] Lloyd, 'Two Monumental Brasses', pp. 66–8. Lloyd (p. 66, n. 1) gives the date of her marriage to Stanley as 1482 (and of Stafford's will 2 October 1481), citing the *Testamenta Vetusta* of Nicholas Harris Nicolas (London, 1826), p. 324. Here Nicolas observes that the manuscript note of the will reads 1471 but that Dugdale's abstract has 1481, which he thinks likely since the will is noted as proved 4 May 1482. Nevertheless, the date of Stafford's death was 4 October 1471 and of Lady Margaret's remarriage early June 1472 (*ODNB*). The will is dated 2 October 1471, and probate was granted on 4 May 1482 (TNA: PRO, PROB 11/7, ff. 34–34v.).

[48] 'And also we haue yeuen *and* gra*u*nted to our*e* seru*au*nt Edith Fowler*e* late wif of Thomas Fowler wydowe certeyn parcelles of the said maners [Maxey's] lond*es and* ten*ementes* to the yerely value by estimac*i*on of xl*i*.' (St John's College, *Collegium Divi Johannis Evangelistae*, p. 116/89–92). This property passed to Elizabeth Lisle, one of Queen

December 1505 Lady Margaret had bought as an endowment for Christ's College the manor of Roydon in Essex;[49] in 1507 Edith acquired a small adjacent property in order to endow a chantry for herself and her husband at Christ's.[50] She was dead by 3 August 1514,[51] but her husband's death appears not to have been recorded. One might suspect he was older than her, given his service with Edward IV and the fact that Edith was his third wife. Lloyd suggests he died 'two or three years earlier' than 13 March 1511, the only dated record of her as widow.[52] In fact, unknown to anyone who has written on this brass, Lady Margaret's accounts record his death in late February 1506: 'Item in reward unto a seruant þat came from my lady Davers bryngyng worde of the decesse of m*aister* Foller'.[53]

John Syclyng

In the same chapel is another brass. It has lost its inscription, probably at Dowsing's visit, but Lloyd argued that it commemorates John Syclyng, first master of Christ's (Plate 14).[54] Syclyng had been a fellow of God's House from at least 1486 (concurrently of Corpus Christi from 1487) and was proctor of God's House 1490–96 and then master. Fisher and Syclyng had long experience of working together; indeed, they had both been in London on University business at the time of Fisher's first meeting with Lady Margaret in 1494. In 1501, at the time of an important case of 'town vs gown' arbitrated by Lady Margaret, Syclyng was senior proctor to Fisher's vice-chancellor.[55]

Lady Margaret's accounts have numerous references to dealings with Syclyng in the years 1504–06. At first he is 'm*aister* Syklyng maist*er* of Goddes Howse in Cambryge',[56] but after the foundation of Christ's in 1505 the new title is used:

    Katherine's gentlewomen, 3 August 1514 (Lloyd, 'Two Monumental Brasses', p. 71). For Maxey see note 5 above.

49 SJCA, D91.21, pp. 3, 58, 62, 77, 148. For the details of the purchase from Robert Radcliffe, son of the attainted John, Lord Fitzwalter, see Jones and Underwood, *The King's Mother*, p. 221.

50 Jones and Underwood, *The King's Mother*, p. 165, n. 79; Lloyd, *The Early History of Christ's College*, p. 339. Her obit was observed by the college until such things ceased in the mid-1540s, and the land was not sold until 1914 (Lloyd, 'Two Monumental Brasses', pp. 77–8).

51 See note 48 above.

52 Lloyd, 'Two Monumental Brasses', p. 72.

53 SJCA, D91.21, p. 98. The previous dated entry is 27 February and the next entry is the last day of February.

54 Lloyd, 'Two Monumental Brasses', pp. 78–82. For a modern description of the brass, see Lack, Stuchfield and Whittemore, *Cambridgeshire*, p. 24 (p. 25 for a rubbing of the brass).

55 Some details here are from the record cards of Malcolm Underwood. See too Underwood, 'The Lady Margaret and her Cambridge Connections', 67; Jones and Underwood, *The King's Mother*, pp. 90–1, 217; Lloyd, *The Early History of Christ's College*, pp. 203–6, 210.

56 'Item delyvered to Jamys Morice to delyver unto <the *canc.*> m*aister* Syklyng maist*er* of Goddes howse in Cambryge towardes the byldynge of the same delyvered the xxii day of Juyne … <lxvi *li.* xiii *s.* iiii *d. canc.*>' (SJCA, D91.21, p. 35, 22 June 1505). Compare similar entries at pp. 28, 71, 97, 99, 114, 160, and for Syclyng's expenses visiting Lady Margaret at Collyweston (with four fellows of God's House), Croydon, and Hatfield, see

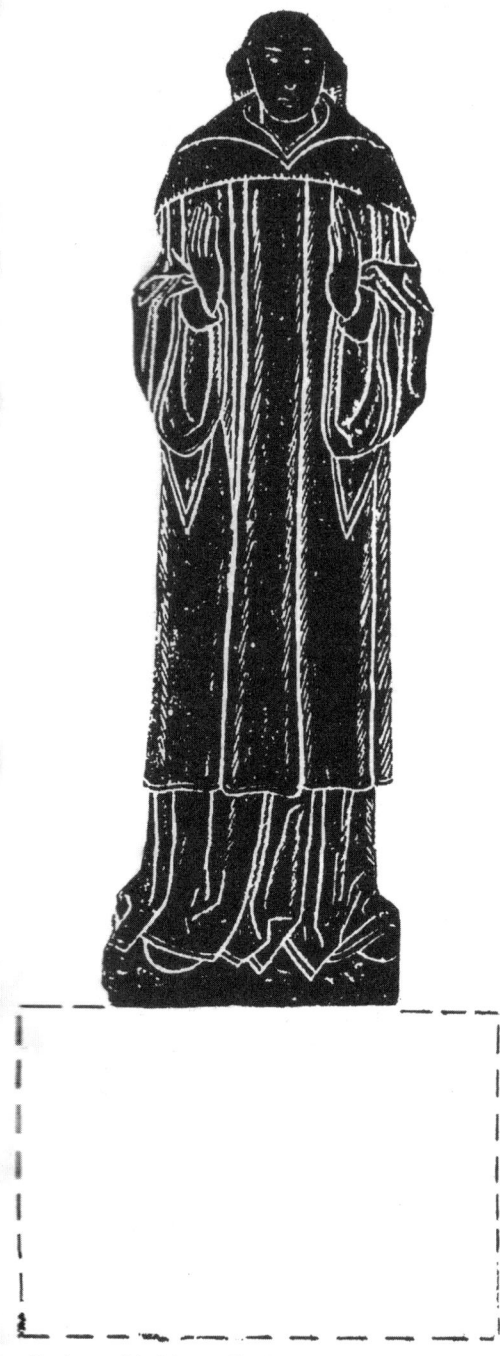

14: Brass of John Syclyng (?) (d.1506), first Master of Christ's College, Christ's College chapel, Cambridge.

Item delyvered another tyme [...] by the hand*es* off m*aster* chancellere and m*aster* controllere [i.e. Hornby and Fothede] toward þe forseid repar*acio*nes off Cristes Collage in Cambrigge to þe hand*es* off m*aster* Sykelyng.[57]

Amongst the 'sum of all the whole allowance and payments' of the year 14 January 1506 to 14 January 1507 is the record of £599 18*d.* 'delyuerd at divers tymes unto m*astyr* Scykelyng toward*es* the beldyng of Cristis Collage'.[58] Syclyng died in the autumn of 1506, but it is not until the year's end summary for 1507 that his death is confirmed by the payment of £21 to his executors, Robert Chapell and Thomas Nunn, fellows of Peterhouse and Christ's respectively, and Simeon Fyncham, priest of St. Benet's: 'Money payd to m*aster* Sikelyng*es* executo*urs* ffor the sup*er*plussage of his accompte ffor Cristez College ... xxi li.'.[59]

Henry Hornby

Just as the attribution of the Christ's College brass to Syclyng is not entirely certain, it is even less so with the brass attributed to Henry Hornby in Little St. Mary's or St. Mary the Less (Plate 15), which had been known as St. Peter outside Trumpington Gate and was used by Peterhouse as its chapel until a new one was built 1628–32.[60] To the south-east of the chancel there is a three-quarter-length brass effigy lacking its foot inscription: this was presumably removed at the time of Dowsing's visits on 21 and 29–30 December 1643 and was certainly already missing when William Cole visited in the 1740s.[61] It is dated *c.*1500 in Lack, Stuchfield, and Whittemore, who suggest that it commemorates John Warkworth, master of Peterhouse (d.1500).[62] After Warkworth, Thomas Denman, one of Lady Margaret's physicians, was briefly master, followed by Hornby from 1501 until his death in 1518.[63] Since the

pp. 16, 56, 127. SJCA, D91.21 covers 14 January 1505 to 14 January 1507. For a discussion of the whole process, see Jones and Underwood, *The King's Mother*, pp. 215–22.

[57] SJCA, D102.10, p. 108 (undated beyond citing the twenty-first year, i.e. between 22 August 1505 and 21 August 1506). In SJCA, D91.21, Christ's College replaces God's House from the year's end 1505 (p. 71).

[58] SJCA, D91.21, pp. 152, 160.

[59] SJCA, D91.19, p. 52. His will is dated 24 September 1506 (Lloyd, 'Two Monumental Brasses', p. 81), but money for Christ's was still being delivered to him as late as 21 September 1506 (SJCA, D91.21, p. 127). Thereafter he is not mentioned and money is delivered instead to Lady Margaret's usher of the chamber, Robert Merbury (pp. 135, 138). For the names of the executors, see Lloyd, 'Two Monumental Brasses', p. 81.

[60] In Hornby's will (TNA: PRO, PROB 11/19, ff. 43v–44v.) it is referred to as St. Mary of Canterbury or Blessed Mary and Peter outside Trumpington Gate.

[61] Cooper, ed., *The Journal of William Dowsing*, pp. 155–61, 192–4. 'We pulled down ... divers superstitious letters in gold' (*ibid.*, p. 156).

[62] Lack, Stuchfield and Whittemore, *Cambridgeshire*, pp. 68, 70 (p. 71 for a drawing of the brass). See too Cooper, ed., *The Journal of William Dowsing*, p. 194.

[63] *BRUC*, pp. 187, 313–14.

brass represents a doctor of divinity in cap and robes,[64] Hornby seems a more likely candidate than Warkworth who is only recorded M.A. and B.Th., not D.D.[65]

However, it is not entirely certain that Hornby was buried at Peterhouse: he may have been buried at Clare College, where he seems to have been a fellow, or at Tattershall, where he was warden.[66] According to his will (16 March 1518), a tomb was to be built in whichever chapel was nearest to his place of death and exequies were to be performed at once.[67] Provision was made for ceremonies a week after his death at the two places where he had not been buried. In all these his family and Lady Margaret Beaufort were to be remembered, and the members of the college rewarded. A priest should be employed to celebrate for a year in his burial place, the priest being his own chaplain, should he be buried at Peterhouse.

Ten poor scholars were to be supported at the University (to the sum of £20), three poor scholars at Peterhouse were to receive clothing annually and their lectures paid (to the sum of £40, to be put into the common chest where Warkworth's money was kept), and three of the neediest sizars were to have 5s. each a year (to the sum of £60). To St. John's he left his largest parchment breviary, to be chained in the chapel, and his parchment missal; all the books from Edmund Hanson's library were to be rebound and given to the library at St. John's.[68] To the library at Clare he left seven volumes of Hugh of Vienne and Augustine's *De civitate dei*, and to Peterhouse four volumes of the Bible with Nicholas of Lyra's commentary and four books of the college's choosing. Other bequests were to his family, the poor in all his livings, and the religious houses where he was a member of the confraternity. He left altar cloths to the altar of St. Thomas in the priory of St. James, East Deeping (and a corporal),

---

[64] The effigy wears the *capa clausa* of a D.D. (also found on brasses of doctors of canon law). I am indebted to Sir John Baker for answering my requests for information, and the statement here on Hornby's academic dress, as well as the one on Ashton's (note 80 below), is based on my understanding of Sir John's responses. Any errors are my own. On the *capa clausa*, see J.H. Baker, 'A Comparison of Academical and Legal Costume on Memorial Brasses', pp. 90–105 in this volume.

[65] *BRUC*, pp. 618–19 *sub* Warkworth, John. The suggestion (without further justification) is that of Rogers, 'Cambridgeshire Brasses', p. 315.

[66] *ODNB*; T.A. Walker, *A Biographical Register of Peterhouse Men and Some of Their Neighbours from the Earliest Days (1284) to the Commencement (1616) of the First Admission Book of the College, Part 1 1284–1574* (Cambridge, 1927), p. 95. The references to Clare in Hornby's will (TNA: PRO, PROB 11/19, ff. 43v–44v.) make his association with the college certain, despite Emden, *BRUC*, p. 313 sub Hornby: 'Yorks. Son of George and Emma. Stated to have been sometime Fellow of Clare and of Michaelhouse [Harrison, 24, Walker i.94] but no evidence found to support either of these claims'.

[67] If he was buried at Peterhouse, his chantry chapel may have been on the opposite side (i.e. the south side) from Warkworth's (R. Willis and J. Willis Clark, *The Architectural History of the University of Cambridge, and of the Colleges of Cambridge and Eton*, 4 vols. (Cambridge, 1886), i, pp. 57–9, iv, no. 3 (Fig. 2)).

[68] Hanson had succeeded Hornby at Tattershall in 1508 (Jones and Underwood, *The King's Mother*, p. 132); he had died in 1511 (D. Lepine, *A Brotherhood of Canons serving God: English Secular Cathedrals in the Later Middle Ages* (Woodbridge, 1995), p. 148). There is no record of his books, or of Hornby's donation of books, at St. John's. I am grateful to Kathryn McKee, the Special Collections librarian, for checking the college's provenance index, benefactors' lists, and library catalogue.

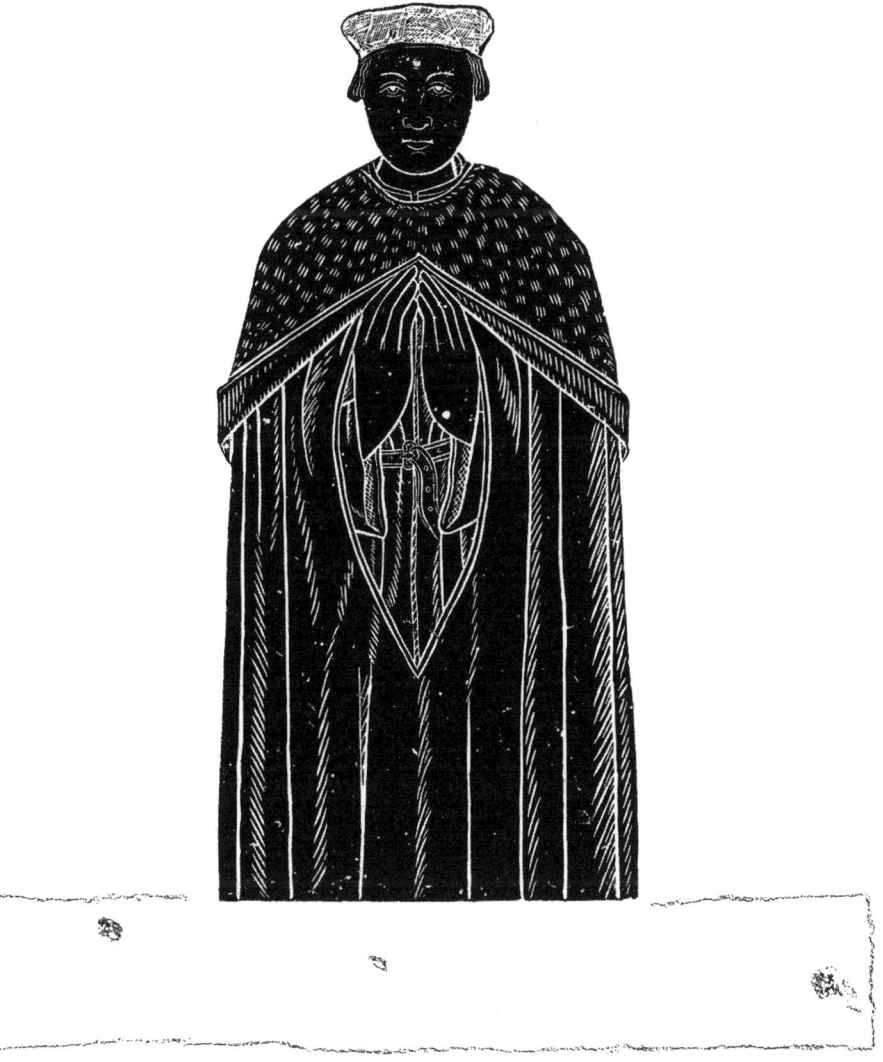

15: Brass of Henry Hornby (?) (d.1518), Master of Peterhouse, former secretary
and dean of Chapel, later chancellor to Lady Margaret Beaufort,
St. Mary the Less, Cambridge.

to the Guild of the Blessed Mary in Baston (with Lent vestments), and to
Warkworth's chapel in Peterhouse (purple velvet with vestments).[69]

The brass may not be that of Hornby, but even if it is not, he is in fact
commemorated elsewhere in Peterhouse. Until the early 1750s panelling
in the Combination Room displayed a series of sixteenth-century and
later panel-portraits of former masters, with the names and dates of those

---

[69] For altar fittings found hidden at Peterhouse in 1650, see Cooper, ed., *The Journal of
William Dowsing*, p. 158.

portrayed painted on them. Eighteen of these are now in the Hall, fixed to the dais and to the late-nineteenth-century screen opposite it. Second from the left on the screen is Hornby, dated 1516 (Plate IX).[70] In view of this it is interesting that Nicholas Rogers has suggested that the brass at St. Mary the Less was 'perhaps derived from contemporary portrait-painting'.[71]

Hugh Ashton

There is no doubt about the memorial to Hugh Ashton, Lady Margaret's receiver-general and (by the time of her death) controller of her household. The dominant monument in the north part of the ante-chapel of St. John's College chapel (George Gilbert Scott, 1866–69) is a brightly painted transi tomb which depicts a robed Ashton above a skeletal cadaver (Plates X a–c).[72] Ashton refers to his chantry in his will: his body is to be buried at St. John's 'before the awter where the preest*es* of my foundacion shall synge', 'and there in the wall to be made my similitude in ij ymag*es*. one lyvely and an other dedely'.[73] In fact, he was buried in York Minster.[74] His monument at St. John's was moved from the old chapel when it was demolished for the new one,[75] and it is in Scott's new chapel that it was accorded greater honour than it had had for most of its existence.[76]

---

[70] Royal Commission on Historical Monuments, *City of Cambridge*, ii, p. 160; Willis and Clark, *Architectural History*, i, p. 65 (no. 11).

[71] Rogers, 'Cambridgeshire Brasses', p. 315.

[72] For the old and new chapels, see Willis and Clark, *Architectural History*, ii, pp. 280–308, 324–50.

[73] TNA: PRO, PROB 11/21, ff. 24–24v. In a letter of 12 May 1520 from the president, John Smyth, to Nicholas Metcalfe, master 1518–37 (see further below), who was in London at the time, Smyth mentions as one reason why he has not left Cambridge for Lincoln: 'We haue many warkmen … for mast*er* Ascheton chapell' (SJCA, D94/500). SJCA, D57.92 records the 1522 fulfilment of Ashton's will in relation to his chantry ('This is the bill of parcells lade owt ffor the bulding of m*aster* ashton Chapell') and his scholars ('This is the byll of parcells lad owt for m*aster* ashton scollers in sant Johns Colleg in Cambryge'). For a transcription, see C.H. Cooper, *The Lady Margaret: A Memoir of Margaret, Countess of Richmond and Derby*, ed. J.E.B. Mayor (Cambridge, 1874), pp. 254–6.

[74] The will refers to his burial at St. John's ('where my body shall rest'), although it is clear that he died at York (see further below). Two of the executors were York clerics (the dean of the Minster and a canon and prebendary), as were the witnesses (the provost of St. William's College and the chamberlain of the Minster), and the notaries were York residents. (For this I am grateful to Professor Claire Cross, as for much useful correspondence on the matter of Ashton's illness and death in York.) Ashton had earlier been ill in London, since he asks for 100*s*. to be given to his cousin Osbern's wife 'for suche paynes as she toke wi*th* me in my sekenes in London'.

[75] Also moved were the arches of the piscina and the stalls of the old chapel (*The Builder*, 15 May 1869). The piscina is in the south wall of the chancel of the new chapel, while the twenty-two most easterly stalls were in the original chapel.

[76] Having discovered that the old chapel was the converted chapel of the original Hospital of St. John, Scott had in fact suggested incorporating it into the new chapel as the south aisle. 'This, however, being considered hardly compatible with the practical uses of a college chapel, was not adopted, and a wholly new chapel was determined on' (*The Builder*, 15 May 1869). For the details that follow, see Willis and Clark, *Architectural History*, ii, pp. 287–88; St. John's College, *Collegium Divi Johannis Evangelistae*, pp. 15–16; A.C. Crook, *From the Foundation to Gilbert Scott: A History of the Buildings of St. John's College*

The chantry in the old chapel had protruded from the north wall of the ante-chapel, with windows east, west, and north.[77] Despite major changes during the reigns of Henry VIII and Edward VI, the chapel had been restored to its former state during Mary's reign under the master, George Bullock. However, when Mary died in 1558, Bullock was deprived and went into exile abroad, and the new master, James Pilkington, appropriated Ashton's chantry for his own use (it was next to the Master's Lodge which was at this time between the Hall and the chapel).[78] The altar had been ripped out in Elizabeth's reign. Briefly restored as a chapel when William Beale was master (1634–44), it was desecrated in the Civil War, and at the time of Scott's restoration was again part of the domestic offices of the Master's Lodge, walled off from the chapel itself. The footprint of the old chapel is marked in the grass in First Court at St. John's, and the original position of Ashton's chantry can be ascertained today by the fact that Thomas Baker (1656–1740), the famous antiquary of St. John's and an Ashton fellow himself (although technically ejected for refusing to swear the oath of abjuration), was buried next to it, as he wished.[79]

The Ashton memorial consists of a marble altar-tomb with two effigies, the upper one on a marble slab with a brass fillet-inscription, and the lower one visible through three open arches in each long side. There are several oddities and inconsistencies about the whole structure. The cadaver lies in a loose shroud and wears a cap. The effigy above wears a white-sleeved surplice over a red-sleeved cassock, with a fur almuce (shoulder cape, worn in choir services) and a black cloak, the *capa nigra* of a master of arts, with a hood worn over it. The M.A. accords better with his status than the 'Dr. Hugh Ashton' which is recorded in the present-day inscription attached to the tomb. The surplice, almuce, and cassock all suggest an ecclesiastical rather than a University context and are more likely to refer to his final preferment as archdeacon of York.[80]

Cambridge 1511–1885 (Cambridge, 1980), pp. 18, 20; Rex, 'The Sixteenth Century', p. 61.

[77] The building expenses (note 73 above) refer to work carried out by Cobb, the stonemason, and Grene, the smith, as well as a bricker and a plumber (for glazing the windows). The materials largely comprised freestone, bricks, lime, sand, chalkstone, and lead for a total sum of £45 16s. 8d. Invaluable for details of the 1640s improvements to the old chapel, as well as the 1880s construction of the new chapel, are the college rentals (SJCA, SB4.1–88) which date from 1555–1985.

[78] For Mary's reign and the masterships of Bullock and Pilkington, see Rex, 'The Sixteenth Century', pp. 49–63.

[79] 'Just as long as Baker's memorial stone remains within the outline of the Old Chapel in First Court, so shall we know exactly where the antechapel and Ashton's chantry were' (Crook, *From the Foundation to Gilbert Scott*, p. 19). For Baker, see *ODNB*. For Baker's full comments on the Ashton chantry, see T. Baker, *History of the College of St. John the Evangelist, Cambridge*, 2 vols., ed. John E.B. Mayor (Cambridge, 1869), i, pp. 93–6. The book has always been the first resort of the scholar of St. John's.

[80] For Ashton's M.A., see note 20 above. The scarlet cassock has perhaps been misunderstood (or painted afresh) as the festal gown of a D.D., who would wear a scarlet, not a black, *capa*. 'J.A.C.' (John Crook, hereafter Crook) refers to the effigy as 'in full canonicals', i.e. the dress of a clergyman or ecclesiastic ('Babes, Sucklings, and Hugh Ashton's

The tomb is covered with an elaborate canopy of freestone or clunch with moulded and shafted supports.[81] Ashton's rebus (an ash tree and a tun or barrel) is in the spandrels of the arches and on the twisted pinnacles in the middle of the wrought-iron grille which encases the tomb-chest and which has a broad band bearing another inscription. The grille itself was made by Cornelius Symondson, who also made the grille around Lady Margaret's tomb in Westminster Abbey.[82] In 1637–38 the restoration of the chapel involved cleaning the bars and the six 'great postes', and providing new ironwork for twenty-two 'pikes', four fleur-de-lys, six tuns, and 'a new Crowne'.[83] Thereafter the monument was neglected until the building of the new chapel led to its removal late in 1868, when it was set up in the new chapel 'ready for extensive restoration'.[84] The effigies have been much restored, especially the hands, feet, and probably the face of the upper effigy.[85] The grille was also restored, by Edmund Beales of Cambridge, although the six large posts and the smaller posts between them (the 'pikes') must be original.[86] How much of the stone canopy has been restored is hard to judge, but it seems likely, given the precarious history of the chapel, that the canopy and surrounds were indeed extensively restored.[87]

The bearing of this on the present essay relates to the two brass inscriptions, one around the tomb, the other around the grille. Perhaps for the first

---

Tomb', *The Eagle*, 75 (1993), pp. 29–32, at p. 29). (*The Eagle* is the college magazine of St. John's.)

[81] For a careful description of the whole ensemble (within the entry for St. John's), see Royal Commission on Historical Monuments, *City of Cambridge*, ii, pp. 187–202 (p. 191 and Plate 243).

[82] S. Bradley and N. Pevsner, *The Buildings of England: Cambridgeshire* (New Haven and London, 2014), p. 202. For Lady Margaret's grille (1526–29), see 'R.F.S.' (R.F. Scott, hereafter Scott), 'Notes from the College Records', *The Eagle*, 18, no. 105 (December, 1894), pp. 1–10; R.F. Scott, 'On the Contracts for the Tomb of the Lady Margaret Beaufort, Countess of Richmond and Derby, mother of King Henry VII, and Foundress of the Colleges of Christ and St. John in Cambridge; with some illustrative documents', *Archaeologia*, 66 (1915), pp. 365–76, at pp. 373–6.

[83] Willis and Clark, *Architectural History*, ii, p. 288, n. 4. There are six large iron struts ('postes') at the four corners and in the middle of each long side, and twenty narrower and shorter iron struts ('pikes') between the large struts on the north and south sides. The fleur-de-lys may refer to the cresting of the monument, the tuns are part of the rebus topping each large strut, and the crown may refer to the square crowns within which these tuns rest.

[84] Crook, *From the Foundation to Gilbert Scott*, pp. 90–114, at p. 108. The authors of *Collegium Divi Johannis Evangelistae* (A.C. Seward and T.G. Bonney) noted in 1911 that Ashton's monument, 'enclosed by a contemporary iron grille', had been removed to the new chapel (p. 15).

[85] Royal Commission on Historical Monuments, *City of Cambridge*, ii, p. 191.

[86] Crook, *From the Foundation to Gilbert Scott*, pp. 109–10.

[87] The Scott scholar Professor Gavin Stamp is of the opinion that George Gilbert Scott's son, also George Gilbert Scott (1839–97), would have been involved in the chantry work (*pers. comm.* August 2015): 'I believe that GG junior had a considerable hand in what happened. He was partly resident in Cambridge, both as an undergraduate and as a Fellow of Jesus in the mid-1860s and I know that he was instrumental in finding homes for some of the furnishings of the old Chapel – e.g. the screen going to Whissendine Church in Rutland. I am convinced that it was Scott junior who was responsible for bits of the old master's Lodge &c. being installed in the new master's Lodge, so I can well believe that he would have taken a close interest in reconstructing the Ashton tomb.'

time after Scott's work at St. John's, the tomb was restored in 1945 under the direction of Professor E.W. Tristram. The effigy was painted (somewhat garishly) by Mr. Toller, the college painter, who had painted the Front Gatehouse a decade earlier; the grille was removed, cleaned of 'dirt and rust', and put back in position by Mr. Topper, senior.[88] This seems to have resulted in two sections of brass being wrongly replaced. The brass on each side is made up of two sections, the south ones correctly placed from west to east (1) and (2), but the north ones (which one would expect to be (3) and (4), i.e. continuing round the blank east side to the north side) are now (4) and (3). It seems likely that this is an error that happened at the time of the 1945/46 restoration.[89] The grille inscription should correctly read:

(1) PRIDIE NONAS IANUARI[I] PERPETVO ANNVIS EXEQUI/ (2) IS CELEBRATIS PRESES MAGISTRO AC SENIORI V S. / (3) [S]OCIVS QVILIBET XII D. SCOLASTICVS ITEM / (4) QVILIBET VI D. EX PIA DEFVNCTI INSTITVCIO[NE]

(4 January in perpetuity after the annual exequies have been celebrated, the president to the master and to the senior fellow 5s., each fellow 12d., likewise each scholar 6d. out of the pious foundation of the dead man).

Even with this rearrangement, the brass inscription is oddly poor Latin.[90] As for the brass fillet around the tomb itself, that has its own problems, particularly in relation to the date it gives for Ashton's death. It is in part so discoloured now as to be hard to read, but it is clear from Willis and Clark's transcription that it should read (south side, west to east (1), and then (2) north side, east to west):

(1) HIC SITVS EST HVGO ASSHETON ARCH[IDECA]NVS EBOR' QUI AD CHRISTIANE RELIGIONIS AVGMENTVM SOCIOS DVOS EX LANCASTR' TOTIDEMQVE SCHOLARES SOCIVM ET SCHOLAREM EBOR' COM' SOCIVMQUE ET SCHOLAREM (2) DVNELM' DIOC' ORIVNDVS SVIS IMPENSIS PIE INSTITVIT ATQUE SINGVLIS A SE INSTITVTIS SOCIIS

---

[88] Crook, 'Babes, Sucklings, and Hugh Ashton's Tomb', p. 31. 'Clifford Evans thinks that a specialist in wrought iron must also have been involved, but that trail is now cold' (*ibid.*, p. 32). For details of the care taken with the Front Gatehouse, see 'The Painting of the Front Gate', *The Eagle*, 50, no. 221 (June 1938), pp. 249–53.

[89] The inscription appears to have been correctly placed in 1886 (Willis and Clark, *Architectural History*, ii, p. 350). The problem is elucidated with humour by John Crook ('Babes, Sucklings, and Hugh Ashton's Tomb'). The Latin transcriptions and translations are my own, with the aid of Willis and Clark for the transcriptions and of my Latinist friend Mr Peter Howell, formerly of Royal Holloway College, University of London, for the translations. The missing or illegible parts of the inscriptions are in square brackets here and below.

[90] There is no verb ('should give' must be understood after 'preses'), and the nominative cases ('socius', 'scolasticus') assume another omitted verb ('should receive'). The –NE of INSTITUCIO is missing, as is the –I of IANUARII, and the S– of SOCIVS is partly lost. It may be that other parts of the original inscription have been lost.

CONSVETVM SOCIORVM STIPENDIVM SOLIDIS XL ANNVIS ADAUXIT
OBIIT IX CALEN' DECEMB' AN' M D XXII

(Here is placed Hugh Ashton archdeacon of York who to the increase of
the Christian religion piously instituted at his own expense two fellows
from Lancashire and the same number of scholars, a fellow and a scholar
from the county of Yorkshire, a fellow and a scholar from the diocese of
Durham, and for those individual fellows instituted by him increased the
usual stipend of Fellows to 40s. a year.[91] He died 23 November 1522.)[92]

The brass fillet gives Ashton's date of death as 23 November 1522; his will is
dated 7 December 1522 and was proved on 9 March 1523. The discrepancy
was noted by Baker and puzzled him.[93] The grille gives 4 January as the date
of his obits, presumably the day of his burial, as required by his will.[94] However,
the confusion is to some extent explained by the event of 12 July 1557, when
the then master, George Bullock, accompanied by fellows and scholars, visited
York expressly to view Ashton's place of burial.[95] Interestingly, the record of
their visit includes a transcription of the words engraved on the York tomb
(presumably part of a longer inscription):

Hic situs est Hugo Ashton archidiaconus Eboracensis qui ad Christianae religionis
augmentum socios ii e Lancastria totidemque scolares, sociumque et scolarem
Eboracensis, sociumque et scolarem Dunelmiensis diocesis oriundos, suis impensis
pie instituit, atque singulis a se institutis sociis supra consuetum sociorum
stipendium solidis quadraginta adauxit; obiit nono Calend. decembris anno
Domini 1522.[96]

[91]   The will refers only to his having already established four fellowships and now establishing four scholarships (no place of origin is mentioned).

[92]   For the Latin, cf. Willis and Clark, *Architectural History*, ii, p. 350. The nominative 'oriundus' (descended from) appears to have no referent (other than Ashton himself, in
which case a further phrase would appear to be missing). See further note 96 below.

[93]   'There must be a mistake in the inscription [on the brass fillet], for his will is dated
December 7 an. 1522, and proved March 9. There can be no mistake in the will, for the
codicil to it is dated the same day, viz. Dec. 7' (Baker, *History of the College of St. John the
Evangelist, Cambridge*, i, p. 94, fn. 4).

[94]   In a Memorandum to his will Ashton left a quarter of his plate to St. John's on the understanding that the master and fellows would 'kepe a yerely obite for me the day of my
buriall foreuer in the said college'.

[95]   Baker, *History of the College of St. John the Evangelist, Cambridge*, i, pp. 94–5. The visit
(recorded in the 'Thin Red Book', SJCA, C7.11, f. 74.) was prompted by a Sampson
Wyvell of Masham, Yorkshire, although his reason for doing so is unrecorded (*ibid.*, i,
p. 346 (no. 61)). The date 1557 is assumed from the document's reference to 'ye xii
day of July in ye third & fourth yere of our soueraigne lord & lady the kynges & quenes
maiestyes most godly reygnes' (Baker's '12 Jul. 3 and 4 Ph. and M.'), although 12 July
1557 would today be recorded as 3 and 5 Philip and Mary (and 12 July 1556 as 2 and 4
Philip and Mary).

[96]   Reproduced in *The Funeral Sermon of Margaret Countess of Richmond and Derby ... Preached
by Bishop Fisher in 1509*, ed. J. Hymers (Cambridge, 1840), pp. 228–9 (no. 13), originally edited by Baker and with his Preface. I have compared the text given by Baker
with the original in the 'Thin Red Book' (see note 95 above) and there are no substan-
tive differences. It may be noted that the Latin 'oriundos' of the York transcription is

The only material difference between this and the inscription on the brass fillet at St. John's is that in the York inscription the York scholar and fellow are to come from the diocese (according to the most likely interpretation of '*sociumque et scolarem Eboracensis … diocesis oriundos*'), but in the St. John's inscription they are to come from the county (*SOCIVM ET SCHOLAREM EBOR' COM' … ORIVNDVS*).[97] What is strange is that the record of the 1557 visit does not mention that the inscription is the same as at St. John's. Since the visit was during the reign of Philip and Mary, when the chapel was restored to its former state under the master, George Bullock (the same master who visited York),[98] one must assume not only that it served to ascertain the whereabouts of Ashton's body, but that it expressly led to the brass fillet being inserted around his tomb at St. John's. Even if this is the case (and it seems very likely), the fact that York recorded the wrong date of death is still strange. One can only assume that an error was made in the original inscription or (perhaps more likely) the later transcription.[99] There is no record extant in York, and in October 1645 the brass was stripped from the grave stones there and used to repair the fabric and bells.[100]

When Ashton died in 1522 he had been archdeacon of York for six years and was a residentiary canon and prebendary (as he had been at St. Stephen's chapel, Westminster, where his will made provision for an obit, as it did at York). A memorial window was set up for him in St. Michael le Belfrey, York, when the church was rebuilt after his death (1525–37).[101] The church always attracted the wealthy and important, situated as it is adjoining the Minster on the south-west side. Successive antiquarians recorded the Ashton window, with

---

preferable to the erroneous 'oriundus' of the St. John's inscription. Baker appears to note this improvement by italicising *oriundos* (*History of the College of St. John the Evangelist, Cambridge*, i, p. 94).

[97] The will makes plain that the place of origin was agreed already: 20 marks were to be raised from a debt owed by John Mundy, the London goldsmith. Of this, 15 marks (£10) were to be spent in exhibitions for four scholars 'after the fourme as my ladies scolers be there [i.e. at St. John's] founden'. (For the preference for fellows and scholars from nine northern counties in the Christ's and St. John's statutes, see further below.) The remaining 5 marks (£3 6s. 8d.) should go to 'the augmentacioun of the lyving and exhibicioun of my said four scolers so by me founded yf I doo it not myself'. There were also four fellows 'which they be already bounden perpetually to fynde afore tyme to pray for me by their comen seall'. The will makes plain that the augmentation should go to the scholars, not the fellows.

[98] On Bullock's actions as Marian Master, see Rex, 'The Sixteenth Century', pp. 51–9.

[99] His death '*nono Calend. januarii*' ('*januarii*' rather than '*decembris*') would provide a death date of 24 December, and his delayed burial until 4 January would then be explained by the intervening Christmas obligations. However, one might note that the use of *Calendae* to mean 'month' (i.e. he died 9 December) would be unusual but not unprecedented, both in classical Latin (C.T. Lewis, C. Short, *A Latin Dictionary* (Oxford, 1966), *sub Kalendae*, II) and in medieval Latin (R.E. Latham and D.R. Howlett, *Dictionary of Medieval Latin from British Sources* (London, 1975–2013), *sub Kalenda*, 1e). Medieval Latin also allows the use of 'kalenda' in the singular to mean 'day', as in '*tali kalenda obiit frater N.*' ['on such a day died brother N.'] from the Customary of St. Augustine's Canterbury (*ibid., sub Kalenda*, 3).

[100] Lindley, *Tomb Destruction and Scholarship*, p. 120. The paving was replaced between 1731 and 1738 (S. Badham and J. Dent, 'New Light on Lost Brasses in York Minster', *TMBS* 19:3 (2016), pp. 235–48).

[101] There is no provision for this in his will.

a Latin inscription, the quartered arms of Ashton (probably, and unusually, quartered with St. Hugh) and the arms of SS Peter, Paul, and William (for the Minster); the figures of SS Peter, Paul, William, and Hugh were represented in the main lights of the window.[102] There are now seven windows of *c*.1530 in the north and south aisles. Although the north was completely rearranged in the 1960s and the south aisle is also altered, an image of St. Hugh (Ashton's namesake) survives in the third window from the east in the south aisle, recognisable by his pet swan at his feet (Plate XI).[103]

John Fisher

Ashton's endowment of eight northern fellowships and scholarships, four for Lancashire and two each for Yorkshire and Durham, was not unusual for one familiar with Lady Margaret's own preferences.[104] She had spent time in the north-west of England, and she herself favoured northerners in the statutes of Christ's. After her death that bias was continued by her close confidant John Fisher, bishop of Rochester in his preparation of the statutes for St. John's. Fisher himself was from Beverley in the East Riding of Yorkshire, and he endowed four fellows and two scholars at St. John's, all to be from Yorkshire or Richmondshire, of which Lady Margaret was countess.[105] In both

---

[102] 'Orate p[ro] a[n]i[m]a magistri Hugoni[s] de Asheton quondam canonici residentiarij eccl[es]ia cathedralis Ebori cujus devotione hoc fenestra vitrata fuit A[nno] d[omi]ni M quingentesimo …' (C.M. Barnett, 'Memorials and Commemoration in the Parish Churches of Late Medieval York', 2 vols. (unpub. D.Phil. thesis, University of York, 1997), i, p. 306) (as recorded by Barnett from Dodsworth, but the bracketed expansions are my own). For details of the antiquarians and their transcriptions, see Barnett, 'Memorials and Commemoration', i, pp. 200–1, 303–6. Baker recorded the same inscription, but as on glass at St. Leonard's Hospital, York (*History of the College of St. John the Evangelist, Cambridge*, i, p. 4, where Baker gives the inscription below a Latin verse of his own in honour of Ashton). This appears to be an error on Baker's part which has found its way into Ashton's ODNB entry, to whose author, Professor Claire Cross, I am grateful for the convincing suggestion that Baker found the detail in F. Drake, *Eboracum* (1736), where Drake quotes from Dodsworth in a section on St. Michael le Belfrey which occurs just after one on St. Leonard's (hence Baker's mistake).

[103] Light a, window sIV. P. Gibson, 'The Stained and Painted Glass of York', in *The Noble City of York*, ed. Alberic Stacpoole and others (York, 1972), pp. 67–233, at pp. 195–201. At the time Gibson was superintendent of the Glass Workshop of the York Glaziers' Trust. The three in the north aisle were put there in the 1960s, made up of jumbled glass from the north-east window. The inscriptions are also new, based on Roger Dodsworth's early-seventeenth-century transcriptions. The donor figures do not necessarily relate to these inscriptions. The south aisle contains four ancient (but not unaltered) windows. I am grateful to Sarah Brown, Director of the York Glaziers' Trust, for further information on these windows. For the medieval glass at St. Michael-le-Belfrey, specifically 'the largest quantity of pre-Reformation glass picturing Thomas Becket to survive in England outside of Canterbury Cathedral', see R. Koopmans, 'Early Sixteenth-Century Glass at St. Michael-le-Belfrey and the Commemoration of Thomas Becket in Late Medieval York', *Speculum*, 89 (2014), pp. 1040–100, at p. 1047.

[104] Thomas Baker (an Ashton fellow himself, as noted above) had been born in County Durham.

[105] Rex, 'The Sixteenth Century', p. 16.

colleges, 'half the original foundation places were to be taken by men from nine Northern counties'.[106]

Hornby, Ashton, and Fisher were arguably the household servants closest to Lady Margaret, and all three were amongst the executors of her will. No others came from her household, except for her kinsman Sir John St. John, her chamberlain.[107] In Lady Margaret's last year, 1509, she no longer signed her accounts on each page; instead these three scrutinised and signed them. As executors who had worked intimately with Lady Margaret and her household, they were the prime movers in securing the future of St. John's after her death: 'Fisher seeking help at court, Hornby supervising affairs in Cambridge, Ashton assisting Hornby to manage such revenues as were available'.[108] All of them lived to see the college established, officially in 1511 (although the formal opening ceremony was not until 29 July 1516, the seventh anniversary of Lady Margaret's month's mind).[109]

However, Fisher's was the pre-eminent role in securing the foundation of St. John's, and he must be considered co-founder with Lady Margaret. He did all the necessary networking and fundraising after her death on 29 June 1509, coercing her grandson Henry VIII into giving more than he wanted (although he held back from the full extent with which she had planned to endow the college)[110] and, as noted above, using his own money towards its foundation and to establish scholarships and lectureships. Without him St. John's would not exist today. He had planned to donate even more, including his magnificent library, but the college was deprived of all his bequests at his execution.[111]

Work had started on Fisher's chantry chapel at St. John's on 16 June 1525. It was in the prime position, north of the chancel, filling the space between

[106] M. Underwood, 'John Fisher and the Promotion of Learning', in *Humanism, Reform and the Reformation: The Career of Bishop John Fisher*, ed. B. Bradshaw and E. Duffy (Cambridge, 1989), pp. 25–46, at p. 28. See Powell, 'Lady Margaret Beaufort as Patron', *passim* (pp. 115–16 for the statutes of Christ's and St. John's). For full details of the statutes of both colleges, see H. Rackham, *Early Statutes of Christ's College, Cambridge* (Cambridge, 1927) and *Early Statutes of the College of St. John the Evangelist in the University of Cambridge*, ed. J.E.B. Mayor (Cambridge, 1859). For the successive versions of the statutes of St. John's, particularly in relation to the promotion and demotion of northerners, see Underwood, 'John Fisher and the Promotion of Learning', pp. 25–2, 33–3, 38–3; Rex, 'The Sixteenth Century', pp. 18–20, 33–9, 43–4, 49, 80–2.

[107] For the other executors see note 33 above.

[108] Jones and Underwood, *The King's Mother*, p. 235.

[109] For the early history of the college, see Rex, 'The Sixteenth Century'; Crook, *From the Foundation to Gilbert Scott*; St. John's College, *Collegium Divi Johannis Evangelistae*.

[110] He had promised £2,800 in lieu of his grandmother's estates but gave only £1,200 (Scott, 'Notes from the College Records', *The Eagle*, 19, no. 108 (December, 1895), pp. 1–15, at p. 1).

[111] On Fisher, see *ODNB*; Rex, *The Theology of John Fisher*; Bradshaw and Duffy, eds., *Humanism, Reform and the Reformation*; M. Dowling, *Fisher of Men: A Life of John Fisher, 1469–1535* (Basingstoke and New York, 1999). For Fisher's endowments and other intended and actual gifts to St. John's, see Scott, 'Notes from the College Records', *The Eagle*, 35 (1914), pp. 2–35; Jones and Underwood, *The King's Mother*, pp. 234–50; Underwood, 'John Fisher and the Promotion of Learning', pp. 35–41; Rex, 'The Sixteenth Century', pp. 5–32 (Rex sub-titles his contribution 'Fisher's College').

the college chapel and the old infirmary of the Hospital of St. John.[112] He himself had rooms in the Master's Lodge, which at that time was linked to the west end of the chapel.[113] The names of the masons and glazier are all preserved in the college records, and the master-mason at Ely, a man called Lee, came to give advice and provide a sketch of the tomb, which was under construction in 1532/33. In the event, as with Ashton, Fisher's body was never laid in it: after his execution on 22 June 1535, it was first buried at All Hallows Barking, but was then moved to St. Peter ad Vincula at the Tower – his head, as was customary, had been spiked on London Bridge and then thrown into the Thames.[114]

As Richard Rex has remarked, 'The systematic elimination of Fisher's memory at St. John's College, Cambridge, should properly be seen as part of the government's attempt to strangle the potential martyr's cult at birth.'[115] In 1540 Fisher's rebus (a fish and an ear of wheat) was chiselled from his tomb and from the arches of his chantry chapel, and the chancel stall ends were re-carved. The college, however, fulfilled his exequies for some years after his death, restoring his commemoration, and to some extent his chantry, in Mary's reign. Over time, however, it suffered further, becoming in the mid-seventeenth century a chamber for the chapel clerk (with a chimney), and then part of the chapel seating.[116] It was when the room was needed for further lumber that the tomb was uncovered, in its dismantled state. A sketch was made at the time, showing a Renaissance tomb with figures holding a blank garlanded inscription and blank shields at either end encircled in a garland (Plate 16), 'exactly like those on the Tomb of the Foundress of the College in the Chapel of Henry 7 at Westminster'.[117] This was the observation of William Cole, who witnessed the removal of the parts of what he assumed

---

[112] For the chantry, see Scott, 'Notes from the College Records', *The Eagle*, 35 (1914), pp. 27–33 (based on SJCA, D106.6); Willis and Clark, *Architectural History*, ii, pp. 282–6; Crook, *From the Foundation to Gilbert Scott*, p. 10.

[113] See the plan in Willis and Clark, *Architectural History*, iv, no. 21 (Fig. 15).

[114] The story that it grew more lifelike each day reached the Continent and fuelled the furore over Fisher's execution (*ODNB*). Thomas More was executed two weeks after Fisher (6 July), but his daughter Margaret Roper secured possession of her father's head, which was eventually buried with her (*ODNB*). On Fisher's death in relation to the issue of martyrdom, see D. Harry, 'Marriage and Martyrdom: The Death of John Fisher Reconsidered', in *Saints and Cults in Medieval England*, ed. Powell, pp. 124–39.

[115] *ODNB*. For the fate of the chantry and the expunction of Fisher's memory, see Rex, 'The Sixteenth Century', pp. 37, 43–4, 54, 61. Even as late as the 1930s there was little wish to accord Fisher the honour due him in relation to St. John's (p. 61).

[116] It was known as 'Iniquity' because its inhabitants could not be seen by the dean (Crook, *From the Foundation to Gilbert Scott*, pp. 17–18).

[117] Quoted by Scott, 'Notes from the College Records', *The Eagle*, 35 (1914), pp. 31–2. Lady Margaret's tomb, like that of her son and Elizabeth of York, was made by Pietro Torrigiano. See P. Lindley, '"The singuler mediacions and praiers of al the holie companie of Heven": Sculptural Functions and Forms in Henry VII's Chapel', in *Westminster Abbey: The Lady Chapel of Henry VII*, ed. T. Tatton-Brown and R. Mortimer (Woodbridge, 2003), pp. 259–93.

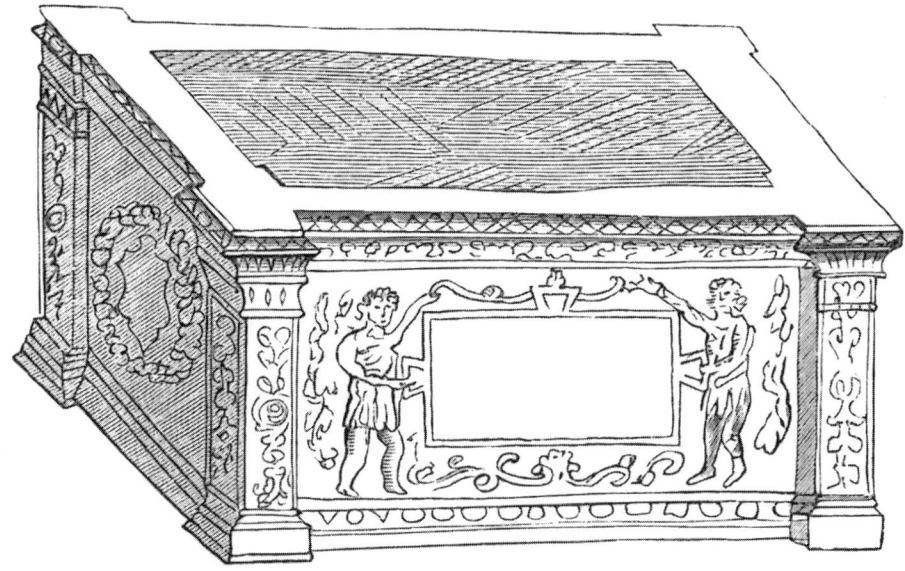

16: Lost tomb of St. John Fisher, bishop of Rochester (d.1535).

had been 'designed for one of the first masters of the College' to the alleyway outside the chapel, where it was ruined within a year.[118]

However, not all traces of Fisher's chantry had been removed, and Scott piously reconstructed in the new chapel the three arches which had served as its entrance from the old chapel. The opening ceremony of the new chapel took place on 12 May 1869, but it was not until July that these three arches were rebuilt as blind arches in the south wall of the ante-chapel.[119] Fisher's arms had combined his family arms and those of the see of Rochester, where he was bishop. In 1540 the Rochester arms had been untouched and only the Fisher arms chiselled out, and today, in the middle arch, one can see a defaced right spandrel and a left spandrel carved with the arms of the see of Rochester. The flanking arches are similar, though narrower: today the left spandrels have the shield of arms of the see of Rochester, while the right spandrels are Fisher's family arms quartered with his rebus.[120]

---

[118] Scott, 'Notes from the College Records', *The Eagle*, 35 (1914), p. 32. See Willis and Clark, *Architectural History*, ii, pp. 285–6 for an account and the sketch of the tomb by Coles's colleague, Mr Essex. (Above, plate 16).

[119] Crook, *From the Foundation to Gilbert Scott*, pp. 110, 112.

[120] The original carving quartered the arms of the see of Rochester with the Fisher family arms (Baker, *History of the College of St. John the Evangelist, Cambridge*, i, p. 91, who notes the former 'yet remaining' and the latter 'now erased').

Nicholas Metcalfe

When Fisher died in 1535, the master of St. John's was his former chaplain and archdeacon, Nicholas Metcalfe, who had taken over in 1518 from the first master, Robert Shorton, and the short-lived second master, Alan Percy.[121] Metcalfe survived his bishop by only four years. He had been Fisher's right-hand man throughout the establishment of St. John's and is recorded often in Lady Margaret's accounts in the last year of her life. In the executors' accounts he is reimbursed for payments made to Syclyng for Christ's College, for buying papal bulls, for preparing books of privy seal for Christ's, and (more homely) his mother is given pecuniary gifts both before and after Lady Margaret's death.[122] He stood with Fisher and others in the conservative faction opposing Henry VIII. In 1531 both he and Shorton signed a protestation in the lower house of Convocation in the early stages of Henry's move to be recognised as supreme Head of the Church.[123] Although he submitted in the royal visitation of the University in October 1535, four months after Fisher's execution, he and others were said by the Visitors to show 'greate pertinacite ... to their olde blindenes' and to be best replaced.[124]

This indeed happened. A brass tablet originally in the old chapel at St. John's is now fastened to the south-east pier of the tower in the ante-chapel of the Scott building (Plate 17). It records:

> *Nicolaus metcalfus huius Collegii magister viginti annos quarto die Julii magistratum excessit [et preces] ad deum [vestras vehementer orat] Anno domini m° CCCCC° xxxvii°*

(Nicholas Metcalfe master of this college for twenty years gave up his mastership 4 July [and fervently prays for your supplications] to God. AD 1537)

The text above places within brackets words which have been defaced, presumably during Dowsing's visit on 29 December 1643.[125] Only 'ad deum' ('to God') is left alone, although in fact the prayers were requested for a

---

[121] *ODNB*; Underwood, 'John Fisher and the Promotion of Learning', pp. 36–41; Rex, 'The Sixteenth Century', pp. 27–36.

[122] SJCA, D91.24.2, pp. 96, 97; D91.24.2, p. 52; D91.24.2, p. 59; D102.1 (1509), f. 4; D91.24.2, p. 59. Metcalfe's accounts in connection with Fisher's foundation at St. John's (29 September 1524 to 29 September 1534) survive as SJCA, D106.6 (Scott, 'Notes from the College Records', *The Eagle*, 35 (1914), pp. 27–35).

[123] *ODNB*.

[124] Quoted by Rex, 'The Sixteenth Century', p. 33 and n. 10.

[125] Dowsing recorded: '44 with Cujus animae propitietur deus, and one with Orata pro anima; 20 former, ten last' (Cooper, ed., *The Journal of William Dowsing*, p. 175). As Dowsing's editor notes, 'Dowsing's entry is incoherent, but probably indicates that he found some memorial inscriptions to reform' (p. 177). See pp. 175–8 for an interesting description of the chapel as it was shortly before, and at the time of, Dowsing's visit.

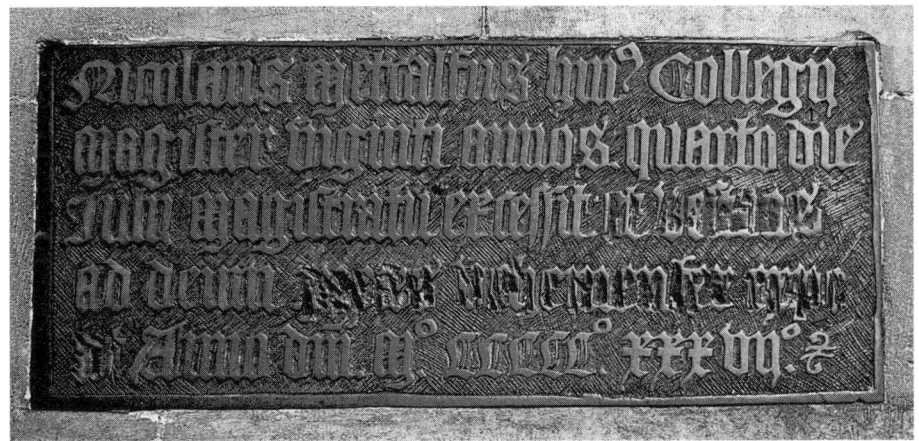

17: Brass tablet commemorating Nicholas Metcalfe (d.1539),
St. John's College chapel, Cambridge.

living man, not for the dead, since it commemorates the termination of his
mastership, an act of revenge to cleanse St. John's of Fisher's influence.[126]

Thomas Watson, the last Catholic bishop of Lincoln, recalled that Metcalfe
'was in trooble before my Lord privy seall, then Lord Cromwell, and shortly
after I was present in the Colledge Chaple [*sic*] when he returnyng home dyd
in the presence of all the fellows resygne the Maystershippe, saying that he
was commaunded so to do, whych he dyd with weepyng tears'.[127] The brass is
usually seen as a record of the esteem in which he was held by the fellows.[128]
It may be the case, however, that it was set up by Metcalfe himself, in agony
of soul. The wording of the request for prayers is not conventional, and, as
noted above, Metcalfe did conform after losing his mastership: as University
proctor he helped to administer the oaths of succession and supremacy in
1536.[129] He died in 1539.

THE LEGACY OF COMMEMORATION

This essay has dealt with the architectural evidence for the commemoration of
men (and one woman) who served Lady Margaret Beaufort, directly or
indirectly, and whose memorials survive in Cambridge. Interestingly, none
can categorically be said to have been buried in Cambridge. Lady Margaret
herself was not buried there. She may at one time have intended to be buried

[126] Rex, 'The Sixteenth Century', pp. 32–3 (and, for the aftermath, pp. 33–6). For the
universities' varied responses to the problems of the latter part of Henry VIII's reign, see
M. Dowling, *Humanism in the Age of Henry VIII* (London, Sydney, Dover NH, 1986), pp.
82–101.

[127] Quoted by Rogers, 'Cambridgeshire Brasses', p. 316.

[128] Rex, 'The Sixteenth Century', p. 33. Thereafter the college became anti-Papist; as late as
the 1930s there was opposition to raising the profile of Fisher (P. Linehan, 'The
Twentieth Century', in *St. John's College Cambridge: A History*, ed. Linehan, pp. 397–639,
at pp. 541–3).

[129] Dowling, *Humanism in the Age of Henry VIII*, p. 91.

with her parents at Wimborne Minster;[130] later there seems to have been an intention that she should be buried with her first husband, Edmund Tudor, at the Austin canons house at Bourne, near Maxey Castle;[131] later still there may have been an intention (at least on her husband's part) that she should be buried with Thomas Stanley in the Austin canons house of Burscough in Lancashire.[132] Thereafter she considered St. George's chapel, Windsor, as a place of burial, but her final decision, taken with her son, was to be buried in Westminster Abbey.[133]

Of those of Lady Margaret's household discussed above, none was buried in an abbey, cathedral, or friary. The facts that they were buried (or, at least, commemorated) in Cambridge and had served the founder of two colleges there explain their wish to be buried in the chapels of her foundations, Christ's College (Edith Fowler) and St. John's College (Hugh Ashton and John Fisher), or of their own college (Henry Hornby). As we have seen, the most ostentatious (certainly today, and not unspectacular then) was the transi tomb of Hugh Ashton, not an academic but a northerner whose tomb is anyway a cenotaph.

The commemorative culture of the late Middle Ages encompassed many different ways in which the living might seek to earn salvation after death. A lavish tomb was not mere ostentation (although the opportunity to display heraldry and heritage was important) but a means by which a priest might be supported and masses said for the dead and the living. Lady Margaret's will lists many religious foundations where prayers would be said for her soul, and the wills of Hornby and Ashton both specify that prayers should be said for Lady Margaret, as well as for their immediate families. In Ashton's case he specified that his four scholars should always pray for 'my said ladies soule and myn my paren*tes* and benefactours'.[134] Fisher did not leave a will (which does not mean he did not make one), but his gratitude to and respect for Lady Margaret are well recorded.[135] Masses would also be said by fraternities

---

[130] Her parents' tomb was an important memorial for her, which she maintained in life and after death. See Jones and Underwood, *The King's Mother*, pp. 30, 173, 178, 232–40.

[131] Scott, 'Notes from the College Records', *The Eagle*, 18, no. 105 (December, 1894), pp. 1–10 at pp. 1–4. Tudor had been buried at the Grey Friars in Carmarthen after his death on 3 November 1456. The plan was to move his body to Bourne; however, it remained in Wales, and he was moved to St. David's cathedral after the dissolution.

[132] See Steer, 'The Plantagenet in the Parish', pp. 67–8.

[133] Windsor was a plan of the 1490s, which she cancelled on 28 April 1499; the previous July her son had confirmed his decision to be buried at Westminster (Jones and Underwood, *The King's Mother*, pp. 206–8). See the essays in Tatton-Brown and Mortimer, eds., *Westminster Abbey: The Lady Chapel of Henry VII*, esp. M. Condon, 'God Save the King! Piety, Propaganda and the Perpetual Memorial', and 'The Last Will of Henry VII: Document and Text', and C. Wilson, 'The Functional Design of Henry VII's Chapel: A Reconstruction', pp. 59–98, 99–140, 141–88. Henry VIII was buried at Windsor, although he may at one time have intended burial at Westminster (*ibid.*, p. 187).

[134] Lady Margaret is mentioned twice in his will, but he does not find it necessary to specify more than 'my ladie'.

[135] Not least in the funeral sermon he preached at her month's mind on 29 July 1509 ('Month's Mind of the Lady Margaret', in *The English Works of John Fisher*, ed. J.E.B. Mayor, Early English Text Society, Extra Series, 27 (London, 1876), i [no more parts published], pp. 289–310).

to which the deceased had belonged, and pardons and indulgences were other means of safeguarding the immortal soul. Lady Margaret belonged to many fraternities: for example, a 1478 letter of fraternity survives from the Grande Chartreuse for Thomas Stanley and his two wives, one dead and one living, and his family; Lady Margaret also acquired many indulgences, such as one of 1476 in consideration of her support of the war against the Muslims in Turkey.[136]

In the cases of Hornby, Ashton, and Fisher, there was the additional charitable act of founding scholarships to the colleges in which they planned to be buried, even if they could not emulate Lady Margaret by founding the colleges themselves. For those who could not found a college (the majority), the founding of a grammar school or scholarships for a grammar school, or the establishment of scholarships and fellowships at a college might be within reach, and we have seen that Hornby left money for exhibitions at Peterhouse and Ashton at St. John's, while Fisher funded them during his lifetime. As for commemorative acts, such as the bequest of books, chapel furnishings, and the like, Hornby's will, with such bequests, has been discussed above. Hornby was, of course, Lady Margaret's former dean of chapel and at his death master of Peterhouse, and his will reflects that status. Hugh Ashton was much more an administrator and his will is typical of a man of business: there are no books, but debts are handled and disposal is made of land, money, and plate.[137] Unlike Ashton, John Fisher's plans for his own chantry at St. John's were far advanced during his lifetime, and he supported the college by books, money, and fundraising in the early years when the burden of its foundation fell most on him. He thought it more valuable to spend money on creating theologians at St. John's than on 'my relatives and other vanities'.[138] His fine library was to go to St. John's after his death but was instead diverted to the king who had signed his death warrant, Lady Margaret Beaufort's own grandson.[139]

Lady Margaret left books in her will to her immediate family and household, but she also gave books during her lifetime, not just as gifts, but as acts of charity.[140] Her furnishing of the library at Christ's College (as of the chapel) must be seen as more than the expected action of a founder, but also as an act of commemorative charity by which love of God (divinity was the focus of her colleges) and learning might be spread and, importantly, remembered.[141]

---

[136] Scott, 'Notes from the College Records', *The Eagle*, 20, no. 114 (December, 1897), pp. 1–21 at pp. 19–20; Scott, 'Notes from the College Records', *The Eagle*, 19, no. 113 (June, 1897), pp. 1–21 at pp. 16–19. See too S. Powell, 'Lady Margaret Beaufort and her Books', *The Library*, Sixth Series, 20 (1998), pp. 197–240 at p. 216, n. 122, pp. 219–20.

[137] The bequest of a tenement at Lathom (the location of the principal residence of Thomas Stanley and Lady Margaret Beaufort), as well as a tenement and lands in Mawdesley, under four miles away (his sister had married a man of the surname Mawdesley) show that he had maintained his connections with the north-west.

[138] Quoted (without reference) by Rex, 'The Sixteenth Century', p. 16.

[139] On the loss of his extensive library, see Rex, 'The Sixteenth Century', p. 32, and, for an attempt to recreate at least part of his library, Rex, *The Theology of John Fisher*, pp. 192–203.

[140] Powell, 'Lady Margaret Beaufort and her Books', pp. 201–2 and *passim*.

[141] Details of the plate, books, and vestments she gave to Christ's College are extant today: Scott, 'A List (Preserved in the Treasury of St. John's College) of the Plate, Books and

However, her acts of charity in relation to books seem to have been ingrained and might be much smaller, and thriftier. For example, in an inventory of her chapel, in which she and Fisher seem to have discussed what might be disposed of and where, one entry is cancelled: 'Item a lyttyll olde mes boke off parchment sum tyme kyvered with clothe off golde & clasped with ii claspstaff sylver & gylted cuius 2m folium supplices', and below is written in Fisher's hand: 'My ladys grace hath the kyveryng & the claspes & bade the dean to gyff the boke to sum poor churche & [so *above line*] the sayde dean gaff the sayde boke unto the parishe church off Badhampton at the desyre off Sir Robert Whitlege.'[142] Most of the items went to the chapel of Christ's College, and her furnishing of the chapel and of the library of the college may be seen not only as a stage in her endowment of the college, but also as a service to learning and piety.

David Harry has argued that not just the bequest of books but their writing and publishing may be seen as acts of commemorative charity.[143] Not only did Lady Margaret bequeath and gift books, she also translated two herself, and arranged the printing, not just of those books, but of other devotional books printed by Caxton, de Worde, and Pynson.[144] She also encouraged others to write for her: Hornby prepared a mass of the Holy Name at her request,[145] and she sponsored the printing of Fisher's sermons on the seven penitential psalms, *The fruytfull saynges of Dauyd*,[146] and his funeral sermon for Henry VII.[147] Fisher was in a position not just to write but also to arrange and perhaps subsidise the printing of his own books. After Lady Margaret's death he published (in Latin) on theological subjects such as the controversy over St. Mary Magdalene.[148] Similarly, for a European scholarly readership,

---

Vestments bequeathed by the Lady Margaret to Christ's College', *Communications of the Cambridge Antiquarian Society*, 9 (1899), pp. 349–67. See too Powell, 'Lady Margaret Beaufort and her Books', pp. 237–8.

[142] SJCA, D102.13, p. 42. For other items given in this way, see S. Powell, 'Textiles and Dress in the Household Papers of Lady Margaret Beaufort (1443–1509), Mother of King Henry VII', in *Medieval Clothing and Textiles, 11*, ed. R. Netherton and G.R. Owen-Crocker (Woodbridge, 2015), pp. 139–57, pp. 147–8.

[143] D. Harry, 'William Caxton and Commemorative Culture in Fifteenth-Century England', in *The Fifteenth Century, XIII: Exploring the Evidence: Commemoration, Administration and the Economy*, ed. L. Clark (Woodbridge, 2014), pp. 63–79.

[144] For her translations and print sponsorships, see Powell, 'Lady Margaret Beaufort and her Books', pp. 211–39.

[145] Powell, 'Lady Margaret Beaufort and her Books', pp. 208–11. She also appointed others to translate for her, such as Caxton and Edmund Hatfeld (*ibid.*, pp. 206, n. 56, 227–8 [but Edmund, not William]).

[146] John Fisher, *This treatise concernynge the fruytfull saynges of Davyd the kynge and prophete* (London, 1508), STC (2nd edn.), 10902; John Fisher, *This treatyse concernynge the fruytfull saynges of Davyd the kynge and prophete in the seven penytencyall psalms* (London, 1508), STC (2nd edn.), 10903.

[147] John Fisher, *This sermon folowynge was compyled [and] sayd in the cathedrall chyrche of saynt Poule within ye cyte of London by the ryght reuerende fader in god Iohn̄ bysshop of Rochester, the body beyinge present of the moost famouse prynce kynge Henry the. vij. the. x. day of Maye, th yere of our lorde god. M.CCCCC.ix. whiche sermon was enprynted at the specyall request of ye ryght excellent prynczesse Margarete moder vnto the sayd noble prynce and Countesse of Rychemonde and Derby* (London, 1509 & 1509–10), STC (2nd edn.), 10900–1.

[148] *Theology of John Fisher*, pp. 65–77.

he opposed Luther in print, and when Henry VIII threatened the Church arguably more dangerously than Luther had done, he wrote (and published abroad) in defence of the king's marriage to Katherine of Aragon.[149]

Finally, however, it was the example of Lady Margaret to her household servants, especially those who served her closest, Hornby, Ashton, and Fisher, which set a model by which they might emulate her, in acts of commemoration and acts of charity, perhaps in reality indistinguishable from each other. Fisher's month's mind eulogy of Lady Margaret is entirely in terms of the model she set to others, and it ends with her death-bed example, which, he twice reiterates, may be recalled by many present as he preached:

> [D]yvers here present can recorde how hertly she answered whan the holy sacrament contaynynge the blessid Jhesu in it was holden before her, and the questyon made untyl her whether she byleved that there was verayly the Sone of God that suffred his blessyd passyon for her and for all mankynde upon the crosse. Many here can bere recorde how with all her herte and soule she raysed her body to make answere thereunto and confessed aassuredly that in the sacrament was conteyned Cryst Jhesu the Sone of God that dyed for wretched synners upon the crosse, in whom holly she put her truste and confydence … And so sone after she was aneled she departed and yelded up her spyryte into the handes of Our Lorde. Who may not nowe take evydent lyklyhode and conjecture upon this that the soule of this noble woman whiche so studyously in her lyf was occupyed in good werkes and with a faste fayth of Cryst and the sacramentes of his Chirche was defended in that houre of departynge out from the body, was borne up into the countre above with the blessyd aungelles deputed and ordeyned to that holy mystery?[150]

[149] For an overview, see S. Powell, 'The Secular Clergy', in *A Companion to the Early Printed Book in Britain*, ed. V. Gillespie and S. Powell (Cambridge, 2014), pp. 150–75, at pp. 159–62. For a list of Fisher's publications in the context of a comprehensive account of them, see Rex, *The Theology of John Fisher*, p. 273. For his English works 1520–35, see *English Works of John Fisher, Bishop of Rochester: Sermons and Other Writings 1520 to 1535*, ed. C.A. Hatt (Oxford, 2002). Hatt is currently completing an edition of Fisher's earlier works.

[150] 'Month's Mind of the Lady Margaret', ed. Mayor, p. 308, l. 28 – p. 309, l. 21 (but edited here according to the conventions described in note 14 above). It was printed by Wynkyn de Worde in 1509: John Fisher, *Here after foloweth a mornynge remembrau[n]ce had at the moneth mynde of the noble prynces Margarete countesse of Rychemonde [and] Darbye moder vnto kynge Henry the. vii. [and] grandame to oure souerayne lorde that nowe is, vppon whose soule almyghty god haue mercy* (London, 1509), STC (2nd edn.), 10891.

CHAPTER 8

'The Stones are all disrobed':
Reasons for the Presence and Absence of
Monumental Brasses in Cambridge

Nicholas Rogers

The university city of Oxford, with its twenty-one pre-nineteenth-century colleges and fourteen medieval parish churches, is blessed with a rich patrimony of monumental brasses. There are no fewer than 117 pre-eighteenth-century brasses and evidence in the form of either indents or antiquarian records of a further 326.[1] Cambridge is less fortunate. The County Series volume lists forty-one surviving brasses and evidence of at least 152 lost ones.[2] Why should this be? One obvious reason is that Oxford was always a larger community. Cambridge only has sixteen pre-nineteenth-century colleges. A good measure of relative size is that Alfred Emden's list of pre-1500 members of the University of Cambridge runs to 695 pages, whereas the Oxford equivalent requires 2,242 pages.[3]

Cambridge before the University was shaped by its strategic position at a river crossing, commanding a network of roads and providing access to the Fenland waterways. It was a mint town from the reign of Edgar and at the time of Domesday Book had at least 373 house plots (compared with 946 in Oxford).[4] Its location encouraged its development as a trading centre; from 1211 Cambridge was the home of one of the major English fairs: Stourbridge

[1] For Oxford brasses, see M. Stephenson, *A List of Monumental Brasses in the British Isles*, rev. edn. (London, 1964), pp. 397–426, 789; J. Bertram, 'The Lost Brasses of Oxford, I: College Chapels', *TMBS*, 11:4 (1972), pp. 219–52; *idem*, 'The Lost Brasses of Oxford, II: The Cathedral and City Churches', *TMBS*, 11:5 (1973), pp. 321–79.
[2] W. Lack, H.M. Stuchfield and P. Whittemore, *The Monumental Brasses of Cambridgeshire* (London, 1995), pp. 20–83. See also 'The Brasses of Cambridgeshire', *TMBS*, 2:7 (1896), pp. 249–75 for further details of Cambridge brasses.
[3] A.B. Emden, *A Biographical Register of the University of Cambridge to 1500* (Cambridge, 1963); *idem*, *A Biographical Register of the University of Oxford to A.D. 1500*, 3 vols. (Oxford, 1957–59).
[4] *VCH, Cambridgeshire*, i (London, 1938), pp. 357, 359; H.E. Salter, *Medieval Oxford*, Oxford Historical Society, 100 (Oxford, 1936), pp. 22–3.

Fair.[5] In the thirteenth century there were sixteen parishes in Cambridge, but of these one did not survive the depopulation of the Black Death and another was redeveloped out of existence when King's was founded.[6] By 1279 there were almost 550 occupied house plots, together with seventy-five shops, suggesting a total population of four to five thousand.[7] As early as 1329 a townsman, Eudo de Helpringham, was commemorated by a brass.[8] The late medieval civic elite provided a significant clientele for marblers, as can be seen on the floors of Great St. Mary's (St. Mary's in the Market), the main town church, and St. Edward's (Plate 18).[9] Although there are difficulties in assessing the total population from the 1524–25 lay subsidies, estimates of 3,900 and 4,600 have been proposed, of which approximately 1,300 were members of the University.[10] The development of Cambridge as a university town thus alleviated the effects of late medieval population decline.

It was convenience of access which attracted the refugee scholars from Oxford in 1209. The earliest members of the University worshipped in nearby parish churches, several of which effectively became college chapels.[11] St. Michael's lent its name to Michaelhouse, which was absorbed into Henry VIII's not so new foundation of Trinity College. St. Bene't's served as the chapel of Corpus Christi. Peterhouse, the first Cambridge college to be founded, derived its name from the original dedication of Little St. Mary's. The members of the Clare and Trinity Hall originally worshipped in St. John Zachary, and after that church was demolished had their own aisles in St. Edward's, where they would customarily be buried. For example, John Puregold, fellow of Trinity Hall, willed in January 1526 that he should be buried in St. Edward's with his first wife Johane under the stone of Thomas and Alice Roger.[12] Puregold was a civil lawyer and, unusually in pre-nineteenth-century Cambridge, a married academic. He stipulated that upon the end of the stone there should be 'a litell superscription of my name in plate for a remembrance'.

One factor which affected both Oxford and Cambridge was that the academic population was a transient one. Unless impeded by death, most fellows would move on to benefices elsewhere. Similarly, medieval heads of house might hope for higher ecclesiastical positions, even bishoprics. Alternatively, they could retire in old age to the comfort of a rectory or canonry. This possibility explains the way in which Walter Hewke, master of Trinity Hall, is depicted on his brass in processional vestments (Plate 5). His

[5]   *VCH, Cambridgeshire*, iii (London, 1959), pp. 92–5; on Stourbridge and other local fairs see also J.S. Lee, *Cambridge and its Economic Region, 1450–1560* (Hatfield, 2005), pp. 114–41.

[6]   On these churches see *VCH, Cambridgeshire*, iii, pp. 123–32.

[7]   F.W. Maitland, *Township and Borough* (Cambridge, 1898), p. 101.

[8]   Lack, Stuchfield and Whittemore, *Cambridgeshire*, p. 55, illus. on p. 56.

[9]   In St. Mary the Great a further eight indents are now lost, and at St. Edward there are at least six lost indents: Lack, Stuchfield and Whittemore, *Cambridgeshire*, pp. 66–8.

[10]   Lee, *Cambridge and its Economic Region*, pp. 28–9.

[11]   Cf. D.R. Leader, *A History of the University of Cambridge*, i: *The University to 1546* (Cambridge, 1988), pp. 68–9.

[12]   CUL, UA, VCCt. Wills I, ff. 42v–45.

will confirms what the unfinished date in the inscription suggests, that his brass was 'redy bought and paide for' in his lifetime, when he was uncertain where he might be buried.[13] This brass could serve as well at Holywell (Hunts.), where he was rector, as at Trinity Hall, where he was master.[14] Of the thirteen masters of Peterhouse between 1382 and 1589, John Neweton (1382) became treasurer of York, William Cavendish (1397) dean of Bocking and John Botelsham (1397) bishop of Rochester.[15] Several other masters contrived to combine the mastership with another office: Thomas of Barnard Castle (1400) was canon of Lanchester, John Holbroke (1421) chaplain to the king, Thomas Lane (1436) canon of Lichfield.[16] Thomas Deynman (1510), physician to Henry VII and the Lady Margaret, was also master of St. Mary Bethlehem Hospital, London, and chose to be buried there.[17] On the other hand, Deynman's successor, Henry Hornby, who was also canon of Southwell and Lincoln and master of Tattershall, elected to be buried in Little St. Mary's, where he had established a chantry (Plate 15).[18] Andrew Perne, master from 1554 to 1589, whose religious vacillations gave rise to the verb 'pernare', doubled as dean of Ely and in his old age resided and was buried in Lambeth.[19]

A primary obligation upon the members of medieval colleges was to pray for their founders and benefactors, a function that survived the Reformation in the form of the collegiate Commemoration of Benefactors. This aspect of college life is expressed architecturally at King's in the enfilade of side chapels, providing spaces for the private Masses of priest fellows and for the establishment of chantries. By the 1480s some at least of these side chapels were roofed in.[20] The first interment to be commemorated by a brass was that of William Towne (d.1496), not a provost (as stated by Mill Stephenson) but a foundation fellow who gave 60 marks to the college for the observation of his obit.[21] Of the thirteen provosts between the foundation of the college

---

[13] TNA: PRO, PROB 11/19 ff. 69–69v.

[14] Emden, *Cambridge*, p. 303.

[15] Emden, *Cambridge*, pp. 76, 129, 421.

[16] Emden, *Cambridge*, pp. 39, 309, 349.

[17] Emden, *Cambridge*, p. 187.

[18] TNA: PRO, PROB 11/19 ff. 43v–44v; Emden, *Cambridge*, pp. 313–14. He made provision for a brass: '*Item volo quod ematur lapis marmoreus ad ponendum supra corpus meum habens ymaginem et scripturam secundum discrecionem executorum meorum*'. The brass commemorating a doctor of divinity at Little St. Mary's almost certainly commemorates Hornby (cf. N. Rogers, 'Cambridgeshire Brasses', in *Cambridgeshire Churches*, ed. C. Hicks (Stamford, 1997), p. 315).

[19] T.A. Walker, *A Biographical Register of Peterhouse Men*, 2 vols. (Cambridge, 1927–30), i, pp. 177–8; in his will, made in 1588, Perne had expressed a wish to be buried either in Ely Cathedral or the chancel of Little St. Mary's or 'otherwise where it shall please Allmightie god to ende the vncertaine race of my painefull pillgramage vpon this slippery earth' (E. Leedham-Green, 'Perne's Wills', in *Andrew Perne: Quatercentenary Studies*, ed. D. McKitterick, Cambridge Bibliographical Society, Monograph No. 11 (Cambridge, 1991), p. 93.

[20] R. Willis and J.W. Clark, *The Architectural History of the University of Cambridge, and of the Colleges of Cambridge and Eton*, 4 vols. (Cambridge, 1886), i, pp. 474–5.

[21] Emden, *Cambridge*, p. 592; Lack, Stuchfield and Whittemore, *Cambridgeshire*, pp. 31, 36, illus. on p. 32.

in 1441 and 1558, seven died in office, but only three, provosts Argentein (Plates 8a&b), Hacumblen and Brassie, were buried in King's College chapel.[22] Richard Atkinson, who died of the plague in 1556, may have been buried at King's but there is no surviving monument. Walter Field, who died in 1499, made provision for his burial either in his chapel at King's or at the college of St. Elizabeth, Winchester, where his parents were buried.[23] Richard Hatton, who was also a canon of St. Stephen's chapel, Westminster, expressed a preference to be buried in this royal chapel where he also requested an 'honest' marble stone with an image and inscription in his will of 1509.[24] Another provost with a conflict of loyalties was John Doget, who was also treasurer of Chichester, chancellor of Salisbury and rector of Odiham (Hants.). When he died in 1501 he was buried in accordance with his will in Salisbury Cathedral.[25]

Of the remaining provosts, William Millington was deprived of his post in 1447 for refusing to swear obedience to new statutes for the college. He remained in Cambridge, however, and in 1466 was buried in the south chancel aisle of St. Edward's church.[26] John Chedworth, the second provost, became bishop of Lincoln, where he was commemorated by a brass.[27] Also promoted to bishoprics were the Lutheran Edward Fox, who was rewarded with Hereford for his efforts in the king's 'great matter', and his more conservative successor George Day, who, until his imprisonment under Edward VI, was both provost and bishop of Chichester, where he was buried in 1556 under a brass-bearing table-tomb.[28] John Cheke, who had supplanted Day, made his peace with the Marian regime and was buried in St. Alban, Wood Street, where he had a 'fair plated Gravestone'.[29] It is not known for certain where Robert Wodelarke, the third provost, was buried, but as the founder of St. Catharine's it is most likely he was interred in the old chapel of that college.[30]

In the fifteenth and early sixteenth centuries royal patronage favoured Cambridge rather than Oxford. No fewer than four colleges were founded by members of the royal family. It may have been as a consequence of the increase in building activity that a marbler was attracted to Cambridge, establishing a workshop which lasted from *c.*1506 to 1541. As yet no document has surfaced which provides him with a name, and indeed his situation in

---

[22] On Provost Hacumblen's commemorative arrangements see N. Pickering, 'Provost Robert Hacumblen and his Chantry Chapel', in *King's College Chapel 1515–2015: Art, Music and Religion in Cambridge*, ed. J.M. Massing and N. Zeeman (London, 2014), pp. 96–113.

[23] TNA: PRO, PROB 11/11, f. 262v; Emden, *Cambridge*, p. 223.

[24] TNA: PRO, PROB 11/16, ff. 155–155v.

[25] TNA: PRO, PROB 11/12, ff. 127–8; Emden, *Cambridge*, pp. 190–1.

[26] Emden, *Cambridge*, pp. 417–18.

[27] J. Bertram, *Lost Brasses* (Newton Abbot, 1976), p. 174, fig. 27; D. Lepine, '"Pause and pray with mournful heart": Late Medieval Clerical Monuments in Lincoln Cathedral', *TMBS*, 19:1 (2014), pp. 15–40 at p. 25, fig. 5.

[28] C.E.D. Davidson-Houston, 'Sussex Monumental Brasses, Part II', *Sussex Archaeological Collections*, 77 (1936), pp. 131–2.

[29] John Stow, *The Survey of London*, ed. A. Munday and H. Dyson (London, 1633), p. 309.

[30] Emden, *Cambridge*, pp. 645–6; J.H. Baker, 'Wodelarke, Robert (*d.*1481?)', *ODNB*.

Cambridge, first deduced by Herbert Haines, is based on the distribution pattern of his brasses.[31] His stylistic roots seem to lie in the Suffolk school of brasses. It is possible that he was in some way connected with the master mason John Wastell, who worked on the last phase of King's College chapel.[32] The characteristics of this Cambridge marbler's work were ably set out by Roger Greenwood. His figures are usually small in scale (though King's and Little St. Mary's show him well able to work on a larger scale (Plates 8a&b and 15)). Hair is shown in matted locks, and women frequently wear a curious flat cap. Praying hands are shown in a naturalistic pose, the fingertips just touching. Children are typically presented on a quadrangular plate. Many of these diagnostic features can be identified on indents, which is fortunate, since outside the college chapels (including Little St. Mary's in that group), Cambridge is singularly lacking in surviving brasses of the Cambridge school. An inspection of the floors of city churches, most notably Great St. Mary's and St. Edward's (Plate 18), gives us a sense of how much we have lost. Malcolm Norris expressed the opinion that the 'product of the workshop is perhaps indicated best by the indents on the floor of St. Mary the Great'.[33] In addition to those indents which can be assigned positively to Cambridge, there are numerous non-Purbeck slabs which may once have held locally produced brasses.

We have very little knowledge as to what was lost from Cambridge religious houses at the Dissolution. Of Barnwell Priory, the most important foundation in Cambridge, nothing remains apart from the Cellarer's Checker and the *capella ad portas* of St. Andrew the Less.[34] Prior to the levelling of the site in 1810–12 John Bowtell recorded fragments of indents found in the cemetery.[35] Will evidence indicates that the Grey Friars, Black Friars, Austin Friars and, to a somewhat lesser extent, the White Friars were popular burial places for townsfolk, local gentry and academics. It is likely that many of these graves were commemorated by brasses. For example, in 1521 Hugh Rankyn, alderman, willed to be buried in the Greyfriars under the same stone as his father and grandfather.[36] This suggests an identifying inscription, and therefore either a brass or incised slab. The only surviving monument that can be associated with a Cambridge religious house is a Purbeck marble slab, now in Jesus College chapel, with the indents of a marginal inscription in separate Lombardics commemorating friar John de Pykenham, master of Sacred Theology, 'Prior of this place'.[37] Where 'this place' was has yet to be determined. The use of

[31]   H. Haines, *A Manual of Monumental Brasses* (Oxford, 1861; repr. Bath, 1970), p. xxix; J.R. Greenwood, 'Haines's Cambridge School of Brasses', *TMBS*, 11:1 (1969), pp. 2–12.
[32]   On Wastell, see J. Harvey, *English Mediaeval Architects: A Biographical Dictionary down to 1550*, rev. edn. (Gloucester, 1984), pp. 316–24; F. Woodman, 'Wastell, John (*d. c.*1518)', *ODNB*.
[33]   Lack, Stuchfield and Whittemore, *Cambridgeshire*, p. iii.
[34]   A. Taylor, *Cambridge: A Hidden History* (Stroud, 1999), pp. 61–3.
[35]   *The Observances in use at the Augustinian Priory of S. Giles and S. Andrew at Barnwell, Cambridgeshire*, ed. J.W. Clark (Cambridge, 1897), pp. xxv–xxvi.
[36]   J.R.H. Moorman, *The Grey Friars in Cambridge 1225–1538* (Cambridge, 1952), pp. 66, 253.
[37]   Lack, Stuchfield and Whittemore, *Cambridgeshire*, p. 31.

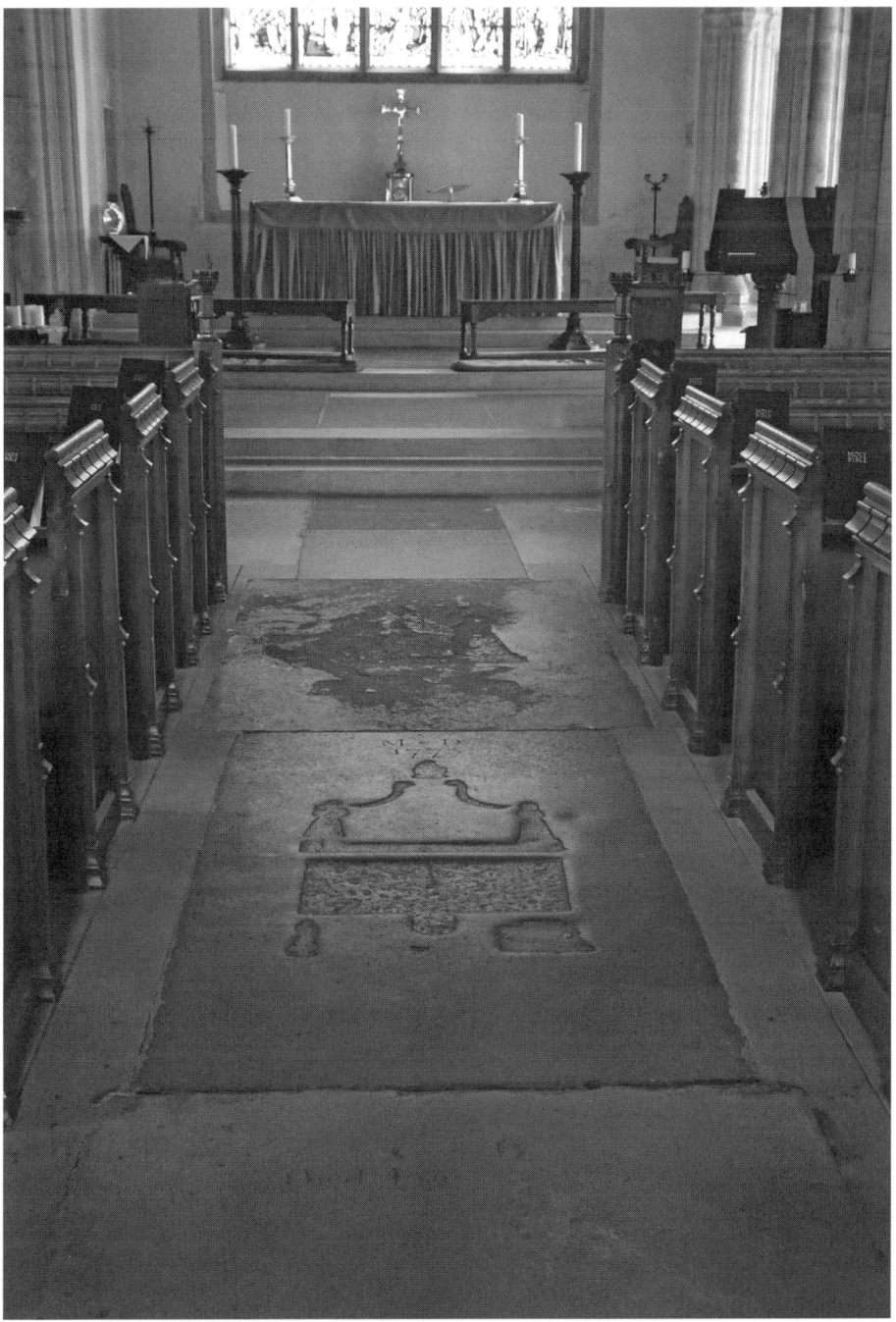

18: Indents in the nave of St. Edward's, Cambridge.

the title 'prior' rather than 'guardian' appears to eliminate the Franciscans, but it could be any one of the other three Cambridge friaries. The slab was reused for a small inscription plate, which itself has been lost. Some of the last products of the Cambridge school are palimpsests, representing spoil from the Dissolution. The only item with a secure provenance came from Chicksands Priory (Beds.),[38] but a reference to Stow-cum-Quy on one of the other inscriptions may point to a Cambridge origin.[39] Another inscription commemorates one Margaret Siday, possibly a member of the Siday family who were Cambridge tenants of Queens' College.[40]

It is possible that the more obviously Catholic imagery on Cambridge brasses was removed at an early stage of the Reformation, in the reign of Edward VI. The crucifix on the Argentein brass in King's (Plate 8a) and the Virgin surrounded by angels on the Billingford brass at St. Bene't's (Plate 2) are more likely to have gone then than in the Civil War. It is customary to blame William Dowsing for the loss of brasses in Cambridge.[41] It is true that he and his colleagues were responsible for the anonymity of many East Anglian brasses where only the indents have survived. But their activities were but one phase of a prolonged process of destruction in the name of religion. To return to the disparity between Oxford and Cambridge, it is evident that the greater religious conservatism of Oxford helped protect brasses in the sixteenth and seventeenth centuries. In 1995, there were only four surviving pre-Reformation brasses in Cambridge parish churches, three of which were to academics, and distributed over three churches. In Oxford there are eight, distributed over four churches, only one of which commemorates an academic. From the 1610s onwards the Town Corporation of Cambridge was dominated by Puritans. Dowsing's silence regarding popish inscriptions in Holy Trinity,[42] the location of the town lectureship, or in Great St. Mary's, where the conduct of services was denounced to Archbishop Laud in 1636,[43] suggests that there may have been a clean sweep of the brasses in these churches prior to the 1640s.

A contemporary Royalist writer described Dowsing as going 'round the Country like a Bedlam',[44] and his diary certainly displays pronounced angelophobia and a Pavlovian reaction to the phrase '*Orate pro anima*'. However, Dowsing has been more aptly characterised by John Morrill as a 'bureaucratic Puritan', acting in strict accordance with the Parliamentary Ordinance of

---

[38]   J. Page-Phillips, *Palimpsests: The Backs of Monumental Brasses*, 2 vols. (London, 1980), p. 85 (2C1), pl. 155.

[39]   Page-Phillips, *Palimpsests*, p. 85 (4C1), pl. 155.

[40]   Page-Phillips, *Palimpsests*, p. 85 (3C1), pl. 155. In 1535 William Siday had recently leased a tenement in Great St. Mary parish from Queens' College (CCCA, CCCC09/08/280).

[41]   For a full discussion of Dowsing and his activities, see T. Cooper, ed., *The Journal of William Dowsing*, (Woodbridge, 2001).

[42]   Cooper, ed., *Journal of William Dowsing*, p. 204. Dowsing did, however, spend Christmas Day 1643 breaking down '80 popish pictures' in Holy Trinity.

[43]   Cooper, ed., *Journal of William Dowsing*, pp. 196–7.

[44]   T. Cooper, 'Dowsing at Cambridge University', in *Journal of William Dowsing*, ed. Cooper, p. 53.

1643 against 'Monuments of Superstition and Idolatry'.[45] Dowsing provides a tally of inscriptions taken up in accordance with his commission from the earl of Manchester, sometimes giving the reason for their elimination: 'At Peter's parish, December 30 ... we took 3 popish inscriptions for prayers to be made for their soules';[46] 'Giles' parish, December 30, we ... tooke 2 popish inscriptions';[47] '1643/4, January 1. Edward's parish, we ... took off 10 superstitious inscriptions.'[48] At 'Benet Temple ... there was seven superstitious pictures, 14 cherubim, and 2 superstitious ingraving: one was to pray for the soul of John Canterbury, and his wife.'[49] Here we have one of those moments when Dowsing reveals some form of antiquarian sensibility: 'And an inscription of a mayd Praying to the Son and Virgin Mary, 'twas in lating, Me tibi-Virgo pia genitor [*recte genitrix*] commendo Mariæ [Maria]; A maid was born to me which I commend to you oh Mary (1432). Richard Billingford did comend this his daughters soul.'[50] This account reveals Dowsing's inability to recognise academic dress and the very narrow limits of his Latinity. But it also serves to demonstrate that Dowsing only acted against the element of the monument that he found objectionable.

In the town churches Dowsing was dealing with wardens who, though they might have grumbled at his fees or the cost of reglazing, were essentially in accord with his religious views. These were the people who had elected Oliver Cromwell as their M.P. Mr. Russell, the churchwarden at 'Benet Temple', lent Colonel Cromwell £300 to pay his soldiers.[51] Trouble came in the colleges. Here Dowsing's legal authority was challenged and the religious rationale of his iconoclasm disputed.[52] In several college chapels, such as Peterhouse and Pembroke, where burials did not take place, Dowsing and his accomplices merely had to break down cherubim and superstitious letters in gold. St. John's College chapel, which had previously served St. John's Hospital, yielded a rich crop of forty-five offensive inscriptions.[53] Some of his inspections seem to have been less than thorough. At Trinity Hall, where he liaised with Thomas Cullier, an '*Orate pro anima*, on a gravestone' was noted and duly removed.[54] But Walter Hewke, with his popish apostles and offensive prayer for his soul in English, was completely overlooked. Was he hidden by the communion table? At King's, where Dowsing was faced with 'one thousand superstitious pictures' which, by means that are still unclear, survived to delight us now, it is uncertain what, if any, damage to the brasses can be assigned to 1644

---

45 J. Morrill, 'William Dowsing and the Administration of Iconoclasm in the Puritan Revolution', in *Journal of William Dowsing*, ed. Cooper, pp. 1–28, at p. 17.
46 Cooper, ed., *Journal of William Dowsing*, p. 191.
47 Cooper, ed., *Journal of William Dowsing*, p. 192.
48 Cooper, ed., *Journal of William Dowsing*, p. 195.
49 Cooper, ed., *Journal of William Dowsing*, p. 168.
50 Cooper, ed., *Journal of William Dowsing*, p. 169.
51 Cooper, ed., *Journal of William Dowsing*, pp. 168–9.
52 See S.L. Sadler, 'Dowsing's Arguments with the Fellows of Pembroke', in *Journal of William Dowsing*, ed. Cooper, pp. 56–66.
53 Cooper, ed., *Journal of William Dowsing*, p. 175.
54 Cooper, ed., *Journal of William Dowsing*, p. 174.

rather than any other phase of iconoclasm.[55] The missing foot inscription on the Hacumblen brass looks like his work. A different approach is adopted on the Towne brass, where the offensive clauses have been chiselled out. On the Argentein brass, where the crucifix has gone, the '*Orate pro anima*' has been left. Brassie's missing prayer scroll was a casual loss in the eighteenth century. Indeed, William Cole recorded seeing a parchment request for prayers, covered in horn, attached to the door of Brassie's chantry.[56]

The systematic removal of offensive monuments in Cambridge, sanctioned by the earl of Manchester as commander of the Eastern Association and in accordance with a Parliamentary Ordinance of 1643, contrasts sharply with the situation in Oxford, which served as the Royalist headquarters during the first part of the Civil War. Such losses as occurred there were casual. The chief casualties were the brasses in the cloisters at New College, apparently removed when the cloisters were in use as an arsenal and presumably drafted as *matériel* by an enterprising quartermaster.[57] Even during the Commonwealth, the only recorded losses in Oxford were cases of petty pilfering by workmen.[58]

Whereas *pietas* might help to preserve anonymous figures of former fellows in Cambridge college chapels, in a busy parish like St. Edward's there was no incentive to preserve figures that no longer had any meaning. If the effigies survived Dowsing, they were soon removed to enable the slabs to be recycled (Plate 19). The notes of Francis Blomefield and Cole bear witness to a gradual process of loss through neglect in the eighteenth century. At St. Peter's, where Blomefield thought all the stones were 'disrobed', Cole was still able to draw a late fifteenth-century civilian in a gown, a pair of beads suspended from his belt and with evangelist symbols in quadrilobes at the corners, but devoid of inscription.[59] All that survives of this is a cut-down slab (Plate 20). In St. Botolph's, Blomefield recorded 'a fine antient Altar Tomb by the S. Side of the Altar, but all the Brasses are reaved, it had an Effigies and Circumscription'.[60] This is the forlorn academic now propped up in the north aisle of the nave (Plate 21). At St. Giles, Blomefield saw before the pulpit the brass of a man in armour with shields of arms and a rebus, the inscription lost.[61] By Cole's time only the shields remained. The details of heraldry given by Blomefield and Cole enable it to be identified plausibly as the brass of John Beton, mayor and M.P. for Cambridge. When St. Giles was rebuilt in the nineteenth century the now brass-less slab was removed to the churchyard, where it was last seen *c.*1890.[62] A Purbeck marble slab in the south choir aisle of St. Edward's with indents from a London A workshop of a man in armour and wife of *c.*1400, recorded as intact by Cole, was subsequently cut

[55] Cooper, ed., *Journal of William Dowsing*, pp. 179–86.
[56] Cooper, ed., *Journal of William Dowsing*, pp. 185–6.
[57] Bertram, *Lost Brasses*, pp. 23–4.
[58] Bertram, *Lost Brasses*, p. 27.
[59] F. Blomefield, *Collectanea Cantabrigiensia* (Norwich, 1750), p. 62; Lack, Stuchfield and Whittemore, *Cambridgeshire*, p. 72, illus. on p. 71.
[60] Blomefield, *Collectanea Cantabrigiensia*, p. 68.
[61] Blomefield, *Collectanea Cantabrigiensia*, p. 64.
[62] Lack, Stuchfield and Whittemore, *Cambridgeshire*, p. 59, illus. on p. 53.

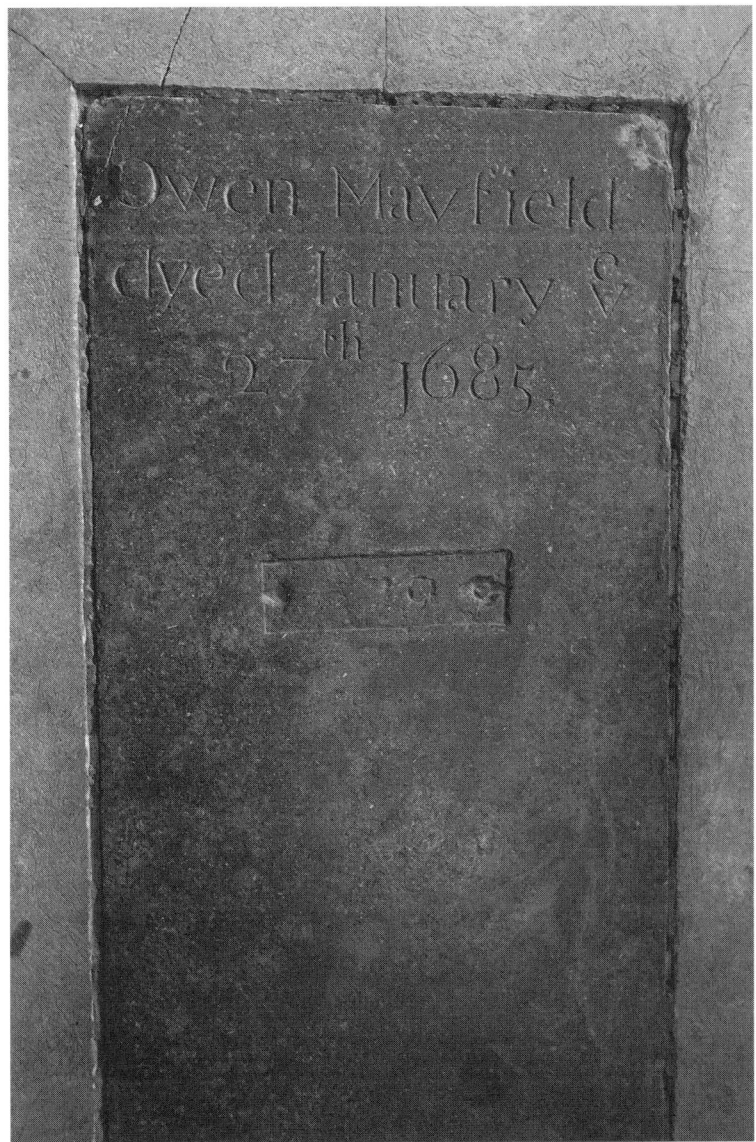

19: Slab with indent, appropriated for later monument of Owen Mayfield (d.1685), St. Edward, Cambridge.

up and only survives in fragments at the west end of the church.[63] Also lost in the eighteenth and early nineteenth centuries were several post-medieval inscription plates, possibly mostly casualties of church restorations. For example, at St. Bene't's we have lost the brasses of Golsen Arisen, a Dutch clockmaker (d.1609), and James Cranidge, 'Master of the Worthy Noble

---

[63] Lack, Stuchfield and Whittemore, *Cambridgeshire*, p. 57.

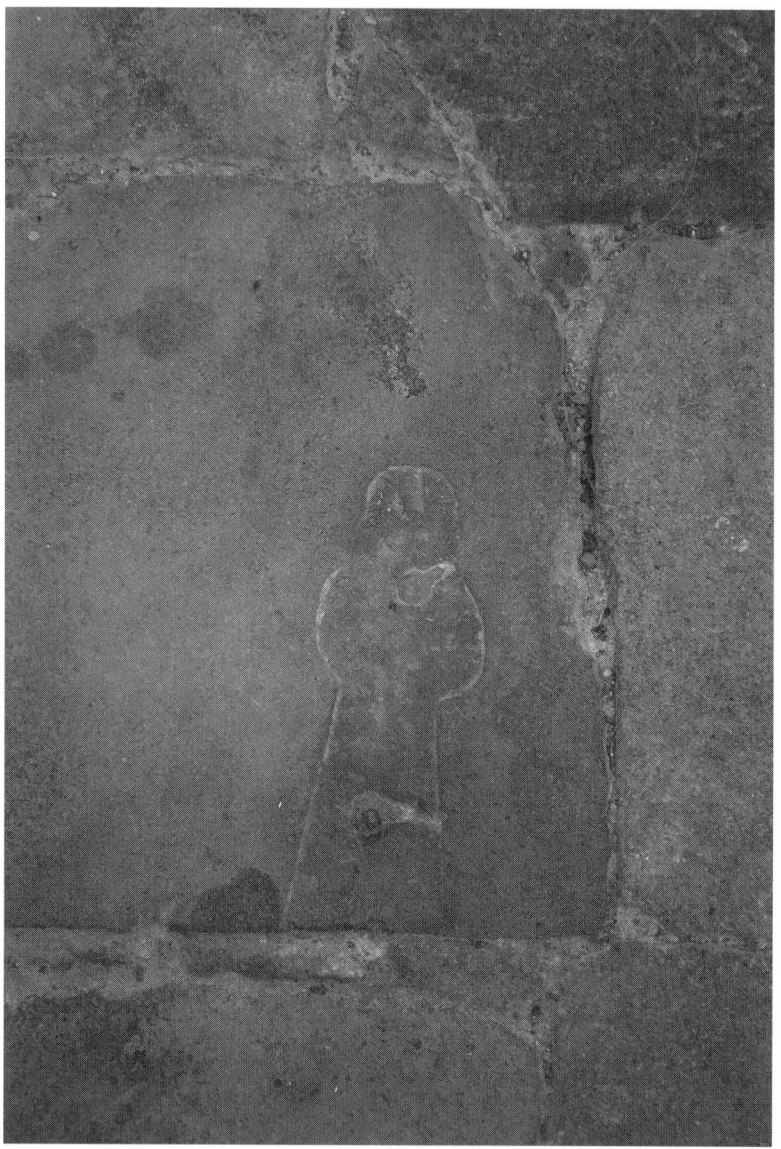

20: Indent of civilian, St. Peter, Cambridge.

Art of Defence' (d.1617).[64] When All Saints in the Jewry was demolished in 1864 the slab of an important early fifteenth-century brass, possibly that of Richard Holme, master of King's Hall, was left in the churchyard rather than being transferred to the new church in Jesus Lane. The slab was still visible in 1970, but can no longer be seen and is probably covered by the gravel surface in the churchyard.[65]

[64] Blomefield, *Collectanea Cantabrigiensia*, p. 46; Lack, Stuchfield and Whittemore, *Cambridgeshire*, p. 52.
[65] Lack, Stuchfield and Whittemore, *Cambridgeshire*, p. 20, illus. on p. 21.

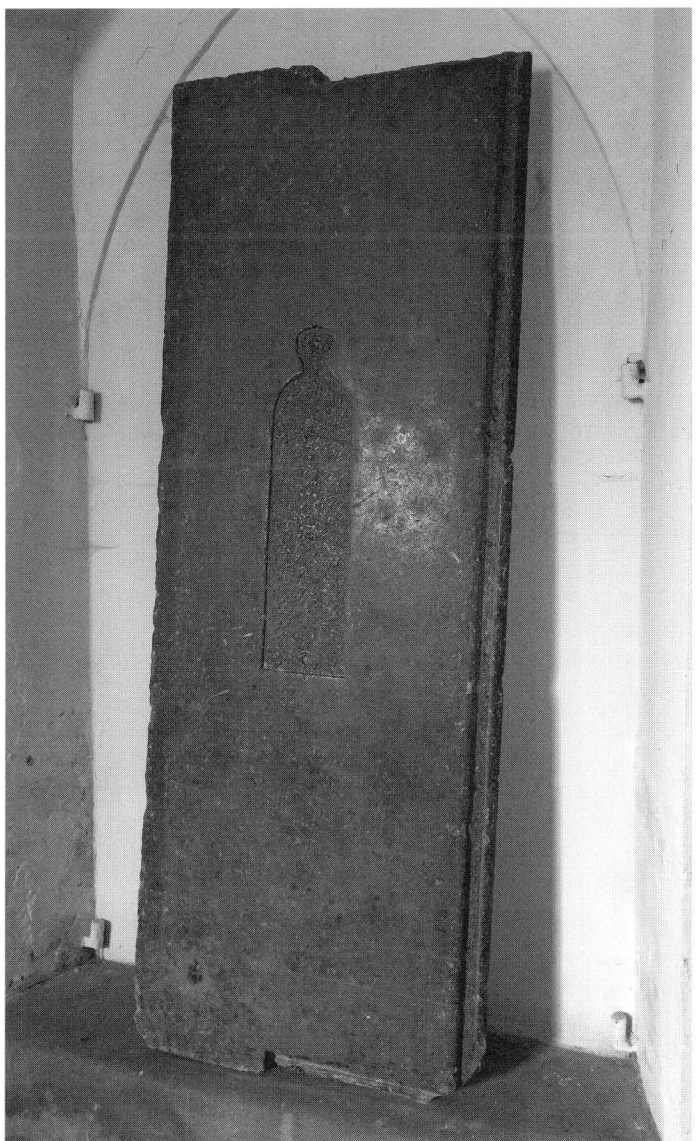

21: Indent of academic, St. Botolph, Cambridge.

When new college chapels were built at St. John's, by George Gilbert Scott, and at Queens', by Bodley, some care was taken to preserve the brasses. At St. John's the brasses are displayed in a somewhat haphazard way, and some notable evidence of indents was lost in the demolition of the old chapel.[66] The mural arrangement of the Queens' brasses reflects their disposition in the

[66] See P. Cockerham, 'A Lost Tomb from St. John's College, Cambridge', *TMBS*, 14:4 (1989), pp. 268–72 for an indent lost when the old chapel was demolished in the 1860s. For indents on the site of the old chapel see Lack, Stuchfield and Whittemore, *Cambridgeshire*, pp. 61–2.

old chapel following the 1773 repaving.[67] The late nineteenth and twentieth centuries saw stabilisation in the condition of Cambridge brasses, thanks to a better appreciation of their historical value, which manifested itself above all in the birth in 1887 of the Cambridge University Association of Brass Collectors. In 1895 Walter Hewke acquired a new head, modelled on the Gygur brass at Tattershall, through the good offices of the Reverend C.G.R. Birch of the Monumental Brass Society.[68] However, losses continue. The most distressing in recent years was the theft in May 2008 of the figure of Richard Billingford, the one element of the Billingford brass left by Dowsing.[69] Fortunately this was recovered in 2017.[70] If one excepts theft, Cambridge brasses are reasonably safe, but indents are threatened both by casual wear and ill-conceived church reorderings.

In many ways the pattern of loss of brasses in Cambridge is typical of English towns, with its phases of iconoclastic destruction and censoring of texts in the sixteenth and seventeenth centuries, followed by destructive neglect in the eighteenth century and destructive restoration in the nineteenth.[71] The presence of the University undoubtedly enhanced the opportunities for patronage and may well have provided the crucial incentive to encourage a marbler to settle in Cambridge. Furthermore, institutional conservatism ensured that the cull of monuments was not as severe as it might have been in a region ideologically uncongenial to the preservation of medieval monuments.

[67] Willis and Clark, *Architectural History*, ii, p. 41.

[68] C.G.R. Birch, 'Note on the Brass of Dr Walter Hewke, Trinity Hall, Cambridge', *TMBS*, 2:6 (1895), pp. 223–4. The original head had gone by 1750 (Blomefield, *Collectanea Cantabrigiensia*, p. 105). Birch suggests that it was lost when the brass was moved to the ante-chapel in 1729. On this brass, see C.G. Daunton and E.A. New, 'Patrons and Benefactors: The Masters of Trinity Hall in the Later Middle Ages', pp. 61–89 in this volume.

[69] *MBS Bulletin*, 108 (May 2008), p. 142, illus. on p. 141.

[70] *MBS Bulletin*, 134 (February 2017), p. 662, illus. on p. 661.

[71] For a general summary of the process of destruction see Bertram, *Lost Brasses*, pp. 11–42.

Bibliography

MANUSCRIPT SOURCES

British Library (BL), London

Add. Ch. 35381–35402. Deeds relating to Baldock, Hertfordshire, 1446–1586.

Add. MS 5814, 5861. William Cole, Collections for the history of King's College and the county of Cambridgeshire.

Add. MS 8835. Wardrobe book of Edward I.

Cotton MS Galba, E XIV. John of Newbury, Compotus of the household of Isabella, late queen of England (d.1358), 30 September 1358–4 December 1359.

Cotton MS Vitellius XII. The Register of the Grey Friars of London containing a list of burials and monuments in their church.

Egerton MS 2849. The mortuary roll of Lucy of Hedingham, *c*.1225–1230.

Harley MS 6114, Harley MS 6865, Add. MS 5954 and Add. MS 5955. Thomas Hatcher, *Catalogus praepositorum, sociorum, et scholarium Collegii Regalis Cantabrigiae, a tempore fundationis ad annum 1572* ('Catalogue of the Provosts, Fellows and Scholars of King's College Cambridge from the date of the foundation to the year 1572').

Royal MS 14 CIX. 'Liber Iohannis Wardeboys Bachilaurei theologie et abbatis'.

Seals, xxxvi, 243. Convent of Grey Friars, Cambridge, seal of vice-custos.

Sloane MS 1726. Codex membranaceus.

Cambridge University Library (CUL)

EDR, G/1/1, G/1/3, G/1/5. Ely Diocesan Records, registers and act books of the bishops of Ely, Simon Montacute (inst. 1337) and Thomas de Lisle (inst. 1345), John Fordham (inst. 1388), William Gray (inst. 1454).

MS Ii.III.3. A Collection of Astronomical Texts.

UA Collect. Admin. 3. Old Proctor's Book, *c*.1390–*c*.1483

UA, Vice-Chancellor's Court, inventories.

UA, Wills I. Vice-Chancellor's Court, register of wills, 1501–58.

Cambridgeshire Archives (CA), Cambridge Record Office

Archdeaconry of Ely, will register 1, 1529–44.
City/PB Box X70/1–10, X71/1–10. Cambridge borough treasurers' accounts, 1422/23–1435/36, 1483/84–1500/01.

Canterbury Cathedral Archives

CCA-DCc/Register/F. Priory and Chapter Registers, *Sede Vacante* Register, 1500–03.

Clare College Archives, Cambridge

CCGB/1/1/5. Copy of 1359 college statutes.

College of Arms, London

MS CGY 647. A record of tombs from London churches and religious houses, thought to have been made by Thomas Benolt, *c.*1505, with several additions to *c.*1530.

Corpus Christi College Archives (CCCA), Cambridge

CCCCo1/G/1/2 (former reference: XXXI.3 (N.3)). Bede rolls of Gild of St Mary, *c.*1280–*c.*1350.
CCCCo1/G/1/11 (former reference: XXXI. 24). Grant of 7*s.* to John son of William le Combere, 1302.
CCCCo1/G/1/17 (former reference: XXVII. 2). Grant of two messuages in Cambridge to the gild of St Mary, 1307.
CCCCo1/G/1/19 (former reference: CCCA, XXX1, 28). Will of Alan de Welles, 1316.
CCCCo1/G/2/1. Minutes of the Gild of Corpus Christi, 1350–58.
CCCCo1/GF/1. Licence granted on petition of Henry Duke of Lancaster for the gilds of Corpus Christi and the Blessed Mary of Cambridge to found and house a 'house' of scholars, and to acquire for them the advowson of St Benedict's, 1352.
CCCCo1/P/53 (former reference: XXXI. 92). Copy of will of Thomas Lolleworth, 1383.
CCCCo9/o8/280 (former reference: IX 25.c). Great St Mary's parish deeds, counterpart of lease to John Smith and Isabel his wife of a tenement, 1535.

Gonville and Caius College, Cambridge

MS 173/94. Thomas Hatcher, *Catalogus praepositorum, sociorum, et scholarium Collegii Regalis Cantabrigiae, a tempore fundationis ad annum 1572* ('Catalogue of the Provosts, Fellows and Scholars of King's College Cambridge from the date of the foundation to the year 1572').

Huntingdonshire Archives, Huntingdon

AH15/1/2. Archdeaconry of Huntingdon, Wills, vol. 2, 1481–86, 1500–26.

Inner Temple Library, London

MS Add 188. Miscellaneous or Additional Manuscripts, four illuminated folios of the courts at Westminster Hall, *c.*1460.

Jesus College Archives, Cambridge

Jesus/Nuns/Gray/29. Will of Roger Mason, 5 July 1392.
Jesus/Nuns/Gray/144a. Will of William Mast, baker, 3 December 1432.
Jesus/Nuns/Gray/360. Will of John Grenelawe, 1 February 1432.

King's College Archives (KCA), Cambridge

KC/18. Foundation grant by Henry VI of lands and privileges to benefit his King's College of St. Nicholas and Our Lady at Cambridge, 1446.
KC/56. King's College register.
KCA/22. College inventories, sixteenth century.
KCA/344, KCA/345. Purveyance of chapel books, 1443, and vestments, *c.*1445.
KCA/684. Volume of inventories/lists.
KCA/687. College inventories, sixteenth century: typescript transcripts by Sir William St. John Hope and Provost James.
KCA, Coll 2/23. College inventories, original notes and transcripts.
KCAR/3/3/1/1/1. Ledger Book I.
KCAR/4/A/3. Mundum Books, 1448–1554.
KCE/716. Cartulary.
KCHR/3/12. Transcription of KCE/716 by John Saltmarsh.

Lambeth Palace Library (LPL), London

Reg. Sudbury, Reg. Courtenay, Reg. Arundel 1. Registers of Archbishops of Canterbury Simon Sudbury, 1375–81, William Courtenay, 1381–96, and Thomas Arundel 1396–1408, Register 1.

London Metropolitan Archives

DL/A/A/004/MS09531/004 (former reference: Guildhall Library MS 9531/4). Diocese of London, bishops' register, 1405–24, 1431–34 with copies of earlier documents.
DL/C/B/004/MS09171/005–006 (former reference: Guildhall Library MS 9071/5–6). Diocese of London, commissary court registers of wills, 1449–66, 1467–83.

Lincolnshire Archives, Lincoln

DIOC/REG/3. Episcopal Register of Bishop John Dalderby, 1300–20
DIOC/REG/7. Episcopal Register of Bishop Thomas Bek, 1342–47.

The National Archives: Public Record Office (TNA:PRO), London

C 1/299/52. Chancery pleadings. Mayor, bailiffs and burgesses of Cambridge v William Barbour and Elizabeth, executrix and late the wife of William Adam. Refusal to make a conduit in Cambridge market-place, as required by the will of Thomas Pomell, 1504–15.
C 143/367/3. Inquisitions taken as a result of applications to the Crown for licences to alienate land. John, duke of Lancaster, to grant the manor of Landbeach, with the advowson of its church, and messuages and land in Cambridge, Barnwell, Grantchester, and Coton, to the master and scholars of Corpus Christi College, 1369–70.
E 101/93/12. King's Remembrancer: Account of expenses of the chamber of lady de Clare, 1351–53.
E 403/59, E 403/72. Exchequer of Receipt: Issue Rolls and Registers, William de Louth (Luda), 1289, and Mary, the king's daughter, 1291.
LC 2/1. Lord Chamberlain's Department: Records of Special Events. Accounts of Funerals and Mournings.
PROB 10. Bundles of original wills proved in the Prerogative Court of Canterbury.
PROB 11. Registers of wills proved in the Prerogative Court of Canterbury.

Norfolk Record Office, Norwich

HARE 2817, 199X5, HARE 2818, 199X5. Hare Collection, abstracts of leases and deeds relating to Shouldham.
Norwich Consistory Court will registers 10, (Betyns, 1457–71), 11 (Jekkys, 1464–72), 25 (Popy, 1501–04).

Peterhouse Library, Cambridge

MS 82. Giles of Rome, Thomas Aquinas, thirteenth century.
MS 85. Nicholas of Lyre, second half of fourteenth century.
MS 223. Augustine, Richard FitzRalph, &c, fifteenth century.

St. John's College Archives (SJCA), Cambridge

C7.11 'Thin Red Book', college register, *c*.1516–42.
D57.92. Accounts for the building of Ashton's chantry and for his scholars, n.d.
D91.15. Inventory of chapel stuff and other household plate and service books, n.d., *c*.1509.
D91.16. Accounts of the treasurer of household (William Bedell), 1506–07.

D91.17. Accounts of the cofferer (James Clarell), 1498–99.

D91.19. Accounts of the treasurer of the chamber (Miles Worsley), 1507–09.

D91.20. Accounts of the cofferer (Miles Worsley), 1502–05.

D91.21. Accounts of the cofferer, 1505–07.

D91.24.2. Accounts of Lady Margaret's executors, 1509–19.

D94/500. Letter from the president, John Smyth, to Nicholas Metcalfe, master, 12 May 1520.

D102.1. Account of treasurer of the chamber (Robert Fremingham), 1509.

D102.10. Book of receipts and payments, 1499–1509.

D102.13. Inventory of chapel stuff, n.d., *c.*1509.

D106.6. Metcalfe's accounts in connection with Fisher's foundation, 1524–34.

SB4.1–88. College rentals, 1555–1985.

Trinity Hall Archives, Cambridge

TH MS 20. The Master's Statue Book.

THAR/6/1/2/3. Will of Dr. Hewke, 1517.

THAR/8/2/2/12/2/2. Evidence on the bequest of the Griffin Inn to Trinity Hall by Walter Hewke, 1518.

THAR/8/2/2/16/1. Feoffment. John Smith to Walter Hewke and others of a messuage, garden and adjoining land in All Saints with Jesus Lane on the south and the west abutting upon Bridge Street by the Dolphin, 1516.

THHR/2/4/1/4. Miscellaneous documents, *c.* 1400–*c.* 1740.

PRINTED PRIMARY SOURCES

Abstracts from the Wills and Testamentary Documents of Printers, Binders and Stationers of Cambridge from 1504 to 1699, ed. G.J. Gray and W.M. Palmer (London, 1915).

Acta Franciscana e tabulariis Bononiensibus deprompta, ed. B. Giordani, I, *AF*, 9 (Florence, 1927).

Annals of Cambridge, ed. C.H. Cooper, 5 vols. (Cambridge, 1842–1908).

Baker, Thomas, *History of the College of St. John the Evangelist, Cambridge*, ed. J.E.B. Mayor, 2 vols. (Cambridge, 1869).

Bedfordshire Wills proved in the Prerogative Court of Canterbury 1383–1548, ed. M. McGregor, Bedfordshire Historical Record Society, 58 (Bedford, 1979).

Caius, John, *The Works of John Caius, M.D. Second Founder of Gonville and Caius College and Master of the College 1559–1573*, ed. E.S. Roberts (Cambridge, 1912).

Calendar of Close Rolls, HMSO, 46 vols. (London, 1892–1963).

Calendar of Fine Rolls of the Reign of Henry III Preserved in the National Archives, ii: *1224–1234*, ed. P. Dryburgh and B. Hartland (Woodbridge, 2008).

Calendar of Patent Rolls, HMSO, 54 vols. (London, 1891–1916).

Calendar of Wills Proved and Enrolled in the Court of Husting, London A.D.1258–A.D.1688, ed. R.R. Sharpe, 2 vols. (London, 1890).

Cambridge Gild Records, ed. M. Bateson, Cambridge Antiquarian Society, Octavo Series 39, (Cambridge, 1903).

Cartulary of the Hospital of St John the Evangelist, Cambridge, ed. M. Underwood (Cambridge Records Society, 2008).

Chartulary of the High Church of Chichester, ed. W.D. Peckham, Sussex Record Society, 46 (Lewes, 1946).

Chroniques de London, ed. G.J. Aungier, Camden Society Old Series, 28 (London, 1844).

Churchwardens' Book of Bassingbourn, Cambridgeshire 1496–c.1540, ed. D. Dymond, Cambridgeshire Records Society, 17 (Cambridge, 2004).

Collection of Ordinances and Regulations for the Government of the King's Household, ed. J. Nichols (London, 1790).

Constitutiones Generales Ordinis Fratrum Minorum, I (Saeculum XIII), ed. C. Cenci and R.G. Mailleux, *AF*, 13, nova series, documenta et studia, 1 (Grottaferrata, Rome, 2007).

Constitutiones Generales Ordinis Fratrum Minorum, II (Saeculum XIV/1), ed. C. Cenci and R.G. Mailleux, *AF*, 17, nova series, documenta et studia, 5 (Grottaferrata, Rome, 2010).

Documents relating to the Additional Endowments and Trust Funds of King's College, Cambridge (Cambridge, 1875).

Documents relating to the University and Colleges of Cambridge, 3 vols. (London, 1852).

Drake, Francis, *Eboracum* (London, 1736).

Dugdale, William, *Origines Juridiciales, or Historical memorials of the English laws*, 3rd edn. (London, 1680).

Early Statutes of the College of St John the Evangelist in the University of Cambridge, ed. J.E.B. Mayor (Cambridge, 1859).

Elizabeth de Burgh, Lady of Clare (1295–1360): Household and other Records, ed. J. Ward, SRS, 57 (Woodbridge, 2014).

English Episcopal Acta 29, Durham 1241–1283, ed. P.M. Hoskin (Oxford, 2005).

Fifth Report of the Royal Commission on Historical Manuscripts, Part 1: Report and Appendix (London, 1876).

Fisher, John, *This treatise concernynge the fruytfull saynges of Davyd the kynge and prophete* (London, 1508), STC (2nd edn.), 10902.

———, *This treatyse concernynge the fruytfull saynges of Davyd the kynge and prophete in the seven penytencyall psalms* (London, 1508), STC (2nd ed.), 10903.

———, *This sermon folowynge was compyled [and] sayd in the cathedrall chyrche of saynt Poule within ye cyte of London by the ryght reuerende fader in god Iohn⊠ bysshop of Rochester, the body beyinge present of the moost famouse prynce kynge Henry the. vij. the. x. day of Maye, th yere of our lorde god. M.CCCCC.ix. whiche sermon was enprynted at the specyall request of ye ryght excellent pryncesse Margarete moder vnto the sayd noble prynce and Countesse of Rychemonde and Derby* (London, 1509 & 1509–10), STC (2nd edn.), 10900–1.

———, *Here after foloweth a mornynge remembrau[n]ce had at the moneth mynde of the noble prynces Margarete countesse of Rychemonde [and] Darbye moder vnto kynge Henry the. vii. [and] grandame to oure souerayne lorde that nowe is, vppon whose soule almyghty god haue mercy* (London, 1509), STC (2nd edn.), 10891.

————, *The English Works of John Fisher*, ed. J.E.B. Mayor, Early English Text Society, Extra Series 27 (London, 1876).

————, *English Works of John Fisher, Bishop of Rochester: Sermons and Other Writings 1520 to 1535*, ed. C.A. Hatt (Oxford, 2002).

Fortescue, J., *De Laudibus Legum Anglie*, ed. S.B. Chrimes (Cambridge, 1942).

Francesco d'Assisi Scritti, ed. C. Paolazzi, Spicilegium Bonaventurianum, 36 (Grottaferrata, Rome, 2009).

Fratris Thomae vulgo dicti de Eccleston Tractatusde adventu Fratrum Minorum in Angliam, ed. A.G. Little (Manchester, 1951).

Fuller, Thomas, *The History of the University of Cambridge from the Conquest to the year 1634*, ed. M. Prickett and T. Wright (London, 1840).

————, *The History of the University of Cambridge, and of Waltham Abbey*, ed. J. Nichols (London, 1840).

The Funeral Sermon of Margaret Countess of Richmond and Derby … Preached by Bishop Fisher in 1509, ed. J. Hymers (Cambridge, 1840).

Grace Book A: Containing the Proctors' Accounts and other Records of the University of Cambridge for the years 1454–1488, ed. L.S. Mordaunt (Cambridge, 1897).

Grace Book B, ed. M. Bateson, 2 vols., Cambridge Antiquarian Society, Luard Memorial Series, 2, 3 (Cambridge, 1903–05).

'Heliae Cortonensis epistola encyclica de transitu Sancti Francisci', in *Fontes Francescani*, ed. E. Menestò, S. Brufani, G. Cremascoli, E. Paoli, L. Pellegrini and S. da Campagnola, Collana diretta da Enrico Menestò, Testi, 2 (Assisi, 1995).

Leland, John, *Joannis Lelandi Antiquarii de Rebus Britannicis Collectis*, ed. T. Hearne, 6 vols. (London, 1770).

Liber memorandorum Ecclesie de Bernewelle, ed. J.W. Clark (Cambridge 1907).

The Observances in use at the Augustinian Priory of S. Giles and S. Andrew at Barnwell, Cambridgeshire, ed. J.W. Clark (Cambridge, 1897).

Register of Henry Chichele archbishop of Canterbury 1414–1443, ed. E.F. Jacob and H.C. Johnson, Canterbury and York Society, 42, 45, 46, 47, 4 vols. (Oxford, 1937–57).

Register of William Bateman, Bishop of Norwich, 1344–1355, ed. P.E. Pobst (Woodbridge, 1996).

Registrum Hamonis Hethe, Diocesis Roffensis, A. D. 1319–52, ed. C. Johnson, Canterbury and York Society, 48–9, 2 vols. (Oxford, 1948).

Roberti Grosseteste episcopi quondam Lincolniensis Epistolae, ed. H.R. Luard, RS, 25 (London, 1861).

Rotuli Hundredorum, ed. W. Illingworth and J. Caley, 2 vols. (London, 1812–18).

Salimbene de Adam, Cronica a.1168–1287, ed. G. Scalia, Corpus Christianorum Continuatio Mediaevalis, 125, 125a, 2 vols. (Turnhout, 1998–99).

Statuta Academiae Cantabrigiensis (Cambridge, 1785).

Statuta Antiqua Universitatis Oxoniensis, ed. S. Gibson (Oxford, 1931).

Stow, John, *The Survey of London*, ed. A. Munday and H. Dyson (London, 1633).

————, *A Survey of London*, ed. C.L. Kingsford, 2 vols, (Oxford, 1908).

Testamenta Eboracensia; or Wills registered at York, ed. J. Raine and J.W. Clay, Surtees Society, 4, 30, 45, 53, 79, 106, 6 vols. (London, 1836–1902).

Testamentary Records of the English and Welsh Episcopate, 1200–1413: Wills, Executors' Accounts and Inventories, and the Probate Process, ed. C.M. Woolgar, Canterbury and York Society, 102 (Woodbridge, 2011).

Vasari, Giogrio, *Le vite de' più eccellenti pittori, scultori e architettori nelle redazioni del 1550 e 1568*, ed. R. Bettarini *et al.*, 11 vols (Florence, 1966–87).

Warren's Book, ed. A.W.W. Dale (Cambridge, 1911).

Wills of the Archdeaconry of Sudbury 1439–1474: Wills from the Register 'Baldwyne': Part I: 1439–1461, ed. P. Northeast, SRS, 44 (Woodbridge, 2001).

Wills of the Archdeaconry of Sudbury 1439–1474: Wills from the Register 'Baldwyne': Part II: 1461–1474, ed. P. Northeast and H. Falvey, SRS, 53 (Woodbridge, 2010).

SECONDARY SOURCES

Aberth, J., 'The Black Death in the Diocese of Ely: The Evidence of the Bishop's Register', *Journal of Medieval History*, 21 (1995), pp. 275–87.

Allen, M., and Davies, M., eds., *Medieval Merchants and Money: Essays in Honour of James L. Bolton* (London, 2016).

à Wood, Anthony, *Fasti Oxonienses, or Annals of the University of Oxford by Anthony à Wood* (London, 1815–20).

Badham, S., 'Evidence for the Minor Funerary Monument Industry 1100–1500', in *Town and Country in the Middle Ages: Contrasts, Contacts and Interconnections, 1100–1500*, ed. K. Giles and C. Dyer, Society for Medieval Archaeology Monograph, 22 (Leeds, 2005), pp. 165–96.

Badham S., and Cockerham, P., eds., *'The beste and fayrest of al Lincolnshire': The Church of St. Botolph, Lincolnshire, and its Medieval Monuments*, British Archaeological Reports, British Series, 554 (2012).

Badham, S., and Dent, J., 'New Light on Lost Brasses in York Minster', *TMBS*, 19:3 (2016), pp. 235–48.

Baker, J.H., 'The Dress of the Cambridge Proctors', *Costume*, 18 (1984), pp. 86–97.

———, *The Order of Serjeants at Law*, Selden Society Supplementary Series, 5 (London, 1984).

———, 'Doctors wear Scarlet: The Festal Gowns of the University of Cambridge', *Costume*, 20 (1986), pp. 33–43.

———, 'An Outline History of the Legal Robes now Worn in England and Wales', in *Court Dress: A Consultation Paper issued on Behalf of the Lord Chancellor and the Lord Chief Justice* (1992).

———, *Monuments of Endlesse Labours: English Canonists and their Work 1399–1900* (London, 1998).

———, *The Men of Court: A Prosopography of the Inns of Court and Chancery and Courts of Law*, Selden Society Supplementary Series, 18 (London, 2012).

———, 'English Judges' Robes 1350–2008', in *Collected Papers on English Legal History*, ed. J.H. Baker (Cambridge, 2013), ii, pp. 812–31.

————, 'The Mystery of the Bar Gown', in *Collected Papers on English Legal History*, ed. J.H. Baker (Cambridge, 2013), ii, pp. 857–67.

Bainbridge, V., *Gilds in the Medieval Countryside: Social and Religious Change in Cambridgeshire c.1350–1558* (Woodbridge, 1996).

Barnett, C.M., 'Commemoration in the Parish Church: Identity and Social Class in Late Medieval York', *Yorkshire Archaeological Journal*, 72 (2000), pp. 73–92.

Barron, C.M., 'The Parish Fraternities of Medieval London', in *The Church in Pre-Reformation Society: Essays in Honour of F.R.H. Du Boulay*, ed. C.M. Barron and C. Harper-Bill (Woodbridge, 1985), pp. 13–37.

Barron, C.M., and Burgess, C., eds., *Memory and Commemoration in Medieval England* (Donington, 2010).

Barron, C.M., and Harper-Bill, C., eds., *The Church in Pre-Reformation Society: Essays in Honour of F.R.H. Du Boulay* (Woodbridge, 1985).

Bertram, J., 'The Lost Brasses of Oxford, I: College Chapels', *TMBS*, 11:4 (1972), pp. 219–52.

————, 'The Lost Brasses of Oxford, II: The Cathedral and City Churches', *TMBS*, 11:5 (1973), pp. 321–79.

————, *Lost Brasses* (Newton Abbot, 1976).

Bertram, J., ed., *Monumental Brasses as Art and History* (Stroud, 1996).

Binski, P., and New, E.A., eds, *Patrons and Professionals in the Middle Ages* (Donington, 2012).

Birch, C.G.R., 'Note on the Brass of Dr Walter Hewke, Trinity Hall, Cambridge', *TMBS*, 2:6 (1895), pp. 223–4.

Bihl, M., 'Statuta generalia Ordinis edita in Capitulo generali an.1354 Assisii celebrato, communiter Farineriana appellata (Editio critica et analytica)', VI, no.17, in *AFH*, 35 (1942), pp. 35–112, pp. 177–253.

Blomefield, F., *Collectanea Cantabrigiensia* (Norwich, 1750).

————, *An Essay towards a Topographical History of the County of Norfolk*, 11 vols. (London, 1805–10).

Bordua, L., '*Master* Plans of Devotion or Daily Pragmatism? The Dedication and Use of Chapels and Conventual Spaces by the Friars and the Laity at the Santo 1263–1310', *Il Santo: Rivista Francescana di storia dottrina arte*, 51 (2011), pp. 491–510.

Bott, A., *The Monuments in Merton College Chapel* (Oxford, 1964).

Boyle, L.E., 'Aspects of Clerical Education in Fourteenth-century England', in *The Fourteenth Century*, ed. P.E. Szamarch and B.E. Levy (New York, 1977), pp. 19–32.

Bradley, S., and Pevsner, N., *The Buildings of England: Cambridgeshire* (New Haven and London, 2014).

Bradshaw, B., and Duffy, E., eds., *Humanism, Reform and the Reformation: The Career of Bishop John Fisher* (Cambridge, 1989)

Brooke, C.N.L., 'The Churches of Medieval Cambridge', in *History, Society and the Churches: Essays in Honour of Owen Chadwick*, ed. D. Beales and G. Best (Cambridge, 1985), pp. 60–77.

————, *A History of Gonville and Caius College Cambridge* (Woodbridge, 1985).

————, 'The Dedications of Cambridge Colleges and their Chapels', in *Medieval Cambridge: Essays on the Pre-Reformation University*, ed. P. Zutshi (Woodbridge, 1993), pp. 7–20.

Brown, A.D., *Popular Piety in Late Medieval England: The Diocese of Salisbury 1250–1550* (Oxford, 1995).

Brown, P., *The Cult of the Saints: Its Rise and Function in Latin Christianity* (Chicago, 1981).

————, *The Ransom of the Soul* (Cambridge, MA, 2015).

Burgess, Clive, '"For the Increase of Divine Service": Chantries in the Parish in Late Medieval Bristol', *Journal of Ecclesiastical History*, 36 (1985), pp. 46–65.

————, 'A Service for the Dead: The Form and Function of the Anniversary in Late Medieval Bristol', *Transactions of the Bristol and Gloucestershire Archaeological Society*, 105 (1987), pp. 183–211.

————, 'Strategies for Eternity: Perpetual Chantry Foundation in Late Medieval Bristol', in *Religious Belief and Ecclesiastical Careers in Late Medieval England*, ed. C. Harper-Bill (Woodbridge, 1991), pp. 1–32.

————, '"Longing to be prayed for": Death and Commemoration in an English Parish in the Later Middle Ages', in *The Place of the Dead: Death and Remembrance in Late Medieval and Early Modern Europe*, ed. B. Gordon and P. Marshall (Cambridge, 2000), pp. 44–65.

————, 'Chantries in the Parish, or "Through the Looking-glass"', in *The Medieval Chantry in England*, ed. J.M. Luxford and J. McNeill (Leeds, 2011), pp. 100–29.

————, 'Obligations and Strategy: Managing Memory in the Late Medieval Parish', *TMBS* 18:4 (2012), pp. 289–310.

————, 'Fotheringhay Church: Conceiving a College and its Community', in *The Yorkist Age*, ed. H. Kleineke and C. Steer (Donington, 2013), pp. 347–66.

Campbell, M., 'Medieval Founders' Relics: Royal and Episcopal Patronage at Oxford and Cambridge Colleges', in *Heraldry, Pageantry and Social Display in Medieval England*, ed. P. Coss and M. Keen (Woodbridge, 2002), pp. 125–42.

Carter, M., '"hys … days here liven was". The Monument of Abbot Robert Chamber at Holm Cultram (Cumbria)', *Church Monuments*, 27 (2012), pp. 38–52.

Cartlidge N., 'A Debate with Death: John Rudyng's Brass in St. Andrew's Church, Biggleswade', *TMBS*, 19:2 (2015), pp. 94–100.

Cherry, B. and Pevsner, N., *The Buildings of England: Devon* (New Haven and London, 2nd edn., 1989; repr. with corrections 1991).

Clark, L., Jurkowski, M., and Richmond, C., eds., *Image, Text and Church, 1380–1600: Essays for Margaret Aston* (Toronto, 2009).

Clark, L., and Rawcliffe, C., eds., *The Fifteenth Century XII: Society in an Age of Plague* (Woodbridge, 2013).

Clark-Maxwell, W.G., 'Some Letters of Fraternity', *Archaeologia*, 75 (1924–25), pp. 19–60.

Clarke, P.D., ed., *The University and College Libraries of Cambridge*, Corpus of British Medieval Library Catalogues, 10 (London, 2002).

Clayton, H.J., *The Ornaments of the Ministers as Shown on English Monumental Brasses*, Alucin Club Collections 22 (London, 1919).

Cobban, A.B., *The King's Hall* (Cambridge, 1969).

——, *The Medieval English Universities: Oxford and Cambridge to c.1500* (Aldershot, 1988).

——, *English University Life in the Middle Ages* (London, 1999).

——, 'English University Benefactors in the Middle Ages', *History*, 86 (2001), pp. 288–312.

Cockerham, P., 'A Lost Tomb from St John's College, Cambridge', *TMBS*, 14:4 (1989), pp. 268–72.

——, 'Bishops, Deans and Canons: Commemorative Contexts across Two Centuries at Exeter Cathedral', *TMBS*, 19:4 (2017), pp. 277–300.

Colvin, H.M., *The History of the King's Works*, 6 vols. and map vol. (London, 1963–82).

Combes, H., 'William Abell: Parishioner, Churchwarden, Limnour, Stationer in the Parish of St Nicholas Shambles in the City of London', *The Ricardian*, 12 (2000), pp. 120–32.

Condon, M., 'God Save the King! Piety, Propaganda and the Perpetual Memorial', in *Westminster Abbey: The Lady Chapel of Henry VII*, ed. T. Tatton-Brown and R. Mortimer (Woodbridge, 2003), pp. 59–97.

Cooper, C.H., *The Lady Margaret: A Memoir of Margaret, Countess of Richmond and Derby*, ed. J.E.B. Mayor (Cambridge, 1874).

Cooper, T., ed., *The Journal of William Dowsing: Iconoclasm in East Anglia during the English Civil War*, (Woodbridge, 2001).

Coss, P., *The Foundations of Gentry Life: The Multons of Frampton and their World 1270–1370* (Oxford, 2010), pp. 154–63.

Coss, P., and Keen, M., *Heraldry, Pageantry and Social Display in Medieval England* (Woodbridge, 2002).

Crawley, C., *Trinity Hall: The History of a Cambridge College, 1350–1975* (Cambridge, 1976).

Crook, A.C., *From the Foundation to Gilbert Scott: A History of the Buildings of St John's College Cambridge 1511–1885* (Cambridge, 1980).

Crook, J., 'Babes, Sucklings, and Hugh Ashton's Tomb', *The Eagle* (Magazine of St John's College), 75 (1993), pp. 29–32.

Danbury, E., 'Security and Safeguard: Signs and Symbols on Boxes and Chests', in *Signs and Symbols*, ed. J. Cherry and A. Payne (Donington, 2009), pp. 29–41.

Dark, K.R., 'Archaeological Survey at Sidney Sussex College Cambridge 1984', *Proceedings of the Cambridge Antiquarian Society*, 74 (1985), pp. 81–4.

Davidson-Houston, C.E.D., 'Sussex Monumental Brasses, Part II', *Sussex Archaeological Collections*, 77 (1936), pp. 130–94.

Delorme, F., 'Diffinitiones Capituli Generalis O.F.M. Narbonensis (1260)', in *AFH*, 3 (1910), pp. 491–504

Dobson, R.B., *The Peasants' Revolt of 1381*, 2nd edn. (London, 1983).

——, 'The Monastic Orders in Late Medieval Cambridge', in *The Medieval Church: Universities, Heresy and the Religious Life*, ed. P. Biller and R.B. Dobson, Studies in Church History Subsidia, 11 (Woodbridge, 1999), pp. 239–69.

Dohar, W., *The Black Death and Pastoral Leadership: The Diocese of Hereford in the Fourteenth Century* (Philadelphia, 1995).

Dowling, Maria, *Humanism in the Age of Henry VIII* (London, Sydney, Dover NH, 1986).

——, *Fisher of Men: A Life of John Fisher, 1469–1535* (Basingstoke and New York, 1999).

Doyle, E., 'William Woodford, O.F.M.: His Life and Works together with a Study and Edition of his *Responsiones contra Wiclevum et Lollardos*', *FS*, 43 (1983), pp. 17–187.

Druitt, H., *Costume on Brasses*, 2nd edn. (London, 1970).

Duffy, E., *Stripping of the Altars: Traditional Religion in England c.1400–c.1580* (New Haven, 1992).

——, 'Salle Church and the Reformation', in *Saints, Sacrilege and Sedition: Religion and Conflict in the Tudor Reformation*, ed. E. Duffy (London, 2012), pp. 83–108.

Emden, A.B., *A Biographical Register of the University of Oxford to A.D. 1500*, 3 vols. (Oxford, 1957–59).

——, *A Biographical Register of the University of Cambridge to 1500* (Cambridge, 1963).

Evans, T.A.R., and Faith, R.J., 'College Estates and University Finances, 1350–1500', in *The History of the University of Oxford*, ii: *Late Medieval Oxford*, ed. J.I. Catto and R. Evans (Oxford, 1992), pp. 635–707.

Farnhill, K., *Guilds and the Parish Community in Late Medieval East Anglia, c.1470–1550* (York, 2001).

Fowler, K., *The King's Lieutenant: Henry of Grosmont, First Duke of Lancaster 1310–1361* (London, 1969).

Gibson, P., 'The Stained and Painted Glass of York', in *The Noble City of York*, ed. Alberic Stacpoole and others (York, 1972), pp. 67–233.

Gillespie, V., 'Medieval Hypertext: Image and Text from York Minster', in *Of the Making of Books, Medieval Manuscripts, Their Scribes and Readers: Essays Presented to M.B. Parkes*, ed. P.R. Robinson and R. Zim (Aldershot 1997), pp. 206–29.

Gillespie, V., and Ghosh, K., eds., *After Arundel: Religious Writing in Fifteenth-Century England* (Turnhout, 2011).

Greenwood, J.R., 'Haine's Cambridge School of Brasses', *TMBS*, 11:1 (1969), pp. 2–12.

Hackett, M.B., *The Original Statutes of Cambridge University: The Text and its History* (Cambridge, 1970).

Haines, H., *A Manual of Monumental Brasses* (Oxford, 1861; repr. Bath, 1970).

Haines, R.M., 'Associates and Familia of William Gray and his Use of Patronage whilst Bishop of Ely, 1458–1474', *Journal of Ecclesiastical History*, 25 (1974), pp. 225–48.

Hall, C.P., 'The Gild of Corpus Christi and the Foundation of Corpus Christi College: An Investigation of the Documents', in *Medieval Cambridge: Essays on the Pre-Reformation University*, ed. P. Zutshi (Woodbridge, 1993), pp. 62–92.

Hargreaves-Mawdsley, W.N., *A History of Academical Dress in Europe until the end of the Eighteenth Century* (Oxford, 1963).

Harris, J.R., *The Origin of the Leicester Codex of the New Testament* (London, 1887).

Harry, D., 'William Caxton and Commemorative Culture in Fifteenth-Century England', in *The Fifteenth Century XIII: Exploring the Evidence: Commemoration, Administration and the Economy*, ed. L. Clark (Woodbridge, 2014), pp. 63–79.

———, 'A Cadaver in Context: The Shroud Brass of John Brigge revisited', *TMBS*, 19:2 (2015), pp. 101–10.

———, 'Marriage and Martyrdom: The Death of John Fisher Reconsidered', in *Saints and Cults in Medieval England*, ed. Susan Powell (Donington, 2017), pp. 124–39.

Harvey, J., *English Mediaeval Architects: A Biographical Dictionary down to 1550*, rev. edn. (Gloucester, 1984).

Hatcher, J., 'Commemoration of Benefactors Address, 4 December 2009: "For the Souls of the Departed in the Mortality and after the year of the Lord 1349 and after"', *The Letter* (Corpus Christi College, Cambridge), 89 (2010), pp. 14–23.

Heseltine, P.J., *The Figure Brasses of Cambridgeshire* (St. Neots, 1981).

Heslop, T.A., 'The Alabaster Tomb at Ashwellthorpe, Norfolk: Its Workmanship, Cost and Location', in *Patrons and Professionals in the Middle Ages*, ed. E.A. New and P. Binski (Donington, 2012), pp. 333–46.

Hicks, C., ed., *Cambridgeshire Churches* (Stamford, 1997).

Holder, N., 'Medieval Foundation Stones and Foundation Ceremonies', in *Memory and Commemoration in Medieval England*, ed. C.M. Barron and C. Burgess (Donington, 2010), pp. 6–23.

Holt, R., and Rosser, G., 'Introduction: The English Town in the Middle Ages', in *The Medieval Town: A Reader in English Urban History, 1200–1540*, ed. R. Holt and G. Rosser (London, 1990), pp. 1–18.

Homan, R.L., 'Old and New Evidence of the Career of William Melton, O.F.M.', *FS*, 49 (1989), pp. 25–33.

Humphries, K.W., ed., *The Friars' Libraries* (London, 1990).

James, M.R., *A Descriptive Catalogue of the Manuscripts other than Oriental in the Library of King's College, Cambridge* (Cambridge, 1895).

———, *A Descriptive Catalogue of the Manuscripts in the Library of Gonville and Caius College*, 2 vols. (Cambridge, 1907–08).

Jennings, B., *The Grey Friars of Richmond* (Richmond, 1958).

Jones, M.K., and Underwood, M., *The King's Mother: Lady Margaret Beaufort, Countess of Richmond and Derby* (Cambridge, 1992).

Jones, P.M., 'The College and the Chapel', in *King's College Chapel 1515–2015: Art, Music and Religion in Cambridge*, ed. J.M. Massing and N. Zeeman (London, 2014), pp. 161–79.

Kingsford, C.L., *The Grey Friars of London* (Aberdeen, 1915).

Kinsey, R., 'The Location of Commemoration in Late Medieval England: the Case of the Thorpes of Northamptonshire', in *Memory and Commemoration in Medieval England*, eds. C.M. Barron and C. Burgess (Donington, 2010), pp. 40–57.

———, 'Each According to their Degree: The Lost Brasses of the Thorpes of Northamptonshire', *TMBS*, 18:4 (2012), pp. 311–33.

Kleineke, H., 'The Library of John Veysy (d. 1492), Fellow of Lincoln College, Oxford, and Rector of St. James Garlickhithe, London', *The Library*, 17:4 (December 2016), pp. 399–423.

Kleineke, H., and Steer, C., eds., *The Yorkist Age* (Donington, 2013).

Knowles, D.M., *The Monastic Order in England: A History of its Development from the times of St. Dunstan to the Fourth Lateran Council, 940–1216* (Cambridge, 1963).

Koopmans, R., 'Early Sixteenth-Century Glass at St Michael-le-Belfrey and the Commemoration of Thomas Becket in Late Medieval York', *Speculum*, 89 (2014), pp. 1040–1100.

Lack, W., Stuchfield, H.M., and Whittemore, P., *The Monumental Brasses of Cambridgeshire* (London, 1995).

———, *The Monumental Brasses of Hertfordshire*, (Stratford St. Mary, 2009).

Latham, R.E., and Howlett, D.R., *Dictionary of Medieval Latin from British Sources*, 17 vols. (London, 1975–2013).

Lawrence, C.H., ed., *The Letters of Adam Marsh*, Oxford Medieval Texts, 2 vols. (London, 2006–10).

Leader, D.R., *A History of the University of Cambridge*, i: *The University to 1546* (Cambridge, 1988).

Lee, J.S., 'The Trade of Late Fifteenth-century Cambridge and its Region', in *The Fifteenth Century II: Revolution and Consumption in Late Medieval England*, ed. M.A. Hicks (Woodbridge, 2001), pp. 127–39.

———, *Cambridge and its Economic Region, 1450–1560* (Hatfield, 2005).

———, 'The Role of Fairs in Late Medieval England', in *Town and Countryside in the Age of the Black Death: Essays in Honour of John Hatcher*, ed. S. Rigby and M. Bailey (Turnhout, 2012), pp. 407–37.

———, 'Piped Water Supplies Managed by Civic Bodies in Medieval English Towns', *Urban History*, 41 (2014), pp. 369–93.

———, 'Decline and Growth in the Late Medieval Fenland: The Examples of Outwell and Upwell', *Proceedings of the Cambridge Antiquarian Society*, 104 (2015), pp. 137–47.

———, '"'Tis the sheep have paid for all": Merchant Commemoration in Late Medieval Newark', *TMBS*, 19:4 (2017), pp. 301–27.

———, 'Trinity in the Town', in *A History of Trinity College, Cambridge*, eds. E. Leedham-Green and A. Green (forthcoming).

Lee-Warner, J., 'Petition of the Prior and Canons of Walsingham, Norfolk, to Elizabeth, Lady of Clare c.1345', *Archaeological Journal*, 26 (1869), pp. 166–73.

Leedham-Green, E., 'Perne's Wills', in *Andrew Perne: Quatercentenary Studies*, ed. D. McKitterick, Cambridge Bibliographical Society, Monograph 11 (Cambridge, 1991), pp. 79–119.

———, *A Concise History of the University of Cambridge* (Cambridge, 1996).

Leedham-Green, E., and Webber, T., eds., *The Cambridge History of the Libraries in Britain and Ireland*, 3 vols. (Cambridge, 2006).

Lepine, D., *A Brotherhood of Canons Serving God: English Secular Cathedrals in the Late Middle Ages* (Woodbridge, 1995).

———, '"A stone to be layed upon me": The Monumental Commemoration of the Late Medieval English Higher Clergy', in *Monuments and Monumentality across Medieval and Early Modern Europe*, ed. M. Penman (Donington, 2013), pp. 158–70.

———, '"Pause and pray with mournful heart": Late Medieval Clerical Monuments in Lincoln Cathedral', *TMBS*, 19:1 (2014), pp. 15–40.

Lewis, Charlton T., and Short, Charles, *A Latin Dictionary* (Oxford, 1966).

Lindenbaum, S., 'London after Arundel: Learned Rectors and the Strategies of Orthodox Reform', in *After Arundel: Religious Writing in Fifteenth-Century England*, ed. V. Gillespie and K. Ghosh (Turnout, 2011), pp. 187–208.

Lindley, Philip, '"The singuler mediacions and praiers of al the holie companie of Heven": Sculptural Functions and Forms in Henry VII's Chapel', in *Westminster Abbey: The Lady Chapel of Henry VII*, ed. T. Tatton-Brown and R. Mortimer (Woodbridge, 2003), pp. 259–93.

———, *Tomb Destruction and Scholarship: Medieval Monuments in Early Modern England* (Donington, 2007).

Linehan, P., ed., *St John's College Cambridge: A History* (Woodbridge, 2011).

———, 'The Twentieth Century', in *St John's College Cambridge: A History*, pp. 397–639.

Little, A.G., 'Records of the Franciscan Province of England (Cotton Charter, XXX, 40)', in *Collectanea Franciscana*, I, ed. A.G. Little, M.R. James and H.M. Bannister, BSFS, 5 (Aberdeen, 1914), pp. 141–53.

———, *Franciscan Papers, Lists and Documents* (Manchester, 1943).

Lloyd, A.H., 'Two Monumental Brasses in the Chapel of Christ's College', *Proceedings of the Cambridge Antiquarian Society*, 33 (1933), pp. 61–82.

———, *The Early History of Christ's College, Cambridge: derived from contemporary documents* (Cambridge, 1934).

Loewe, A., 'Michaelhouse: Hervey de Stanton's Cambridge Foundation', *Church History and Religious Culture*, 90 (2010), pp. 579–608.

Lomas, K. and Cornell, T., eds., *Bread and Circuses: Euergetism and Municipal Patronage in Italy* (London, 2003).

Lovatt, R., 'Two Collegiate Loan Chests in Late Medieval Cambridge', in *Medieval Cambridge: Essays on the Pre-Reformation University*, ed. P. Zutshi (Woodbridge, 1993), pp. 129–65

———, 'Hugh of Balsham, bishop of Ely 1256/7–1286', in *Pragmatic Utopias: Ideals and Communities, 1200–1630*, ed. R. Horrox and S. Rees Jones (Cambridge, 2001), pp. 72–7.

———, 'College and University Book Collections and Libraries', in *The Cambridge History of the Libraries in Britain and Ireland*, ed. E. Leedham-Green and T. Webber, 3 vols. (Cambridge, 2006), i, pp. 152–77.

Lovatt, R., and Lovatt, M., 'The Religious Life of the Townsmen of Medieval Cambridge', in *Catholics in Cambridge*, ed. N. Rogers (Leominster, 2003), pp. 4–21.

Lucas, H.S., 'Diplomatic Relations between England and Flanders from 1329 to 1336', *Speculum*, 11 (1936), pp. 59–87.

Luxford, J.M., 'The Collegiate Church as Mausoleum', in *The Late Medieval English College and its Context*, ed. C. Burgess and M. Heale (York, 2008), pp. 110–39.

Luxford, J.M., and McNeil, J., eds., *The Medieval Chantry in England* (Leeds, 2011).

Luxford, J.M., and Michael, M.A., eds., *Tributes to Nigel Morgan – Contexts of Medieval Art: Images, Objects and Ideas* (Turnhout, 2010).

Maitland, F.W., *Township and Borough* (Cambridge, 1898).

Marks, R., 'Picturing Word and Text in the Late Medieval Parish Church', in *Image, Text and Church, 1380–1600: Essays for Margaret Aston*, ed. L. Clark, M. Jurkowski and C. Richmond (Toronto, 2009), pp. 162–202.

Marks, R., and Williamson, P., eds., *Gothic: Art for England 1400–1547* (London, 2003).

Marmion, D., and Thiessen, G.E., *Trinity and Salvation: Theological, Spiritual, and Aesthetic Perspectives* (Bern, 2009).

Mason Neal, J., ed., *Illustrations of Monumental Brasses*, 5, Cambridge Camden Society (Cambridge, 1842).

Massing, J.M., and Zeeman, N., eds., *King's College Chapel 1515–2015: Art, Music and Religion in Cambridge* (London, 2014).

Montagu Benton, G., 'Essex Wills at Canterbury', in *Transactions of the Essex Archaeological Society*, new series, 21 (1933–37), pp. 234–69.

Moorman, J.R., *The Grey Friars in Cambridge, 1225–1538* (Cambridge, 1952).

Morgan, V., and Brooke, C., *A History of the University of Cambridge*, ii: *1546–1750* (Cambridge, 2004).

Morrill, J., 'William Dowsing and the Administration of Iconoclasm in the Puritan Revolution', in *The Journal of William Dowsing: Iconoclasm in East Anglia During the English Civil War*, ed. T. Cooper (Woodbridge, 2001), pp. 1–28.

Munby, A.N.L., 'Notes on King's College Library in the Fifteenth Century', *Transactions of the Cambridge Bibliographical Society*, 1 (1951), pp. 280–6.

Nelson, A.H., ed., *Records of Early English Drama: Cambridge*, 2 vols. (Toronto, 1989).

New, E.A., 'Seals and Status in Medieval English Towns: A Case-study of London, Newcastle and Durham', in *Good Impressions: Image and Authority in Medieval Seals*, ed. N. Adams, J. Cherry and J. Robinson (London, 2008), pp. 35–41.

———, 'The Brass and Seal of John Trillek (d. 1360), Bishop of Hereford: Comparative Thoughts', *TMBS*, 19:1 (2014), pp. 2–14.

Nicolas, Nicholas Harris, *Testamenta Vetusta* (London, 1826).

Norris, M., *Monumental Brasses: The Memorials*, 2 vols. (London, 1977).

Oates, J.C.T., *Cambridge University Library: A History* (Cambridge, 1985).

Orme, N., 'The Medieval Schools of Cambridge, 1200–1550', *Proceedings of the Cambridge Antiquarian Society*, 104 (2015), pp. 125–36.

O'Sullivan, D., *In the Company of the Preachers: The Archaeology of Medieval Friaries in England and Wales*, Leicester Archaeology Monograph 23 (Leicester, 2013).

Oxford Dictionary of National Biography, eds. H.C.G. Matthew and B. Harrison, 60 vols. (Oxford, 2004).

Oxford English Dictionary online. http://www.oed.com/

Page-Phillips, J., *Palimpsests: The Backs of Monumental Brasses*, 2 vols. (London, 1980).

Palmer, W.M., *History of the Parish of Borough Green Cambridgeshire*, Cambridge Antiquarian Society, 54 (1939).

Parker, R., *Town and Gown: The 700 Years War in Cambridge* (Cambridge, 1983).

Penman, M., ed., *Monuments and Monumentality across Medieval and Early Modern Europe* (Donington, 2013).

Pfaff, R., *New Liturgical Feasts in Later Medieval England* (Oxford, 1970).

Pickering, N., 'Provost Robert Hacumblen and his Chantry Chapel', in *King's College Chapel 1515–2015: Art, Music and Religion in Cambridge*, ed. J.M. Massing and N. Zeeman (London, 2014), pp. 96–113.

Pollard, G., 'Medieval Loan Chests at Cambridge', *Bulletin of the Institute of Historical Research*, 17 (1939–40), pp. 113–29.

Powell, S., 'Lady Margaret Beaufort and her Books', *The Library*, sixth series, 20 (1998), pp. 197–240.

——, 'Lady Margaret Beaufort as Patron of Scholars and Scholarship', in *Patrons and Professionals in the Middle Ages*, ed. P. Binski and E.A. New (Donington, 2012), pp. 100–21.

——, 'The Secular Clergy', in *A Companion to the Early Printed Book in Britain*, ed. V. Gillespie and S. Powell (Cambridge, 2014), pp. 150–75.

——, 'Textiles and Dress in the Household Papers of Lady Margaret Beaufort (1443–1509), Mother of King Henry VII', in *Medieval Clothing and Textiles 11*, eds. R. Netherton and G. R. Owen-Crocker (Woodbridge, 2015), pp. 139–57.

Powell, S., ed., *Saints and their Cults in the Middle Ages* (Donington, 2015).

Rackham, H., *Early Statutes of Christ's College, Cambridge* (Cambridge, 1927).

Rackham, O., 'Why Corpus Christi?', in *Corpus within Living Memory: Life in a Cambridge College*, ed. M.E. Bury and E.J. Winter (London, 2003), pp. 9–17.

Raines, F.R., *The Fellows of the Collegiate Church of Manchester*, ed. F. Renaud (Manchester, 1891).

Rex, R., *The Theology of John Fisher* (Cambridge, 1991).

——, 'Lady Margaret and her Professorship 1502–1559', in *Lady Margaret Beaufort and her Professors of Divinity at Cambridge 1502 to 1649*, ed. P. Collinson, R. Rex and G. Stanton (Cambridge, 2003), pp. 19–56.

——, *Henry VIII and the English Reformation*, 2nd edn. (Basingstoke, 2006).

——, 'The Sixteenth Century', in *St John's College Cambridge: A History*, ed. P. Linehan (Woodbridge, 2011), pp. 5–92.

Reynolds, D., ed., *Christ's: A Cambridge College Over Five Centuries* (London, 2005).

Ringrose, J., 'The Medieval Statutes of Pembroke College', in *Medieval Cambridge: Essays on the Pre-Reformation University*, ed. P. Zutshi (Woodbridge, 1993), pp. 93–127.

Rogers, N., 'Cambridgeshire Brasses', in *Cambridgeshire Churches*, ed. C. Hicks (Stamford, 1997), pp. 303–19.

———, 'Charter upon Act of Parliament for the Foundation of King's College, Cambridge', in *The Cambridge Illuminations: Ten Centuries of Book Production in the Medieval West*, ed. P. Binski and S. Panayotova (London, 2005), pp. 379–81.

———, 'The Frenze Palimpsest' in *Tributes to Nigel Morgan – Contexts of Medieval Art: Images, Objects and Ideas*, ed. J.M. Luxford and M.A. Michael (Turnhout, 2010), pp. 223–40.

Röhrkasten, J., *The Mendicant Houses of Medieval London 1221–1539* (Münster, 2004).

———, 'Friars and the Laity in the Franciscan Custody of Cambridge', in *The Friars in Medieval Britain*, ed. N. Rogers (Donington, 2010), pp. 107–24.

Rosser, G., 'Communities of Parish and Guild in the Late Middle Ages', in *Parish, Church and People: Local Studies in lay religion 1350–1750*, ed. S. Wright (London, 1988), pp. 29–55.

Royal Commission on Historical Monuments, *An Inventory of the Historical Monuments in the City of Cambridge*, 2 vols. (London, 1959).

Rubin, M., *Charity and Community in Medieval Cambridge* (Cambridge, 1987).

———, *Corpus Christi: The Eucharist in Late Medieval Culture* (Cambridge, 1991).

———, 'Religious Culture in Town and Country: Reflections on a Great Divide', in *Church and City 1000–1500: Essays in Honour of Christopher Brooke*, ed. D. Abulafia, M. Franklin and M. Rubin (Cambridge, 1992), pp. 3–22.

Rutledge, E., 'An Urban Environment: Norwich in the Fifteenth Century', in *The Fifteenth Century XII: Society in an Age of Plague*, ed. L. Clark and C. Rawcliffe (Woodbridge, 2013), pp. 79–99.

Rutledge, P., 'The Will of Oliver Wyth, 1291', *A Miscellany*, Norfolk Record Society 56 (Reading, 1991), no.152, pp. 9–30.

Sadler, S.L., 'Dowsing's Arguments with the Fellows of Pembroke', in *The Journal of William Dowsing: Iconoclasm in East Anglia During the English Civil War*, ed. T. Cooper (Woodbridge, 2001), pp. 56–66.

St. John's College [T.G. Bonney], *Collegium Divi Johannis Evangelistae 1511–1911* (Cambridge, 1911).

Saltmarsh, J., 'The Muniments of King's College', *Proceedings of the Cambridge Antiquarian Society*, 33 (1933), pp. 83–97.

———, 'The Founder's Statutes of King's College, Cambridge', in *Studies presented to Sir Hilary Jenkinson*, ed. J. Conway Davies (London, 1957), pp. 337–60.

Salway, P., 'Excavations on the Franciscan Site in Sidney, 1958', in *The Bull and the Porcupine* (1959), pp. 35–9.

———, 'Sidney before the College', in *Sidney Sussex College, Cambridge: Historical Essays in Commemoration of the Quatercentenary*, ed. D.E.D. Beales and H.B. Nisbet (Woodbridge, 1996), pp. 3–34.

Saul, N., *Death, Art, and Memory in Medieval England: The Cobham Family and their Monuments 1300–1500* (Oxford, 2001).

——, *English Church Monuments in the Middle Ages: History and Representation* (Oxford, 2009).

——, 'Patronage and Design in the Construction of English Medieval Tomb Monuments', in *Patrons and Professionals in the Middle Ages*, ed. P. Binski and E.A. New (Donington, 2012), pp. 316–32.

——, 'Fotheringhay Church, Northamptonshire: Architecture and Fittings', in *The Yorkist Age*, ed. H. Kleineke and C. Steer (Donington, 2013), pp. 367–79.

——, *Lordship and Faith: The English Gentry and the Parish Church in the Middle Ages* (Oxford, 2017).

Schofield, J., 'Excavations on the Site of St Nicholas Shambles, Newgate Street, City of London, 1975–9', *Transactions of the London and Middlesex Archaeological Society*, 48 (1997), pp. 77–135.

Scott, R.F., 'Notes from the College Records', *The Eagle* (Magazine of St John's College), 18, no. 105 (December, 1894), pp. 1–10.

——, 'Notes from the College Records', *The Eagle*, 19, no. 113 (June, 1897), pp. 1–21.

——, 'Notes from the College Records', *The Eagle*, 20, no. 114 (December, 1897), pp. 1–21.

——, 'Notes from the College Records', *The Eagle*, 35 (1914), pp. 27–35.

——, 'A List (Preserved in the Treasury of St John's College) of the Plate, Books and Vestments bequeathed by the Lady Margaret to Christ's College', *Communications of the Cambridge Antiquarian Society*, 9 (1899), pp. 349–67.

——, 'On the Contracts for the Tomb of the Lady Margaret Beaufort, Countess of Richmond and Derby, mother of King Henry VII, and Foundress of the Colleges of Christ and St. John in Cambridge; with some illustrative documents', *Archaeologia*, 66 (1915), pp. 365–76

Searle, W.G., *The History of the Queens' College of St Margaret and St Bernard in the University of Cambridge 1446–1560*, Cambridge Antiquarian Society Publications, 9 (1867).

Shepard, A., 'Contesting Communities? "Town" and "Gown" in Cambridge, *c.*1560–1640', in *Communities in Early Modern England: Networks, Place, Rhetoric*, ed. A. Shepard and P. Withington (Manchester, 2000), pp. 216–34.

——, 'Litigation and Locality: the Cambridge University Courts, 1560–1640', *Urban History*, 31 (2004), pp. 5–28.

Siraut, M., 'Accounts of Saint Katherine's Guild at Holy Trinity Church, Cambridge: 1514–37', *Proceedings of Cambridge Antiquarian Society*, 67 (1977), pp. 111–21.

Salter, H.E., *Medieval Oxford*, Oxford Historical Society, 100 (Oxford, 1936).

Slater, L., 'Defining Queenship at Greyfriars London, *c.*1300–58', *Gender and History*, 27 (2015), pp. 53–76.

Somerville, R., *History of the Duchy of Lancaster, i: 1265–1603* (London, 1953).

Spain, J., *The Pilgrimage to Our Lady of White Hill: Antiquaries, Local Historians and the Formation of an Historical Tradition* (Cambridge, 2013).

Staniland, K., 'Civil Costume on Brasses', in *Monumental Brasses as Art and History*, ed. J. Bertram (Stroud, 1996), pp. 40–7.

Starkey, D., 'A Royal Saint at Work: Henry VI, Henry VII and the Tudor Transformation of Cambridge', in *Saints and Cults in Medieval England*, ed. Susan Powell (Donington, 2017), pp. 80–100.

Steer, C., 'Royal and Noble Commemoration in the Mendicant Houses of London, *c*.1240–1540', in *Memory and Commemoration in Medieval England*, ed. C.M. Barron and C. Burgess (Donington, 2010), pp. 117–42.

———, 'The Plantagenet in the Parish: The Burial of Richard III's Daughter in Medieval London', *The Ricardian*, 24 (2014), pp. 63–73.

———, 'The Canons of St Paul's and their Brasses', *TMBS* 19:3 (2016), pp. 213–34.

———, '"For quicke and deade memorie masses": Merchant Piety in Late Medieval London', in *Medieval Merchants and Money: Essays in Honour of James L. Bolton*, ed. M. Allen and M. Davies (London, 2016), pp. 71–89.

———, 'Monuments of the Dead in Early Franciscan Houses, *c*.1250–*c*.1350', in *The English Province of the Franciscans (1224–c.1350)*, ed. M.J.P. Robson (Leiden, 2017), pp. 405–25.

———, 'The Franciscans and their Graves in Medieval London', in *The Franciscan Order in the Medieval English Province and Beyond*, ed. M. Robson and P. Zutshi (Amsterdam, 2018), pp. 115–38.

Stephenson, M., *A List of Monumental Brasses in the British Isles*, rev. edn. (London, 1964).

Stöber, K., *Late Medieval Monasteries and their Patrons: England and Wales, c. 1300–1540* (Woodbridge, 2007).

Stokes, H.P., *The Chaplains and the Chapel of the University of Cambridge (1256–1568)*, Cambridge Antiquarian Society Publications, Octavo Series 41 (Cambridge, 1906).

Sutton, A.F., and Visser-Fuchs, L., '"As dear to him as the Trojans were to Hector": Richard III and the University of Cambridge', in *Richard III and East Anglia: Magnates, Gilds and Learned Men*, ed. L. Visser-Fuchs (Richard III Society, 2010), pp. 130–42.

Swanson, R.N., *Church and Society in Late Medieval England* (Oxford, 1989).

Sweeting, W.D., 'Cambridge Friars in 1533', *Fenland Notes and Queries: A Quarterly Antiquarian Journal for the Fenland, in the Counties of Huntingdon, Cambridge, Lincoln, Northampton, Norfolk, and Suffolk*, 5 vols. (Peterborough, 1891–1909), iv, no. 712, pp. 71–2.

Tait, H., 'The Hearse-Cloth of Henry VII belonging to the University of Cambridge', *Journal of the Warburg and Courtauld Institutes*, 19 (1956), pp. 294–8.

Tatton-Brown, T., and Mortimer, R., eds., *Westminster Abbey: The Lady Chapel of Henry VII* (Woodbridge, 2003)

Taylor, A., *Cambridge: A Hidden History* (Stroud, 1999).

Thomson, R.M., *A Descriptive Catalogue of the Medieval Manuscripts in the Library of Peterhouse, Cambridge* (Cambridge, 2016).

Thrupp, S., *The Merchant Class of Medieval London 1300–1500* (London, 1948).

Tout, T.F., 'The Household of the Chancery and its Disintegration', in *Essays in History presented to Reginald Lane Poole*, ed. H.W.C. Davis (Oxford, 1927), pp. 46–85.

Turner, D., and Saul, N., 'The Lost Chantry College of Lingfield', *Surrey Archaeological Collections*, 98 (2014), pp. 153–74.

Underwood, M.G., 'The Lady Margaret and her Cambridge Connections', *Sixteenth Century Journal*, 13 (1982), pp. 67–82.

——, 'John Fisher and the Promotion of Learning', in *Humanism, Reform and the Reformation: The Career of Bishop John Fisher*, ed. B. Bradshaw and E. Duffy (Cambridge, 1989), pp. 25–46.

——, 'The Impact of St. John's College as Landowner in the West Fields of Cambridge in the Early Sixteenth Century', in *Medieval Cambridge: Essays on the Pre-Reformation University*, ed. P. Zutshi (Woodbridge, 1993), pp. 167–88.

——, 'A Cruel Necessity? Christ's and St John's, Two Cambridge Re-foundations', in *Pragmatic Utopias: Ideals and Communities, 1200–1630*, ed. R. Horrox and S. Rees Jones (Cambridge, 2001), pp. 84–96.

——, 'Religion and the University to 1535', in *Catholics in Cambridge*, ed. N. Rogers (Leominster, 2003), pp. 22–37.

Venn, J., *Alumni Cantabrigienses: A Biographical List of All Known Students, Graduates and Holders of Office at the University of Cambridge, from the Earliest Times to 1900*, Part 1: *To 1751*, 4 vols. (1922–27).

The Victoria County History of the Counties of England (London, 1900– in progress).

Vincent, N., 'The Wonderful Will of William of Wendling (d.1270)', *Nottingham Medieval Studies*, 45 (2001), pp. 68–96.

Wade, E.M., 'Cambridge Borough', 'Blankpayn, John, of Cambridge', and 'Maisterman, Richard, of Cambridge and Duxford, Cambs.', in *The History of Parliament: The House of Commons 1386–1421*, ed. J.S. Roskell, L. Clark and C. Rawcliffe, 4 vols. (London, 1992), i, pp. 286–91; ii, pp. 249–50; iii, p. 670.

Wade, E.M., and Woodger, L. S., 'Herries, John (d.1418), of Cambridge', in *The History of Parliament: The House of Commons 1386–1421*, ed. J.S. Roskell, L. Clark and C. Rawcliffe (London, 1992), iii, pp. 356–7.

Walker, T.A., *A Biographical Register of Peterhouse Men and Some of Their Neighbours from the Earliest Days (1284) to the Commencement (1616) of the First Admission Book of the College*, 2 vols. (Cambridge, 1927–30).

Way, A., 'Mortuary Roll, sent forth by the Prior and Convent of Ely, on the death of John de Hothom, Bishop of Ely, deceased, January, A.D.1336–7', *Cambridge Antiquarian Communications*, 1 (1851–59), pp. 125–39.

White, P.W., *Drama and Religion in English Provincial Society, 1485–1660* (Cambridge 2008).

Williams, G., 'Ecclesiastical Vestments, Books, and Furniture, in the Collegiate Church of King's College, Cambridge, in the Fifteenth Century', *The Ecclesiologist*, 20 (1859), pp. 304–15; 21 (1860), pp. 1–7; 24 (1863), pp. 99–102.

Willis, R., and Clark, J.W., *The Architectural History of the University of Cambridge and of the Colleges of Cambridge and Eton*, 4 vols. (Cambridge, 1886, vols. 1–3 reprinted, 1988).

Wilson, D.M., and Hurst, J.G., 'Medieval Britain in 1959', *Medieval Archaeology*, 4 (1960), pp. 134–65.

Wilson, J., *Memorabilia Cantabrigiae: or, An account of the different colleges in Cambridge: biographical sketches of the founders and eminent men, with many original anecdotes, views of the colleges, and portraits of the founders* (London, 1803).

Wood, R.A., 'The Ownership of Books amongst the London Rectors in the Late Fourteenth and Fifteenth Centuries', *Medieval Prosopography* (forthcoming).

Woodcock, T., *Legal Habits: A Brief Sartorial History of Wig, Robe and Gown* (London, 2003).

Wooding, Lucy, 'From Foundation to Reformation, 1421–1558', in *The History of Manchester Collegiate Church and Cathedral*, ed. J. Gregory (Manchester, forthcoming).

Wright, S.J., ed., *Parish, Church and People: Local Studies in lay religion 1350–1750* (London, 1988).

Zutshi, P., ed., *Medieval Cambridge: Essays on the Pre-Reformation University* (Woodbridge, 1993)

Zutshi, P.N.R., and Ombres, R., 'The Dominicans in Cambridge 1238–1538', *Archivum Fratrum Praedicatorum*, 60 (1990), pp. 313–73.

UNPUBLISHED THESES

Barnett, C.M., 'Memorials and Commemoration in the Parish Churches of Late Medieval York', 2 vols. (unpublished D.Phil. thesis, University of York, 1997).

Fowler, K., 'Henry of Grosmont, first duke of Lancaster, 1310–61' (unpublished Ph.D. thesis, University of Leeds, 1961).

Steer, C., 'Burial and Commemoration in Medieval London, *c.* 1140–1540' (unpublished Ph.D. thesis, University of London, 2013).

Walker, P.M., 'Fashioning Death: The Choice and Representation of Female Clothing on English Medieval Funeral Monuments 1250–1450' (unpublished University of Manchester Ph.D., 2013).

Index